THE KOGAN PA

MATURE
STUDENT'S

HANDBOOK 1990

THE KOGAN PAGE

MATURE STUDENT'S

HANDBOOK 1990

MARGARET KORVING

KOGAN
PAGE

First published in 1989 by
Kogan Page Ltd, 120 Pentonville Road, London N1 9JN

Typeset from author's disks by Saxon Printing Ltd., Derby.

Printed and bound in Great Britain by Richard Clay, The Chaucer Press,
Bungay.

British Library Cataloguing in Publication Data
The Kogan Page Mature Student's Handbook: full-time, part-time
 and distance learning courses.
 1990 –
 1. Great Britain. Vocational education
 370.11'3'0941

ISBN .i.1-85091-964-X

Contents

Open and Distance Learning Courses

Degree and Advanced Courses

General Information

Preface

If you have picked up this book, you probably feel your life could be better in some way. You may wish to improve your work or home life, your leisure time or your prospects. The ideas, profiles and lists of courses in *The Mature Student's Handbook* can help you change your life a little, or a lot.

You may already know you want to train for a completely new career. If so, 'Retraining and New Skills Courses' will open your eyes to the wide range of opportunities for late starters. These include mature-entry courses at schools of nursing, radiography, occupational therapy, physiotherapy and chiropody. Colleges, polytechnics and universities also have a huge choice of courses – from catering to violin-making and from teaching to computing.

If you want to broaden your academic horizons, 'Pre-Entry, Sample and Access Courses' can help you brush up your education. 'Open and Distance Learning Courses' show you ways to qualify in your own time. In 'Degree and Advanced Courses' you can find details of entry concessions for mature students, plus information about part-time and full-time degrees. If you want to work for yourself, check 'Small Business and Self-Employment Courses'.

Not sure which route to take? Then take time to 'Examine Your Life' – see page 9 – to help you decide your priorities. Then turn to page 23 where you'll find 'New Directions for Late Starters' – career fields where maturity can be an asset. Enjoy your choice and the rest of your life and remember, it's never too late to *make a fresh start*.

Margaret Korving

Examine Your Life

For more than 20 years I have been answering questions from readers of national newspapers and magazines on the subjects of changing careers, returning to education or making more of abilities that people feel are being wasted in their present jobs. It's an immensely enjoyable and satisfying job and I've learned a tremendous amount from readers' experiences of changing direction in later life and the difficulties and joys it can bring.

So many of my letters come from 'late starters' that I decided to research and write this book as a source of ideas and factual information for people who have had to put off training for their dream career (or perhaps trying for a place at college) and who at last find themselves able to start planning their future.

For most people, there are many personal factors that have to be sorted out before they can choose the right course for their needs. That's why the courses section of this book has been preceeded by these pages to help anyone who's not quite sure what kind of course to go for. (If you *are* sure – go straight to the index and you'll find directions there to the courses you want in your home region.) If not, read on to find out how you can make a satisfying choice that will meet your personal needs.

WHY? WHAT? HOW? WHEN? WHERE?

Often the question that has to be answered before any suggestions can be made is *why* the reader wants to make a change. You can completely change your lifestyle by taking up a new career or going into higher education, but it's important to be sure that this change is taking you in the right direction. Do you feel strongly enough about your project to see it through?

It's also important to know *what* is your main objective in changing. It takes a lot of effort to turn your back on a boring but safe job, or study after work, or live on a grant. You need to be sure that the long-term aim is something you really want, what you personally will get out of it, and how it will affect those whose views and comfort matter to you.

You also have to consider *how* you are going to manage your change. Most mature people have commitments; if not a family to maintain, then a mortgage to repay, or sometimes an unusual difficulty. I remember one reader who first had to find a dog-minder for the large and energetic dog she couldn't leave shut in the house when she was at college. It proved a lot more difficult than deciding which course to take.

Commitments can also affect *when* you can attend courses or start training. Increasingly colleges are offering courses between 9.30 a.m. and 3.15 p.m. to suit parents with children at school, and this year, the number of part-time Nurse training courses has increased too. Another valuable development is that of evening degree courses, joining those of the Open University and the vocational courses of The Open College in making it possible for people to prepare for a change while earning a living or maintaining a home.

A final factor that comes up frequently in the letters I answer is *where* courses are offered. Most adults are not free to toss their bonnets over the windmill and travel hundreds of miles away to take up a new training in a strange town. They need to know what's available within travelling distance of their homes. That's why in each section of this book, courses are arranged in regions – London and Middlesex, Southern and Eastern, Central, Northern, Wales and Western, Scotland and Northern Ireland.

Once you've sorted out the why, what, when, how and where of your change, you can concentrate on finding the right match for your requirements in the course lists. Here are some ideas for you to consider in the light of your own situation.

WHY DO YOU WANT TO CHANGE?

YOU NEED A NEW JOB
Redundancy is nothing unusual these days, but you may have to retrain or move to where the work is, or employ yourself (using redundancy money to set up in business). Or you may be able to organise a mixture of part-time, voluntary and self-employed work. You can keep your right to benefits (and get an extra allowance) by retraining under the Employment Training Scheme which is locally organised to provide people with the skills needed by local employers. You can also take a college course that occupies no more than 21 hours a week without losing benefits under the 21-hour rule (details in 'Costs and Grants' section).

YOU NEED MORE MONEY
Get it by improving your qualifications on an evening class or home study basis and prepare yourself for promotion or a new job. Or retrain for something that pays better, or lets you earn in your spare time with a newly acquired freelance skill. You might also reduce your outgoings by moving into a new social circle with other students who are also on a limited budget or by getting a job with 'perks' – subsidised accommodation, say, or a company car.

YOU'D LIKE MORE FRIENDS

Find these by training for work that is more companionable (in a big hospital, say) or by switching to a work/study area that attracts mainly men or mainly women, if you want to meet the opposite sex. Give up your job to study at college, where you'll have the chance to make friends who share your interests. If you can't manage this, start on a spare-time course that lets you meet new people.

YOU'RE BORED WITH YOUR JOB

You may not need to change your work as such; just the place where you do it (by moving from the country to the town, for instance). If you have transferable skills, you could change employers – say from being a secretary in a commercial firm to being secretary to a novelist or on a farm. You can retrain for a new career, set up a small business in your free time, take a course to prepare you for voluntary work – or study something so demanding that you'll need your boring job for a rest. Taking a spare-time course doesn't mean you *have* to change jobs.

YOU'RE AT A LOOSE END

All of a sudden, the family is grown up and you're free to please yourself. Or you've finally paid that mortgage and can take early retirement – to do what? You can get help with decision-making through a New Opportunities or Wider Opportunities course (see 'Pre-Entry, Sample and Access Courses'). You may also be able to follow that dream to go to university – there are often substantial entry concessions for mature students. Perhaps you could use your choice of course to make a move to the seaside/country/city – wherever you fancy living – and build up a new set of interests and friends through your study contacts.

YOU WANT BETTER PROSPECTS

You may be unqualified, or have outdated skills, or no real skills at all, so that you need to restart and retrain. College courses and home-based study through The Open College can give you a fresh start. Perhaps you need extra knowledge – computer know-how, for instance – so that you can divert into a more promising job area. You could put yourself into a different promotion category by taking exams you missed out on at school. Some people though, have 'paper qualifications' but no practical skills, or may want to catch up on subjects like art or music or literature that they've never really had time to think about. Daytime, evening and home study courses are widely available to satisfy these particular needs.

YOU NEED SOMEWHERE TO LIVE

You can look for jobs that traditionally have residential perks and train for them as a mature student. Then again, some educational courses will give you a roof over your head while you learn (most universities and polytechnics have accommodation for a large proportion of students). Student nurses and students for the paramedical professions can usually be resident during their training. Once you have a steady job, getting rooms and flats is usually easier. Organisations like banks and building societies, which provide home loans, normally need evidence of earnings to grant a mortgage. An employer's reference can help you get accommodation, too.

YOU'RE RESPONSIBLE FOR OTHERS – BUT NEED A CHANGE
If you have to look after children, or an elderly or disabled person, the answer may be self-employment, unemployment plus home-based study, or finding a way to train for jobs with unsocial hours (so that others can 'home sit' while you work evenings, nights or weekends). Job-sharing is another possibility once you have skills to offer. Or you can follow a home/study/work/leisure plan with other responsible relatives, or maybe people you meet through a single-parent, or carers' group. If you live far from a bus route or are scared of late night travel after evening classes, distance learning or short holiday courses (while a friend stands in for you at home) may widen your horizons. Once you start digging for information, you meet other people who have tackled the same kind of problem – their solutions may be new to you. The Open University, The Open College and Open Learning Federations are reaching out to people with commitments to make it easier for them to improve their circumstances.

NEEDS, PROBLEMS AND PRIORITIES

The three sections that follow illustrate familiar problems experienced by people who want to make a fresh start, they should help you decide which are the most important factors in your life that you must take into account when you are choosing a new direction. Examples are in question-and-answer form, as they are usually presented to careers advisers. No two people have exactly the same needs, problems and priorities, but you can often identify ways to tackle your own situation from the answer to someone else's problem.

WHAT ARE YOUR NEEDS

INDEPENDENCE
'I need a skill, qualification or training that will mean I can earn something for myself, regardless of where I may move, and my previous skills. I need to extend my abilities and add to my knowledge to feel secure.'
   Take a look at skills you can take with you, maybe to let you set up in a small way at home – for instance, musical instrument technology, or motorcycle maintenance, or a universally useful training such as selling or dressmaking or lorry driving that you could earn from in any part of the country.

STATUS
'I want to take a course with an end product that shows I have worked hard and achieved a recognised target. I won't be really satisfied until I have a national qualification, or a job or business of my own that gives me a place in society.'

Check courses that lead to nationally recognised qualifications, like City and Guilds awards, the BTEC Higher National Diploma or Certificate, or to the award of a professional institute like the Institute of Marketing or the Association of Accounting Technicians. If you're thinking of a small business, learn the ropes first – the 'Small Business and Self Employment Courses' section of this book lists a range of possibilities from running a guest house to owning a shop. (People are more likely to invest in you if you can show you've trained for your business.)

COMPANIONSHIP
'I want to make contact with people who share my interests, so I can feel part of a group and have the pleasure of talking over subjects I find interesting without feeling I might be boring people.'

Many universities, polytechnics and colleges offer this sort of opportunity – you might begin by reading the reports included in the 'Degree and Advanced Courses' section from students at Hatfield Polytechnic (Southern and Eastern Region). Dotted through the book you'll find more examples of people who have met others like themselves as the result of taking a study course. It may not have been their primary reason for studying – often they had to retrain, or needed qualifications for promotion – but making new friends with the same interest was a bonus.

CREATIVITY
'I need to do something that develops the creative side of my nature. It's all very well being useful and capable, but I have ideas and imagination, and I won't be satisfied until I have tried my hand at creating something original.'

Throughout this book you'll find examples of 'creative' courses from working in silver to floristry and from writing to wrought ironwork. Opportunities are not simply on a leisure course basis. Mature students may be accepted on high-level art and design courses on the basis of work they have done in their own time so as to make up a portfolio to show admissions tutors. Check both the 'Retraining and New Skills Courses' and 'Degree and Advanced Courses' sections.

CONTRAST
'My life is dull and predictable. There's no variety in my job and my responsibilities involve doing the same thing at the same time, most days. I am looking for a new career or outside interest that will be a complete contrast to everything else that I have done.'

How about book and archive conservation? Or training to be a tour manager? Or taking a Registered Nurse course – many schools accept candidates aged up to 50 and a few consider people over that age. Those are just three possibilities. You may find more if you skim through the 'New Directions for Late Starters' lists on page 24.

SERVICE

'I want to get some skills that will let me be useful to people who need help. There's nothing basically wrong with the way I live at present except that I feel I could be contributing instead of just being sorry for people. You know what they say – 'if you're not part of the solution, you're part of the problem.'

Many of the colleges in this book have devised special courses for people who want to contribute to the community. The range is vast, from training for voluntary service at Rockingham College in Rotherham to postgraduate courses in art and drama therapy at Hertfordshire College of Art. Paramedical careers – chiropody, occupational therapy, physiotherapy and radiography – all accept mature students and they are welcomed into social work training. Each year the age limits for training seem to go up in these health and welfare occupations, and not just because the supply of young entrants is running out. Increasingly, training authorities write to me and say how valuable the 'life experience' of mature entrants has proved to be.

WHAT ARE YOUR PROBLEMS?

FEAR OF FAILING

'I disliked school and got out as soon as possible. Even though I have to get qualifications to get a job (or to get out of a boring one) I dread going back to the classroom and making a fool of myself in a crowd of teenagers, just as I used to make a fool of myself at school.'

You can ensure that you will be with people who have to face similar problems if you choose a 'Basic Literacy/Numeracy' course, or a 'Fresh Start' or 'Return to Learn' course – or if you begin at home, using a distance-learning course (see 'Open and Distance Learning Courses').

POOR SCHOOL RECORD

'I didn't dislike school, but I didn't get much out of it, either. I did well in a few subjects that I liked, but there aren't many opportunities for people without English and Maths which I failed. And it's hardly likely I'll pass them after all these years if I couldn't do it when I was young.'

Courses from The Open College include 'Make it Count' – how to do basic arithmetic, and 'The Writing Course' to help you write well. These are good preliminaries to GCSE courses which you can take at college or by home study. Or look at 'Access' courses, which are designed for mature people and have no entry qualifications. Incidentally, if you need direct personal help, teachers who advertise in local papers that they coach children for reading, writing and arithmetic will often willingly take adults. Sometimes they'll even visit your home to teach you.

CAN'T KEEP UP

'I've tried taking evening classes but I can't seem to keep up because I keep missing classes, owing to overtime and shift work. What I need is something adaptable. A "plan-it-yourself" course would be ideal, but I don't know that I have the staying power to work away at a distance-learning course on my own. Any ideas?'

You're the sort of person for whom flexible study courses have been devised. 'Flexistudy' courses were evolved by the National Extension College, and many colleges of further education use them. There are also various adaptations of this system in which you learn mostly at home with access to a local tutor for help and encouragement. The word 'Open' attached to a course usually means flexible learning methods as well as flexible entry requirements. See 'Open and Distance Learning Courses'.

LEFT SCHOOL WITH NO QUALIFICATIONS
'My daughter showed me some of the things she had to learn for GCSE and it would be quite beyond me. Finding out how little I know has made me even keener to catch up (because coping at work has shown me I'm not incapable of learning). But I do need to start from scratch. There weren't GCSEs or O-levels in my day! Is there any kind of preparatory course for people in my situation?'

No problem. 'Basic Skills' courses start from the beginning; they may be called 'Pathway' or 'Gateway' since colleges tend to use their own titles for the same kind of course, but you can easily pick out those designed for beginners. Some colleges also run some special courses for new immigrants (or old immigrants who have never quite got to grips with the language of their adopted country). 'Open College' schemes are another possibility, including Study Skills, and you may be able to do much of the work at home. Look at the range of 'Pre-Entry, Sample and Access Courses' for examples, and ask your student daughter to collect prospectuses or leaflets from local colleges, where you'll find the latest ideas for people who are restarting in education.

FAILED A-LEVELS
'I gave up after two attempts at A-levels. Now I'm stuck, with no hope of ever getting to university, which was always my dream. Yet I'm not a fool and I find it easy to pick up theory related to my job. Is there any way in which I can offer my job qualifications instead of A-levels for entry to a degree course, because I do still want to go to university?'

Universities, polytechnics and colleges are ahead of you! They've discovered that people with work-related qualifications (many of which involved studying in the evenings as well as holding down a day job) are a very good bet when it comes to degree course study. Warwick University's research showed they do better than conventional school-leaver entrants with A-levels. You can offer BTEC (or the old ONC/D or HNC/D) or many professional course qualifications instead of A-levels, or you can take one of the specially-designed 'Access' courses for mature students instead of A-levels, to prepare for degree level work. Each university, polytechnic and college listed in 'Degree and Advanced Courses' indicates its concessions for mature students including all the alternatives to A-levels that satisfy the entry requirements.

EXAM NERVES
'I don't want to take exams. They always made me sick with nerves at school and I never did myself credit. But I do find certain subjects interesting, and I'd like to pick up where I left off in some areas, if only I can avoid tests. Any chance of colleges taking people who *don't* want to pass exams and get qualifications?'

University Extra-Mural courses are primarily for people who study for pleasure and interest. But you can also become an Associate Student or in some cases a Visiting or Listening Student – this is particularly true of polytechnics. It means you pick out a single course from a degree or similar study course, and just attend the lectures or practical demonstrations for that particular course. You can do the course work, but it's entirely up to you whether you want to enter for the exam. Birmingham Polytechnic and Hatfield Polytechnic are examples of polytechnics offering this sort of scheme. Many Open University courses are also designed for non-examination candidates – people who want to learn for the pleasure of studying. And there are plenty of short courses open to non-examination students, including day schools, evening courses, Saturday study days and summer schools. Middlesex Polytechnic, for example, offers a well-established summer school. And it's worth remembering that you can also take an exam course without applying to take an exam! In other words, if you want to study GCE A-level English Literature, you can go on the course, but won't be forced to fill in the exam entry form and pay your exam fee.

WHAT ARE YOUR PRIORITIES?

GUARANTEED JOB PROSPECTS
'I need to qualify for a new job. I'm prepared to learn full time and work hard, but there must be a genuine chance of a job at the end of it and I must stand a chance of getting that job. How can I pick a course with real prospects of employment?'

Look in the newspapers for opportunities to be trained by specific employers – for example, to run an off-licence or a service station or as a school meals cook. Consider the health professions, especially those for which the Department of Health provides training bursaries; that's a good indication of need. The identification 'TA-sponsored' means a course funded by the government under Employment Training (explained on page 346) which will combine college study and work experience in occupations where there is a demand for new blood. If ever you're not sure about job prospects, get advice from trade unions, professional associations and employers federations – it's in their own interest to encourage new trainees in skill shortage areas and not to encourage people to enter already crowded fields.

CHANCES OF PROMOTION
'I have a job, but my prospects are poor and I want to study to improve my future. Any course I take must be a recognised one that employers will approve, and it will have to fit in with my work, because I can't afford to give

up – I might not be able to get back into a job again. Can I make sure of choosing the right course?'

No-one is likely to give you an unconditional guarantee, but trade unions and professional associations (see above) will advise on recognised courses and areas where particular skills are in short supply. For example, the Royal College of Nursing has drawn attention to the shortage of specially-trained Intensive Care Nurses; a trained nurse who takes a post-Registration ITU course should find plenty of job opportunities. The Department of Education and Science's 'Teaching as a Career' Unit has advertised widely for people to train for shortage areas in teaching – maths, physics, business studies, craft, design and technology. Training allowances, bursaries and/or grants are usually provided for people taking extra courses in 'shortage skills' areas. BTEC Continuing Education Units often provide the opportunity to update on a single aspect of your work, such as 'Using Word Processors'. There's also been a huge expansion of Open Learning facilities (see page 234) which means you can learn when it suits you. And in many jobs there are opportunities to go on short updating courses, either arranged by your firm (look on the company noticeboard and in the organisation's magazine), and conducted during working hours, or run by some outside body in the evenings. Don't overlook the value of an Open University degree or an Open Business School qualification or a London University external degree. Employers are generally impressed by people who demonstrate that they care enough about improving their prospects by studying in their spare time, even if the subject doesn't directly relate to their present job. (Having a degree can also open up a range of second career possibilities.)

I WANT A SAFETY NET

'My job is quite a good one, but these days you never know what's around the corner. I'd like to add a second string to my bow. Then, if I should be hit by redundancy, I'd have something else I could turn to for a living. But the course will have to be in my own time – evenings, weekends, holidays – and of course, something that welcomes mature students. What are the choices?'

Dozens. You could take a part-time degree or open learning course, or spend part of your holiday time and money on an intensive private course in some special skill – anything from lorry-driving to word-processing. Or you could take evening classes in a creative skill like cake-icing or upholstery-making, or in a maintenance skill such as carpentry, or horticulture which would give you scope for spare-time, home-based employment. Check the course lists for your region and also the 'Information Sources' list at the end of the book for more ideas.

I CAN ONLY STUDY DURING SCHOOL HOURS

'I want to prepare to go back to work when my children are old enough for school. I can study part of the day or take an evening class, and my priority is to find something that will demonstrate that I have a brain and haven't let it go rusty while I've been at home. What are the choices?'

This depends on where you live. Some places have courses from 10 a.m. to 3 p.m. designed especially for people like you. Any course under the 21-hour rule (see 'Costs and Grants') might be arranged in such a way that it fits into school hours. The European Social Fund (courses identified as 'ESF-sponsored') puts up some money for courses specifically designed to suit 'women returners', especially for women who want to train for jobs that are not traditionally women's work, such as building or engineering. If you're not sure what might be best for you, look out for daytime courses with titles like 'New Opportunities for Women' or 'Wider Opportunities' (likely to be listed in the 'Pre-Entry, Sample and Access Courses' section).

I DON'T KNOW HOW TO CHOOSE

'I've spent a lifetime in the wrong job. Now I want to make a complete change. Quite what to do I'm not sure, but if I could find a list of all the possible jobs and courses, I daresay I could find something for myself. Is there anywhere that lists all the choices and entry requirements?'

I don't know of one single directory that covers all you want to know, but to begin with ideas for careers you might research, any good careers guide kept in public libraries, such as The Daily Telegraph Careers A-Z, Equal Opportunities *or the* Careers Encyclopedia *will be helpful. Colleges often put on courses that let you sample a range of skills and study areas – look for titles like 'New Opportunities', 'New Directions', 'Multi-Skills'. On page 24 I've listed examples of careers where maturity is often an asset. Remember that Jobcentres and commercially-run employment agencies can usually tell you what kind of people are in demand in your area. Having located the range of likely jobs, you can look first in this book for courses devised or attracting 'late starters'. If there's nothing specifically for mature students, turn to the* Directory of Further Education *or the* Directory of Independent Training and Tutorial Organisations, *both of which should be in your local public library. You may be lucky enough to find an Educational Guidance Service in your area – ask the librarian. Otherwise, the Head of Adult Continuing Education at your local college, polytechnic or university may be able to advise you on tracking down elusive courses.*

EDUCATION IN RETIREMENT

'All my life I've gone out to work to earn the money to go to work and earn the money. Now (as I'm taking early retirement/have had a windfall/have discovered I can get a mature student's grant) I want to study for my own satisfaction. Exactly how do I begin?'

The whole wide world of learning – academic, creative, practical, inventive – is out there waiting for you. Sandwell College in Liverpool told me about one 82-year-old who did well in signwriting. Hatfield Polytechnic introduced me to a number of 70-year-olds enjoying a degree course in Contemporary Studies. And Hensol Hospital in Mid-Glamorgan has a number of students in their 50s currently tackling nurse training. I suggest you begin by leafing through your regional lists of courses in each section of this book to get an idea of choices within easy travelling range. Then get free prospectuses, and if you have a dream that you want to follow up, but which doesn't seem to be covered, track down a professional institute/trade body concerned with it and ask them about training. (See the 'Information Sources' section, page 351 for further details.) Never hesitate to write to a college's Adult/Continuing Education Department for advice. As the percentage of young people in the country declines, colleges of all kinds are setting out to attract mature students, and that means anyone from 21 upwards. Some colleges will gladly introduce you to other 'late starters' who will tell you what it's like to enjoy learning for its own sake, and how they started. Polytechnics are particularly good in this respect.

I CAN'T AFFORD A COURSE THAT COSTS MUCH

'I am unemployed and it's as much as I can do to survive on benefits, without paying for classes. People tell me there are 'special courses for the unemployed'. What are they about and how do I find out about them?'

First get a leaflet from your local DSS office about the 21-hour rule, whereby you can retain your right to benefits while you study, as long as you keep to certain basic rules about when you take classes (explained more fully in the 'Costs and Grants' section). Look through the other sections for ideas for courses. Apart from courses under Employment Training (free, and you keep your benefit entitlement plus£10 a week), many colleges put on courses especially for unemployed people. Often the 'unwaged'/ are eligible too – this lets in people who can't actually look for work outside the home because they have a child to care for (colleges may have creches for which children of single parents or anyone else with special problems gets priority). Some courses also attract special ESF training benefits – check these out. In industries where there have been large-scale redundancies, there may be special retraining schemes with extra financial benefits; ask your trade union if you think this could be a possibility. The Open University has provision for helping students in financial difficulty – they'll send you details on request.

ANY IDEAS FOR COPING WITHOUT A GRANT?

'I started out on a course and was given a grant, but I gave it up halfway. Now my LEA says I'm not eligible for another grant. All the careers I look at seem to require a degree like the one I first tried for. How can I get a degree without a grant?'

Take your degree part time, by day or in the evening, or take an Open University degree. It will be worth the same as any conventional full-time degree – in some employers' eyes it will be worth more, because everyone knows how much work is involved in studying in your spare time, after working. Part-time postgraduate courses are also widely available if you have 'graduate status' but need to upgrade your knowledge or add a vocational slant to your education. Incidentally, degree study hours often make it possible to hold down a part-time or evening or weekend job as well as study. Many people manage to combine study for an evening or OU degree with full-time work.

I CAN PAY FOR TRAINING, BUT IS IT SAFE TO GO TO A 'PRIVATE' COLLEGE?

'I have redundancy money which I could invest in a course of training or study, but I must make sure I'm spending it wisely; when it's gone, it's gone.

How can I discover which courses are recognised, and also what demand there might be for people with particular qualifications which can be obtained quickly through a "crash" course?'

In the case of a job-related course, check it out with the appropriate professional or trade body; for instance, if it's a catering course, the Hotel, Catering and Institutional Management Association; if it's an antiques repair course, with the British Antique Dealers' Association, and so on (libraries can help you find addresses). In the case of an education course, ask the local Education Authority, the Educational Guidance Centre, if there is one, or the Jobcentre. Special-interest magazines, with titles like The Grocer, The Bookseller, Construction News *have articles about labour demand in the occupations they serve. You can usually look at them in the public library reading room, though you may have to ask the librarian to help you find a copy if they're not on display for readers.*

GRANTS – HOW MUCH, WHERE, FROM WHOM?

'There's no question of my being able to finance a course. Though I need to make a change, it's either got to be through getting a job with an organisation that trains me with pay, or by doing a course that attracts a grant. How does anyone find out which courses get grants?'

The section of this book headed 'Costs and Grants' lists addresses you can contact about grants. Colleges themselves also sometimes know about sources of finance. For instance, there might be a scholarship in memory of a past student that they can award, or a local fund that they can tap into. Or they may know of a loans scheme, whereby you can pay back when you're qualified and have found a job. The Career Development Loans scheme is described in 'Costs and Grants' which also covers grants from your local education authority and bursaries for paramedical courses of training.

WHERE CAN I FIND LISTS OF INTENSIVE COURSES?

'Because of my job (teacher, actor, nurse, sales representative) I can only manage short, intensive 'crammer' courses – or maybe a summer holiday course, or weekend courses. How do you track these down?'

There's a nationally recognised guide called the Directory of Independent Training and Tutorial Organisations *published by Career Consultants and available in public libraries. Summer schools get advertised in the Sunday newspapers, such as the* Sunday Telegraph, Sunday Times, Observer. *Weekend and other short courses are listed in the* Residential Short Courses Guide *(£1.15) by post from the National Institute of Adult Continuing Education, 19b de Montford Street, Leicester, LE1 7GE).*

IS THERE SUCH A THING AS A MOBILE COURSE?

'My husband is in the services and we move every two years or so. What courses can I take, moving from college to college. I can't leave my family to study, even if I did get a grant.'

It's never easy to move between colleges but it's getting easier thanks to ECCTIS. This stands for the Educational Counselling and Credit Transfer Information

Service. 'Credit Transfer' is fast catching on, particularly among polytechnics and briefly, it enables you to move from one course to another being credited for the work you do in each one. There's a fuller description in the Introduction to 'Degree and Advanced Courses'. ECCTIS records on computer all the facilities that exist to transfer between courses in the same subject but in different parts of the country. There is an ECCTIS Handbook *which may be available in your library; otherwise seek help from the Continuing Education Department of the nearest polytechnic. Any college belonging to an Open College Federation – explained in the Introduction to 'Open and Distance Learning Courses' – is likely to take you, whatever level of study you've reached. And Open University and courses from The Open College also provide the facility you need, for stopping when you have to move, and re-starting where you left off when you are ready.*

I CAN ONLY TAKE A COURSE SOMEWHERE CLOSE TO HOME. WHAT IS THERE FOR ME IN NORTHAMPTON?
'My husband encourages me to return to work and train for a proper career this time instead of the routine job I had before marriage. But I can't leave the district as I have a family to consider. I know big cities have plenty of choice but what might there be for me, living in Northampton?'

This is why The Kogan Page Mature Student's Handbook *is organised in regions, by town names. To take 'Retraining and New Skills Courses' as an example, if you look up Northampton in the 'Central England' section, you'll find you can consider courses in business, fashion, social work, chiropody, radiography and occupational therapy – and that doesn't include all the opportunities that might be available with a degree at Nene College, Northampton. By all means check your own town's offering in each section of the book, but consider places that are just a bus ride away – they may have an entry too. This applies wherever you live, and for any readers within commuting distance of a big city like London or Edinburgh, it's worth taking into account courses a train ride away too. Good hunting!*

New Directions for Late Starters

Since this book was first published in 1988 (under the title *Make a Fresh Start*), there has been a striking change in public attitudes to mature students. Employers who formerly put an upper age limit of 30 or 35 in their vacancy advertisements now often mention no age limit at all. Many, facing a dearth of school-leaver applicants, are actively pursuing 'returners' and even 'early retirers'.

As I write in April 1989, my own local paper carries an advertisement for speech therapists, 'full time, part time or jobshare'; there's a restaurant offering four hours' work daily, with free lunch; the supermarket wants people of any age to work any convenient shifts and the further education college is promoting its 'school hours only' Access course. National newspapers often have advertisements from local authorities, some of whom now consider applicants regardless of sex, race, religion, disability *and* age. Even the Civil Service Commission, issuing a careers guide for graduates, includes several opportunities which carry the message 'no upper age limit'.

Meanwhile, in researching opportunities for late starters in schools of nursing, radiography, physiotherapy, occupational therapy and chiropody for *The Mature Student's Handbook*, I am impressed by their efforts to attract and keep mature entrants. One school of occupational therapy says it has people of 50 and 51 in its first year. A famous London school of nursing is among those which considers candidates aged up to 50, and adds that it would give careful consideration to well-motivated candidates above that age. One nursing school's upper age limit for entry to training is 55.

Obviously each college principal, like each employer, is guided by experience in considering mature entrants. Personality and background must play a part in selection. Someone with a sound scientific background is likely to be able to absorb the medical and technical aspects of a paramedical training much more readily than someone who has no science O-levels. The person who has taken part in community life, either by doing a part-time job of some kind or joining in voluntary work, is an attractive training proposition for work with people, whether it's a BEd for teacher training, an Institute of Personnel Management course or the Certificate of Qualification in Social Work.

Published age limits for entry to a training course may well be affected by the physical health, past experience and personality of the individual candidate. I always advise mature applicants for jobs to add a passport-size photograph to their c.v.'s to help selection committees visualise them as individuals. Some of the colleges and training establishments in this book offer counselling interviews before application – this is true of polytechnics and universities as well as nursing and paramedical schools. Everyone concerned can benefit from this experience.

In the section that follows, I have listed some work areas where maturity can often be a plus factor. They are by no means the only occupational fields where 'late starters' are welcome but they will give you some examples to set you thinking where your own skills, personality and ambition might be welcomed:

CATERING, INCLUDING LICENSED PREMISES

Cooking, waiting, room service, bar work – in hotels, guest houses, holiday camps, company training centres, student hostels. Cooking and domestic services in hospitals and schools including boarding schools. Working on licensed premises (maturity often essential) e.g. managing a pub, running an off-licence, in charge of drinks service in a club or hotel. Running a works social club. Managing a wine bar. Running the bar in a golf or other sports club. Working for an outside catering firm, responsible for drinks and hire of glasses.

COMMUNITY WORK

Social worker (for local authority, charity, voluntary unit, in residential home). Warden of old people's home or sheltered accommodation. Caretaker of private residential development for the elderly (opportunities increasing rapidly). Care assistant in state/private old people's home, nursing home. Counsellor (paid or unpaid work – the latter can give you the experience to be accepted for training for paid work), in marriage guidance (now called 'Relate'), with teenagers, with cancer or AIDS patients, drug/alcohol-dependent people, depressed or anxious people, those suffering from under/overeating problems, the suicidal, the bereaved. Working as a play leader, in a playgroup or sometimes in a children's ward. Running a youth club, helping at a day centre for handicapped or lonely or elderly people. Home helping (includes welfare work as well as domestic aid – clients in all age groups). Training as, or working with, a funeral director.

TEACHING

In areas that are in short supply in schools – Maths; Physics; Business Studies; Craft, Design and Technology – where it can be valuable to have come from industry and be able to show teenagers where your subject fits into the employment scene. Similarly, at college, passing on your work skills, whether you teach Welding or Word Processing. Local colleges often invite people to write to them with details of any subject they can offer. They may be prepared to try offering a course like Making Silk Flowers or Tax Tips for the Self-Employed if they know they have a suitable instructor available. After you've brought up a family, training to teach nursery/infant or primary school children, where your own experience could be a useful basis for your college study. Teaching basic Literacy and Numeracy to adults – perhaps beginning as a volunteer tutor, then getting the offer of paid work at a college. Teaching English as a Foreign or Second language, in colleges or by private coaching. Acting as a correspondence course tutor, marking work and advising students by letter or phone. Teaching your hobby – swimming, dressmaking, public speaking. Driving Instruction (for those who can pass Department of Transport exams).

SELLING
Direct sales – to friends and neighbours, by party-plan or mail-order catalogue. Some people work their way up to senior supervisory positions from a modest start of this kind. Telephone sales – promoting insurance and saving schemes, or perhaps something like a building modernisation scheme. Industrial or technical sales, using previous career knowledge, e.g. as an engineer or chef or nurse, to obtain sales training with pay from a manufacturer, so that you can sell scientific or technical or medical products. People who have worked in retail selling (anything from china and glass to food and drink) can often use their product knowledge as the foundation for paid sales training with a manufacturer. Moving on from being an industrial or commercial sales person, you might become a manufacturer's agent at any age, using contacts made during your career. Companies looking for agents advertise in national newspapers (in the business section) and in special-interest magazines.

THERAPIES
Not all the therapies in the following list are practised in NHS hospitals or can be gained in the community through the NHS. Where one can work in a particular therapy under the NHS, with approved training, I have used the symbol 'NHS'. Acupuncture, Alexander Technique, Art Therapy (NHS), Bach Flower Therapy, Chiropractice, Diet Therapy (NHS), Dramatherapy (NHS), Herbalism, Homeopathy (NHS), Horticultural Therapy (NHS), Hypnotherapy, Industrial Therapy (NHS), Massage (not to be confused with Physiotherapy), Music Therapy (NHS), Naturopathy, Occupational Therapy (NHS), Osteopathy, Physiotherapy (NHS), Psychotherapy (NHS), Radiotherapy (NHS). These are examples of therapies in which a mature approach can be welcome. Some, though, have demanding entrance requirements – some schools have concessions for mature students. If you are embarking on the conventional entry requirements for a specific course, check with the professional body concerned that you won't have reached the upper age limit for training before you qualify. Read college entries

carefully; there may well be alternatives to the GCSE/A-level entry requirements asked of school leavers if you are a mature candidate.

CARING OCCUPATIONS

Apart from those mentioned under 'Social Work' you can train as a
Registered Nurse up to age 45 in most health authorities, up to 50 in some,
and occasionally, over 50. Age limits are quoted in nursing school entries in
the 'Retraining and New Skills' section. Mature students are now often
considered by nursery nursing courses leading to the National Nursery
Examination Board certificate and there are a few extended courses for
people with home responsibilities. Experience as a nursing auxiliary in a
hospital or nursing home, or a care assistant in a home or day nursery can
stand you in good stead if you want to train for a professional qualification
when children are at school. Medical Reception Work (including Appointments Clerk in hospital) Medical Secretarial Work and Practice Administration, for a health centre, is often very suitable for mature people. A modest-
part time job can develop into a full-time career. Mature people are often
preferred as Ward Clerks in hospitals. Beauty Therapy and some of its
specialities – Epilation or Cosmetic Camouflage, for instance – are good
mature entrant areas. Hairdressing is a very useful training that enables you
to set up your own business, in a salon or as a visiting stylist.

SERVICES

Many an engineer turns Technical Illustrator or Technical Author. Building
Craft skills can lead to Site Supervision, or individual skills can be
redirected, e.g. a carpenter and joiner may become a Shopfitter or Kitchen
fitter. Automobile engineering bodywork skills can convert to Car Restoration services. Green-fingered gardeners with artistic and sales interests can
retrain in Floristry. Experienced campers and caravanners can do seasonal
work as Campsite Couriers or Caravan Site Wardens (it helps to have basic
maintenance skills, first aid and a language if you want to work abroad).
Much-travelled people can train as Tour Guides. Find yourself a chance to
work on an exhibition stand as a demonstrator of something you know
about, and lo! you have experience of demonstrating, which lets you try
agencies to get more of the same work with different products or services.
Knowledgeable about computers and/or electronics? The home computer
owner who can't justify a service contract may be very glad to call up your
services if you advertise computer repairs.

OFFICE SKILLS

The more you have, the better your job chances, but remember to *select* from
your range when you apply for jobs that ask for specific abilities. You could
scare off an employer if you offer all that he asks for and a great deal more.
Skills you can choose from: Typing, Audio Typing, Shorthand Typing,
Word Processing, Book-keeping, Costing, Computerised Accounts, Filing,

Computerised Information Storage, Ordering and Re-Ordering, Stock Checking, Telephone and Reception Skills, Telex, Fax, Photocopier Operation, VAT Records, PAYE calculations, DSS deductions, Mailing List Operation, Progress Chasing (orders, debts), Official Returns (e.g. farm, tax, health), Statistics Collection, Transport Booking and Timing (planes, trains, car hire, route planning and estimating), Dispatch by Red Star or other Courier Service at home or abroad, including Insurance, Customs Declaration Forms – still think you know all about office work? Job specialities include Accounts Technician, Legal Executive, Office Services Manager, Personnel Office Assistant (diversification – Employment Agency Interviewer), Conference Executive, Hotel Receptionist, Information Clerk (e.g. at an Airport), Advertisement Sales Clerk, Freight Forwarding Assistant, etc. etc. Your age may limit where you start, but as we all know, 'It's not where you start, but where you finish' that matters.

Get the skill, get the job – and you can then get going!

PRE-ENTRY, SAMPLE AND ACCESS COURSES

The 'toe-in-the-water' approach to changing your life

Introduction

All the courses in this first section of *The Mature Student's Handbook* are introductory in some way. They may be designed to let you sample a range of skills and careers to see which interests you. They may be courses to prepare you for higher education, beginning with the all-important subject of 'Study Skills' – how to listen, how to take notes, how to remember, how to construct an essay.

Some of them begin right at the beginning with basic literacy and numeracy. Others are adult versions of GCSE or A-levels – courses devised specially to suit mature people. Many of these pre-entry courses are designed for all comers. They have titles like 'Fresh Start' or 'Return to Study' which tell you that the tutors are expecting a range of people to turn up from many different backgrounds and levels of education, all setting out to tackle something new together.

Breaking the Ice

Assuming, though, that you've decided to change your life by taking a course, why bother with an introductory session?

If you are 100% certain that the career change you're making is the right one, and you know you have all the necessary pre-entry qualifications, then, by all means, skip this section and turn to one of the others – 'Retraining and New Skills Courses', 'Small Business and Self-Employment Courses', 'Open and Distance Learning Courses' or 'Degree and Advanced Courses'. You will find a wide choice of possible courses to apply for straight away.

The Confidence Gap

For most people, though, changing direction isn't quite as straightforward. If you have been at home, say, for ten or fifteen years, bringing up a family, then even going out to a GCSE evening class with a crowd of strangers may seem daunting.

In the same way, if you've done the same job all your life, even if you know you've never liked it, you will be taking something of a jump in the dark when you decide to give it up and retrain for something new. You need to think carefully about what is going to be involved, for you, and perhaps also your family.

Taking on a part-time course can be a challenge, too. You'll be committing yourself to spending a lot of your free time studying, for most courses have a homework element. It takes a little while to get into the way of it and it's usually better to make a gradual start, rather than overload yourself and find you have to keep dropping subjects or classes.

The factors to be clear about before you decide on a particular course of study are (1) to be sure that the content is something that will hold your attention (2) that the final qualification or skill gained is something you will value and (3) that you're going to be able to cope with the work.

Taking a pre-entry course can be a very good idea. It's a 'toe-in-the-water' approach that lets you sample the sort of topics you have to learn about and see how you get on with them – and indeed, the other students and the tutors.

Sifting through the options

For some people, too, there can be a problem in sorting through the choices. It's easy enough to decide that you've had enough of your present lifestyle and you want to change it. But how can you be sure you're making a wise choice of course from all the hundreds available? You may be eligible for training to take up a dozen different careers, but knowing which one is right for you may be hard to discover. Taking a 'taster' or 'pre-entry' course could help you make up your mind.

With a higher education course – for a degree, higher diploma or professional qualification – you need to take even greater care. You are likely to be committing yourself for several years of study, examinations and living on a grant (if you get one). Beginning with an 'Access' course that shows you both what you'll be expected to study and the level of work you'll be expected to do is a way of testing your motivation as well as giving you a launch pad into university, polytechnic or college.

What the titles mean

Colleges often invent their own titles for courses, and prospective students may not be entirely sure what they mean. The only certain way of finding out is to write or call on the college and ask for particulars of the specific course. But there are also some popular titles to look for in the course lists:

Access courses are usually preparatory courses for higher education (HND or degree entry), though in the last year or so, some *Access to Nursing* courses have been devised too. On this sort of course, you are prepared for mature student entry to an advanced level of study. It's an alternative to the long haul through GCSEs and A-levels and the subjects you study are taught in a way that is appropriate for adults. Access courses usually include some time brushing up your study skills, which is helpful if you have been a long way away from learning. You don't usually need any entry qualifications and some courses are part time or in school hours only.

Return to Learn and *Fresh Start* courses will often involve taking a range of short introductory courses to help you catch up with new methods of learning, and also to decide if you want to go any further with a particular subject.

Someone who's taken a Return to Learn course may decide to go on to an Access course. Someone else might decide to go for a retraining course or apply directly as a late starter for a degree. There's usually a certain amount of personal counselling on this sort of course to help people decide what to do next.

Open in the title of a course may mean 'open to everyone – you don't need any entry qualifications' or 'out in the open', i.e. you can do most of your studying at home by distance-learning methods. There's a fuller explanation in the introduction to 'Open and Distance Learning Courses', but because many colleges belong to Open College Networks, providing courses at levels from beginner to advanced, and mention their beginners' courses as asuitable starting point for 'returners', I've specified where they say they are offered in this section of the book.

Sampling courses have many titles. You may find that they're called 'New Directions' or 'New Opportunities for Women' or 'Wider Opportunities' or 'Replan'. There's a very good description of a 'Wider Opportunities for Women' course in the Durham: New College Durham entry in the Northern course lists of this section. The make-up of each course is different, but the idea is the same; to show people the range of choices open to them, and either give them talks about different occupations and the training available, or give them the chance to sample a skill, perhaps in a 'Drop-In Workshop'. The workshops may offer a range of different occupations, from basic plumbing to beginners' computing, or they may concentrate on providing the facilities and tution for one subject, like a Communcations Workshop or a Mathematics Workshop – see 'Halifax' in the Northern courses listed in this section.

Obviously you'll find other titles for preparatory courses have been used by colleges. *Polyprep* is pretty clear in itself, but Hatfield Polytechnic's entry in the Southern and Eastern list of courses in this section explains it more fully. *Gateway* can be a tricky one, as it may mean that the college concerned is a Gateway centre for courses from The Open College, providing tutorial support for students (see 'Open and Distance Learning Courses').

Sometimes, though, a college may have been describing its own particular preparatory course for mature students as a 'Gateway' course for years, and wouldn't want to change the name because that's the way it's become known in their district.

As always, if in doubt – ask. Most colleges who supply information for *The Mature Student's Handbook* emphasise that they are interested in welcoming mature students, and they often have someone who acts as a student counsellor or mature student adviser. You can track down this sort of person by phoning up and asking the person who answers 'Can you put me through to the person who deals with queries from mature students, please?' – or by naming the particular course that interests you, and asking if you can speak to the course tutor.

GCSE and A-level courses: some colleges offer what they call 'Mature GCSE' courses – meaning that special courses are put on for adult students. Otherwise, you may find you can join a group of school-leavers preparing for GCSE or A-levels, on an 'in-fill' basis – that means where there's space available. As the number of people leaving school falls, so more spaces are likely to become available in college GCSE and A-level courses, so don't be afraid to ask about these. It seems likely that in the future, there will be many more mature people joining teenagers at college and the college authorities will be glad to have them, to keep up the numbers for their classes.

Costs and Grants

There's a special section at the end of this book on this subject. Just for now, you may like to know that if by chance, a course is described as 'TA-sponsored' then it means the government's Training Agency has funded it, and it could well be free. If a course is described as 'under the 21-hour rule', then it's been planned to take advantage of the Department of Social Security rule that allows people receiving benefit (because they are unemployed or disabled, for instance) to study for up to 21 hours a week without losing their entitlement to benefit. You have to satisfy certain requirements – see the 'Costs and Grants' section of this book.

For some courses you may get a discretionary grant from your local education authority (LEA). Courses at Adult Residential Colleges often attract mandatory grants or a bursary. Where this has been identified by the organisers, I've mentioned it in the entry. Some students finance themselves by borrowing money, and in this connection the government's Career Development Loans might be a possibility (see 'Costs and Grants' section).

NB: Don't overlook the possibility of a pre-entry course in the 'Open and Distance Learning' section of this book, if you'd prefer or need to start learning at home. Check the 'Degree and Advanced Courses' section too, for details of *Associate Student* courses, which let you dip into undergraduate degree courses at university, polytechnic or college, to study one unit or topic that for you could be an introduction to a more extensive course.

THE COURSE LISTS

Courses are listed in order of town name, within regions. The full address of each college is given in the regional address lists at the end of the book.

I list colleges under their location, instead of their title, because often the name of a college doesn't suggest where it is situated. For example, Cassio

College is in Watford and Hertfordshire College of Building is not in Hertford, as you might expect, but in St Albans.

By identifying colleges according to their location, I hope to make it possible for people to see what might be on offer at a range of towns within reach of their home base or job. (Sometimes it's easier to go on to a course from work than go home and come out again for an evening's study.)

In compiling *The Mature Student's Handbook* I wrote in March 1989 to every UK university, polytechnic, college of higher education and college of further education. (New for 1989 are colleges of nursing, chiropody, physiotherapy, occupational therapy and radiography – see 'Retraining and New Skills Courses'.)

Some, which featured in the 1988 edition, had not returned updated or corrected entries by the time the book went to press a month later. In many cases, this could well have been because noamendments to their entries were needed, since many of the colleges which did reply in time simply confirmed last year's entry, in some cases adding new courses developed in the last 12 months. All the same, if you see an entry preceded by (1988), it has been included on the assumption that the college concerned wished to make no changes.

Finally, if you contact your local college, you may well find extra courses on offer – courses that were not confirmed when the book went to press, or have been introduced very recently to satisfy a local demand.

I am always delighted to know about new courses – and indeed, to hear readers' views of the courses they have taken, for future editions. Please write to me through the publisher, Kogan Page, whose address is at the front of the book.

THE REGIONS

Colleges and training centres with entries in this book are grouped into six regions as follows:

London and Middlesex	London area, including Middlesex. *Many colleges in Southern and Eastern England may also be accessible from London.*
Southern and Eastern England	Kent, Sussex, Surrey, Hampshire, Berkshire Buckinghamshire, Hertfordshire, Bedfordshire, Essex, Cambridgeshire, Suffolk, Norfolk.
Central England	Oxfordshire, Hereford and Worcester, Northamptonshire, Leicestershire, West Midlands, Shropshire, Staffordshire, Derbyshire, Lincolnshire, Nottinghamshire.

Northern England	Cheshire, Lancashire, Merseyside, Humberside, West Yorkshire, South Yorkshire, North Yorkshire, Cumbria, Durham, Tyne and Wear, Northumberland.
Wales and Western England	Avon, Gloucestershire, Wiltshire, Dorset, Devon, Cornwall, Gwent, South Glamorgan, Mid Glamorgan, West Glamorgan, Dyfed, Powys, Gwynedd, Clwyd.
Scotland and Northern Ireland	Dumfries and Galloway, Borders, Strathclyde, Lothian, Central, Fife, Tayside, Grampians, Highlands, Co. Antrim, Co. Armagh, Co. Down, Co. Fermanagh, Co. Londonderry, Co. Tyrone.

London and Middlesex

London – General

A guide *Cross-Ilea Access Courses 1989-90* is published by the Inner London Open College Co-Ordinating Committee. The courses listed are normally designed to prepare students for entry to specific higher education courses at colleges, polytechnics and universities (where some places may be reserved for 'Access' students). Some provide entry to a wide range of degree, diploma or professional courses – Business Studies, Engineering, Humanities, Law, Nursing, Social Sciences, Social Work, Teaching, Technology, Speech Therapy and Fashion Design are among the options. Academic entry requirements are not usually needed.

The guide is normally available in public libraries, or you can get a copy free from any of the following addresses: North & East London Open College Network, The Marlborough Building, 383 Holloway Road, London N7 0RN; Central & West London Open College, 115 New Cavendish Street, London W1M 8JS; Greenwich & Lewisham Education for Adults Network, South East London College (Breakspears 329), Lewisham Way, London, SE4 1UT; Open College of South London, Manor House, 58 Clapham Common North Side, London SW4 9RZ.

Birkbeck College

Access course. Open Routes. Provisional First Year entry scheme (see 'Degree and Advanced Courses'). University of London Preparatory Course in Mathematics, 1 year, part time. (For language preparatory courses, see City and East London College.) Contact The Registrar on 01-631-6561 (24-hour recording facility).

Camden Training Centre

(1988) Returners (for women) part time. Open Door English as a Second Language, part time.

Central London Adult Education Institute (formerly City Lit)

Fresh Horizons, with range of subjects, plus study skills and tutorials to catch up on missed opportunities and prepare for higher education, full time or part time, day or evening. Breakthrough, to build up confidence in reading, writing and discussion skills, part time, day or evening. Study Session, part time, day or evening. Open Study, part time, evening, study skills, plus own choice of subjects.

Central London: Polytechnic of Central London
Accepts Access course students from Kingsway College. Modern Engineering Foundation course for students with Arts/Humanities A-levels who wish to pursue a technological career, full time. Certificate of Continuing Education for mature students thinking of returning to education (mode not specified).

City and East London College
Access to Social Work Foundation course (students from ethnic minorities) full time, linked to Diploma in Social Work of Polytechnic of North London. Access Preparatory BEd course (students from Caribbean community) full time, linked to Polytechnic of North London degree. Similar part time course available for all candidates, also linked to PNL. Access Preparatory BEd course (students from the Bangladeshi community and other bilingual applicants who wish to become primary school teachers) linked to course at Thames Polytechnic. Access to HND and BA Business Studies at Polytechnic of North London (for people from ethnic minorities, especially black women) full time. Access to Modular BA Humanities at Polytechnic of North London, part time. Access to Nursing at Princess Alexandra School of Nursing, The London Hospital (for students bilingual in English and a language such as Bengali, Somali or Chinese, resident in Tower Hamlets or Hackney), part time. Preparatory courses in languages for students preparing to enter Birkbeck College, University of London to read Classics, French, German or Spanish, evening. University preparation course for those aiming to take Arts or Social Science degree courses, linked to Essex University (other universities and polytechnics also possible), full time or part time. Access preparatory course in physical and social sciences, linked to modular degree at City of London Polytechnic, part time. Access to Modular BSc Social Sciences degree at North London Polytechnic (including Librarianship), part time. Access to Speech Therapy training (for bilingual students) linked to City University, Central London Polytechnic or University College, London, part time.

Access: viewpoints
'During the Access course, we've studied English Literature, which has taken up a main section, Communications – developing our skills of verbal and oral communication – Study Skills, which everybody on the course needed, and Maths, which played quite an important part. We've also touched on Psychology, Philosophy and some Sociology, and for the last term, we've been going to the Polytechnic where we will be doing our degree, for an introduction to our specialist subject.'

(Access student, City and East London College)

'For a long time, higher education establishments have been aware that A-levels are not very good predictors of performance on degree courses, and that there was scope for a one-year course that concentrated on the skills needed for an autonomous student to take a degree course. Access courses are an attempt to give a second chance to people who, through no fault of their own, haven't got to where they ought to be. They provide an alternative to A-levels which is less broad in content but equally deep, and therefore more suited to adult students.'

(Spokesperson, City and East London College)

City Lit
- see Central London Adult Education Institute, above.

City University
(1988) Open Study, part time, day or evening, for adults wishing to return to higher education.

College for the Distributive Trades
Access to Higher National Diploma in Distribution course, part time, under 2l-hour rule. Mature students may be admitted without formal qualifications to this course, which contains specialist units in the areas of Distribution, Management, Marketing, Advertising & Public Relations, Fashion and Textiles Merchandising.

Cordwainers College
BTEC First Diploma in Design (Leathercraft) full time, 1990, depending on validation. Primarily designed as Foundation course for 16-year-olds but may also be suitable for adults. Currently being offered as college Pre-Diploma course for 1989 students.

East London: Polytechnic of East London
Accepts Access students on a wide range of degree courses. Conversion courses available for candidates with Arts/Humanities A-levels who wish to study Engineering or Technology (Higher Introductory Technology and Engineering Conversion Courses – HITECC).

Goldsmiths' College: University of London
Access courses in: Art and Communications; Social Studies; Education; Literature and Drama; and other schemes which may be used as evidence of sustained mature age study including Performance Skills; Making Experience Count; University of London Diplomas and Certificates in Anthropology, Field Archaeology, Art History, Economics, History, Literature, Film and Television Study, Psychology and Sociology.

London: University of London
Does not provide Access courses, but does accept a large number as satisfying General Entrance Requirement. (See 'Degree and Advanced Courses'.)

Middlesex Polytechnic
Return to Study courses in subjects like Psychology, Economics, Social Work, Geography for mature students considering full-time or part-time degree or other higher education courses. Also Pre-degree course for mature students returning to study; Returning to Learning course for older people. Certificate course, part of Modular Certificate/Diploma/Degree scheme (see 'Degree and Advanced Courses'). All-ages Summer School, many options and chance to earn credits for a degree.

Summer School: viewpoints
'I came last year to the Summer School because I thought it sounded interesting, and the year before that I'd been on another course run by Middlesex Poly, which was called 'Return to Learning' to see if I would like the atmosphere – and I did like it. I live in Brighton, and managed my first Summer School by commuting up and down. That year I did the Foundation of English Literature, and this year I did one of the courses that lead from that – 'The Short Story'. The course is three afternoons a week and you have to leave quite an amount of time for reading and writing essays. Apart from that, the grounds are very beautiful and you can reach the underground fairly easily to get to London. At last year's Summer School, I took the course exam and got a credit. Then I went for an interview at Sussex University, which is near where I live, and they were very interested in the fact that I'd spent my summer getting this credit. In fact they have accepted me unconditionally for next term to take a degree – presumably based on attending two Summer Schools.'

(Summer School student, Middlesex Polytechnic)

'The actual tuition that a student receives comprises perhaps 10 or 12 hours a week for five weeks, but students are also entitled to have a free run of the campus, which is sited so that they have easy access to London, while they're also located in a glorious country park setting. We have all sorts of sports and leisure facilities and have laid on a wide social programme for students. There's a well-stocked library, special facilities for art and music, and the Summer School students are free to take advantage of any of these aspects of the campus.'

(Spokesperson, Middlesex Polytechnic)

Morley College
(1988) English and Maths workshops, part time or evening. Second Chance English, Second Chance Maths and Second Chance French, part time. Study Skills, part time. Fresh Start in Social and Community Studies, Fresh Start in Science, Fresh Start in the Humanities, Fresh Start in Languages, daytime or evening classes, all available under 21-hour rule for unemployed people (see 'Costs and Grants'). Open University Preparatory Course (Saturday mornings). University of London External Degree Preparatory Course in English,

evenings. Wide range of introductory courses in subjects as diverse as Basic Art and Elementary Arabic. Part of Open College of South London (see 'Open and Distance Learning Courses'). Studies/Humanities, part time.

Newham Community College
Access by Independent Learning, part time, day or evenings; leads to Diploma of Higher Education courses at East London Polytechnic or to other courses (e.g. BEd, Certificate of Qualification in Social Work) at East London Polytechnic and other higher education centres. Return to Learn, part time, day; to improve basic education, to acquire or improve skills, e.g. Typing, Computing, Book-keeping, help progress to employment or other college courses, e.g. BTEC vocational courses or Access. Return to Learn courses are available at five centres within the borough. College says: 'Late start for parents – some creche places available.'

North London College
Courses under 21-hour rule include Business Skills for Adults, Adult Foundation and ESL Adult Foundation/Word Processing, and for students aiming at higher education, Preparation for Higher Education (also offered as an evening course).

North London: Polytechnic of North London
Wide choice of Access courses through City and East London College, Haringey College, Kingsway College, South London College, Southwark College and Waltham Forest College. Also 'Women into Architecture and Building' part-time course, satisfying entry requirements for PNL degrees in Architecture and Interior Design. HITECC course, a foundation course leading on to degree courses in science and engineering subjects, including Polymers, Chemistry, Physics, Computer Electronics, Computing and Electronic and Communication Engineering. Foundation course in Women's Studies (may be a pathway into evening degree), evenings. A letter from a Polytechnic spokesperson says 'Whatever unique identity belongs to this Poly, it concerns our commitment to mature students, second-career trainers and 'second chancers' ... over 60% of our population is over 2l at entry, and in some faculties (e.g. Social Studies) 90% of students are in this category.'

Paddington College
Access courses, all taking place between 10 a.m. and 3 p.m. during term, duration one year: Computing Access, linked to degree or HND at Central London Polytechnic; Science Access, linked to degree or HND in various sciences and associated subjects (e.g. Life Sciences, Environmental Science at Central London Polytechnic or HND Food Technology at Polytechnic of the South Bank – can also lead to courses in Chiropody, Physiotherapy, Osteopathy etc.). Engineering Access, linked to degree or HND at Central

London Polytechnic. Teaching Access (for students with an intimate knowledge of the Caribbean or Asian communities) linked to BEd degree at Middlesex Polytechnic. Threshold courses, same hours and duration as Access, roughly equivalent to A-levels, for adults who did not complete their education when younger, leading to degrees in Arts and Sciences. Threshold courses also available part time day or evening. Pre-Access preparatory course, part time, may lead to any Access course. Pre-Chiropody course, leading on to State Registered Chiropody at the Chelsea School of Chiropody, Paddington College, part time (15 hours per week). English and Study Skills, for students whose first language is not English, afternoons only. Also one-year courses, normally 10 a.m. – 3 p.m. in English, Study Skills and Fresh Opportunities, with substantial education and careers advice, for adults wishing to return to education or re-train. Special provision for students whose first language is not English. Introduction to Business for Bilingual students (20 hours per week).

South Bank: Polytechnic of the South Bank
Involved in 16 Access courses run by local FE colleges. Access courses with links into: Law; Built Environment; Business Studies; Maths, Science and Computing; Physical Sciences; Electrical and Electronic Engineering; Mechanical Engineering; Environmental Engineering; Health; Biotechnology and Environment; Languages; Social Sciences; Nursing; Teaching; Food Technology; Home Economics; Hotel, Catering and Institutional Management; Nutrition with Biology. The last-named leads to eligibility for registration as a State Registered Dietician.

South East London College
(1988) Preparatory BEd course (students from ethnic minorities) in conjunction with Goldsmiths' College, full time. Preparatory BEd course (Design and Technology) in conjunction with Thames Polytechnic, full time. Special GCSE/GCE A-level courses for adults (housewives, shift workers etc.) between 10 a.m. and 3 p.m. in various subjects. Foundation course for Information Technology users, part time, day and evening. Electronics for Women (no previous knowledge or particular mathematics standard required) part time, 9.30 a.m. to 3.15 p.m. ESF-funded one-year full-time (school hours and terms) preparatory course for women wishing to become Engineering Technicians, probably leading to City and Guilds awards. Preparatory courses for City and Guilds 726 Information Technology award, full time, part time or evening.

South London College
(1988) Access courses in: Business Studies, Food Studies, Engineering, Geology, Health, Biology and Environment; for Pharmacy Technicians, in Social Administration. Adult Foundation courses in Business Studies, Food Studies, Social and Community Work. Mode not specified but all the

courses listed above are organized in association with the Open College of South London, so it's reasonable to expect that flexible study arrangements will be available.

South West London College

(1988) Return to Study, full time. Access into Professional Accountancy, leads into Chartered Association of Certified Accountants' course, full time. Second Careers (three days). Foundation courses in Counselling, full time. Part of Open College of South London. Directed Private Study (see 'Open and Distance Learning Courses').

Thames Polytechnic

Sites at Woolwich, Dartford, Avery Hill, Wapping, Shadwell. Wide range of courses for mature students on several sites. Short courses, 'taster courses' workshops and training for work. Access courses to prepare for entry into higher education and teacher-training courses. Free advice from Greenwich Education and Training Advice Education Shop (01 834 2993).

Tottenham College of Technology

Access to Nursing, students aged 21 and over. Up to 21 hours, 5 days per week, one of which will be spent undertaking practical experience arranged by Enfield & Haringey School of Nursing.

Uxbridge College

Open Access, part time (GCSE. A-, A/S-levels). Management and New Opportunities courses for women, part time. Access to Higher Education: Social Science, Science, Nursing.

West London Institute of Higher Education

Fresh Start, part time (evenings) can lead to entry to degree courses. Options in American Studies, Beliefs and Values in World Religions, English, History, Understanding Britain. Past students have moved on to a part-time BA, a full-time BEd and a high-level course in local government administration.

Westminster College

(1988) Access to BA Home Economics and Teacher's Certificate at South Bank Polytechnic, full time. Access to BEd Primary Education at South Bank Polytechnic.

Willesden College of Technology

Access to Science, full time. Gateway to Study, full time (17-hour course). Preparatory courses for Open University (Maths, Science, Social Science, Humanities) evenings.

Southern and Eastern England

Basildon College of Further Education
Return to Study, Access course to higher education and employment. GCSE/A-levels, Foreign Languages – all with hours to suit mature students. Also flexible learning opportunities in many subjects.

Basingstoke Technical College
Access – Pre-Degree course, part time, under 21-hour rule and full time. Foundation Course in Art and Design, part time. Open University Preparatory course, evenings. GCSE/A-levels for mature students, part time, day and evening and full time. Basic Literacy/Numeracy, part time, evening. Employment Training courses including Women Returning to Work and Preparation course for entry to Nurse training.

Bedford College of Higher Education
(1988) Access to BEd Primary Education, full time. Also, subject to CNAA approval, Access to BEd (Hons) Secondary – Physical Education or Indian Dance, full time. Access to BA (Hons) Combined Studies, full time.

Borehamwood: De Havilland College
- see under Welwyn Garden City.

Bracknell College
Return to Work, part time.

Brighton Polytechnic
(1988) HITECC conversion course for people of A-level standard but without A-level Maths and Physics (or similar qualifications) wishing to prepare for entry to advanced courses in Engineering or Technology. Well-motivated mature candidates are welcome and may be able to offer work experience in lieu of A-levels. Certificate in Art, Craft and Society scheme, part time, provides opportunity for 'second chance' education and may support entry to more advanced courses.

Bromley College of Technology
(1988) Return to Study, part time.

Cambridge College of Further Education
(1988) Pre-School Playgroups Association Foundation course, part time.

Cambridge: Cambridgeshire College of Arts & Technology
Being amalgamated with Essex Institute of Higher Education; no information about courses available during this process.

Canterbury College of Art
(1988) Foundation course in Art, full time. Mature students welcome.

Canterbury College
GCSE/A-levels for mature students, selected academic subjects, part time. Open University Pre-Foundation course, part time. Access courses, part time. Open College courses and other Open Learning courses. Women into Engineering, part time.

Canterbury: University of Kent at Canterbury
New Opportunities for Women, part time. Access courses: Humanities, Social Sciences; Maths, Natural Sciences (the last two are currently being planned). Study Days; Study Evenings; Gateway courses. All these are part time. Also a range of general education courses (not leading to a qualification) is available.

Continuing Education at Kent: viewpoint
'The students on our courses come from all walks of life: housewives, train drivers, unemployed and retired people, school teachers and manual labourers; adults of all ages and previous educational histories. Some come just for the pleasure of study; some with the definite intention of proceeding to further studies.

Students of our Access courses have identified several unexpected gains: most mentioned new confidence, supportive friendships and intense mental stimulation. They gained "encouragement and an appetite for learning" ... "a restoration of confidence in one's ability to write" ... "a sense of achievement in learning" ... "the enjoyable company of the other students on the course also provided an unexpected bonus" ... "the group discussions stimulated my tired little grey cells beyond recognition."

(Spokesperson, School of Continuing Education, University of Kent)

Colchester Institute
Access course, part time, under 21-hour rule. Open University preparatory course, part time. GCSE/A-level for mature students,full time, part time, under 21-hour rule. Basic Literacy/Numeracy full time, part time, under 21-hour rule. Multi-Skills, full time, part time, under 21-hour rule. Open Learning Scheme (see 'Open and Distance Learning Courses').

Croydon College
(1988) Wide range of courses for unemployed people including Basic Numeracy and Literacy and Wider Opportunities for Women as well as Jobsearch training schemes.

Dunstable College
'We are continually developing flexible programmes on a modular basis for people wanting to update or retrain. For example, the GCSE/A-levels are scheduled for half mornings, to assist women's needs. (See also 'Retraining & New Skills' and 'Open & Distance Learning Courses'.)

Eastleigh College of Further Education
(1988) Access courses in Humanities and Technology, full time and part time.

Epsom – North East Surrey College of Technology
A-levels for mature students, part time, between 10 a.m. and 2.15 p.m. Flexilearning (see 'Open and Distance Learning Courses'). Back to Study – short course. Basic Numeracy, evenings. Access course preparing adults for degree in Sciences at Brunel University or Kingston Polytechnic.

Guildford College of Technology
Access to BEd degree at Kingston Polytechnic, part time. Access to degrees in Science and Engineering at University of Surrey. Return to Study, part time. GCSE part-time provision.

Hastings College of Arts and Technology
Mature students accepted on GCSE and 'A' level courses.

Hatfield Polytechnic
New Opportunities for Women, part time. Polyprep, part time (leads to a Certificate in Preparatory Studies). *Associate Student* scheme, part time (see 'Degree and Advanced courses'). Learning in Later Life, part time. Polyphysics, part time. HITECC conversion course for people of A-level standard but without A-level Maths and Physics (or similar qualifications) wishing to prepare for entry to advanced courses in engineering or technology. Well-motivated mature candidates are welcome and may be able to offer work experience instead of A-levels. This college is very sympathetic to mature students.

Polyprep: viewpoints
'On the Polyprep course, they give you four or five different subjects. Study Skills; English; we did a little bit of Anthropology, which was very exciting, knowing how it all started, a little bit of Biology; then we had Numeracy – which I failed dismally. But the lecturers taking us seemed to be specially

picked, they let you down very lightly. There was no embarrassment in front of other students. Nobody knows what marks you get, except between you and the lecturers. It's done very tactfully. At the end of the course, you'd have to be very bad, you'd have to flounder in all the subjects, not to find at least one thing to do that's interesting. At the end, the lecturer said to me, "If you really wanted to, and you've got the gumption to try, you could do a degree course." Well, for a retired person looking for a new role, this was absolutely marvellous.'

(Polyprep (now undergraduate) student, Hatfield Polytechnic)

'We have been in the business of designing routes back for mature students since about 1970, and we have quite a variety of routes back. We tend to design a route for a target group. For instance, we pioneered the New Opportunities for Women courses. Polyprep is for men and women who want to come back into higher education. They use the course to re-acquaint themselves, or perhaps acquaint themselves for the first time, with how to study. It's quite tough. They come in for two days a week and it's an 18-week course. They have to read and de-gut a book, present written work, do all the things all students have to do and most of them get turned on by this, even if they're petrified at first. It's a tool of analysis for the student and a measure of their potential ability.'

(Spokesperson, Hatfield Polytechnic)

Havering Technical College
(1988) Access course, linked to chosen degree subject(s) and college/polytechnic/university, part time. Fresh Start, part time. Open Learning (see 'Open and Distance Learning Courses').

Hemel Hempstead: Dacorum College
(1988) Fresh Horizons for Women, part time. Return to Learn, part time, enables adults to get a first qualification in English and Maths (see also 'Open and Distance Learning Courses').

King's Lynn: Norfolk College of Arts & Technology
(1988) Open Access course (English Literature, History, History of Art, Social Science) linked to University of East Anglia – school hours, Tuesday, Wednesday, Thursday. Access to Nurse Training, linked to Queen Elizabeth Hospital, King's Lynn – Thursday mornings (creche available) or evenings.

Kingston Polytechnic
Wide range of Access courses available from local FE colleges to allow entry to BEd, BA and BSc degrees at the Polytechnic. Contact Admissions Office for advice and information.

Luton College of Higher Education
(1988) Access to Further Education (for multi-ethnic students) part time, under 21-hour rule. New Horizons for Women, part time. Open University Preparatory course, part time. GCSE/A-level for mature students, part time.

Morden: Merton College
Arts Access to Higher Education; Applied Sciences Access to Higher Education; Social Sciences Access to Higher Education; Languages Access to Higher Education. All are one-year part-time courses for unqualified people over the age of 21. Students may apply to undertake BA, BSc or BEd courses at many universities, polytechnics and colleges of higher education. Access to BEd with Music – four term part-time or full-time course leading to study at Kingston Polytechnic. Return to Study – part-time day or evening course for anyone who wishes to improve their study skills and discover their future study direction.

Merton: Institute of Adult Education
Access, Fresh Start, New Directions, Extra-Mural University and Workers Educational Association classes. Saturday schools.

Newbury College
Return to Study scheme to suit individuals; can include GCSE, A-levels, BTEC National awards, various technical courses. Also evening course in Study Skills. TA-sponsored Restart full time and other Training Agency sponsored courses for unemployed people.

Norwich City College of Further and Higher Education
Access courses to University of East Anglia, full time or part time. 'Options'; Return to Study, part-time summer course; 'Way In' – GCSE Return to Study for Adults, part time; New Opportunities for Women, part time. Open Learning (see 'Open and Distance Learning Courses'), College Certificate in Community and Welfare Studies, full time or part time.

Portsmouth: Highbury College of Technology
(1988) Adults Pre-Degree full time and part time, leads to degrees at West Sussex Institute of Higher Education (and elsewhere). Wider Opportunities for Women, part time. Flexistudy and Open Learning courses (see 'Open and Distance Learning Courses').

Portsmouth College of Art, Design & Further Education
Return to Study and GCSE/A-level courses through Portsmouth Open Learning Programme (see 'Open and Distance Learning Courses').

Reading College of Technology
Access to higher education in the Social Sciences or in the Natural Sciences, two-year course with Berkshire County Council awards available. Full-time

GCSE and GCE AS and A-level courses of one and two years duration in 20-plus subjects. Mature students welcome.

Richmond Adult and Community College
Study Plan scheme, validated by the University of Oxford Delegacy. Fresh Start, part-time, modular, accredited daytime Access course in Humanities and Social Sciences. Art Access, part-time, accredited modular course, options including Design, Drawing, Painting, 3-D Computer Graphics. Business Studies, part-time, accredited Access programme. Fresh Start, Art and Business Studies programmes can provide access to higher education or re-entry to work. Gateway, part-time, modular accredited course for people who wish to return to study but prefer to progress at their own pace. Options currently include English Language and Literature, Study Skills, History, Sociology, Maths.

St Albans: City College
Mature students welcomed on infill basis on any part-time GCSE/A-level course. Access, full time, but hours mainly 9.30 a.m. to 3 p.m. Leads to university and polytechnic entrance.

Slough: Langley College of Further Education
Return to Study, part time.

Southampton Technical College
Access, part time, to La Sainte Union College of Higher Education degrees in English, Modern Languages, European Studies or Theology and will assist Access to BEd. Wider Opportunities for Women, part time. GCSE/A-levels/AS levels/BTEC courses, full time or part time; some GCSE courses with special 'mature student' syllabuses. Flexistudy courses (see 'Open and Distance Learning Courses').

Southampton: University of Southampton
Return to Study, part time, though Adult Education Department.

Southend College of Technology
Access course (to suit individual aims and directions), full time or part time. TA-sponsored New Opportunities for Women, part time. Return to Study, part time, 10 a.m. – 3 p.m. to suit parents. Learning Workshops – Literacy, English Language Support (for students whose first language is not English), Mathematics and Numeracy, Social Science, Computing, Languages, Office Skills - a 'season ticket' system is available for those who want to drop in as and when they wish. Adult students welcome to join courses in the main timetable for 16-19 year-olds; possibilities include Entry into Media Occupations, Pre-Social Worker course, Introduction to Assertiveness. Also Open Learning (see 'Open and Distance Learning'). This college is very sympathetic to adult students. Ask for the 'On course' free brochure.

Stevenage College
Pre-GCSE, GCSE/A-level for mature students. Basic Literacy/Numeracy, all full time or part time.

Surbiton: Hillcroft Adult College
Residential. Women Only. CNAA Modular Certificate, can lead to higher education, training or employment. No entry requirements, students receive mandatory grant. Also part-time Return to Learning and Linked Learning, short residential follow-up, during Easter or Summer (see 'Degree and Advanced Courses' for more details).

Sutton College of Liberal Arts
Return to Study, part time. Open University preparatory courses, part time. Women Back to Work, day and evening. Office retraining. GCSE, 'A' and A/S level examinations.

Tonbridge/Tunbridge Wells: West Kent College
Access to Higher Education. Access to Nursing for mature students. Return to Study. Part-time GCSEs (evenings). Part-time A-levels (evenings and day time courses for adults). Ask for part-time prospectus.

Watford: Cassio College
(1988) New Opportunities for Women, part time. Introduction to Counselling, part time and evenings (can lead to advanced courses at Stevenage or Hatfield). GCSE and A-level courses, full time, part time and evenings. Improve your Maths/English (suitable as pre-entry to GCSE). Pre-Nursing (with provision to take GCSEs), full time or part time. City and Guilds, part-time day courses in Cookery, Fashion, Embroidery and Flower Arranging, all classfied by college as suitable pre-entry courses.

Watford College
HITECC conversion course for people of A-level standard but without A-level Maths and Physics (or similar qualifications) wishing to prepare for entry to advanced courses in engineering and technology. Well motivated mature candidates are welcome and may be able to offer work experience in lieu of A-levels. Pre Higher Education course, full time, for those wishing to enter teaching of social sciences. GCSE/A-levels for mature students, full time and part time. Open Access to New Technology, part time (Multi-Skills). Wider Horizons courses by arrangement for those preparing for Open University or similar. (See also 'Open and Distance Learning Courses'.)

Welwyn Garden City: De Havilland College (also at Borehamwood and Hatfield)
(1988) Access to Further and Higher Education, part-time, modular, programmes from nine to twenty hours per week. Return to Study, part

time. Social Studies for Adults, part time. European Studies, part time. GCSE/A-levels for mature students, part time and special evening course in English. Spectrum – courses for adults with special learning needs, full time and part time; part-time help on one-to-one basis with reading, writing, spelling and basic maths (can be in student's or tutor's home). Artprep (for young students, but mature candidates also welcome), full time, part time by arrangement. Open Learning (see 'Open and Distance Learning Courses').

Wimbledon School of Art
The school says: 'Significant mature student entry to Art Foundation course', full time.

Central England

Abingdon College
Access courses designed to meet entry requirements for Oxford Polytechnic degree courses, full time or part time. GCSE/A-levels for adult students, part time or on infill basis. Return to Study/Pre-Access courses designed for students returning to education (including study skills, educational/vocational advice etc.). Basic Education in English or Numeracy, on individual basis, evenings. Courses for students with special needs (physical or educational) part time. Open Learning scheme (see 'Open and Distance Learning Courses').

Birmingham: Birmingham Polytechnic
Associate Student Programme (see 'Degree and Advanced Courses'). Listening and Visiting Student Programme – range of about 200 subjects from Media Studies to Maths, Accountancy to Fine Art, part time about two hours per week per subject. May lead to degree entry.

Visiting Student Programme: viewpoint
'I was a clerical worker with absolutely no opportunity for promotion, so I started going to night school. I did an O-level first of all, and went on and passed that, and did an A-level – by which time I'd got so engrossed in the education system, I really wanted to become a full-time student. But then the disaster came. I failed an A-level. I'd already applied to come to the Polytechnic, so I rang up, praying I could get on still, and received an awful lot of sympathy. A Visiting Student Counsellor was contacted about me. He then contacted me and said would I like to join the Visiting Students, so I jumped at the chance. They told me that if I worked hard, I'd be able to get on to the full-time degree course. I'm unemployed at the moment and I think millions of other people ought to take up this opportunity and do this.'
(Visiting student, Birmingham Polytechnic)

'Visiting and Listening students attend lectures and seminars we are running for our existing students. Visiting students are eligible to take the assessment or examination in the unit or course they are studying. Listening students may or may not be eligible to take the assessment, but if attendance is satisfactory, the student gets a transcript to show this. Most Listening students are sitting in on the courses in order to update their professional knowledge and skills.'

(Spokesperson, Birmingham Polytechnic)

Birmingham: Bournville College of Further Education
Access to Higher Education. Access to RGN (Nursing) training. Foundation to Learning. New Opportunities for Women. Women Into Technology (full time). Return to Work. Adult Preparation Training. Training Foundation courses in, e.g. Care, Catering, Data processing, Office Skills, Creative Design, Funeral Directing (by distance learning). Time on Your Hands. Mature students also join all GCSE and A-level classes and entry concessions are made. Most courses can be taken part time, day or evening. (See also 'Retraining & New Skills Courses'.)

Birmingham: Matthew Boulton College
(1988) Mature students' Alternative Admissions schemes, part time, to BEd and BA courses at Birmingham Polytechnic (no qualifications required). Alternative Admissions study skills course, part time, for mature students wishing to apply to various universities/polytechnics. GCSE, part time and evenings. New Opportunities for Women, part time. Preparatory Studies, part time, for those who need an introduction to study skills before starting other courses, Open University Preparatory Course, part time.

Bridgnorth and South Shropshire College of Further Education
Return to Work Programme for women, part time, school hours only. New Horizons (Caring, Business Studies or GCSE/A-levels) full time, part time or under 21-hour rule. Opportunities in Electronics and Engineering.

Chesterfield College of Technology and Arts
(1988) Access (Social Studies, Creative Design, Science and Technology, Environmental Studies) part time, under 21-hour rule. GCSE/A-level mature students' course, part time, under 21-hour rule. Basic Literacy/ Numeracy, part time under 21-hour rule. Open Learning (see 'Open and Distance Learning Courses').

Coventry: Henley College
(1988) Adult Literacy/Numeracy. Pre-GCSE Maths. How to Study Effectively. Taking Stock – course covers Life Patterns and General Health Care. Modes unspecified, ask college. 'Gateway' centre for courses from The Open College.

Coventry Polytechnic
New Opportunities for Women, part time, school hours only. Return to Learn (afternoon or Saturday morning). *Associate Student* scheme and 21-

hour rule courses (see 'Degree and Advanced Courses'). HITECC conversion courses for people of A-level standard but without A-level Maths and Physics (or similar qualifications) wishing to prepare for entry to advanced courses in engineering or technology. Well-motivated mature candidates are welcome and may be able to offer work experience in lieu of A-levels.

Derby: Derbyshire College of Higher Education
Gateway course, part time, between 10 a.m. and 3 p.m. for mature students to explore their capabilities and options. Pathway I, follow-up course, same attendance pattern, introducing Contemporary English Literature and Human Studies, with Study Skills and Numeracy. Pathway II, same attendance pattern, extends knowledge through a selection of several subjects. Certificate awarded on successful completion of the two Pathway courses can be used as alternative Access to degrees taught by the college (see 'Degree and Advanced Courses').

Dudley College of Technology
(1988) Access to Polytechnic Higher Education in Humanities, Social Sciences, Business Studies, Information Technology, Social Work, Science and Technology under 21-hour rule. Access course to Afro-Caribbean/Asian hairstyling, under 21-hour rule. Return to Study, part time. GCSE/A-levels, all age groups, full time, part time or evenings. Basic Literacy/Numeracy – wide range of courses, including English and Communications Workshop. Women's Access course and a General Entry course for Craft, Design and Technology, full time or under 21-hour rule.

Hinkley College of Further Education
(1988) 'Alternative Programme' for unemployed people under 21-hour rule. Wide range of skills and subjects, from Antique Restoration to Access course, all ability levels catered for, can lead on to other college courses.

Keele: University of Keele
(1988) Foundation Year (an introduction to the three-year Honours degree programme) is an excellent basis for mature students or for students not completely decided about their course requirements, according to the university. (See also 'Degree and Advanced Courses'.) Extra-mural courses in association with Lichfield College, part time.

Kettering: Tresham College
(1988) General Education Workshop, part time, course designed for individual students. Adult Basic Education, evenings. English and Maths Workshop for mature students, times to suit individuals. Gateway Workshop for mature students, half-day units, choices to suit individuals (includes Information Technology, Word Processing, Shorthand, Typewriting, Office Systems etc.). GCSE for mature students (two centres). Infill

opportunities on wide range of GCSE and A-level courses. Open University Preparatory Course. Open Learning Courses. Multi-Skills Workshop (see also 'Retraining and New Skills Courses', 'Open and Distance Learning Courses', 'Small Business and Self Employment Courses').

Kidderminster College
Replan courses for unemployed people, under 21-hour rule; options are: Introduction to Welding, Photography, Word-Processing and Music Keyboard. Return to Learning, part time. Open Access programmes, part time. 'Open Office' part time. Flexistudy (see 'Open and Distance Learning'). Adult Basic Education (including English as a second language) part time.

Leamington Spa: Mid-Warwickshire College of Further Education
Open Access (Life Sciences) leading to degree entry requirements of Coventry Polytechnic, part time, school hours. Open Access (Business Studies) leading to higher education, part time, school hours. Fresh Start, part time, school hours or evenings – introduction to study and range of courses. GCE A-levels for mature students, part time, school hours only. English as a Second Language for Workseekers, part time, school hours only. GCSE/A-levels, part time on infill basis. New Opportunities for Women, part time, mornings only. Second Chance to Learn (in association with Workers Educational Association) part time. Many part-time introductory and specific skills courses for unemployed adults (see 'Retraining and New Skills Courses'). Open Learning provision (see 'Open and Distance Learning Courses').

Lichfield College
This college is in the process of expanding its adult and community education facilities. At present it offers Basic Literacy/Numeracy on an individual basis, GCSE/A-level courses on an infill basis and many art and special-interest courses (see 'Retraining and New Skills Courses').

Loughborough: Co-operative College
Residential adult college owned by British Co-operative Movement, which provides full-time education for mature people as well as management courses for staff from Co-operative shops and Co-operative banks. Offers full-time Diploma in Policy Studies for people aged 23 and over without any prior qualifications (course covers social, business, historical and political issues, including community development, economic trends, national policies, political institutions and commercial and voluntary organisations). Selection by interview; experience in voluntary or community activities is a distinct advantage. Grants available to cover fees, course expenses, maintenance, allowances for dependents and personal expenses.

Loughborough Technical College
(1988) Access, part time or under 21-hour rule. Return to Learn, full time and part time. Gateway, part time. Open University Preparatory Courses, part

time. Mature students' GCSE/A-level, full time and part time. Basic Literacy and Numeracy, full time and part time. Basic Skills Workshop – Reading/Writing/Numeracy. Open Learning (see 'Open and Distance Learning Courses'). This college shows extra consideration for students with special needs - disabilities or learning difficulties – and has equipment that can be loaned to students for the period of their course (e.g. Microwriters, Braille writers etc.).

Newark Technical College
Return to Study/Return to Learn, full time, part time and under 21-hour rule. Mature Matriculation, full time, part time and under 21-hour rule. Open University Preparatory course, part time. GCSE/A-level mature students course, full time, part time, and under 21-hour-rule. Basic Literacy/Numeracy, full time, part time and under 21-hour rule. TA-sponsored Restart, part time. Drop-in scheme.

Newcastle-under-Lyme College
Intensive GCSE and GCE 'block-timetabled' courses for adults. Replan provision as part of general Staffordshire scheme, details from college. Access course for mature students. Direct link with Keele University possible.

Nottingham: South Nottinghamshire College of Further Education
Return to Study. Open University Preparatory Courses. GCSE and A-level mature student courses. Basic Literacy/Numeracy. Second Chance/Wider Opportunities. Drop-in scheme for Literacy and Numeracy. Modes not specified – ask college.

Nottingham: Trent Polytechnic
Access programme in liaison with local colleges of further education. HITECC Diploma Foundation course, to provide people with a good working knowledge of Engineering Sciences, Maths and Computing. The course attracts a wide variety of students ranging from 18–20-year-olds with arts backgrounds to more mature students who may not have studied for many years. Applications are welcomed from mature candidates who show strong motivation and who preferably have an O-level in Mathematics and some work experience. All candidates are interviewed. The course leads directly into HNDs and degrees at the Polytechnic in Computing, all types of Engineering, Mathematics and BEd courses in Mathematics and Sciences or Craft, Design and Technology. Also *Associate Student* scheme (see 'Degree and Advanced courses'). Open Programme provides a wide range of one-off events and short courses, designed to meet or 'stimulate' particular interests. This gives the opportunity to enter the Polytechnic and to become familiar with it. Open Programme clients may subsequently choose to consider further courses of study for which decision advice and guidance is

available. For details of Open Programme events and courses, telephone 0602 4l8248, extension 2333/2158.

Oswestry College
Basic Literacy and Numeracy Skills. Mature GCSE. Access to Higher Education via A-levels and BTEC National level.

Oxford Polytechnic
There are a number of local Access courses in the county which prepare students for entry into higher education. These courses are mainly Humanities and Social Science courses and are avaiable at the five colleges of further education in the county – Oxford, Abingdon, Henley, West Oxfordshire (Witney) and North Oxfordshire (Banbury). There is also a Science Access course at the Oxford College of Further Education. Applicants with no previous qualifications are welcome. Alternatively, there is a 20th Century Studies course run by North and West Oxford Community Education Centre which will also prepare students for entry into higher education. HITECC conversion course for people of A-level standard but without A-level Maths and Physics (or similar qualifications) wishing to prepare for entry to advanced courses in Engineering or Technology. Well-motivated mature candidates are welcome and may be able to offer work experience in lieu of A-levels.

Redditch College
It is proposed that this college should merge with North Worcestershire College to become North East Worcestershire College, so the range of courses may be affected when this happens. (1988) GCSE courses for mature students, full time. GCE A-level courses for mature students, full time. Pre-Nursing and Pre-Social Work courses for mature students, full time. Basic Skills (Literacy and Numeracy), part time, under 21-hour rule. Open Learning scheme (see 'Open and Distance Learning Courses'). Flexistudy (see 'Open and Distance Learning Courses').

Retford: Eaton Hall International
Certificate in Teaching English to Speakers of Other Languages – preliminary course; combines distance learning and residential block. Entered here at college's request as it is seen as a preparatory course for Teaching English as a Foreign Language (see 'Retraining & New Skills Courses').

Shrewsbury College of Arts and Technology
Access course to Higher Education. Attendance 3 days per week.

Solihull College of Technology
(1988) GCSE/A-level courses for mature students including adult unemployed. Flexistudy. Also Open College facilities (see 'Open and Distance Learning Courses').

Stafford College of Further Education
(1988) Open Access course in 20th-Century Life, evenings, can lead to a degree course at Staffordshire Polytechnic. Open Learning Access courses are available in a variety of GCSE,GCE and Business Studies subjects. Also Introductory Course in Catering, leading to City and Guilds certification, for people currently employed in the hotel, catering and tourist industries who wish to improve their career prospects.

Stoke-on-Trent – Cauldon College of Further and Higher Education
Access course in English, Sociology, History, Psychology, Study Skills, part time, day or evening, leading to degree courses at Staffordshire Polytechnic, Keele University and other higher education institutions.

Stoke-on-Trent: Staffordshire Polytechnic
(1988) 'Sampler' courses, part time, day or evening – choose from Computing, Politics, Law, Sociology, Economics, Business and Management Studies, History. Also *Associate Student* scheme (see 'Degree and Advanced Courses'). Study Experience Course in Economics; degree preparation for unqualified candidates who want to 'test the water' – evenings or afternoon and evening. Open College course, part time, in association with Stafford College of Further Education and Telford College of Arts and Technology. HITECC conversion course for people of A-level standard but without A-level Maths and Physics (or similar qualifications) wishing to prepare for entry to advanced courses in Engineering or Technology. Well-motivated mature candidates are welcome and may be able to offer work experience in lieu of A-levels.

Stoke-on-Trent Technical College
College states: 'Accessibility is paramount in this Potteries College that specialises in Technology. On the grounds that "It's people that count!", there are programmes across the board. The attractiveness of returning to learning through Access programmes is taken up, particularly for women and for people wishing to get into technology; there are vocational programmes of the most imaginative kind in Employment Training to set up new opportunities or to give the chance of retraining...' (See also 'Open and Distance Learning' and 'Retraining & New Skills courses'.)

Stourbridge College of Technology and Art
(1988) GCSE, full time and part time. NB: College says, 'Mature students particularly welcome and do not always have to conform to (standard) entry requirements.'

Stratford-upon-Avon: South Warwickshire College of Further Education
(1988) Access to Higher Education (times to suit family commitments or part-time employment) in association with Coventry Polytechnic and the

University of Warwick – various course options. Twentieth Century Studies, full time, for mature students, moderated by university and polytechnic representatives. Open Access to Science, between 10 a.m. and 3 p.m., can lead to courses in subjects as diverse as Biotechnology and Primary Teaching. Open Access to Engineering, between 10 a.m. and 3 p.m. can lead to various courses including Engineering Science, Systems Engineering (involving Computerisation). Return to Learn (includes counselling sessions) part time.

Sutton Coldfield College of Further Education
(1988) Access course, part time. Alternative Admission scheme, part time. Open University Preparatory Course, part time. Pre-GCSE, part time. GCE A-level mature students course, part time. Basic Literacy/Numeracy, part time. New Opportunities for Women, part time.

Tamworth College of Further Education
(1988) Access course, full time, an alternative to the traditional A-level route for mature students who want to acquire the skills to study in higher education.

Walsall: West Midlands College of Higher Education
(1988) Access to BEd degree, full time, in association with former Warley College of Technology (now part of Sandwell College).

Warley/West Bromwich: Sandwell College
(1988) Amalgamation of Warley College of Technology and West Bromwich College of Commerce and Technology. Access to BEd degree at West Midlands College of Higher Education, Walsall, full time, applicants from ethnic minorities particularly welcomed. Basic English, English as a Second Language, English for Immigrants, all part time. Women in the Community (confidence-building, women's rights and history) part time. Assertiveness Training (women and ethnic minorities), part time.

Warwick: University of Warwick
(1988) The Open Studies Programme offers day and evening courses in a variety of subjects; no entry qualifications are required. Certificate courses, based on the Open Studies Programme are offered part time in Women's Studies, and are planned in Archaeology, Local History and Counselling. Certificate-level study can be a stepping stone to a part-time degree course. (See also 'Degree and Advanced Courses'.)

Wellingborough College
GCSE for mature students, part time under 21-hour rule. GCE A-level, same conditions. City and Guilds Information Technology, BTEC First Certificate and BTEC National Certificate in Caring Services, part time, under 21-hour

rule, during school hours. Return to Study, Access and Open University Preparatory Courses are also available, modes not specified – ask college.

West Bromwich: see Warley/West Bromwich

Witney: West Oxfordshire Technical College
Access to Further Education – 20 hours per week. Access to Higher Education – 20 hours per week. This college requests also that certain of its Agricultural (Stud and Stable Husbandry – Thoroughbred Industry) courses are entered in this section: (a) Certificate Course, working in trainers' yards as stud grooms, secretaries, head lads. Some school achievements necessary. (b) Diploma – Mature GCSE, OND/C acceptable. Ability in other management disciplines considered.

Wolverhampton: Bilston Community College
Access to Higher Education, part time. Wide choice of specialisations including Art and Design, Business/Computer Studies, Race Relations, Engineering, Sciences (Biology, Physics), Library and Information Studies, Psychology etc. Can lead to degree/HND entry or professional course. Adult Skills course, part time, wide choice of skills from car body repair to computer programming (see 'Retraining and New Skills Courses'). City and Guilds Information Technology. Pathway I, part time: general education with emphasis on English and Maths for mature students; may be preparation for higher education. Basic Education for adults who have not studied for many years and need help with speaking and writing English – could be particularly useful for ethnic minority students – part time under 21-hour rule. Also Women-Only courses, funded by European Social Fund, all 20 hours per week for 32 weeks, e.g. Women Re-Entrants; Vocational and Language Training for Women (may be very helpful for those Asian women who have a poor command of English); Women and New Technology; Women in Science and Engineering; Women in Supervision and Management; Women and Self-Employment; Women and Craft Design Technology. NB: This college appears to be particularly sympathetic to the needs of unemployed adults and anyone with a problem to overcome, whether it's lack of former education, disability or language difficulties. A range of opportunities is available for adults with basic education needs and it is becoming increasingly possible to commence training at any time of year, including the summer months.

Wolverhampton: Wulfrun College of Further Education
(1988) Access. Return to Learn. Mature Matriculation. Open University. GCSE/A-level Opportunities. Multi-Skills. Basic Literacy/Numeracy courses – mode unspecified – ask college. (See also 'Open and Distance Learning Courses'.)

Northern England

Altrincham: South Trafford College of Further Education
Access to higher education, part time, under 21-hour rule. Return to Study, part time, under 21-hour rule. GCSE/A-level for mature students, full time, part time, under 21-hour rule. Basic Literacy/Numeracy, part time, under 21-hour rule. English as a Second Language, part time. Flexistudy (see 'Open and Distance Learning Courses'). Wider Opportunities for Women (see 'Retraining & New Skills' at college's request).

Ashington: Northumberland College of Arts & Technology
Adult foundation programme – guidance and access for adults seeking further and higher education or employment. Drop-In Centre, for support with writing, spelling and study skills; GCSE and GCE A-level – extensive menu available – access September each year. Mature entrants course for entry to Institute of Clerks of Works. Access to higher education course in Science and Engineering – September each year.

Ashton-under-Lyme: Tameside College of Technology
Threshold, full time or part time under 21-hour rule – aimed at access to degree/higher diploma courses at universities, polytechnics and colleges, via Manchester Open College Federation.

Barrow-in-Furness College of Further Education
(1988) Mature students' full time, part time and evening courses to suit individual needs for GCSE/A-level courses; also 'Drop-In' facilities. (See 'Open and Distance Learning Courses'.)

Blackburn College
Return to Learning, part time or full time, individually planned. Basic Skills to Pre-GCSE level, part time or full time, individually planned. English Language support courses for bilingual students. Communicating Across Cultures (groups or individuals from minority ethnic groups). Also Open College (see 'Open and Distance Learning Courses').

Bolton Institute of Higher Education
Associate Student scheme (see 'Degree and Advanced Courses'). Polymaths, which can lead to degree course, part time, evenings.

Bradford: Bradford and Ilkley Community College
(1988) Preliminary Course in Art and Design, part time, for mature/ unemployed students. Electronics for Women, part-time Foundation course, school hours and terms only. Basic Technology courses for Women, including Motor Vehicle Craft Studies, Vehicle Body Repair and Refinishing and Electronics. Return to Learn, part time. Certificate for Mature Students (Humanities and Social Sciences) full time or part time, to prepare for entry to higher education or professional training. Certificate for Mature Students (Business Studies) part time – successful students are eligible for the HND or HNC course in Business Studies. Access course to BEd or Postgraduate Certificate in Education, part time, for people from the Indian subcontinent who are fluent in more than one language and with an overseas qualification, such as MA or BA. Access to Bilingual Employment (ABLE) full time, for people who speak Urdu, Punjabi or Bengali together with English, and want to improve their chances of finding a bilingual job; may also open doors into further education.

Bradford: University of Bradford
The University recently introduced a range of Foundation Year Courses in Engineering. The courses are designed to enable candidates without conventional qualifications for entrance to Engineering degree courses to convert to engineering. To qualify for these courses candidates do not require passes in specific subjects at GCE A-level. A GCE pass at Ordinary level/GCSE at Grade B or higher in both mathematics and at least one physical science is normally required. Candidates can also qualify with approved alternative qualifications – for example in the Scottish Certificate of Education or Certificate of Sixth Year Studies, the Irish School Leaving Certificate or a BTEC National or Higher National Certificate in Sciences, Business Studies or Computer Studies. Mature students with a similar level of achievement in mathematics and physical sciences are also welcome to apply. Successful completion of the Foundation Course enables candidates to continue to a conventional degree course in Chemical Engineering, Civil Engineering, Electrical and Electronic Engineering or Mechanical Engineering.

Bridlington: East Yorkshire College of Further Education
(1988) Access to Higher Education, part time. Return to Study, part time. Pre GCSE, part time. GCSE/A-levels for mature students, part time. Basic Literacy/Numeracy, part time. New Opportunities for Women/Wider Opportunities, part time. Drop-In scheme. Multi-Skills, part time. Also Open Learning (see 'Open and Distance Learning Courses').

Burnley College
Gateway for Women (introduction to further education and vocational retraining). Access (counselling and advice for adults returning to further

education – does not appear to be a substitute for A-levels). Open College (adult entry into higher education – ask for details). Open College (Maths and Numeracy Workshop). NB: modes unspecified – ask at the college.

Consett: Derwentside College
Higher Education Foundation Certificate, part time, can lead to a range of degree/diploma courses at polytechnics in North East England. Open University Preparatory Course, part time. GCSE/A-level for mature students, part time, under 21-hour rule. Basic Literacy/Numeracy, part time, under 21-hour rule. Office Skills for the Unemployed; Employment Training (see Retraining & New Skills). Adult Basic Education Course, part time, individually planned.

Dewsbury College
Access course for ethnic minority students, full time, linked to Social Sciences courses at Leeds Polytechnic, Sheffield City Polytechnic, Bretton Hall College, Bradford & Ilkley Community College. Fresh Start (Continuing Opportunities Programme) for unemployed people, under 21-hour rule – can lead to Access or other courses. Breakthrough course for all adults, part time, under 21-hour rule, can lead to Access or other courses. New Opportunities for Women, part time, school hours, one day a week. Basic Skills Workshop, part time, under 21-hour rule. Study from home (see 'Open and Distance Learning Courses'). Creche support available.

Doncaster Health Authority
Access course to Nursing, one day (9 a.m. – 4 p.m.) at Doncaster Royal Infirmary, and one evening (6 p.m. – 8 p.m.) at Doncaster Metropolitan Institute of Higher Education, Waterdale. Course lasts 12 weeks.

Durham: New College Durham
New Beginnings – basic numeracy and literacy course, part time. Wider Opportunities for Women, part time. Scope – skill-sampling course for unemployed people, part time. Open University Preparatory Course, evenings. Open Learning and Flexistudy (see 'Open and Distance Learning Courses').

Wider Opportunities for Women: viewpoint
'Nearly 100% success has been achieved in helping students proceed to work or further training and education. One student does it all – she works part time in a kitchen shop, has taken a training course to qualify as a Citizens Advice Bureau volunteer worker, passed her Marine Navigation certificate and started her own business on a part time basis. That's exceptional, but we find that coming on the course shows women that there *are* many openings for them, even in times such as these, if they can present themselves well and are willing to tackle new activities. Women have the chance to sample

Computing, Catering, Office Technology, Sport, Art and Design, Music and Drama, Welding, Carpentry, Car Maintenance, Painting and Decorating, Bricklaying and Electrical Engineering. Sessions are also held on job search skills and self-presentation.'

(Spokesperson, New College Durham)

Gateshead Technical College
Higher Education Foundation Course (in association with Newcastle College of Arts & Technology) part time over one, two or three years – can lead to degree/diploma courses at Newcastle-upon-Tyne Polytechnic. Adult Literacy/Numeracy, part time, day and evening. Open Learning and Flexistudy (see 'Open and Distance Learning Courses'). Return to Nursing. Mature entry to Nursing.

Halifax: Calderdale College
New Opportunity courses in GCSEs and A-levels for mature students. Access courses are being developed and should be available by September 1989, to include Access to Humanities, Social Science, Business and Technology. The courses will be offered on a full- and part-time basis, and can be studied under the 21-hour rule. Drop-In Mathematics and Communications Workshop. Community Drama course for mature students under the 21-hour rule. Open University Preparatory course, part time. All tuition for people on benefit is free of charge. The college is also developing community-based access points in Calderdale to encourage people back into education. Provision is varied according to the demands of the community and it acts as a feeder into the more formal approach of college.

Workshops with a Difference: viewpoint
'The Communications Workshop houses all the resource materials a student of English and Communications could wish for, with a cheerful, vigorous and helpful staff... The drop-in nature of attendance is bound to suit everyone, whether coming to consult a tutor, use the audio equipment, cameras, word-processors and so on, or simply to practise some of the many communications exercises on file.' ... 'A well equipped, expertly staffed Mathematics Workshop is available to all. More than 100 students a day pass through ... you can work at your own pace, with a teacher at your elbow to provide guidance and support when needed. The workshop is designed to suit all kinds of students, from "starters" to "returners".'

(Spokesperson, Calderdale College)

Huddersfield Polytechnic
HITECC conversion course for people of A-level standard but without A-level Maths and Physics (or similar qualifications) in Engineering or Technology. Well-motivated mature candidates are welcome and may be able to offer work experience in lieu of A-levels. ESF-sponsored Women into Technology course, full time, school hours and terms only.

Kirby College of Further Education
'We welcome mature students on all our courses'. Most feature in the 'Retraining & New Skills' section, but titles which imply the content is preparatory include Pre-Hospital Studies, full time, CCETSW Preliminary Social Care, full time, and GCSE full- and part-time courses.

Lancaster College of Adult Education
Participates in Open College of the North West; part time courses, wide range of subjects. GCSE Mature Students, part time (four subjects only). Languages, from preliminary to advanced certificate and City & Guilds (3 craft subject areas). Music Associated Examining Board exams, various grades.

Leeds Polytechnic
(1988) Skills Training and Career Development Programme, 10 weeks, part time. Course can lead into a wide range of vocational courses (see 'Retraining and New Skills Courses').

Leeds: Park Lane College of Further Education
Mature Matriculation Preparation course, full time or part time. Pre-Degree Study Skills, Open University Preparatory Course, part time. 'Start Afresh' part time for people away from education for some years; includes career planning. Practical Study Skills, part time, to be taken before or during a study course. Assessment Programme for anyone who thinks he/she may have difficulty following the Start Afresh course. Individual Programme to tackle weaknesses or to allow people to start at times between course start dates. (See also 'Retraining and New Skills Courses' for wide range of 21-hour courses.) Pre-degree Law Access course. TA-sponsored Job Club. NB: College is particularly welcoming to mature students.

Leigh College
'All our courses are open to everyone in the community and outside who can benefit from them. Special concessions for the unemployed'. GCSE and A-level courses full time and part time. GCE A or GCSE-linked full-time courses biased towards Expressive Arts, Paramedical, Music. Music Foundation course part time. New Opportunities for Adults, part time. (See 'Retraining & New Skills', 'Small Business', 'Open & Distance Learning courses'.)

Liverpool: South Mersey College
Access course leading to degree and Certificate of Qualification in Social Work (CQSW) entry at universities, polytechnics and institutes/colleges of higher education. Second Chance course, including Open Learning Workshop in Maths and English for adults of all ages without qualifications, wishing to improve basic skills and develop new areas of interest in order to

progress to such courses as GCSE, A-level or Access. Wider Opportunities for Women courses in Construction and Automobile Technologies. Courses in general education to provide women with the confidence to enable them to proceed to other relevant further education courses.

Manchester Polytechnic

(1988) Polymaths, part time, can lead into degree in Mathematics. Certificate in Environmental Studies, part time, can lead into Diploma of Higher Education or degree in Environmental Studies. HITECC conversion course for people of A-level standard, but without A-level Maths and Physics (or similar qualifications) wishing to prepare for entry to advanced courses in Engineering or Technology. Well-motivated mature candidates are welcome and may be able to offer work experience in lieu of A-levels. NB: Excellent free *Mature Students' Handbook* available, from Manchester Polytechnic, All Saints, Manchester Ml5 6BH.

Manchester: South Manchester Community College

'Gateway' general access course for mature students, full time, part time and under 21-hour rule for those who are not certain which subjects they would like to study in higher education: mainly leading to the Diploma in Higher Education at Manchester Polytechnic. 'Pathway' access course under 21-hour rule, includes Local History, Sociology, English Language and Literature, Maths, Study Skills, Computing. Operates during school hours only. 'Threshold' access course, full time, part time and under 21-hour rule, for those who wish to do degrees in Humanities and Social Sciences. 'Vocational' access course, for those who wish to do degrees or diplomas in Social Work or Youth Work and Community Work, and people who need to develop confidence and skills because they have had little academic success at school or since. Courses are widely accepted by universities, polytechnics and colleges of higher education. Playgroup for students' children. Courses lead to qualifications from the Manchester Open College Federation (see 'Open and Distance Learning Courses'). Mature students are warmly welcomed at this college.

Manchester: UMIST (University of Manchester Institute of Science and Technology)

Mature Matriculation Scheme (see 'Degree and Advanced Courses'). Also 'Conversion Course' for people with qualifications that are good (e.g. Arts A-levels, grades BBC or better), but inappropriate for Engineering degree courses. After the first year, the subsequent three years are common with UMIST's existing Engineering degree courses.

Manchester: University of Manchester

New Horizons, part time – a 'taster' course across a wide range of subjects plus study skills; available October-March. Wider Horizons, part time –

extends New Horizons course, but individual units may be taken. Return to Study – distance-learning version of New Horizons (see 'Open and Distance Learning Courses'). Career Studies programme, flexible hours, for people looking for a change.

Manchester: Withington Centre for Community Education

Fresh Start, part time. Return to Study, under 21-hour rule. Open College courses though Manchester Open College Federation, various subjects and levels. Pre-GCSE, part time. GCSE/A-levels for mature students, part time. Basic Literacy/Numeracy, part time. Open Workshops in Modern Office Skills, Maths, English, Book-Keeping, Basic Skills, Business English, English as a Second Language.

Middlesborough: Longlands College of Further Education

(1988) GCSE. Introduction to Computing. Access courses. Women's 'Taster' and Access courses (various vocational areas). Basic Skills (Literacy and Numeracy). Personal Counselling. Scope-type infill provision, for adults seeking to update skills in vocational areas. Prepare for Engineering, Electrical Engineering, Electronic Engineering, Computer Engineering, Information Technology – all these for people without qualifications. Pre-entry 'top up' units for people with qualifications, e.g. Bridging Courses from Electrical Craft level to BTEC Higher Award entry. Access to Higher Education Course, range of modules available.

Middlesborough: Teesside Polytechnic

Access to Humanities, Social Studies, Information Technology, Computer-Aided Engineering, Mathematics, via part-time Access/Gateway programmes. HITECC conversion course for people of A-level standard but without A-level Maths and Physics (or similar qualification) wishing to prepare for entry to advanced courses in Engineering or Technology. Alternative admissions: well-motivated mature candidates are welcome and their work and life experience may be accepted in lieu of formal qualifications.

Nelson: Nelson & Colne College

Under the aegis of the Open College of the North West, the college offers a range of courses at introductory and post-introductory level. These courses tend to concentrate on Study Techniques and the Social Sciences, with some courses on the Law and Business Studies side. These can be taken full or part time. The Continuing Education section offers help with Maths and English on a flexible drop-in basis, which is ideal for adults with other commitments. 'We suggest that any adult wishing to make a fresh start at our college contacts "Stand l8", the college's educational and guidance service. A confidential talk with one of our adult education staff will ensure that prospective students get on to a suitable course – perhaps even at another college! Appointments can be made by ringing Nelson 603151.'

Newcastle-upon-Tyne Polytechnic
(1988) Higher Education Foundation course, in association with Newcastle-upon-Tyne College of Arts and Technology, Gateshead Technical College, Derwentside College, Peterlee College and North Tyneside College. 14 subject modules are available, each one designed to take a year to complete with the student attending college for half a day per week per module. Well motivated mature candidates are welcome and may be able to offer work experience in lieu of A-levels. Also *Associate Student* scheme (see 'Degree and Advanced Courses').

Ormskirk: Edge Hill College of Higher Education
(1988) Return to Study, part time. *Associate Student* part time (see 'Degree and Advanced Courses'). Open College scheme (see 'Open and Distance Learning Courses').

Peterlee College
Employment Training Programme and Adult Education provide opportunities including Drop-in Workshops to develop basic skills, e.g. Maths, Letter Writing, Interview Techniques. Access to Higher Education course for adults, part time. Adult Basic Education Workshop, part-time, drop-in basis. Adult Basic Education, evenings. Flexistudy (see 'Open and Distance Learning' courses).

Preston: Lancashire Polytechnic
Foundation Studies course, part time, to help students assess their suitability for higher education. New Opportunities for Women, specially timed between 10 a.m. and 3 p.m. LEA-sponsored Access course for students from ethnic minorities, part time, leading to entry to a degree course. Foundation course in Science and Technology for Women, full time. HITECC conversion course for people of A-level standard, but without A-level Maths and Physics (or similar qualifications), wishing to prepare for entry to advanced courses in engineering or technology. Well-motivated mature candidates are welcome and are able to offer work experience and prior learning, certificated or not, in lieu of A-levels. *Associate Student* Scheme (see 'Degree and Advanced Courses'). Part of Open College of North West. Detailed advisory interview available for mature students considering return to education. Also free cassette tape on request 'It takes All Sorts'.

Rochdale College of Adult Education
(1988) Preparation for Employment, under 21-hour rule. Job Search Skills and New Technology.

Rotherham: Rockingham College of Further Education
Open College scheme to prepare for higher education, part time, credit-based – acceptable for entry to various universities, polytechnics, colleges.

Flexistudy (see 'Open and Distance Learning courses') and Preparation for Nurse Training.

Rotherham College of Arts & Technology
(1988) Access to Higher Education, full time and part time, leading to Certificate of the South Yorkshire Open College. Women's Access to Information Technology, full time and part time. New Opportunities for Women, part time. Women's Studies, part time. Women's Studies in Multi-Skills Workshop, part time. Access to Employment and Training, under 21-hour rule, for people over 25 who have been unemployed for 12 months or more. Return to Learning, part time (roll-on, roll-off entry) under 21-hour rule, and Return to Study, under 21-hour rule, leading to Certificate of South Yorkshire Open College (see also 'Open and Distance Learning Courses'). Communications for Employment and Training (for students from ethnic minorities who need help with English), under 21-hour rule. PHIT (Physically Handicapped into Information Technology) under 21-hour rule. Multi-Skills Workshop, part time. Special Workshops, including Multi-Skills and English Language support, primarily for those whose first spoken language is Mirpur Punjabi, part time.

Salford College of Technology
Proposed BTEC Continuing Education in Health Studies course, giving access to courses in Nursing, Chiropody, Physiotherapy, Occupational Therapy, Radiography, Social Work and Higher Education. The proposed course would be organised on the basis of 30 weeks of 10 hours attendance and l further week involving two days 10 a.m. – 3 p.m. and one day 10 a.m. – 2 p.m., together with a work placement of 30 days of 4 hours attendance each. No starting date has yet been announced for this course but as and when it goes ahead, it will be open to candidates over 21 who are numerate and literate and have shown some evidence of commitment to work in the health or caring areas.

Sheffield City Polytechnic
(1988) The Polytechnic and other colleges in the region have developed a number of preparatory Access courses which can lead to many of Sheffield City Polytechnic's degree-level programmes. There is also an *Associate Student* scheme, part time (see 'Degree and Advanced Courses'). The South Yorkshire Open College may be contacted through Sheffield City Polytechnic, 36 Collegiate Crescent, Sheffield S10 2BP.

Sheffield: Loxley Tertiary College
Access to Business Studies, full time, successful students guaranteed place at Sheffield City Polytechnic. Women's Access course in Engineering Technology, full time; guaranteed places on degree course at Sheffield City Polytechnic for successful completion. Women's Access course to higher

education, part time - 6 hours per week over 2 years – (South Yorkshire Open College Certification at levels 3 and 4 to meet matriculation requirements of Sheffield City Polytechnic and Sheffield University). Access course in Social and Community Care, part time – 6 hours per week over 1 year – (South Yorkshire Open College Certification at levels 2 and 3 to meet entry requirements of higher level Sheffield Tertiary College courses in the Community Care area; guaranteed places on Parkwood Tertiary College Diploma in Social Care course for successful students). HITECC conversion course, full time, in conjunction with Sheffield City Polytechnic, open to students who have previously studied arts or humanities subjects but not Maths or Science to A-level, who wish to convert to an Engineering discipline, and to mature students with relevant previous experience but no qualifications. Course leads to HITECC Diploma and guaranteed place on Engineering degree or HND course at Sheffield City Polytechnic for successful completion. 'The college provides a range of basic education and return to study opportunities on its two main sites and in ten of its sub-centres. These include GCSE options, and, increasingly, a network of short course provision with an emphasis on South Yorkshire Open College accreditation. Options include Women's Studies, Introductory Information Technology and Health Issues, but there is also an emphasis on responding to the needs of individual adult returners.'

Sheffield: Parkwood College
(1988) A-level Alternative course, to prepare students for higher education, part time. Access course for Asian students part time and full time, including help with mother tongue.

Sheffield: Rother Valley College of Further Education
Access to Higher Education, full time and part time. Return to Learn, part time. Mature Matriculation, full time and part time. GCSE/A-level for mature students, part time. Basic Literacy/Numeracy, part time. New Opportunities for Women/Wider Opportunities, part time. Drop-In scheme, part time. 3-D Studies(Pre-Polytechnic Art and Design degree courses), part time.

Sheffield: Stradbroke College
GCSE and A-level. The college offers approximately 30 subjects at GCSE level and 20+ at A-level, available full or part time. Classes consist of students of mixed ages. 'Our students seem to feel that this enhances the composition of the courses'. Second Chance to Learn, one day a week for two years, can lead to entry to a degree course both at Sheffield Polytechnic and Sheffield University. It is specifically geared to meeting the needs of women – it fits into a school timetable and has creche facilities. Access to Journalism, full time. This is a new course with no formal entry requirements and any applicant over the age of 19 will be considered. Recognised

by the National Council for the Training of Journalists – successful completion will give entry to the formal NCTJ schemes and the prospect of employment with a provincial newspaper. Also recognised by the University of Sheffield where successful students will progress through levels of study to the award of the University's Diploma of Journalism. Preparation courses (summer, evening courses) for mature students entering Higher Education or the Open University. In the autumn, more specific subject-based courses are planned mainly for OU applicants but relevant to others also.

Shipley College
Return to Study skill by Open Learning and by a taught course (part time). These can lead into higher education, BTEC, City and Guilds or GCSE. GCSE/A-level – mature students welcome on infill basis. HELP – this course offers a contribution of GCSE or A-levels in the Humanities and Arts, such as Communications, Literature, Law, Psychology, Sociology, for those thinking of a career such as Social Work or Teaching. Placements can be organised for those with well-formed career plans. Visits and speakers are organised to help students firm up their ideas.

Returning to Work/Study: viewpoint
'It's a first step in helping adults decide in which direction they will proceed – further study or training, or directly securing employment. This course is specially designed for people without educational qualifications. They may have left school early, recently become unemployed or have been out of the job market for several years … As well as participating in a practical Job Search exercise, the course will include a very basic introduction to the computer's role in the workplace, with guidance in 'hands-on' experience … a chance to improve communication skills … individual counselling and plenty of opportunities for discussion in a friendly, relaxed atmosphere with like-minded adults and skilled staff. Attendance is on Mondays between 9.30 and 3 p.m., and no attendance is required during school holidays and half-term breaks. Creche facilities are available.'

(Spokesperson, Shipley College)

Southport College of Arts and Technology
Open College of the North West day and evening courses. Various levels and subjects, for unqualified adults who want to improve job prospects or work towards higher education. Return to Study – GCSE/A-levels, part time, day and evening. Basic English for adults, evenings. English as a Foreign Language, evenings.

Sunderland Polytechnic
Polytechnic Certificate in Art and Design Foundation Studies, full time.

Sunderland: Wearside College

Introductory courses for Women, half a day each a week, to Information Technology and Welding, creche facilities available. Proposed 'taster' courses including hydraulics, pneumatics, bricklaying etc. Telephone enquiries to Elsie Thompson on Wearside 5670794, extension 275.

Wakefield: Bretton Hall College

Mature student courses, part time, for those preparing to return to education, prepare for university matriculation, take Open University Foundation courses. (See also 'Open and Distance Learning Courses'.)

Warrington: North Cheshire College

New Opportunities for Women, part time. Return to Study, part time (self-selected modules). Access courses, part time; many subjects at various levels (level 4 courses can lead into degree studies). 'Jigsaw' Programme, part time, includes Study Skills, Personal Evaluation, Educational Counselling. NB: the Dean of Studies says: 'The college is particularly geared to the needs of those students who wish to "Make a Fresh Start". A variety of course structures enable adult men and women to take advantage of the University of Manchester "Mature Matriculation" provision. All our full-time courses are open to mature students.'

Widnes: Halton College of Further Education

'We accept mature students on all our courses'. GCSE and GCE A-level subjects available. (See also 'Retraining & New Skills', 'Small Business', 'Distance & Open Learning Courses'.)

Wales and Western England

Aberystwyth: Ceredigion College of Further Education (Aberystwyth, Cardigan, Felinfach)
(1988) GCSE A-level for mature students, part time, under 21-hour rule (no specific entry qualifications required). Agriculture, preliminary, part time. Horticulture, preliminary, part time. (See also 'Retraining and New Skills Courses' for short courses with vocational application that can be taken without prior qualifications.)

Aberystwyth: University College, Aberystwyth
The college offers a number of Access courses, some in conjunction with other colleges, for intending mature undergraduates at this or at any other university. A one-year Foundation course in Mathematics & Physics is run by the college with bursaries from the Laura Ashley Foundation for up to 8 students. In conjunction with Ceredigion College of Further Education, the college offers Access courses leading to BTEC qualifications in Microelectronics and Computing. Discussions regarding a Life Sciences Access course are ongoing. Courses in Agriculture are offered in conjunction with both the Welsh Agricultural College and Tresham College, North-amptonshire. Success in any of these courses can lead to a degree course at UCW or elsewhere. Places are guaranteed at UCW for successful candidates on the residential Foundation course, the Microelectronics and Computing course and the Tresham College Access course.

Barnstaple: North Devon College
Access to further education for unemployed people (e.g. to Business Studies, Caring Skills, Catering). Return to Study, part time. GCSE/A-levels – mature students welcome on standard courses. Restart, one week full time and 'Drop In' facility.

Bath: Norton Radstock Technical College
Start courses, part time. Second Step for Women, part time. Adult Basic Education, evenings. Access to Information Technology, mainly evenings. Range of Access courses preparing students to enter higher education or professional training courses, for those who do not have the traditional

entry qualifications. Mature GCSE courses in variety of subjects including Maths, English, Business Studies and Accounts. Several other learning programmes due in September 1989 including Community Care, Business Studies and a general long Pre-Access course.

Bridgewater College
(1988) Women into Work (for women 25 and over, exploring non-traditional areas of work). Access course: Humanities and Social Science, linked chiefly to Bristol Polytechnic. Access course: Science, to higher education, various establishments. Details of times from college. Open Learning (see 'Open and Distance Learning Courses').

Bristol: Brunel Technical College
(1988) Access to Science, part time, under 21-hour rule, timetabled to suit people with domestic commitments. Designed to meet Bristol Polytechnic entrance requirements for one of: HND Applied Physical Sciences, HND Applied Biological Sciences; BSc (Hons) and BSc Scientific Instrumentation, BSc Applied Chemical Sciences (subject to CNAA approval). 'Freeway' Open Learning (see 'Open and Distance Learning Courses').

Bristol: Filton Technical College
Access to Social Science, Humanities, Education and Social Work, part time, currently under 21-hour rule, may lead to degrees of Bristol University and Bristol Polytechnic. Access to Craft, Design and Technology Teaching, in conjunction with Bristol Polytechnic, for women and for people from ethnic minorities. GCSE/A-level courses open to mature students, full time and part time. Adult Literacy – tuition for new readers who may join the evening class at any time. Flexastudy courses (see 'Open and Distance Learning Courses').

Bristol Polytechnic
HITECC conversion course for people of A-level standard but without A-level Maths and Physics (or similar qualifications), wishing to prepare for entry to advanced courses in Engineering or Technology. Well-motivated mature candidates are welcome and may be able to offer work experience in lieu of A-levels. Access students from courses at local technical colleges welcome – see 'Degree and Advanced Courses'.

Cardiff: South Glamorgan Institute of Higher Education
(1988) Diploma in Social and Industrial Studies, full time (grants available), no formal qualifications required. Successful completion of this course may lead to the student's acceptance on vocational courses within the Institute, or on degree courses in the areas of History, Social Sciences and Law, at university or polytechnic.

Cardiff: University of Wales College of Cardiff
Preliminary year and Foundation year courses available in Science and Engineering.

Cardigan – see Aberystwyth: Ceredigion College

Cheltenham: College of St. Paul & St. Mary
(1988) Access to BEd, full time, mainly for students from ethnic minorities. Preparing for Higher Education, part time and full time.

Chippenham Technical College
(1988) GCSE open to students of all ages, full time and part time. Access to Nurse Training for mature students. Job Applications Techniques, evenings. New Opportunities for Women, part time. Adult Literacy/Numeracy, various, part time. Progressive Literacy, evenings. Flexistudy (see 'Open and Distance Learning Courses'). All full-time courses at this college are open to adults.

Dolgellau: Coleg Merionnydd
(1988) Open Learning (see 'Open and Distance Learning Courses').

Exeter College
Access to Higher Education, details from college.

Exeter: University of Exeter
Runs two programmes of Access to higher education courses (one in Humanities and Social Studies, one in Science and Technology) part time and in school hours only, in colleges throughout Devon, Cornwall and Dorset.

Felinfach – see Aberystwyth: Ceredigion College

Haverfordwest and Neyland: Pembrokeshire College
GCSE/A-level mature students, full time. Drop-In scheme for most courses. Pre-Nursing and Modern Office Skills course.

Llanelli: Carmarthenshire College of Technology & Art
(1988) Access to Higher Education. New Opportunities for Women/Wider Opportunities; details from college.

Newtown: Montgomery College of Further Education
'The college accepts mature people on all courses and has done so for some years. There is therefore considerable experience in dealing with "returners", and following a period at college, the record of progression into suitable employment locally or into higher education is good'. Mature students are accepted on GCSE and A-level courses and a wide range of vocational courses (see 'Retraining and New Skills Courses').

Plymouth College of Further Education
New Opportunities for Women Training Programme, full time. Access to Higher Education in Science and Technology – flexible hours and times to

suit individuals. Can lead to the Design & Technology Department of the College of St. Mark & St. John, leading to a BEd qualification in this shortage subject; to various courses at Plymouth Polytechnic based, loosely, around their Combined Sciences degree programme; to the Primary School Science BEd course at the College of St. Mark & St. John; to courses at St. Luke's College, part of Exeter University; to Membership of the Society of Chiropodists, leading to State Registration; to the Secretarial Linguist's course at the College of Further Education, Plymouth. Pre-Nursing and Professional Studies programme. Note also: One day 'Career Change' briefing courses in the following areas: Personnel, Hotel & Catering, Safety, Security, Administrative Management and Computing Systems, Operations Management, Financial Services Management. One and two-day 'Applying for a Job' courses, covering c.v.'s, Application Forms, Interview Techniques.

Pontypool College
Most courses listed by this college feature under 'Retraining and New Skills' but the following titles suggest that the content is preparatory in nature: Drama Foundation course, Music Foundation, PE Foundation course. Courses also available for GCSE and A/level, A/S level subjects. (See also 'Retraining and New Skills Courses'.)

Pontypridd: Polytechnic of Wales
(1988) Access course – Industrial Society and Culture, part time, can satisfy entry to Polytechnic's Humanities degree course, full time or part time. Conversion course for entry to Engineering degrees, details from college.

Salisbury College of Technology
(1988) Basic Literacy/Numeracy, part time. Adult Education Foundation, part time and evenings. Adult Education Extension (about A-level standard), part time and evenings. How to Study (return to study course), evenings, suitable for Open University preparation. Words and Ideas – Spoken Skills, part time, may lead to RSA Spoken English; it can improve interview technique, sales skills. Introduction to Social Sciences, part time. Access course to Higher Education. Open Learning (see 'Open and Distance Learning Courses').

Street: Strode College
Make Your Experience Count, part time. RSA Certificate of Continuing Education, part time. GCSE/A-level, part time

Swansea: Gorseinon College
(1988) Return to Learn, part time. Projected Open University Preparatory Course.

Swansea: University College of Swansea
Access courses in History, Politics, Philosophy, English, Welsh, Sociology, Science and Engineering for mature students, full time and part time. Return to Study and Pre-Access courses also available.

Taunton: Somerset College of Arts & Technology
Access to Higher Education. New Directions for Men, part time and New Directions for Women, part time, both incorporating Second Start. Return to Learn, part time. GCSE/A-level for mature students, part time. New Opportunities for women/Wider Opportunities, part-time. New Directions (Multi-Skills course).

Second Start and New Directions: viewpoints
'There were some of us who desperately needed legal advice, facts about social security benefits, Inland Revenue information. We all had different needs. On the Second Start course, there was always something for you, maybe not every week, but if you weren't actually needing what was provided that week by the person who was coming to give us advice, you could always see why the advice that was being given to other people was important; you were learning indirectly from what they were being given.'

'One of the things that was very interesting involved the self-analytical exercises they gave us. You had actually to draw, in illustrative form, how you saw our life, and it was really interesting. One lady, I remember, did her life looking as if it was a road map and she had roundabouts where she didn't know which of the turnings to take, and they were all marked as different options for her, which I thought was a very clever way of doing it. It's really then that you realise life is full of choices and it's nice to know the options that are open to you.'

'When you've been through a divorce or a bereavement or something of that sort, I think initially you always feel inadequate. Probably it's unjustified, but I think there's always a certain feeling of inadequacy and going into a college means you've got to sort yourself out and say "I can do it. I'm just as good. I might be even better than some of the people who are here"– but you've got to make yourself go.'

(Students, Somerset College of Arts and Technology)

'The classic opportunity that we can give people is to identify needs that they have got and get something done about them, but I think much more important than that is that if you do manage to get over the threshold and join a course, then you have this marvellous experience of finding out that other people have been through precisely the same experience that you have. You've got something to offer not only yourself in that way but other people as well.'

(Spokesperson, Somerset College of Art and Technology)

Tiverton: East Devon College of Further Education
(1988) Return to Learn, part time.

Torquay: South Devon College of Arts & Technology
'Mature students are welcome to apply for admission to most courses at the college. Return to Learn courses, starting three times a year running for 10 weeks can help you make the right choice. The course includes Study Skills, English (Written & Spoken), Maths and Computers, plus lots of careers advice, information and tutorial support. Past students have gone on to Access to HE, A-levels, GCSE, Ruskin College, College of St. Mark & St. John and Open College of the Arts. Some of this year's students are applying to Rolle College, Plymouth Polytechnic and Fircroft College. Fresh Start courses of two days are run at half terms for those wanting to open the door to new horizons.'

Totnes: Dartington College of Arts
'We welcome applications from mature students. As well as encouraging mature students on to our degree courses (see 'Degree & Advanced courses') we have seven other courses, two of which are specifically aimed at people returning to higher education – the Arts Access course and the BTEC Diploma in the Performing Arts'.

Weymouth College
(1988) Open Access service with Teach Yourself units; Learning Resource centre (see 'Open and Distance Learning'). Also free short and block courses in Building, Electronics, Modern Office Skills and Computing.

Yeovil College
Programmes currently on offer include Managing a Career Break, Return to Learn and New Skills New Directions. 'Yeovil College is very experienced at offering opportunities for mature students to make a fresh start. The aim is to open up *all* courses from basic literacy to preparation for higher education, and from basic numeracy to advanced engineering and business qualifications to mature people, and to give them appropriate support and tutorial help during their time at college. Plans are in hand to open a Women's Training Centre in Yeovil, specificially to help women retrain in non-traditional skill areas where there are expected to be job opportunities, e.g. engineering, electronics, construction, motor vehicle etc.'.

Scotland and Northern Ireland

Aberdeen College of Commerce
'We are keen to attract mature students to the college and offer a wide range of subjects at all levels, many of which are aimed at people who wish to gain additional qualifications through part-time study or want to retrain.' (See 'Retraining & New Skills Courses'.) Full-time, part-time and evening courses include General Education and English as a Foreign Language.

Alloa: Clackmannan College of Further Education
SCE subjects, day and evening.

Belfast College of Technology
(1988) No pre-entry provision but many courses for unemployed adults. (See 'Retraining and New Skills Courses.')

Clydebank College
SCE/GCE for mature students. Return to Study. Modular scheme for National Certificate. Details from college. Open Learning Unit (see 'Open and Distance Learning Courses').

Coleraine: University of Ulster
All the following courses are intended to prepare and qualify mature students for entry to degree courses: Certificate in Foundation Studies for Mature Students, full time and part time, available at Magee College and Belfast; Diploma in Combined Social and Behavioural Studies, part time, available at Jordanstown, (qualifies students to be eligible to apply for admission to the second year in a range of full-time social and behavioural sciences courses). Diploma in the Humanities, part time, evenings, available at Jordanstown (new course, 1989 intake; will permit access to the full-time degree of BA (Hons) Modern Studies in the Humanities). Diploma of Higher Education in Irish Studies, full time. Certificate in Foundation Studies in Art and Design, full time. Certificate in Foundation Studies in Music, part time. BTEC HNC Business and Related Studies, part time.

Dundee: Duncan of Jordanstone College of Art
First Year General Course in Art and Design accepts up to 10% of students without formal qualifications but with good portfolio of work.

Dundee: University of Dundee
New Opportunities for Men and Women, part time (especially relevant for entry to Arts and Social Sciences courses at this university). Wider Opportunities for Women course, part time, in association with Dundee College of Further Education.

Edinburgh: Napier Polytechnic of Edinburgh
Open Learning courses (see 'Open and Distance Learning Courses').

Edinburgh: University of Edinburgh
New Horizons, Returning to Work or Study, Career Development course. Access course – prepares adults for entry to undergraduate courses in the Faculties of Arts, Divinity, Law and Social Sciences.

Fermanagh College
'We aim to provide open access for handicapped and able-bodied mature students to the full range of full-time and part-time courses on the Enniskillen campus and in the large number of Outcentres throughout the County'. Pre-entry courses include a Foundation Certificate for mature students wishing to proceed to Higher Education and Adult Basic Education courses including Adult Literacy and Adult Numeracy. (See also 'Retraining & New Skills Courses'.) 'Over recent years an increasing number of mature students have progressed to Higher Education or different occupations on completion of study at Fermanagh College'.

Glasgow: Anniesland College
Access to Business Studies. This course is offered under the auspices of the Scottish Wider Access Programme (SWAP). It is designed in conjunction with universities and central institutions and successful completion guarantees a place on a degree or HND course. All applicants are interviewed for this course. (See also 'Retraining & New Skills Courses' and 'Small Business Courses'.)

Glasgow: University of Glasgow
Department of Adult and Continuing Education. Introduction to Study for mature students, mainly evenings but part time, day possible. Successful completion of the course may lead to entry to the Faculties of Arts, Divinity, Law and Financial Studies (with respect to the Law degree) and Social Sciences.

Glasgow: University of Strathclyde
Return to Study, evenings. Pre-entry course, may lead to entry to degrees in Arts and Social Studies, evenings. Continuing Education Certificates, may lead to entry to part-time degrees (see 'Degree and Advanced Courses').

Inverness College of Further & Higher Education
Modular programme, part time, allowing individuals to plan own Return to Learning. Open University Preparatory course, part time, or 21-hour rule. Open Learning (see 'Open and Distance Learning Courses').

Motherwell College
SCE courses ('H' and 'O' grades) and Access Courses (Science and Technology, Hospitality Services) provide popular routes for mature students to gain entry to higher education. Students with disabilities can be accepted on to most courses and are supported in their studies by the considerable resources of the Special Needs Department.

Newcastle College of Further Education
Pre-School Playgroups, part time, for City & Guilds award. Access, Mature GCSE/GCE A-level. Information Technology, part time. Leisure Management part time.

Newry: the Continuing Education Programme (Southern Education and Library Board
Time for Women, part time. Women in Mind, part time. Women on the Move, part time – these three offered at Crossmaglen, Newry, Kilkeel. Creative Writing, Holiday French, Holiday Spanish, Healthy Living, courses for 60+. Courses for the Volunteer Bureau. Return to Study. Action for Community Employment. Relaxation and Sport for Women. In-Service courses for industry. Personal Development and Career Development. Certificate in Foundation Studies for Mature Students. 'Our approach is one of meeting the needs of people on an ongoing basis. This sometimes means one-day courses or short block courses. We depend on our people telling us what they need and we then facilitate them'.

Paisley College of Technology
Prospective mature students might like to note that Paisley is a participating member of the Scottish Wider Access Programme (SWAP). The scheme involves one year full time-study of National Certificate modules with guaranteed entry to higher education for successful candidates. Information of the full range of subjects available can be obtained from the Gateway Guidance Unit (041 422 1070) or the SWAP Offices (041 553 2471).

Perth College of Further Education
New Moves for Women – aimed at women intending to return to education, training or employment. Full range of SCE Ordinary and Higher Grade subjects. Standard Grade English also on offer and suitable for the mature adult returner. Directed training for Employment Training available across the range of college subjects (see 'Retraining and New Skills Courses').

RETRAINING AND NEW SKILLS COURSES

For people who want to make a complete change or gain new skills to enhance their prospects

Introduction

Since the first edition of *The Mature Student's Handbook* (then titled *Make a Fresh Start*) was published in Spring 1988, two important factors have affected the range of retraining opportunities for adults.

First, what is known as the 'demographic time bomb' has been widely publicised. Colleges, training centres, professional institutes and trades unions have come to recognise that very shortly, the much reduced number of school-leavers available for training (due to a fall in the birthrate in the 70s) will mean that older people have to be recruited and trained.

This has meant an increase of opportunities for mature people in many occupations. Age limits for entry to training have been substantially extended in some professions and employers who at one time would not consider anyone over the age of 35 have had to widen their recruitment to take in the over-40s (sometimes the over-50s).

NATIONAL HEALTH SERVICE CAREERS

Because of this, and because, too, readers of *Make a Fresh Start* have shown a particular interest in careers concerned with health professions, I have added information about late start opportunities to train for careers in nursing, chiropody, occupational therapy, physiotherapy and radiography under the 'Retraining and New Skills' heading, including entry concessions often offered to late starters. Most courses attract a training allowance or bursary or grant (see 'Costs and Grants').

EMPLOYMENT TRAINING

The other major development to have become established since the first edition of *Make a Fresh Start* is the government's Employment Training programme. It replaces a number of schemes previously available, so if you have an old copy of this book you will find, for example, that the 'MSC-sponsored' schemes it included are no more. The old MSC has been replaced by the new Training Agency and all the programmes it sponsors are now covered by the general title of 'Employment Training'. Where a college has one or more of its courses sponsored by the Training Agency under Employment Training, they are identified by the use of 'TA-sponsored' in front of the name of the course.

The exact description of Employment Training that follows has been supplied by the Training Agency:

'Employment Training is a training programme for unemployed adults and is open to all people over 18 and under 60 years of age who have been unemployed for at least 6 months. It aims to help people gain the skills and knowledge needed to compete for jobs in the local labour market. This programme is funded by the Training Agency and all participants will receive a training allowance of at least £10 more than previous benefit. Training will consist of a mix of directed and practical training which will last up to a maximum of 12 months depending on the training needs of each individual. Further information can be obtained from Training Agency Area Offices.'

I would add to this that though some of this Employment Training is being done by employers (most people will have seen the 'We're training the workers without jobs for the jobs without workers' advertisement on TV), much is also being done at further education colleges. As you go through this section, you will see that quite a few entries refer either to Employment Training or to the Training Agency (TA-sponsored courses).

There is also provision within the Employment Training scheme for people who want to set up in business. You'll find details in the introduction to the 'Small Business and Self-Employment' section.

Having given a welcome to this new government scheme, let's remember that you don't necessarily have to take part in a government-funded training scheme to change direction. There have always been careers for which you can train 'on the job'. For example, nurses are accepted for training up to the age of 45 and in an increasing number of nursing schools 50. One or two nursing schools say they consider over-50s. Retailing and catering are occupational areas that attract people of all ages and my local hypermarket is advertising not only for 'returners' but for people who want to work after retirement.

WHERE MATURITY IS AN ASSET

At the beginning of this book I've given a list of jobs where 'mature entrants' are welcomed (pages 23-27). Individual employers may vary in their attitudes to what is 'mature' but all the jobs are in areas where it is a specific advantage to have had some life experience. Other careers, for which courses are listed in this section, welcome candidates across a wide age range.

Quite a few of the jobs on this list do involve retraining, in one way or another. Sometimes you can get in via a degree course (see the 'Degree and Advanced Courses' section). Interestingly, the latest Civil Service careers guide for graduates includes a number of areas where 'No upper age limit' is listed after the job description. Sometimes it is possible to retrain by home study (see 'Open and Distance Learning Courses') and since the advent of The Open College, which concentrates on vocational courses, it's been easier to get job qualifications this way.

FULL TIME OR PART TIME?

Retraining doesn't always have to be full time but there are no part-time courses under Employment Training, a point that the Training Agency stresses.

On the other hand, if you can't find the sort of course you want under ET, there may be something offered to you by a college as a '21-hour-rule course'. This is a concession to help unemployed people who have left full time education but who wish to take up study or attend training courses while continuing to receive benefit. There are rules to be observed (set out in the 'Costs and Grants' section of this book) but if you satisfy them, you can take a college course that involves studying for not more than 21 hours a week, without losing your right to benefit.

A very small number of the courses listed are described as 'ESF-sponsored'. ESF = the European Social Fund, which means the course has been financed by a special grant from the EEC. Often the courses concerned will be of a kind that provide new opportunities for a group regarded as disadvantaged in the career concerned – for instance, a course like 'Women into Construction'. If a course is ESF-sponsored, not only is it likely to be free, but you may get a training allowance too.

In many cases, though, students will have to pay their own fees and finance themselves through their retraining. They may get a discretionary grant from their local education authority (LEA) or perhaps an allowance from some kind of local trust. Colleges are very knowledgeable about sources of grants for their students, and it's always worth asking if former students have obtained a grant or award.

Many colleges reduce fees to a very small amount for unemployed people. Look in prospectuses to see if there is information about a scheme of this kind.

DISCOVERING OPPORTUNITIES

As last year, I wrote to all UK universities, polytechnics, colleges of higher education and colleges of further education seeking information on their 1989/90 opportunities for late starters. Some which did not reply last year have responded enthusiastically this year. Some of last year's entries have been updated with details of new courses and opportunities. But where you see (1988) heading a college's list of courses, it means that no reply was received to a request to update information. It could well be that no updating was needed, but be a little wary when following up courses with the (1988) heading as things may have changed, or be about to change.

A most enthusiastic and helpful response came from schools of nursing, chiropody, occupational therapy, physiotherapy and radiography and the phrase 'We welcome mature entrants' appeared in almost every letter.

There are special entry and application procedures in the case of careers of this kind, and if you are considering one of them, the notes below are important:

Nursing
The statutory academic entrance requirement is that you should possess five GCSE/GCE O-levels at grades A, B or C, or CSE Grade 1, normally including English Language. Some schools also want a pass in Mathematics and occasionally a school will ask for more than five passes.

For mature entrants (and each school can decide for itself when you are mature – it can be anything from 19 to 25) there may be the opportunity to take the UKCC entry test. The UKCC is the United Kingdom Central Council for Nursing, Midwifery and Health Visiting, and there are three different versions of their test (so that if you fail the first time, you can study some more and try a second, different test).

People often ask what this UKCC entry test involves. The Council issues a fact sheet for candidates explaining that it measures 'verbal reasoning, non-verbal reasoning, arithmetic (including graphs and charts) and comprehension, and takes approximately one hour to complete. One or two schools of nursing have mentioned in letters to me that this is a demanding test and that often older age groups find it difficult. Examples of test papers are not available, but your local library may be able to suggest some books for you to look through that have examples of 'verbal reasoning and non-verbal reasoning' tests (they may be called 'intelligence tests') so that you won't be completely taken aback if you're faced with the sort of question that reads 'If window is to open, door is to red, oak, closed, safe?'

All the schools of nursing in this booklet willingly sent details of their courses, but those in England pointed out that applications are handled by the Nurses' Central Clearing House, English National Board, PO Box 346, Bristol, BS99 7FB. They distribute your application to up to six nurse training schools of your choice (and you do have to apply through the NCCH even if you can only accept a place if it's offered at the local hospital which has a part-time training scheme). NCCH provides you with an application package, which you have to complete and return with a fee of £6.

NB: For nursing schools in Scotland, Wales and Northern Ireland, you still apply direct – there is no central system.

Chiropody
For entry to training for this profession, the Society of Chiropodists normally asks for a minimum of two A-levels and 3 GCSEs/O-levels at grades A, B or C, including at least one science at either level. Individual schools can have higher requirements for school-leaver entrants.

However, as you will see from the entries in this book, most schools and departments of chiropody have concessions for mature students. They vary from place to place, so read the entries with care. It is always regarded as a good thing to have observed a chiropodist at work, in a hospital or clinic, or at a school of chiropody, before you make your application. Manual dexterity is valued – if you're good at art or embroidery or working with small tools, this will be in your favour. Student chiropodists can apply for discretionary grants from their LEAs.

Occupational Therapy
Like nursing, there is a central admissions system. You can get details from the Occupational Therapy Training Clearing House, College of Occupational Therapists, 20 Rede Place, London W2 4TU. Individual schools of occupational therapy are very willing to send prospectuses, and several made the point that the expect students to visit different schools and to have observed occupational therapists at work before they make application.

The entry requirements for school-leaver candidates are normally two A-levels and at least three GCSEs/O-levels Grades A–C including English and Biology. There are usually concessions for mature entrants and quite a few graduates subsequently train as occupational therapists. Experience of voluntary work with elderly or disabled people is well regarded. Grants for training are provided by the Department of Health.

Physiotherapy
In the last few years it has been difficult for mature entrants to get a start in physiotherapy because of the great pressure on places from school-leaver entrants. Information now received from schools of physiotherapy suggests that this has been relieved to some extent, and most schools are likely to take a few 'late starters' who have the right academic, personal and physical standards for the course, which is a strenuous one.

A range of academic entry requirements is considered, including BTEC National Diplomas in relevant subjects, but the usual requirement is for candidates to have two A-levels (3 Scottish Highers) in academic subjects, preferably including a biological subject, and five GCSEs (Grades A–C) – the GCSEs to include English and two science subjects. For mature students, individual schools do offer entry concessions which I have listed as notified to me. As with occupational therapy, it is regarded as important for prospective students to have spent time watching a physiotherapist at work so that they know what's involved.

There is a national Clearing House system for applications (which doesn't prevent you writing to individual schools for prospectuses), and you can get details from the Chartered Society of Physiotherapy, 14 Bedford Row, London WC1R 4ED. Grants for training are provided by the Department of Health.

Radiography

courses are of two kinds; diagnostic, which deals with the use of X-ray equipment to help diagnose disease or injury, and therapy, which involves using X-ray equipment to treat disease, usually, but not invariably, malignant disease. Though the academic entrance requirements for both types of course are the same, the temperament and personality for each kind of work is different, and Schools of Radiography strongly advise that people considering radiography careers should arrange to visit both kinds of department and talk to the radiographers about the work they do.

Applicants aged under 25 have to satisfy the College of Radiographers' official academic entry requirements, i.e. have five GCSE or O-level passes, grades A–C to include Mathematics or Physics, a written English subject, a Science subject and two others. At GCE A-level 4 points gained from one or more subject passes will be required (that means you can offer a one grade B pass or two grade D or better passes). There are a number of acceptable alternatives including certain BTEC awards and Open College 'B' units. NB: The Open College referred to here is not The National Open College, which distributes learning packages to use at home or work, but one of the Open College Federations described in 'Open and Distance Learning Courses'.

Radiography applicants who are aged 24 and over by the commencement of their training may be granted entry concessions but have to submit applications on a special green form provided for the purpose. This form has to be accompanied by a supporting statement relating to the applicant's suitability in terms of educational background, work experience and personal qualities prepared by the Principal of the School of Radiography concerned (so your performance at interview will count for a lot).

There is no Clearing House for radiography training applications; you can approach schools directly. Grants for training are provided by the Department of Health.

INITIALS AND THEIR MEANING

Probably the least familiar of the exam titles used by colleges in this section is 'BTEC'. It stands for the Business and Technician Education Council, and they offer awards at First (or preparatory) level, National level (for entrants starting out with a 4 GCSE/O-level of entry requirement) and Higher National level (for entrants starting out with GCSEs and at least one A-level). In many cases there are entry concessions for mature students, especially for the Higher awards (HND/HNC). BTEC also offers Continuing Education units – very useful both for updating purposes and in some instances as a preparation for further advanced training.

BTEC courses are offered in colleges in England, Wales and Northern Ireland. The National level of qualification is aimed at training people who can work at a technician or similarly responsible support level in industry, commerce and public service. The Higher level is aimed at people who would work at senior technician or assistant manager level and BTEC Higher students often continue their education by moving directly into the second or occasionally third year of a degree course.

Scotland's system is called SCOTVEC which stands for the Scottish Vocational Education Council. Students begin at the National level, and make up courses to suit their own career needs from individual modules or units of study. SCOTVEC National Certificates can be used for entry to SCOTVEC Higher National Diplomas and Certificates – you'll find these listed in the appropriate college sections.

HND – OR A DEGREE?

Each has its special value for someone changing direction. HND courses are usually strongly vocational, which is why they are included in the 'Retraining and New Skills' section. They provide you with knowledge and skills of immediate value to an employer. They are also shorter in duration than degrees; two years full time or three years if you take a sandwich course that includes periods of work experience. HNDs are often accepted by professional and trade institutes to as making the holders eligible for at least the junior grade of membership and they may exempt the holder from some professional institute exams.

With a few obvious exceptions like engineering and computing, to say nothing of the BEd for teaching, degrees are not vocational. What they provide is 'graduate status' and that in its turn opens up a range of opportunities for training, either with employers or on a postgraduate course (more about this in the introduction to 'Degree and Advanced Courses'). If you have no specific vocational interest but you know you want to aim at a long-term career, think carefully about the benefits of beginning with a degree, which you may be able to do on a part-time basis. If in doubt, get prospectuses describing both HND and degree courses and compare what they involve and what they offer.

OTHER COURSES

You will find one or two independent (i.e. commercial, private) training centres listed in this section. They have been included usually because they have been strongly recommended by someone known to me, or sometimes by ex-students I have interviewed in my work as a journalist. There is an excellent book called the *Directory of Independent Training and Tutorial Organisations* listing hundreds of independent courses, with details. I've listed it in the 'Information Sources' section of this book and you should be able to see a copy through your local library.

TRAINING IN YOUR OWN TIME

Not everyone wishing to retrain is unemployed. One of the purposes of *The Mature Student's Handbook* is to suggest ways in which people can widen their career horizons by getting some additional training, qualifications or practical skills on a spare-time basis. For many people, the idea of buying a learning package to study at home has great appeal. They can still go on working in their jobs or looking after dependents whilst gaining knowledge and often qualifications, to let them forge ahead when they are free to make a change. If this applies to you, remember to check the 'Open and Distance Learning Courses' section of the book.

OTHER SOURCES OF ADVICE

If you know what you want to retrain for, a good way of finding out about ways to retrain and where courses are offered is to ask the appropriate trade or professional association. Many have lists of approved courses. Some will recommend specific courses for mature people, or suggest colleges where they know late starters will be treated sympathetically. Careers books listed in the 'Information Sources' section will help you track down any particular institute you need to find.

Jobcentres are also knowledgeable about retraining courses, especially free ones, courses for unemployed people and those which attract an allowance. For executives and professionally qualified people, there is a similar free advice service through P.E.R. – Professional and Executive Recruitment – which also publicises retraining courses. P.E.R. offices are listed in the telephone directory.

Educational Guidance Centres, where available, (see the 'Information Sources' section), have advisers to consult and reference books to look in, but as yet, not every town has such a centre. As an alternative, the careers staff at local colleges are often willing to advise potential students (write a short letter first, to see if you can make an appointment to see an adviser). There are also independent careers guidance agencies, which charge a fee for testing your aptitudes and abilities and advising you both on new careers and ways of training for them that will suit your circumstances. The one I know well is Career Analysts, 90 Gloucester Place, London, W1 and I can recommend their service for all ages. Other similar services can be found by studying advertisements in 'Educational' columns of national newspapers.

ALL-KNOWING LIBRARIANS

When all is said and done, the one source of information that is accessible to everybody is the public library service. It may be a huge building in a city centre or just a travelling library in a van, but I have never yet found a library whose staff were not enthusiastic and painstaking in tracking down elusive facts, even in instances where they had to research information from other specialised libraries. Incidentally, you can telephone libraries with questions and the person on duty to deal with queries will look up information or addresses for you if you can't get in to do your own research.

THE COURSE LISTS

Colleges, training schools and training centres are listed according to their location, by town name, in regions. The full address of each college, school or centre is given in the regional address lists at the back of the book.

If you have opened the book at this section, you may wonder why I have chosen this layout. It is because quite often, a college name doesn't indicate where it is situated. For instance, Cassio College isn't in Cassio but in Watford. Hertfordshire College of Building is not in Hertford but at St Albans. By giving the locations of colleges, and grouping them together in regions, I hope you may be able to find several retraining opportunities within travelling distance of your home. *The counties included in each region are listed on pages 35-36.*

If you contact your local college, school or training centre, you may well find more courses on offer – those that were not confirmed when this book went to press, or that have been newly introduced to satisfy demand. Look out in particular for more part-time nurse training courses – many schools of nursing are considering ways of providing them.

I am always delighted to know about new retraining courses and readers' experiences of retraining. Please write to me through the publisher, Kogan Page, whose address is at the front of this book.

London and Middlesex

Bloomsbury College of Nurse Education
Full-time 3-year course and part-time 4-year course leading to Registered General Nurse qualification. Entry to the part-time course is once a year in May and candidates work 30 hours a week, duty shifts being arranged with tutors and ward sisters to take account of school hours and terms. School states: 'We are very happy to accept mature students here at the Bloomsbury College of Nurse Education providing they pass an interview and meet the academic requirements of five GCSEs or O-levels at ABC grades or Grade 1 CSEs. If they do not have these qualifications, they may sit the UKCC entry test. We have no upper age limit.'

Brent & Harrow School of Nursing
Part-time mature entrants course, leading to Registered General Nurse qualification. Course planned to start in Spring 1990. It is planned for 30 hours per week. One weekend per month to be worked, and one 'special duty' either on early start, early finish or late start, late finish. Hours per day will be 9.15 a.m. until 3.45 p.m. five days per week. Night duty will also be included in the final year. Candidates must meet UKCC entry requirements, offering either (a) 5 O-level academic subjects including English Language or (b) a pass in the UKCC entry test, 2 references and an interview. School states: "Candidates should have good reasons for wanting a part-time course, i.e. family or dependants, otherwise they should apply for the full-time course. Candidates should also have a stable home situation and children should be in full-time education."

British Isles Study Programme (Independent College)
Part-time Tour Management training course (lectures on Wednesday and Thursday evenings in Central London) plus 8-day Training Tour. Following graduation, students may take extra intensive training tours in popular regions. In 1989/90 these will include 7 days in Ireland and a long weekend on Hadrian's Wall. This is the recommended training course of the Association of British Travel Agents' National Training Board and leads to City & Guilds Certificate in Tour Management. Applicants must be at least 25 and preference is given to people with foreign language qualifications.

Tour Management: viewpoints

'I am a tour manager working on a freelance basis. The tours that I conduct are very varied, as the itineraries are those requested by overseas travel agents with many specialist interests, e.g. sports, history, cathedrals, agriculture, houses and industry. My next tour will take me to Stratford-upon-Avon, Chester, North Wales, Edinburgh, the Scottish Highlands and the Isle of Skye. After that I will spend a week in Ireland.

In addition to the BISP Tour Manager's course, I have qualified as a York Minister Accredited Guide, and have taken the BISP Graduate Training Tours to Hadrian's Wall, Cumbria and Ireland. I speak English, French and German fluently, and find much of my work in these languages.'

(Former student, British Isles Study Programme)

'The City and Guilds of London Institute specifies exactly what students must absorb to earn the National Certificate; the techniques, the documentation to be dealt with, booking into and out of a hotel, set procedures, what to do if a passport is lost, and so on. The second part of the examination deals with the history, topography and geography of Britain and Ireland. It can include questions on art, stately homes, architecture and general knowledge.

The British Isles Study Programme includes an eight-day tour of Britain during which each student is expected to present a prepared subject to his and her fellow students over the public address system. Each student acts as the 'Duty Tour Manager' for one day. The organiser arranges for problems to arise, such as a coach breakdown, a passenger with a sudden illness, or hotel operational difficulties, to ensure the student can cope.

Prospects are good as the incoming travel industry expands year after year, though in the first year, newcomers may begin with only short engagements. Some people only want to work for a limited period each season. For example, one lady is a school teacher who can only acept work when she's not teaching. Another is a retired Royal Navy Officer, who only wants to work a few weeks each year. Others are actors and only want to work while 'resting'. Others want to work the full season, which means from April to late October.'

(Spokesperson, British Isles Study Programme)

Camberwell Health Authority: King's College Hospital School of Radiography

Full-time 3-year training leading to the Diploma of the College of Radiographers (Diagnostic or Therapy). College states: 'We have accepted mature students in the past and it has been a worthwhile experience, so we are happy to carry on. Entry concessions are possible, but each case is considered on its merits. It would be wise for a candidate without the standard O- and A-levels to write to the College of Radiographers, 14 Upper Wimpole Street, London, WlM 8BN to find out whether he/she were eligible.'

Camden Training Centre
(1988, excluding courses formerly MSC-sponsored.) In association with
Kingsway College, Hackney College, Southwark College, North London
College, Working Men's College, Kilburn Polytechnic, Project Fullemploy,
Co-ops Advisory Group. Range of courses under 21-hour rule: Building
Maintenance, Cookery for the Catering Industry,for City and Guilds 706/1
Call Order Catering, for City and Guilds 700/1. Other courses likey to be
available on a full time basis: Carpentry and Joinery, Microelectronics,
Gardening, Printing, Industrial Clothing Machining, Nursery Nursing for
NNEB Certificate. ESF-sponsored courses: Business Technology for
Women, full time; Building for Women, part time, under 21-hour rule;
Plastering for Women, full time; Carpentry for Women, full time; Introduc-
tory Building for Women, part time, under 21-hour rule; Introduction to
Computing, full time. Women's Introductory Microelectronics/Women's
Microelectronics, mode not specified.

Nursery Nursing: viewpoint
'I'd been unemployed for two years, during which time I'd been working
voluntarily with children at weekends, handicapped children in an adven-
ture playground. Prior to that I'd worked in homes and schools for
handicapped children, and I had thought of going on a comprehensive
nursing course, for children and general nursing. When I saw the nursery
nurse course advertised, I thought it would be a very good preparation – or it
might be entire in itself. We learn about the normal child from 0 to 7,
covering child development, child care and education, spending four days
at the training centre and one day a week out on placement (and the course is
also preceded and followed by placements). My ambition is to get
experience after qualifying and then to do voluntary work overseas in a
Third World country.'
                    (Student nursery nurse, Camden Training Centre)

'All our students are over 25 and take a standard entry test and are
interviewed before acceptance. As well as child care, health, development
and education, their course includes first aid training, social studies,
communication and a creative studies component so that they develop
interests they can share with children.'
                    (Spokesperson, Camden Training Centre)

Central London: Polytechnic of Central London
Sites at Euston, Holborn and around Oxford Circus area. Comprehensive
evening and part-time day Languages Faculty (25 languages) with courses at
several levels. Diploma in English as a Second or Foreign Language, full
time, but attendance arranged between 9.30 a.m. and 1.30 p.m. for those
with home responsibilities. Diploma in Law, full time (for mature stu-
dentswho obtain a Certificate of Eligibility from the Council for Legal

Education). Diploma in Applied Social Studies/Certificate of Qualification in Social Work, full time, for mature students over 30.

Central Middlesex and Hammersmith Hospital Schools of Radiograpy and Radiotherapy

Full-time 3-year course leading to Diploma of the College of Radiographers (Diagnostic or Therapy). Schools state: 'We do accept mature students (over 25) and there are special entry concessions for them under the College of Radiographers regulations if they do not meet the normal requirements. There is no specific upper age limit but obviously, the older a person is, (say over 35) the more care needs to be taken with their suitability and attitude for a profession which can be very demanding, physically and mentally.'

Charing Cross School of Nursing: Riverside Health Authority

Full-time 3-year course leading to qualification of Registered General Nurse. Candidates without statutory academic entry requirements may take UKCC entry test. School states: 'We are prepared to consider mature students and do not have any upper age limit'. NB: Riverside Health Authority includes other schools of nursing including one (Lorna Delve & Banstead School of Psychiatric Nursing, in Epsom, Surrey) which offers a full-time 3-year course leading to the qualification of Registered Mental Nurse.

Chelsea School of Art

Certificate in Interior Decoration, full time, mature students welcome.

College for the Distributive Trades

College says you may be admitted to any course 'as an exceptional case – this usually depends on age and experience'. Options include Furnishing and Interior Design, full time (trade experience or special aptitudes may be accepted in lieu of GCSE/O-levels). BTEC National Diploma and COTAC Certificate course in Travel & Tourism, full time (no maximum age limit; candidates with four GCSE/O-levels or equivalent). Fresh Food Merchandising (older applicants welcome; CSE or similar in two or three subjects). Separate part-time prospectus, includes COTAC, evenings, Commercial Textiles, part-time, evenings. Higher National Certificate in Business and Management Studies, leading to specialism in Travel, Marketing, Advertising and Retailing. All are suitable for adults returning to industry, or retraining for a career change.

Cordwainers College

Leathergoods Diploma, full time, for City & Guilds at Ordinary and Advanced Levels. Leathercraft and Saddlery Diploma, full time, for City & Guilds, Skills Tests and Livery Company awards. BTEC National Diploma in Design (Footwear), full time. BTEC Higher National Diploma in Design (Footwear), full time. BTEC Higher National Diploma in Footwear Manufacture, full time. (BTEC courses start Autumn 1990 subject to approval and validation.)

Ealing Health Authority School of Nursing
Full-time 3-year training courses for Registered General Nurse and Registered Mental Nurse qualifications. School states: 'All our courses are opened to school leavers and mature applicants. There is no upper age limit in operation and every applicant is considered on his/her own merits. We do not have any concession or special entry requirements for mature applicants'.

East London: Polytechnic of East London
Sites at Barking (Schools of Business & Management and Engineering) and West Ham (Schools of Architecture, Art and Design; Science; and Social Sciences). Consideration given to those over 25 with valuable employment experience but without formal entry qualifications. Polytechnic Diploma/ Certificate of Qualification in Social Work, full time, for candidates over 25 with some relevant experience. Diploma in Careers Guidance, full time. Diploma of Higher Education (Multi-Subject), entry concessions possible for mature students; options include Architecture, Business Studies, New Technology and Psychology. DipHE by Independent Study, full time or part time – see below. Polytechnic Postgraduate Diploma in Management (also open to non-graduates – students may be self-employed), part time by self-managed learning. Mature students especially welcome; more than a third of students are over 25. Contact Continuing Education Unit for specialist information.

School for Independent Study: viewpoint
'The School for Independent Study was established to enable students to plan for themselves their own programmes to study in partnership with the specialist areas of the polytechnic. The main age range is from 25 to 40, though students include people aged from 21 to 70. It is very suitable for career change; previous students have included a fireman who became a social worker and a florist who became a journalist. Students have to agree their programmes with tutors, establish that they can get adequate supervision and present work for assessment like any other students. But unqualified people are considered (on science and technology programmes as well as the arts and social sciences) and work schedules can be devised to suit an individual student's circumstances.'
    (Spokesperson, School for Independent Study, East London Polytechnic)

Enfield & Haringey School of Nursing: North Middlesex Hospital
Full-time 3-year courses leading to Registered General Nurse or Registered Mental Nurse qualification. School states: 'We welcome applications from mature students, male and female. The upper age limit is 45 years. We offer all applicants the opportunity to take the UKCC entry test. Tests are held in the School of Nursing once a month, and no charge is made for taking the test.'

Guy's Hospital School of Physiotherapy

Full-time 3-year course leading to Membership of the Chartered Society of Physiotherapy. School states: 'We accept a fair percentage of mature students, entry concessions being specific to each individual case. We do not necessarily specify an upper age limit; this being relative to personal background and candidates' intended opportunity to employ the skills they will have gained for an appropriate and useful length of time ahead.'

Guy's Hospital Radiography Education Centre

Full-time 3-year course leading to Diploma of the College of Radiographers. Centre states: 'We are certainly interested in offering opportunities for mature entrants. It is difficult to itemise fixed requirements, since every applicant is judged on their own merits. I am enclosing the College of Radiographer's standard entry requirements (*see introduction to Retraining section*) but if a mature student seems suitable, we can ask for them to be considered as a "special case", although there would need to be a very strong justification for training for a "very mature" student – but we would not want to be tied to any particular upper age limit.'

Guy's Hospital School of Nursing – see Thomas Guy and Lewisham School of Nursing

Hammersmith Hospital School of Nursing

Full-time 3-year course leading to Registered General Nurse qualification. Mature students accepted, upper age limit 'around 40 years'. Hospital adds: 'Candidates must be passed as medically fit, and must meet the current statutory educational requirements for entry to training. This normally involves them entering and passing the UKCC entry test.'

Hospitals for Sick Children: Charles West School of Nursing

4-year combined Registered General Nurse and Registered Sick Children's Nurse Training. Mature students (over 20 and under 50) considered. School states: 'If an individual over this age was to enthusiastically enquire, we would make an individual judgement about suitability to sustain the rigours of the course.'

Hounslow & Spelthorne Health Authority: West Thames School of Nursing

Full-time (148 week) Registered General Nurse course. Part-time (208 week) Registered General Nurse course. School states: 'We do accept mature candidates for nurse training up to the age of 50 and anyone older is looked at on an individual basis.' Candidates must satisfy the usual entry requirements, i.e. 5 GCSE passes (Grades A–C) or exam equivalent, or a pass in the UKCC entry test.

Islington & Hampstead School of Radiography: Royal Free Hospital

Full-time 3-year training course leading to Diploma of the College of Radiographers (Diagnostic or Therapy). Mature students accepted – no upper age limit. School states: 'Mature students are considered on individual merits/life experience and may be acceptable with no formal qualifications, subject to acceptance by the College of Radiographers.'

King's College London
Full-time 4-year honours degree in Physiotherapy. Application through UCCA (see 'Degree and Advanced Courses'). School states: 'Preference is given to those candidates with three A/AS level subjects at Grades CCD (or above) of which two passes should be in a science subject. It should be noted that most entrants are expected to have six to eight O-level passes including English, Mathematics, Chemistry and a Biological subject at a good grade.'

London College of Fashion
(1988) Certificate in Clothing Production, full time, for those over 21 planning to enter the clothing industry at technician level. You need at least three GCEs/GCSEs including English Language, and the college says 'it is not uncommon for students to be graduates'. Clothing Skills, under 21-hour rule, may lead to City and Guilds award in Garment Making and Wholesale Cutting/ BTEC HND Theatre Studies, full time; candidates with at least two years' experience in the theatre considered without formal entry qualifications, options in Theatrical Costume or Specialist Make-up. Evening courses in Theatrical Hair Skills, Theatrical Wigmaking, Theatrical Make-Up techniques, open to people who participate in amateur dramatics as well as professionals. Trichology, evenings (foundation course for those without science background).

London College of Printing
HND Business Studies with options in Printing and Publishing, Journalism, Publicity and Promotion, full time. Entry concessions possible for those over 21. NB: candidates who successfully complete the course with the Journalism option will also be awarded a Periodical Training Trust Certificate. Certificate in Pre-Entry Periodical Journalism, full time, entry concessions possible for those who show promise as journalists. Foundation in Media Studies, full time, unqualified mature candidates considered if they show ability to undertake the course. Diploma in Photo-Journalism, full time, for practising photographers, writers and journalists, but applications invited from mature students, particularly from ethnic minorities. Diploma in Publishing Production, full time, open to mature students seeking a change of career as well as those with publishing experience. Diploma in Graphic Origination and Reproduction, full time, open to candidates with relevant industrial experience and examples of their work. Diploma in Creative Screen Printing, full time, as above. Certificate in Printing Techniques, full time, for those who have prospects of employment or see career prospects in printing. Certificate in Craft Bookbinding, full time, no formal entry qualification (extended study also possible).

London Foot Hospital and School of Chiropody
Full-time 3-year course open to mature students aged up to 37. Entry concessions possible with regard to the A-level entry requirement according to the individual merits of the applicant.

London Hospital School of Radiography and Radiotherapy
Full-time 32-month course leading to Diploma of the College of Radiographers (Diagnostic or Therapy). School states: 'Mature students can be accepted for training. The upper age limit varies, depending on the working capacity of the person involved - as a rough guide, the maximum limit considered would be 45 years. The entry for mature students (over 24 years of age) does vary from the standard, and is based mainly on the suitability of the person to undergo training and the ability to succeed in the final qualifying examinations. Therefore the individuals are considered on their academic and personal merit.'

London School of Occupational Therapy: West London Institue of Higher Education
Full-time 3-year training course for the Diploma in Occupational Therapy. Mature students accepted, no age limit specified. Entry concessions possible; prospectus states 'For mature students, GCE O-level or equivalent in English Language and at least one A-level from those listed (for school-leaver entrants), together with evidence of study and achievement in the two years prior to entry' will be required. Also: 'All students who wish to join the Diploma course must do so by entrance examination. Intending students must be prepared to keep a day free for the examination and interview.'

Middlesex Hospital School of Physiotherapy
Full-time 3-year course. Mature students accepted (age limits 25–32 in most cases). Entry concessions possible; school states 'We would expect mature applicants to have at least 1 A-level, preferably in a science subject, but failing this, some evidence that they are capable of studying to undergraduate level.'

Middlesex Polytechnic
Six sites, in and around Barnet, Enfield and Haringey. Certificate/Diploma in Higher Education; Modular course, subjects can be vocationally related – e.g. Law, Art and Design, Education, Information Technology. Entry concessions possible for those over 21. DipHE can lead to degrees (see 'Degree and Advanced Courses'). Certificate in Industrial Relations and Trade Union Studies, full time or part time for potential full-time trade union officers; mature students without qualifications and with trade union experience specifically invited to apply. Introduction to Information Technology, full time and part time. BTEC HNC/HND Computer Studies, full

time or part time. For unemployed graduates, TA-sponsored MSc Applied Computing Technology (computer graphics, software, robotics). BTEC HND Mechanical and Production Engineering or Electronic Engineering, full time or part time. Postgraduate Diploma in Housing, part time, unqualified mature students currently employed in Housing are considered. Certificate of Qualification in Social Work, full time, aimed primarily at people aged 25 or over with some experience in voluntary or paid social service.

Middlesex & University College Hospitals Schools of Radiography
Full-time 33-month training leading to the Diploma of the College of Radiographers and to the addition of DCR (T) = Therapy, or DCR (R) = Diagnostic Radiography after one's name. School states: 'We do accept mature students, up to the age of about 45 years. There are entry concessions and special entry requirements for mature students, and those with a good general education should apply for further details. We can arrange for individual students to visit the Schools and spend time in the Radiography and Radiotherapy Departments.'

Morley College
(1988) Many leisure courses, some with earning potential. Examples, all part time: Photography, Calligraphy, Glass Engraving, Craft Bookbinding, Hand and Machine Knitting, Quilt-making and Patchwork, Dressmaking, Toymaking, Jewellery Making, Cookery, Cake-Decorating, Radio Production Skills, Television Training (includes Scriptwriting), Creative Writing – Novels, Plays, Writing for Radio and TV – Woodwork and Picture Framing, Language-learning facilities include Dutch, Norwegian, Polish, Japanese, Chinese. Music courses include Recording Techniques and Popular Composing and Arranging for Instruments (if you want to start your own group). Foundation course for Pre-School Playgroup Leaders. Nominal fee and 21-hour rule arrangements for unemployed/benefit claimants.

North London College
Most NCL courses welcome mature students and are flexible in their entry requirements. Courses specifically designed for adult returners include a 21-hour 3-year NNEB (Nursery Nursing) course aimed at male and female students who (a) have parental responsibilities and/or (b) are bilingual. Other 21-hour courses include Business Skills for Adults, Working in the Community and Preparation for Higher Education (also offered as an evening course). The Sports & Recreation Management course and a unique Community Theatre and Drama Workers' course particularly welcome members of disadvantaged groups, including, on the Theatre course, the 'physically challenged'. Mainstream courses include BTEC National awards in Business & Finance, Health Studies, Leisure Studies, Computer Studies, Media, Performing Arts and Science. BTEC First award courses are available

in some of these areas. City & Guilds courses include 726 (Information Technology Scheme), 779 (Media Techniques – Print & Radio Journalism) and 224 (Electronic Servicing – part time only) and Community Care Skills. Part-time and evening short courses in Business Skills, Media and Computing.

North London: Polytechnic of North London
(Sites in Camden and Islington.) Polytechnic Diploma/Certificate of Qualification in Social Work, full time, open to mature candidates without formal qualifications (under 25s should have five O-levels or three A-levels including English). Diploma in Purchasing and Supply, full time or part time, for graduates or entrants with HND/HNC in Business Studies, or mature students with relevant experience. Diploma in Recreation Management, part time, for graduates or those with HND/professional qualifications, or, exceptionally, for over-27s with HNC or at least four years of management experience. (A range of part-time courses related to recreation is available – ask the Polytechnic.) Other courses which mature entrants might consider as a way of retraining or developing career prospects include Accounting Foundation, full time; Postgraduate Conversion Diploma in Computing (see 'Degree and Advanced Courses'), Diploma in Labour Studies, full time, giving exemption from Stage 2 exams of the Institute of Personnel Management. Also evening degrees (see 'Degree and Advanced Courses').

Paddington College
Medical Records and Computing/Information Technology courses, arranged between l0 a.m. and 3 p.m. for mature students, the latter course particularly for bilingual sudents. Association of Accounting Technicians' Certificate in Accounting. NNEB Nursery Nurse training, full time, for mature men and women with a broad general education. Bilingualism is an asset for this course. Office training for adults – flexible modular packages in office skills and information technology. Motor Vehicle course for adults (20 hours per week). Part-time and full-time courses in Leisure and Tourism, Theatre and Studio Sound and Lighting, Photography.

Paddington College: Chelsea School of Chiropody
Full-time 3-year course leading to the Diploma of the Society of Chiropodists. (Pre-Chiropody course available for candidates without A-levels or sciences.) School states: 'No set upper age limit for mature students but employers discourage us training people over the age of 45 years. All mature students are interviewed prior to being offered a place on the course and each application is judged on its merits.'

Pitman Central College: Southampton Row
(Independent college – see also Wimbledon, in Southern and Eastern England section.) Extensive range of intensive courses in secretarial,

information technology and management subjects, full time, part time and evenings. Options include: 15-week Intensive Secretarial course for graduates and those with A-levels; 6-week Typing, Computing and Office Technology course; l-week Beginners' Typing course; 4-week Keyboarding and Accounts Course; 4-week Legal Secretarial course (day or evening) for those with a typing speed of at least 25 words per minute. Many more choices, including 4-day Word Processing courses, attendance mornings only, during the summer, and 4-week Word Processing and Computer Application courses, evenings, also during the summer. Send for 'Full and Part Time' or 'Evening Courses' brochure.

Secretarial training: viewpoint
'I had been managing a shop, but after a year, the demands of working every Saturday and all through holiday periods (we even opened on Bank Holidays as we catered for the tourist trade) prompted me to change careers. Secretarial training looked a good launch pad with dozens of possible work environments from hospitals to newspapers. I spent my savings on a 15-week intensive course at Pitman Central College, and believe me, it *was* intensive. For the first five weeks there were two hours of shorthand homework every night and we worked hard all day, with only short coffee and lunch breaks. It paid off: at the end of the 15 weeks, all 20 people on the course left with Pitman Certificates of 80 wpm (or more) Shorthand and 40 wpm Typewriting, plus Word-Processing experience. I left college on Friday and started as a secretary in a graphic design agency on Monday. After a year, and substantial salary increases, I was made office administrator, with a receptionist and a junior to help me. I subsequently moved into broadcasting where I am currently working as a Festival Administrator.'
(Former student, Pitman Central College)

Royal Free Hospital and Friern School of Nursing
Full-time 3-year courses leading to qualification of Registered General Nurse or Registered Mental Nurse. School states: 'We do not wish to put an upper age limit, but rather see applicants individually. We offer the UKCC entry test as an alternative to the usual entry requirements. This year (1989) we are allocating half of one of our six intakes of students, specifically for mature candidates.'

Royal Marsden Hospital School of Radiotherapy
Full-time 3-year course leading to Diploma of the College of Radiographers (Therapy). Entry concessions for mature applicants possible, in accordance with the regulations of the College of Radiographers which has a special panel to consider mature candidates, but School of Radiotherapy would expect such applicants to have at least English, Mathematics and a further Science subject at the equivalent of O-levels, plus further education to at least A-level standard. School states: 'The upper age limit would generally

be about 40 years and each candidate would be considered individually, taking into consideration their personality, experience and general education.'

St Bartholomew's School of Nursing: St. Bartholomew's Hospital
Full-time 3-year course leading to Registered General Nurse qualification. School states: 'We certainly welcome mature students. The upper age limit is 45 years. Applicants should have the qualifications laid down by the UKCC (i.e. 5 subjects at GCE O-level or educational equivalent) to include English Language. If applicants do not meet the above requirements, they may take the UKCC educational test as a means of entry.'

St Mary's Hospital School of Physiotherapy
Full-time 3-year course of training leading to a Graduate Diploma in Physiotherapy and Membership of the Chartered Society of Physiotherapy. School states: 'Mature students are considered for entry by the school, but must present evidence of academic achievement.'

St Thomas's Hospital School of Physiotherapy
Full-time 3-year course, upper age limit normally 30 years. School states: 'We expect mature students to have a good background of educational qualifications and to have done some study at a higher level immediately prior to applying. Each student is considered on their individual merits.'

St Thomas's Hospital: South East Thames Regional Radiography Training Centre
Full-time 3-year course leading to the Diploma of the College of Radiographers (Therapy). Centre states: 'We have no particular restrictions regarding the age limit of applicants. However, our attitude to each candidate would need to take into account practical consideration – in particular, the prospective career opportunities of a person after three years or training; and considering the retirement age of 60 years. In other words, provided career opportunities are likely to exist for the candidate and that they fulfilled criteria common to the selection of all applicants, we would be happy to accept mature students. There are special dispensations in the academic criteria for mature entrants – details available from the College of Radiographers.'

South London College
(1988 – excluding courses formerly MSC sponsored.) Electronic Servicing (TV and Audio Equipment and Industrial Equipment) for City and Guilds award, full time. Basic Craft Principles in Electrical/Electronic or Mechanical Engineering, under 21-hour rule. Microcomputer Technology for City and Guilds award, full time. Welding Craft Practice, for City and Guilds award, part time. Welding or Basic Hydraulic Pneumatic Systems or Basic Robotics,

evenings. Electronics for Women, school hours and terms (ESF sponsorship possible). NC/CNC Machine Tool Setting, part time or evenings, for City and Guilds award. NC/CNC Machine Tool Programming, part time or evenings, for City and Guilds award. Refrigeration Mechanics Course (Installation and Service), full time, for City and Guilds award. BTEC National Diploma in Business and Finance, full time, entry concessions possible for over-19s. National Examinations Board for Supervisory Studies (NEBSS) Certificate and Local Government Certificate, part time, for potential supervisors. Work Study, students over 20, part time, day or evening. BTEC National Diploma in Computer Studies, full time, over-19s selected by aptitude test and interview. Information Technology Users courses (various levels) part time. Software Workshops for Information Technology users (business, education, medical) various entry requirements, part time, day or evening. Home Economics for Family and Community Care, for City and Guilds award, full time, possibility of 21-hour rule entry for mature students. Catering Supervision and Managment for City and Guilds award, for over-21s with relevant City and Guilds certificate. The Cookery Certificate, day or evening. Creative Studies (Fashion) part time, for mature students, includes design, cutting, construction, for City and Guilds award; good basis for dressmaking business.

South East London College
(1988, excluding courses formerly MSC-sponsored.) Women-only BTEC National Diploma in Engineering, full time. Women-only BTEC National Certificate in Engineering, part time.

South West London College
(1988) Association of Accounting Technicians' Certificate, full time, no formal entry requirements. Chartered Association of Certified Accountants' Graduate Conversion course, full time. Office Skills for mature students, school hours only, no formal entry requirements. English as a Second Language/Office Skills, mornings only, no formal entry requirements. Adult Secretarial, school hours only, no formal entry requirements. Access to Professional Accountancy, full time, no formal entry requirements. BTEC National/HND and Certificate/HNC Business Studies, full time, entry concessions possible for over-19s. Introductory/Certificate course in Supervisory Studies, part time, for potential supervisors. Institute of Training and Development Certificate, part time, no formal entry requirements.

Thames Polytechnic
(Sites at Woolwich, Dartford, Avery Hill, Wapping, Shadwell.) Retraining and vocational courses on several sites. Mature students are welcome to apply for all full-time and part-time courses; alternative qualifications, relevant experience or evidence of ability related to the chosen course may be accepted instead of normal entrance requirements. Foundation

Diplomas/Certificates in Computing or Mathematics; retraining courses for teachers (Physics, Design Technology, Mathematics); Certificates/Diplomas in Health, Architecture, Landscape Architecture, Management Studies (Health), Personnel Management, Youth and Community Work. BTEC HNC/D courses in Business and Finance, Civil Engineering, Chemistry, Computer Studies, Information Technology, Engineering (Electrical and Electronic or Mechanical), Mathematics, Statistics and Computing, Science (Pharmaceutical).

Thomas Guy & Lewisham School of Nursing
Full-time 3-year course leading to qualification as a Registered General Nurse. No age limit mentioned but school's literature states 'Mature entrants will be considered with five O-level passes or equivalent certificates on an individual basis.' For candidates without statutory academic entrance requirements, the UKCC entry test is available, conducted at the School of Nursing on the first Wednesday of each month. Applications for the UKCC test must be made in writing. Shortened course for graduates (see 'Degree and Advanced Courses').

Tour Management Training Centre
(1988) Independent College – S. Little, Course Manager. Tour Management Training Programme, January–March, part time, leading to City and Guilds award in Tour Management (Europe) and Association of British Travel Agents' Seal of Approval. Knowledge of foreign languages an advantage. Selection by interview each summer.

Uxbridge College
Flexi-skill courses in Typewriting (Beginners and Refresher), Word-Processing, Book-keeping and Audio-Typing. Part time, in modified form, at low cost. Flexible courses developed by women, for women wishing to return to work.

Waltham Forest School of Nursing: Whipps Cross Hospital
Full-time 3-year courses leading to qualifications of Registered General Nurse or Registered Mental Nurse or Registered Nurse for the Mentally Handicapped. School states: 'Mature candidates areencouraged and welcomed – all considered on an individual basis. As an alternative to the usual entry requirements, a pass in the UKCC entry test is acceptable – this test is conducted monthly.'The RMNH course is a new one provided by Waltham Forest Health authority and Waltham Forest College. 'The course commences at Waltham Forest College, eight weeks from the foundation unit, followed by a two-week preparation for the first placement. This will take place in a nursery, followed by further study and placements in mainstream education, residential areas and the community.'

West London Institute of Higher Education
Diploma in Social Work/Certificate of Qualification in Social Work, entry concessions possible for those over 25; preference may be given to those with some social work experience. Diploma in Occupational Therapy, full time, entry concessions possible for mature students. BTEC HND in Computer Studies, entry route available for mature students with some computing experience. Short computer coures, including Introductory Programming, Word-Processing: Wordstar and Word-II, use of spreadsheets and databases. Part-time and evening courses, some devised to meet special needs. See also School of Physiotherapy, below.

West London Institute of Higher Education School of Physiotherapy
Full-time three-year course leading to Graduate Diploma in Physiotherapy. School states: 'We do accept mature applicants and there is no formalised upper age limit. All applications are considered on overall merit and although we do not necessarily expect applicants to meet the standard minimum of 2 A-level passes for acceptance, preference is given to those offering evidence of study to an appropriate standard during the five years preceeding entry to the course.'

Westminster Hospital School of Radiography: Riverside Health Authority
Full-time 3-year course of training leading to Diploma of the College of Radiographers (Diagnostic). College states: 'In common with all Schools of Radiography, we accept mature students. Each candidate is considered individually as we waive our normal entry requirements of 5 GCSEs and 2 A-levels. However, experience has taught us that prospective students, whatever age, do have to have an aptitude for science and technology and like working with people. They must also be prepared to accept that there is a recognised infrastructure which is difficult to overcome. Some mature students have found the hospital environment incompatible with their previous experience ... strongly advise any mature applicant to visit several radiography departments before proceeding with an application.'

Southern and Eastern England

Ashford: South East Kent School of Nursing
Full-time, 3-year course leading to Registered General Nurse qualification. Full-time 2-year course leading to Enrolled Nurse (General) qualification. The school literature states that the training is 'a little over' 3 years or 2 years in each case. No age limit is specified in their leaflets. *Important Note*: For entry to most RGN courses, candidates are required to satisfy statutory entry requirement by offering 5 GCSE (Grades A–C) or GCE O-level or CSE Grade 1 passes including English. At this school, candidates must offer *six* academic subjects including English. For the EN(G) course, an entrance test is available.

Barnet School of Nursing
Full-time 3-year courses leading to qualification of Registered General Nurse or Registered Mental Nurse. Candidates without statutory GCSE/GCE entry requirements may take UKCC entry test. School states: 'We welcome mature applicants for nurse training. Those who have had a job before bring life experiences to nursing and this is of great benefit to patients. Usually we consider applicants aged up to 40 years. However, we might consider somebody older who has some relevant knowledge/skills/expertise to offer. Each is considered on individual merits.'

Basingstoke Technical College
Office Skills Refresher, part time, includes choice of skills training. Mature candidates accepted on full-time Diploma for Personal Assistants, part-time Secretarial/Office Skills, on short courses in Word-Processing Familiarisation, and on infill basis, to part-time Typewriting.

Bracknell College
BTEC National Diploma in Travel & Tourism, full time. BTEC National Diploma in Computing Studies, full time.

Brighton Polytechnic
(1988) BTEC HND Public Administration, full time, entry concessions possible for those aged 21-plus. NB: this policy may apply to other Brighton

HND courses and also part-time HNC courses. Polytechnic Certificate scheme in Art, Craft and Society, part time, special options include Art, Bookbinding and repair, Printmaking, Photography, Three-Dimensional Craft (Wood, Metal, Ceramics or Plastics), Printing and the Graphic Arts. Diploma of Higher Education (Business Studies) part time, open to wide range of candidates, including, for example, those with a teacher's certificate or diploma and, exceptionally, unqualified mature students with adequate business experience. Can lead to a degree (see 'Degree and Advanced Courses'). Polytechnic Certificate course in Computer Studies, part time. Computer Workshops, various levels, from beginner upwards. Postgraduate Diploma in Counselling, part time, for candidates with or without academic qualifications who have substantial experience in the counselling field. Polytechnic Diploma in Creative Embroidery, part time, mainly for teachers, but others who can demonstrate ability considered. Foreign languages, part time, various levels: French, German, Spanish, Greek, Italian, Russian, Portuguese. Certificate in Management Studies, part time, wide range of entry qualifications acceptable; over-25s with suitable business experience need not always have formal qualifications.

Brighton Polytechnic Department of Chiropody
Full-time 3-year course leading to Diploma of the Society of Chiropodists. Polytechnic states: 'We do accept mature students into the Department of Chiropody and there is no upper age limit specified. However, the number of places offered to people who will be significantly over the age of 40 at the time of their registration (that is three years after commencement) is not likely to be more than 10% of the intake. We seem to use the age of 25 as our definition of mature students and we are anticipating that approximately half of our students will be over 25 in future. We welcome mature students and value their contribution. On the whole our experience of mature students with a wide range of entry qualifications has been good and their progress has been comparable with that of 18-year-old entrants from sixth forms.'

Bromley College of Technology
(1988, excluding courses formerly MSC-sponsored.) Electronics Servicing for City and Guilds award, part time, for those employed in the industry and those with a keen interest in it. BTEC Post Experience courses, part time, for people aged 21-plus - main entry criterion is 'ability to benefit'. Options are Computer Studies, Improve your Financial Decision-Making, Making Sense of Marketing. Evening study options include Word-Processing (Introductory to Advanced), Computer Literacy, Audio-Typing, Medical Shorthand.

Bromley School of Nursing
Part-time 3 years and 9 months course leading to Registered General Nurse qualification, organised to coincide with school terms in order that holidays

can be taken at the same time as school children. Each student will work a 30 hour week. Creche facilities are available on both the Orpington and Farnborough sites (places subject to availability). Candidates must have fiveacademic O-levels or equivalent and the upper age limit is 47.

Cambridge College of Further Education
(1988 excluding courses formerly MSC-sponsored.) RSA Book-keeping/ Accounts, evenings. GCSE evenings. Foundation Certificatein Accounting, day and evenings, can lead to Association of Accounting Technicians course. Institute of Marketing Certificate and Diploma, evenings, applicants with sales/marketing experience but without usual qualifications may be admitted. Tee-Line Shorthand, Typewriting and Word Processing, beginners to RSA III, day and evenings. Cake Decoration, for those aiming at high standards for celebration cakes, evenings. Patisserie, afternoons, to meet requirements of hotels, hospitals etc. Cookery for Hotels and Restaurants, City and Guilds 706/1, part-time day release. Breadmaking and Flour Confectionery for City and Guilds 120, part time, for new entrants to and older workers in the bakery industry. Wine and Spirit Association Certificates, part-time useful preparation for work in wine trade, hotels etc. Applications Programming Certificate for City and Guilds 417, part time, to suit computer operators wishing to progress. Community Care in Practice, for people employed, or preparing for work in the community, part time. Pre-School Playgroups Association Foundation course, part time, school hours only. Nursery Assistants course, for those wishing to work with the under-fives. City and Guilds 730 Certificate for Teachers in Further and Adult Education. City and Guilds 734 Certificate in Teaching Students with Special Needs in Further Education. RSA Diploma in the Teaching of Communications. RSA Certificate for Vocational Preparation Tutors - modes unspecified.

Cambridge: Cambridge and Huntingdon Department of Nurse Education
Full-time 3-year course of training leading to the qualifications of Registered General Nurse or Registered Mental Nurse or Registered Nurse for the Mentally Handicapped. Candidates without the statutory GCSE/GCE entry requirements may take the UKCC entry test. Department states: 'We welcome mature candidates, especially if they are local. The upper age limit is 50 years on start of training, and as with all candidates, we expect them to attend an Occupational Health review.'

Cambridge: Cambridge Health Authority School of Physiotherapy
Full-time 3-year course of training leading to Membership of the Chartered Society of Physiotherapy. School states: 'We do accept mature students but would be reluctant to offer a place to anyone over 40 years of age. We recommend that mature students who have done no formal study for some years, complete at least 2 A- levels prior to entry - biology and any other

subject of their choice - possibly broadly related - e.g. psychology or sociology. For those with no science background, we suggest O-level/GCSE Physics or any chemistry/physics combination.'

Cambridge: Cambridgeshire College of Arts and Technology
Is being amalgamated with Essex Institute of Higher Education; no information about courses available during this process.

Cambridge: School of Diagnostic Radiography
Full-time 3-year training course leading to the Diploma of the College of Radiographers (Diagnostic). College states: 'We do accept mature students at this School of Radiography. There is no upper age limit - each case is considered on its merits.' All mature students have to apply to the special panel of the College of Radiographers after acceptance by a training centre with their own statement as to why they want to train, and an academic and personal statement of support by the teaching staff who interviewed them.

Canterbury College of Art - see Kent Institute of Art & Design

Carshalton: Merton & Sutton Health Authority: Carshalton School of Nursing
Full-time 3-year courses leading to qualification as a Registered General Nurse or Registered Nurse for the Mentally Handicapped. For candidates without statutory GCSE/GCE entry requirements, the UKCC entry test is available. School states: 'Mature students welcomed. We offer training to suitable candidates from 18–45 years of age, both men and women.'

Chatham: Mid Kent College of Further & Higher Education
(1988, excluding courses formerly MSC-sponsored.) BTEC National Diploma and HND sandwich, Computer Studies. Mature students without the usual academic qualifications may be admitted in special circumstances. BTEC HND Business Studies, full time, same rules as for Computer Studies. Certificate of Qualification in Social Work, full time, for applicants aged 20–50. Those over 25 do not need formal academic qualifications, though they must satisfy the college that they can meet the academic requirementsof the course. All candidates must have had at least a year's working experience since leaving school (not necessarily in social work). Applications from mature students/ethnic minorities particularly welcome. Association of Accounting Technicians' course, part time, over-21s without usual entry requirements may apply. BTEC Business Studies or Business Studies (Finance), part time, over-21s without usual academic entry requirements may apply. Institute of Legal Executives, part time, over-30s with appropriate experience may be exempted from educational entry requirements. Institute of Purchasing and Supply Foundation course, part time, over-25s with relevant experience may be exempted from educational entry requirements. BTEC Certificate in Management Studies, part time, over-25s who

have held a suitable post for at least three years may be admitted without formal academic qualifications. NEBSS Certificate/Diploma in Supervisory Studies, part time, for employed/potential supervisors, with background to enable them to benefit from the course. Institution of Industrial Managers (formerly Works Managers), part time, over-27s with at least four years industrial experience may be admitted without academic entry requirements. Institute of Personnel Management, part time, over-23s with at least two years relevant experience may be accepted without the minimum academic qualifications. Computer Programming, part time, introductory to advanced. NC/CNC Machine Tool Setting and Operation and NC/CNC Part Programming, part time, for mature students, to update their knowledge. Shorthand, Typewriting and Word Processing, part time, various levels. Medical Reception, part time, open to those without experience in the medical field. Open Learning (see 'Open and Distance Learning Courses').

Chelmsford: Mid Essex School of Nursing
Full-time 3-year training course leading to Registered General Nurse qualification. Full-time 2-year training course leading to Enrolled Nurse (Mental Subnormality) qualification. UKCC entry test available as an alternative to usual GCSE/GCE entry requirements. School states: 'We welcome mature applicants up to the age of 45 years.'

Chichester: West Dean College
(1988) Independent college. Three full-time restoration courses in association with the British Antique Dealers' Association - Antique Furniture, Antique Porcelain and Ceramics, Antique Clocks - and two full-time professional restoration courses - Musical Instrument Making and Book-Binding and the Care of Books. All five courses lead to Diplomas. The college authorities emphasise that Antique Ceramics Restoration and Antique Clocks are 'advanced' courses, though they appear in this retraining section as they enable successful students to acquire a vocational training. Also short (one week or weekend) courses in creative subjects with earning potential, e.g. Cabinet-Making, Calligraphy, Stained Glass, Working with Precious Metals.

Antique Ceramics Restoration: viewpoint
'This course combines a very good basic training in the history of ceramics with practical experience at the same time. We often work from museum photographs of articles in their original condition. Any restoration should be accurate, and ethics come into it. The restoration must be unobtrusive but quite obvious when you look at it from say, about a foot. When I leave I'll find a job that isn't purely commercial, which combines craft with the antiques trade.'

(Student, Restoration course at West Dean College)

Working with Precious Metals: viewpoint
'I'm making a silver coffee pot, which is the most complicated thing I have tackled so far, but I do make other things - boxes, bowls, spoons, small things to make and sell or give as Christmas presents or 25th wedding anniversary presents. The fact that West Dean runs weekend and five-day courses means that they cater both for the person with leisure to fill and those who may want to turn a hobby to professional use, perhaps when they are between careers. If you choose, they can train you to a competent professional level.'
(Student on Working with Silver short course, West Dean College)

Chichester: West Sussex Institute of Higher Education
Nurse training in association with Chichester and Graylingwell School of Nursing, for candidates aged 18–42; courses leading to Registered General Nurse, Registered Mental Nurse, Enrolled Nurse (General) and Enrolled Nurse (Mental).

Colchester Institute
TA-sponsored Import/Export Clerks, full time. TA-sponsored Systems Analysis, full time. TA-sponsored Advanced Office Technology, full time and part time. TA-sponsored BTEC Certificate in Electronics, full time. Mature students welcome and no upper age limit to any of the Institute's courses – admission at the discretion of individual course tutors. Courses that attract late starters are Teaching English as a Foreign Language, full time; Diploma in Vehicle Restoration, full time; Diploma in Book Conservation, full time; Diploma in Leisure and Recreation Studies, full time; HNC Business and Finance, part time. Open Learning (see 'Open and Distance Learning Courses').

Vehicle Restoration: viewpoint
'I left school with really no idea what I wanted to do, and ended up restoring and tuning pianos, which I enjoyed. In the last few years, it's obviously been a dying trade because of the advent of electronic instruments, so when I saw this car restoration course advertised, I jumped at the chance – the philosophy of restoration is very much the same. Though the metalwork, and particularly the welding, involves a lot more than I first thought, the woodwork tools and usages are all the same. What the course has done for me is to give me a lot of skills which will mean I can't be out of work when I leave here. Firms specialising in car restoration are springing up all over the country. I think people are simply getting fed up with the boxes car manufacturers are producing nowadays, all alike in three sizes.'
(Student, Vehicle Restoration Course, Colchester Institute)

Book Conservation: viewpoint
'We also offer a two-year Diploma in the Conservation of Books and Archive Materials, from which students move into a wide variety of jobs: in County

Record Offices and the Public Records Office, in Trinity College, Dublin, and another one works with the National Trust, looking at the problems of book collections in big country houses. Two former students set up independently in Cambridge. Another is off to Glasgow University Library; another went to the National Library in Florence - a lovely place to work. Book and Archive Conservation is an area where it's been estimated in this country alone there will be over 100 jobs coming up in the next five years; in fact there's an absolute mountain of work piling up all the time - millions of documents in need of conservation.'

(Spokesperson, Book Conservation, Colchester Institute)

Croydon College
(1988, excluding courses formerly MSC-sponsored.) BTEC HND Business Studies, full time, possible entry concessions for over-21s. Extended Certificate of Qualifiation in Social Work (CQSW)s full time, but hours 10 a.m. to 3 p.m. only, to suit people with home commitments. Certificate of Qualification in Social Work, full time, conventional hours. For both CQSW courses, those over 25 need not have O-levels but must show evidence of ability to undertake academic work and ideally, have some relevant experience. Estimating and Quantity Surveying, full time, for over-21s with building industry experience. Bookbinding, part time, day or evening. Printmaking, part time (selection by portfolio for practising artists). Certified Diploma in Accounting and Finance for graduates or equivalent. BTEC HNC Business Studies/Public Administration, part time, over-21s without usual qualifications may be accepted at Course Director's discretion. BTEC Certificate in Management Studies, part time, over-25s may be accepted with three years' relevant management experience. Certificate in Marketing, evenings, over-21s with three years' practical marketing experience need not offer formal qualifications. Institute of Personnel Management Course, part time, day and evenings, or evenings only - Part I entry open to people with two A-levels *or* two years' practical experience. Institute of Purchasing and Supply Foundation Course, evenings, people aged 26-plus working in purchasing need not offer GCEs.NEBSS Certificate in Supervisory Management, for candidates of minimum age 21-plus and with supervisory potential. Shorthand/Typing, afternoon or evenings - candidates must be competent in English Language. Service of Food (Silver Service Waiting) evenings, no formal entry requirements. Wine and Spirit Education Trust Certificate/Higher Certificate, no formal entry reqirement. Computer Literacy and Computer Programming, evenings, no formal entry requirement. CNAA Certificate in Further and Adult Education, part time, for those wishing to teach in further and adult education. BTEC National Certificate in Heating, Ventilating and Air Conditioning, part time, day and evening, for draughtsmen/women or site technicians wishing to extend career prospects. City and Guilds Craft Studies in Electronic Engineering, part time, day and evening. Mature, experienced students may be admitted

at Part II level. Mechanical Engineering Craft Studies for City and Guilds 201/5 awards, open to mature students with engineering background. Machine Tool Setting and Operation for NC/CNC leading to City and Guilds 230 award, mature students employed in production engineering considered. Motor Vehicle Craft Studies for City and Guilds 381 award, part time, day or evening, no formal entry requirements. NB: many of these courses are designed for young students, but the college willingly considers mature entrants when space is available.

Dunstable College
Mature students welcomed on all courses. The college provides a wide range of courses in the following areas of work: Engineering, Business Studies, Secretarial, Printing, Graphics, Science, Maths, Caring, Health Studies, Leisure and Recreation and is continually developing flexible programmes on a modular basis for people wanting to update or retrain. College also offers a large number of short courses in Computer Accounts, Desktop Publishing, Interviewing Technique and other subjects all designed to upgrade and retrain people for better jobs.

Dunstable College: viewpoint
'We have just had two women completing our Higher National Certificate in Design. They both combined families and academic work in order to get distinctions in the exam and enhance their job prospects.'
(Spokesperson, Dunstable College)

Eastbourne: Sussex Downs School of Nursing
Full-time 3-year training course leading to the qualifications of Registered General Nurse or Registered Mental Nurse. Applicants without the usual GCE/GCSE entry requirement may take the UKCC entry test. School states: 'We accept mature entrants up to the age of 55 years.'

Epsom: North East Surrey College of Technology
(1988 excluding courses formerly sponsored by the MSC.) Access to Information Technology, part time. Computer Programming, full time. Secretarial Refresher, full time. Clerical Update, full time. BTEC HNC Building Services Engineering (Controls), full time. BTEC HNC Scientific Instrumentation, full time. BTEC HND Business Information Technology, full time. BTEC HND Science (Applied Biology) full time. BTEC HND Construction, full time. BTEC HND Computer Studies, full time. Horticulture for City and Guilds award, part time, in association with Merrist Wood Agricultural College, no formal entry requirements. NEBSS Certificate in Supervisory Management, part time, for potential supervisors. Medical Reception, part time, no formal entry requirements. Typing, Shorthand, Word Processing, part time, no formal entry requirements. BTEC Certificate in Management Studies, evenings, for those who have varied academic

backgrounds, or who are over 25 with at least three years' experience in a post of responsibility. Certified Diploma in Accounting and Finance, evenings. Those over 25 may be allowed to enrol if they have attained a position of responsibility in a career other than accountancy. Short part-time courses with earning potential, leading to College Certificate and City and Guilds award include Fashion, Soft Furnishing, Toymaking, Tailoring, Machine Knitting. Flexilearning (see 'Open and Distance Learning Courses').

Guildford College of Technology
TA-sponsored Employment Training scheme in many areas; details from college. Mature students with five O-levels may apply for the Diploma in Fine Bookbinding, full time. Those with three O-levels may apply for the Design Technician in Printing, full time course.

Guildford: Regional Radiotherapy Education Centre
Full-time 3-year training course leading to the Diploma of the College of Radiographers (Therapy). College states: 'We do accept mature students to the age of 40-42 years. All mature students have to apply to the special panel of the College of Radiographers after acceptance by a training centre with their own statement as to why they want to train, and an academic and practical statement of support by the teaching staff who interviewed them.'

Guildford: South West Surrey College of Nursing
Full-time 3-year courses leading to qualification as a Registered General Nurse or Registered Mental Nurse. Candidates without the statutory academic entrance requirements may be able to take the UKCC entry test. College states: 'We do welcome mature entrants whom normally make up 20/25% of our course members. We do not have an upper age limit, although in practice we would not consider candidates above 50. It should be noted the candidates do need to be physically fit and in good health. We are currently planning considerable change to our nurse education programmes, including the likelihood of introducing the Project 2000 programme of training in 1990. This course will have both full- and part-time members.'

Hastings College of Arts and Technology
Mature students may apply for places on the following courses:(a) Hotel, Catering & Beauty Studies: BTEC First Diploma, BTEC National Diploma (Years 1 and 2), Diploma in Professional Cookery, Cookery and Food Service Diploma (one year or two year), General Catering course, Hotel Reception (one year or two year), Beauty Therapy (one year or two year), Hairdressing (one year or two year), Hairdressing and Beauty (3 year). (b) Business and General Studies: BTEC National Diploma Business Studies, Secretarial courses. (c) Engineering and Science: BTEC National Diploma courses in

Electronics, Mechanical & Production, Computing Technology, General Engineering. BTEC Higher National Diploma in Engineering with options in Mechanical and Production and Electronics.

Hatfield Polytechnic
TA-sponsored Professional Updating for Women, three days a week in college, one day a week and one week's placement with an employer; hours 10 a.m. – 3 p.m. to suit school days. Day nursery facilities available. No fees and travelling expenses are paid. (See also 'Degree and Advanced Courses'.)

Havering Technical College
(1988) Open Learning, includes Shorthand and Typing (see 'Open and Distance Learning Courses').

Hemel Hempstead: Dacorum College
(1988) Offers a series of courses designed to suit individual needs. Courses start every term and require attendance two hours daily for duration of studies. Subjects include Keyboarding Skills, Typewriting (I and II) Word Processing, Shorthand (Beginners, speeds 50-plus, 80-plus). VDU operation. Book-keeping, Wages Preparation.

High Wycombe: Buckinghamshire College of Higher Education
BTEC HND Engineering, full time. BTEC HND Information Technology, full time. BTEC HNC Electronic Engineering, part time. BTEC HNC Mechanical/Production Engineering, part time. BTEC HNC Computer Studies, part time. For these, the college 'particularly welcomes applications from mature students who, while not necessarily possessing formal qualifications, have appropriate industrial experience which is relevant to the course.' Certificate of Qualification in Social Work (CQSW) full time - minimum age of entry is 21 and there is no upper age limit. Previous social work experience is essential for those under 23 and over 40 and desirable for others. There are no formal educational requirements for candidates aged 27-plus. BTEC HND Business Studies, full time or sandwich; exceptionally those without formal qualifications aged 21-plus may be admitted. BTEC HNC Business Studies, part time, regulations as for full time. BTEC HND Business Information Technology, full time - applications from mature students welcomed. Institute of Personnel Management course, evenings - candidates without normal qualifications considered if at least 23 with at least 24 months personnel or related experience. National Examinations Board Course in Supervisory Studies, part time, for potential supervisors/managers over 21; no formal entry qualifications. BTEC Certificate in Management Studies, part time, day and evening; those over 25 may be admitted without formal qualification if they have had at least three years' experience and are holding/have held a position of responsibility.

Ipswich: East Suffolk Health Authority School of Nursing
Full-time 3-year courses leading to qualification as a Registered General
Nurse or Registered Mental Nurse. Candidates without the statutory
academic entrance requirements may take the UKCC entry test. School
welcomes mature applicants and does not specify an upper age limit.

Ipswich: Suffolk College of Higher and Further Education
(1988) Certificate of Qualification in Social Work, full time; candidates 21–45.
Diploma in Residential Day Care, full time, for candidates aged 18–50.
Academic qualifications are not required for the latter course.

Social Work: viewpoint
'I previously worked in engineering and held down my last job, as a chief
estimator, for 18 years. Over the last seven or eight years, I realised I was
very much a square peg in a round hole. I was attracted by social work
because I had served as a borough councillor dealing with problems, so with
my children, aged 13–21 and responsibilities in economic terms diminish-
ing, I realised it was "now or never" if I was going to make a break. There
was a lot of heart-searching and worry, but we've made it, and there's no
looking back now.'

(Student on CQSW course, Suffolk College)

Diploma in Residential and Day Care: viewpoints
'I'd done quite a bit of work with unemployed people and also with a
community relations council. When I was made redundant, I went back to
college for a course in cost accounting, thinking I might go into business, but
that didn't work out, and I finally decided that it would be worth me going
into social work as a paid occupation. The course is valuable, particularly the
placements. For instance, the placement I'm on now is with old people.
Having met a lot of old people living at home, when I was working as a
volunteer, I find it's a very different environment when they are resident in a
home. You have 50 or 60 old people to consider and you have to cater for
their needs 24 hours a day.'

(Student, Residential and Day Care course, Suffolk College)

'There are eight to ten thousand homes in this country providing residential
care for children, old people, handicapped and mentally ill people, in the
voluntary, private and social services sector. They all need properly trained
staff, though it's worth emphasising that staff do not necessarily have to
"live in" and may take sleeping-in duties on a rota basis. Residential social
work is as practically demanding as hotel management, while also calling for
personal and emotional qualities. A residential setting is a complex
organisation, and management responsibilities include food, heating,
upkeep of property, management of grounds, organisation of day and night
shifts and, most important, catering for the needs of individuals. Residential

social workers contribute substantially to the therapy and psychological help given to people in homes. In addition, day care provision for all client groups is now rapidly expanding and is providing excellent career opportunities for people who wish to work regular hours.'

(Spokesperson, Suffolk College)

Kent Institute of Art and Design
(1988) This college is an amalgamation of Canterbury College of Art, Medway College of Design and Maidstone College of Art. In the past, colleges have been prepared to consider under-qualified candidates with relevant work experience and a good portfolio of work in art/craft/design. Policies are not likely to change in this respect as the result of amalgamation and mature students should always enquire.'

Kingston Polytechnic
TA-sponsored 'Women into Management' course, full time - includes general management, finance, marketing, computing and in-company project. Two years' previous business experience at a responsible level required. Postgraduate Diploma in Theatre, Film and Television Design, full time. Formal academic qualifications not always necessary; previous experience in the theatre, film or TV (professional or amateur) needed. BTEC HND Business Studies or Mechanical Engineering, full time, over-21s with four or more years in suitable employment may be admitted without minimum qualifications. Polytechnic Diploma in Personnel Management, over-21s with suitable work experience may be admitted by test and interview. Diploma in Social Work/Certificate of Qualification in Social Work (CQSW) full time, for people aged 30–50 – formal academic qualifications not essential. (See also 'Degree and Advanced Courses'.) Contact Admissions Office for information and advice.

Luton College of Higher Education
(1988) BTEC HND Business Studies, full time, entry concessions possible for those over 21 with suitable business experience. HND Business Studies with Bilingual Administration option, exceptionally, those over 21 may be admitted without the usual entry qualifications at the discretion of the college. HND Public Administration, full time, entry concessions possible for those over 21 with suitable work experience or community experience. HND Computer Studies, full time; mature entrants with suitable work experience given special consideration. HND Business Information Technology, full time, same rule applies. HND Computer Aided Engineering/ HND Applied Electronics, Computer Engineering, Communications Engineering, all full time, mature students considered on merit. Wide range of part time courses, also Open Learning (see 'Open and Distance Learning Courses').

Luton: Luton and Dunstable School of Radiography
Full-time 3-year training leading to Diploma of the College of Radiographers (Diagnostic). School states: 'We do accept mature students. There is no specified upper age limit as such: rather we look at each applicant individually from the point of view of physical and mental fitness in the present and for a projected 10 years' service after qualification. I suppose this sets a practical limit of about 50. As to entry requirements, we can exercise some discretion, subject to the approval of the College of Radiographers, in that relevant experience of life and work can be accepted in lieu of some of the entry requirements. We would still insist on GCSE equivalent in English and Mathematics, and a science or technology background would be encouraging. Again we would look to whether each applicant's ability, application and motivation to study offered a reasonable prospect of success in the course. Our approach would not necessarily apply to other Schools of Radiography - we are all autonomous within the bounds of the minimum national standard and acceptance by the College of Radiographers.'

Maidstone: Mid Kent College - see under Chatham

Morden: Merton College
Beginners' typing, part time (a Return to Work course); Typing and Word-Processing, part time (a Return to Work course). Cooks' Professional course for mature students with some flair for cooking. Motor Cycle Engineering Mechanics, full time, aptitude test. Musical Instrument Repair, full time, aptitude test. Computer-Aided Engineering, full time. BTEC National Diploma in Health Studies, full time This course is vocationally based and has work experience throughout the year in health studies fields, such as Nursing, Radiography, Physiotherapy, Chiropody, Dentistry etc. The college says 'All our courses are open to mature students, and, for most, exemptions from entry requirements are available.'

Motorcycle Engineering: viewpont
'I moved up to Lincolnshire because we could get a house there. I'm married with a young child, but I never seemed to get a job in Lincolnshire. One place went bankrupt before I could get there and other jobs simply fell through. I've always wanted to work with motorcycles but I just didn't have any experience. Firms are willing to take on young people, but not adults without any experience because they're going to have to pay them too much to train. Then I got on to this course. They train you from the beginning, the whole thing - design, frames, cycle parts, engines, fuel injection, electrics. We do a couple of days practical in the workshops and three and a half days in the classroom, plus general studies, plus welding. Meanwhile my family commutes between my mother-in-law in Salisbury, my parents in Teddington and our home in Lincolnshire - but it should all be worth it in the long run.'

(Student, Motorcycle Engineering, Merton College)

Musical Instrument Repair: viewpoint
'I spent 15 years as a self-employed cabinet maker, doing French polishing and antique restoration, and it was my love of music that brought me to this course. My friends are musicians as well. I felt I wanted to repair guitars and make guitars, which is a natural progression from my experience as a cabinet maker (though in fact we learn to repair a very wide range of instruments here). We cover general woodwork and general metalwork, and work on brass instrument repair, woodwind instrument repair, non-fretted stringed instrument repair, the violin family, fretted stringed instrument repair and we also do work on pipe organ design and maintenance.'

(Student, Musical Instrument Repair, Merton College)

Newbury College
Restart and various Adult Education courses sponsored by Berkshire Training Fund for the Unemployed, all free to and specifically for unemployed people. 'Adult job-changers are welcome to enrol for any of the college's courses on a full-time or part-time basis. The opportunities for job change, whether in technological subjects or business studies, are too numerous to list in detail, says the college.

Norwich: Broadland Centres of Nursing & Midwifery Education
Full-time 3-year training leading to the qualifications of Registered General Nurse or Registered Mental Nurse or Registered Nurse for the Mentally Handicapped. Candidates without statutory GCSE/GCE entry requirements may take the UKCC entry test. School states: 'Our school accepts mature students for all courses. The upper age limit for commencing basic nurse training is 45 years.' A special brochure for mature entrants is available free - ask for 'Care for a Change?'

Norwich City College
College Certificate in Community and Welfare Studies, full time or part time, minimum age 25, with an interest in working with people. HND Business Studies, full time, and HND Computer Studies, full time - applicants over 21 may be accepted if they can show ability to benefit from the course. Other HND possibilities include Computer-Aided Engineering, Electronics, Hotel Management and Information Technology. The college hopes to offer HND Business Information Technology. Mature students are accepted on an infill basis on all college courses; options could include College Craft Catering Diploma, full time, (several City & Guilds awards included), City and Guilds Hotel Reception, full time, BTEC National Certificate in Land Use (Valuation and Property Management), full time - mature students with relevant experience considered without qualifications. City and Guilds Technician in Electronic Servicing, full time - mature students with active interest considered for entrance test. Certificate/ Diploma in Furniture-Making, full time, entry by aptitude test. City and

Guilds Recreation and Leisure Studies, full time or part time. 'Re-Entry to Nursing' evenings, for qualified nurses. Association of Accounting Technicians Certificate in Accounting, open entry, no qualifications needed, part time. Secretarial courses including general, legal, medical, linguist, private and post-graduate, full time. Beginners' courses in typing, shorthand and word-processing, part time. Retraining and updating in office skills, part time, day and evening. Also Open Learning (see 'Open and Distance Learning Courses').

Peterborough: Peterborough and Stamford Department of Nurse Education

Full-time 3-year course leading to Registered General Nurse qualification. Normal entry requirements. School states: 'We do accept mature students, the upper limit being approximately 45, but each application is considered individually.'

Portsmouth College of Art, Design and Further Education

Mature students may be accepted for the following: BTEC National Diploma in Design (Communications); BTEC National Diploma in Design (Three-Dimensional); BTEC National Diploma in Retail Marketing, Design and Distribution; Pre-degree Art Foundation.

Portsmouth Health Authority: Queen Alexandra Hospital

Mature Registered General Nurse training course, open to local candidates, aged from 25 to 45; thirty-hour week from 9 a.m. to 3.30 p.m. (32 hours during Midwifery experience). School holidays off. Candidates are expected to do some relevant work, paid or voluntary, before being considered, e.g. work in an old people's home or as an auxiliary in a nursing home. Those without the statutory academic entry requirements may take a special English National Board test to assess their ability to cope with this course, after which advice will be given on a course of study to be undertaken before commencing nurse training. School states: 'This course has been operating for almost 20 years, with always a long waiting list. The training will be incorporated into the new educational system under Project 2000.'

Mature General Nurse Training: viewpoint
'I think the main advantage we have is a worldly experience. When you get into your 30s, you have had your children, you have elderly grandparents, your own parents are becoming more middle aged. Mature nurses have a lot to offer in the sense that we can empathise with the patients and their problems. The disadvantage is that we tend to get more emotionally involved: as mothers and as wives, and as children of elderly parents, we can perhaps sympathise with patients a lot more. People have said "Oh, I

think you must be mad. You've got a husband, you've got a home, your children have grown up - what on earth are you doing studying nursing?" I think it's fulfilling a part of my life that I missed out on earlier on.'

(Mature student nurse, Queen Alexandra Hospital School of Nursing)

'Men are just as welcome as women to come forward, but originally the course was for women with children at school. We test them for tenacity and do tend to send people away saying, "If you haven't done any studying since school, go off and do a bit." We try to get them to demonstrate some sort of discipline of work, so perhaps they may become home helps or help in an old people's home. They never get in the year they apply because we have so many applicants. They bring experience of life, patience and the wish to go in and be good, basic, caring nurses. In time, they become more ambitious, but essentially I don't think they ever lose that basic, caring attitude, whereas at l8, you're raring to get on.'

(Spokesperson, Queen Alexandra Hospital School of Nursing)

Portsmouth: Highbury College of Technology
(1988) This college sent only a prospectus, without comment on mature student entry, but the prospectus included various courses in areas noted for second career opportunities, e.g. Technical Authorship, evenings; Diploma in Driving Instruction, part time; Secretarial and Computer courses, full time and part time.

Portsmouth and South East Hampshire Health Authority School of Radiography
Full-time 3-year course leading to Diploma of the College of Radiographers (Diagnostic). Entry concessions possible for mature applicants in accordance with the regulations of the College of Radiographers which has a special panel to consider mature candidates. School states: 'We welcome applications from mature students for which the upper age limit is 45. There are entry concessions for mature students but applicants have to show they have the ability to study at the level required; therefore some recent study experience is useful in this regard.'

Reading: Bulmershe College of Higher Education
This college is now part of the University of Reading, see below.

Reading College of Technology
Full-time courses are available for mature students as follows: BTEC First and National Diplomas in Hotel and Catering, City and Guilds Food Preparation and Service; BTEC National Diploma in Leisure; City and Guilds Diploma in Hotel Reception and Front Office Practice; BTEC National Diploma in Health Studies; NNEB Nursery Nursing Certificate; City and Guilds Family and Community Care Certificate; City and Guilds Hairdressing and Beauty Therapy Diploma; BTEC First Diploma in Science; BTEC

National Diploma in Computing; City and Guilds 726 Information Technology; BTEC First, National and Higher National Diplomas in Engineering; Office Studies and Information Technology; Secretarial and Information Technology; Intensive Secretarial; Post A-level Secretarial; BTEC First and National Diplomas in Business Studies; BTEC First and National Diplomas in Construction.

Reading: University of Reading

Faculty of Education and Community Studies - Certificate of Qualification in Social Work, full time, for candidates aged 22-50: those over 25 need not necessarily have formal qualifications but must have academic potential and all are expected to have had some experience in paid or voluntary social work. Certificate in Community and Youth Work, full time: only a small number of candidates under 23 are taken - they must have at least five GCE O-levels. Those aged 23-plus must be able to demonstrate a good standard of written ability as well as experience as a volunteer worker, part time or full time, equivalent to a full year's work.(See also 'Degree and Advanced Courses'.)

Richmond Adult and Community College

ESF-sponsored Back to Business course, full time, for women aged 25-plus who have had their careers interrupted; includes updating on Computing and New Business Technology. Wide range of Office Skills courses, part time, including Beginners' Office Technology and Refreshers' Office Technology. A large variety of craft, design and technology courses with earning potential.

Rochester: Mid Kent College - see under Chatham

Romford College of Nursing and Midwifery

Full-time 3-year course leading to qualification as a Registered General Nurse or Registered Mental Nurse, upper age limit on entry 40. Full-time 3-year course leading to qualification as a Registered Nurse for the Mentally Handicapped, upper age limit on entry 50. Full-time 2-year course leading to qualification as an Enrolled Nurse (General) or Enrolled Nurse (Mental), upper age limit on entry 45. The college also states: 'Applicants from age 50 years are assessed on an individual basis.'

St Albans: City College

Business and Secretarial Skills Retraining/Refresher course. Modular: options include Typewriting, Audio Typewriting, Word-Processing, Computer Awareness, Computerised Accounting, Book-keeping, Shorthand, etc. Flexible attendance - all classes between 9.15 a.m. and 3 p.m.

St Albans: Hertfordshire College of Art and Design

BTEC HND Design (Modelmaking) full time, for students from varying backgrounds, previous relevant experience helpful. (Also Art Therapy and Dramatherapy - see 'Degree and Advanced Courses'.)

Modelmaking: viewpoint
'We are always prepared to consider people, whoever they are and whatever their qualifications. Probably most students come from design courses, but we have had film cameramen, people with degrees in geology, people retraining from being made redundant, a number of people from the armed forces, and so on. The course has an excellent relationship with the business and a good employment record. We look at examples of things students have made and also for the potential to deal with other people. Often the client does not have a clear picture in his or her mind as to the nature or purpose of the model to be made, and relies on the modelmaker to interpret and develop the idea. There are about 2000 professional model-makers in Britain, working for architects and designers and working in film and television as well.'

(Spokesperson, Hertfordshire College of Art and Design)

St Albans: Hertfordshire Centre for Building Studies
Students of all ages are acceptable. Short courses and City and Guilds qualification courses with earning potential: Painting and Decorating; Signwriting; Paperhanging; Plumbing; Furniture Construction; Carpentry and Joinery; Welding; Brickwork. BTEC Technician training in Construction, including Civil Engineering, Quantity Surveying, Estimating, Site Management, Building Services, Building Control.

Southampton School of Radiography
Full-time 3-year course leading to Diploma of the College of Radiographers (Diagnostic or Therapy). Age limit not specified but school states: 'We not only accept mature students, we positively encourage mature people to apply to us and we regard this group as a very important recruitment market.'

Southampton Technical College
The College is a Training Manager for Employment Training and is able to offer a wide range of training opportunities for unemployed adults and 'returners' as well as a special programme for women, disabled people and those for whom English is a second language. For lone parents, help may be available for childminding support. The college has a policy of supporting adult students and this is reflected in the fact that over 30% of enrolled students are adults. Careers counselling as well as guidance and support is available to people while participating in Employment Training.

Southampton University Hospitals Combined School of Nursing
Full-time 3-year courses leading to qualification as a Registered General Nurse or Registered Mental Nurse or Registered Nurse for the Mentally Handicapped. Full-time 2-year course leading to the qualification of Enrolled Nurse (General). Candidates aged over 25 who do not possess the

usual GCSE/GCE entry requirements may sit the UKCC entry test. School states: 'We welcome applications from mature students up to the age of 45 years to both our basic and post basic courses.' (Post-basic courses include the opportunity for General Enrolled Nurses to follow a course leading to Registration. A post-registration course leading to the qualification of Registered Sick Children's Nurse is also available.)

Southend College of Technology
Separate brochure of day and evening courses for adults. Includes Office Skills Refresher, part time, 9 a.m. – 3 p.m.; New Technology Typing (Word-Processors, Electronic Typewriters etc.), part time; Word-Processing, from beginner to advanced, part time, day or evening; Audio-Typing for beginners and improvers, part time; Teeline shorthand for beginners, evenings. TA-sponsored Administration/Secretarial skills courses. Music for Adults (includes evening 'Rock College' if you want to start your own group). Women Only evening courses in Car Maintenance and Electricity for Everyday Living and a 3 day a week course for women in Decorating, Engineering and Furniture Construction. Wide range of Engineering courses includes Electronic Computing workshop, Computer Machine Tool Programming, Electronics and Microprocessors for Motor Vehicles (evenings). Courses for teachers (RSA, City and Guilds). Better Care courses for those running residential homes. First Aid for home and in industry. For unemployed people, the college states: 'Every college course is open to you and we are working with the DHSS to simplify arrangements for claiming benefit while you learn. Most unemployed adults are entitled to study for up to 21 hours per week without losing benefit.' Open College (see 'Open and Distance Learning Courses').

Stevenage College
TA-Sponsored Book-keeping, full time. TA-sponsored Secretarial, full time. Extended Certificate of Qualification in Social Work (CQSW) course for people with home responsibilities (school hours only) and/or without conventional qualifications. Care Assistants' course for mature students, for City and Guilds 325. One day a week in college, one day a week in placement, three terms.

Extended Social Work Course: viewpoints
'I worked in a Labour Exchange. I just seemed to administer rules and I felt I wasn't helping the people on the other side of the counter ... I was a foster parent. I heard about the course from a social worker friend who had been on it ... I'd taken an Open University degree and there were no opportunities where I lived, so as I had done community work before I married, I moved to Stevenage from Dorset so I could take this course.'
    'The college takes into consideration that most of the people on the course have children and makes allowances for that. They also offer a lot of support

for those who haven't the academic background ... Being a more mature student gives you a wider scope and a wider field to talk about. Mothers and elderly people feel we're more in tune with what they are going through.'

'We start the course with a preliminary placement. I was in an area social work placement. Then we have a community work placement (I worked in a psychiatric unit), and then I was part time in college and part time on placement in a medical social work department at a local hospital.'

(Students, Social Work Courses, Stevenage College)

'Students come on the course saying "I've only been a Mum for 10 years", "I've only been a foster-Mum", "I've only been looking after my hand-icapped children." We find they come with a lot of talent and a lot of life experience, which is more important than A-levels. In the first year of the course, they catch up on the students with A-levels and the course is a blend of theory and practice; studying social work subjects like child care, mental health, family therapy, social policy and the law, at the same time as putting it into practice in the field. Social work involves counselling, but you are working from a legal perspective. It's a very important role as a local government officer.'

(Spokesperson, Stevenage College)

Sutton College of Liberal Arts
Computers, part time. Typewriting, part time. (See also 'Small Business and Self-Employment Courses'.)

Tonbridge/Tunbridge Wells: West Kent College
TA-sponsored Building Trades course. Part-time day courses in Community subjects, including Care of the Elderly, Childcare, Counselling Skills, Institute of Health Services Management, Medical Reception, Dental Surgery Assisting, National Nursery Examinations Board Certificate in post-qualifying studies, Diploma in Practice Administration, Social Care (in-service students), Teachers of students with Special Needs. Also short courses to update or upgrade people at work, e.g. Information Technology - an Introduction for Managers, and Foreign Languages for Business. Special part-time prospectus available.

Tunbridge Wells: Tunbridge Wells Health Authority (Pembury Hospital)
Full-time 3-year course leading to the qualifications of Registered General Nurse or Registered Nurse for the Mentally Handicapped. Part-time 3 years and 9 months course leading to the qualification of Registered General Nurse. Candidates without statutory GCSE/GCE entry requirements may take the UKCC entry test. Hospital states: 'There is no upper age limit for entry into nurse training with our health authority.'

Watford: Cassio College
(1988) Introductory and Certificate courses in Counselling, part time. Introduction to Bereavement Counselling, part time; Dental Surgery Assistants, part time; Typing, part time; Learn Professional Journalism, part time. Updating Office Skills, part time; Word Processing and Electronic Typing, evenings; PICKUP and short courses in Cookery, Bakery and specialisms within these areas for people wishing to update knowledge and skills. Cookery for the Catering Industry, for City and Guilds 706/1, mode unspecified. NEBSS Supervisory Studies, mode unspecified. Range of specialised short courses (one day or part time evening) in subjects that range from specialist Sugar and Chocolate Work to Telephone Techniques. (See also 'Small Business a:ni Self-Employment Courses', and 'Open and Distance Learning Courses'.)

Watford College
BTEC HND Business Studies (Advertising and Marketing, Business and Financial Administration, Personnel Management options) full time. Those over 21 with relevant work experience but without conventional qualifications may be admitted. Diploma in Advertising, full time, mature candidates with relevant business experience may be accepted on merit. Diploma in Publishing, full time, normally graduate or similar entry; exceptional candidates considered with other qualifications. Printing, Desktop Publishing, Photography and Packaging courses, various modes and entry requirements. Secretarial and Business courses, various modes and entry requirements, including a part-time day secretarial course. NEBSS Certificate in Supervisory Studies, part time, no academic entry requirements for potential supervisors aged 21 and over. BTEC Certificate in Management Studies, part time, no academic entry requirements for candidates aged 23 and over. Certificates in Personnel Practice, Marketing, Sales Management, Production Planning, all part time, entry requirements variable. Wide range of Automobile Engineering courses, full time and part time, including 'Multi-Skills Centre' with facilities for studying body repair, mechanics, electrics, restoration, model engineering, welding, etc. During 1989 plumbing, heating, carpentry, painting and decorating, bricklaying, plastering, tiling and glazing should be added to Multi-Skills. Open Learning (see 'Open and Distance Learning Courses').

Watford: West Hertfordshire School of Nursing
Full-time 3-year courses of training leading to the qualification of Registered General Nurse or Registered Mental Nurse or Registered Nurse for the Mentally Handicapped. Full-time 2-year courses of training leading to the qualification of Enrolled Nurse (General) or Enrolled Nurse (Mental Handicap). For the RGN, RMN and RNMH courses, the UKCC entry test is available for those without the normal GCE/GCSE requirements. For the EN (G) and EN (MH) courses, a school entrance test is offered to those without

formal educational qualifications. School states: 'We are pleased to consider mature candidates up to the age of 45 years.'

Welwyn Garden City: De Havilland College
(1988, excluding courses formerly sponsored by the MSC.) Automatic Systems - CNC Machine Tools, full time; CNC Machining and Computer Aided Design, full time. Computer Aided Engineering, full time. BTEC HNC Engineering Software, part time - appropriate A-level background required, but applications from those with relevant work experience can be considered. Retraining for mature students: Keyboarding for Supervisors and Managerial Skills, full time; Intensive Secretarial, mornings only; Refresher in Secretarial Skills, school hours only. Journalism and Media Studies (A-levels with vocational slant and City and Guilds Media Techniques award) full time, mature students with five O-levels welcome. Science for Industry (A-levels and GCSE with laboratory practice) full time, part time or under 21-hour rule; mature students welcome, including those without formal qualifiations. Social Care (A-levels and GCSE with work experience in social care), full time, part time or 21-hour rule. BTEC National Diploma in Health Studies, full time (suitable preparation for nursing, midwifery, occupational therapy, physiotherapy entry). Special consideration given by the local School of Nursing and Operating Department Assistants' training school to students who complete this course successfully; open to all candidates with three or four O-levels and mature students welcome - those without qualifications interviewed and advised. Counselling, part time.

Wimbledon: Pitman College Wimbledon
Wide range of secretarial studies, information management and office technology courses. Includes 15-week Intensive Secretarial course, full time, 10-week Typewriting, Computing and Information Management Course, full time and 4-week Keyboarding and Word Processing course, full time. For returners, 4-week full-time 'Refresher course' school hours only, covering Shorthand, Typewriting, Audio Typing and Word Processing; students may take Shorthand only or Typing, Audio and Word Processing only and may study all day, or just in the morning (Shorthand) or just in the afternoon (Typing, Audio and Word Processing).

Worthing: Worthing District School of Nursing
Full-time three-year course leading to qualification of Registered General Nurse. Candidates without statutory entry requirements may take the UKCC entry test. School states: 'We accept student nurses from 17 and a half to 50 years. The Health Authority has an equal opportunities policy.'

Central England

Abingdon College
BTEC Certificate in Management Studies, part time – over-25s with suitable experience but no formal qualifications may be eligible. BTEC Certificate in Business Administration, part time – same regulations apply. London Chamber of Commerce and Industry's Private Secretary's Certificate and RSA single-subject examinations, full time. Mature candidates with industrial/commercial experience and a good education may apply. TA-sponsored Audio-Typewriting course, full time – age limits 19-40 with O-level English Language (grades A–C) or equivalent. Open Learning (see 'Open and Distance Learning Courses').

Birmingham: Bournville College of Art
(1988) Part-time courses for all ages, some with earning potential, e.g. Bookbinding; Ceramics, Fashion (for beginners or advanced dressmakers); Photography; Silversmithing and Jewellery; Technical Illustration.

Birmingham: Bournville College of Further Education
The following courses attract adults who wish to change career direction: Training foundation courses in e.g. Care, Catering, Data Processing, Office Skills, Creative Design, Funeral Directing (by Distance Learning). Time on Your Hands. Women's Carpentry. Cookery for City and Guilds 706/1,2 and 3 Cook's Certificate (1 day per week over 3 years). City & Guilds 019/1, 2, 3 and 4 Floristry. City and Guilds 779 Certificate in Media Techniques (Journalism and Radio). Tourist Guides. Basic Secretarial Course. Audio-typing. Typing. Word Processing. Shorthand (Teeline).

Birmingham: Matthew Boulton College School of Chiropody
Full-time 3-year course leading to Diploma of the Society of Chiropodists. School states: 'It has been the Birmingham School of Chiropody's policy for a number of years now to welcome mature students. I am pleased to say no upper age limit applies. We have currently in our first year a student who is in her late 40s. On occasion we may be in a position to waive some of our normal entry requirements. This will of course depend on performance at interview, professional experience and other factors.' NB: College prospectus states that a creche is available at Matthew Boulton College.

Birmingham Polytechnic
Diploma in Social Work (CQSW) full time – over-25s need not have GCEs if they have experience of social work practice, but will be assessed for academic potential. Diploma in Careers Guidance, full time – over-25s with relevant employment experience may be accepted without usual academic qualifications. Certificate in Foundation Studies in Art and Design – exceptionally talented applicants may be taken as special admissions (without O-levels). Institute of Personnel Management Course, part time – course entry requirements relaxed for those aged 23 with at least two years' relevant experience. Certificate in Individual and Family Counselling, part time, candidates working in voluntary counselling considered as well as nurses, health visitors, social workers, youth workers. Certificate in Playwork, part time, for experienced playworkers. (See 'Degree and Advanced Courses' for full-time and part-time courses with special provision for mature students.)

Birmingham: Newman and Westhill Colleges
At Westhill College: Certificate in Community and Youth Work, full time, for those who are at least 20. Over-23s may offer alternatives to academic entry requirements.

Birmingham: Queen Elizabeth School of Nursing
Full-time 3-year course leading to qualification of Registered General Nurse. Candidates without statutory academic entry requirements may take the UKCC entry test. School states: 'The upper age limit for applicants to this school is 47 years of age.'

Birmingham: Birmingham School of Physiotherapy
Full-time 3-year course leading to Membership of the Chartered Society of Physiotherapy. School states: 'This school welcomes applications from mature students provided that their academic background indicates that they will be successful in this course. Although we have no stated upper age limit, we would not encourage students to start training after the age of 45.'

Birmingham: Birmingham School of Radiography
Full-time 32-month course leading to Diploma of the College of Radiographers (Diagnostic). Entry concessions possible for mature candidates without the usual academic entry requirements who are considered by a special panel of the College of Radiographers. School states: 'We are very keen to encourage mature applicants to Radiography training. We do not specify an upper age limit but do take into account the probable years of service following completion of training, and as a result, would consider 45 as approaching the upper limit.'

Birmingham: South Birmingham Health Authority School of Nursing
Full-time 3-year courses leading to qualification of Registered General Nurse or Registered Mental Nurse or Registered Nurse for the Mentally Handicapped. Part-time 4-year course leading to qualification as Registered General Nurse – 30-hour week, school hours, school holidays – 4 weeks' night duty during whole 4 years of training. Candidates without the statutory academic entry requirements may take the UKCC entry test. Upper age limit for all courses is 45.

Bridgnorth and South Shropshire College of Further Education
Updating for unemployed people in Automation and Robotics, part time plus home-based study. Computer-Aided Design – no previous computer experience required, basic drawing skills an advantage, evenings. Computer Numerical Control lathes course for people who have knowledge only of conventional machining methods, evenings. Computer-Aided Engineering, part time, modular (some costs may be reimbursed by TA). BTEC National award courses, full time, for young people, but open to mature applicants with relevant industrial/commercial experience – e.g. Business and Finance; Electronics; Caring Services; Computer Studies; Secretarial and Office Technology. Specialised courses include Tourism and Catering, leading to City and Guilds and RSA awards.

Corby: Tresham College: see under Kettering

Coventry: Henley College
(1988) Basic Skills Training, for people having difficulty in getting work due to lack of attainment at school. Technical Writing. Engineering Skills in CNC/CAD. New Engineering Skills in High Technology. Computing. Office Skills and Technology. Microcomputer Servicing and Maintenance. Food Preparation. Leisure and Recreation Management. Mature students also welcome on BTEC HND in Hotel, Catering and Institutional Management. Modes for these courses not stated – please ask college.

Coventry Polytechnic
Polytechnic Diploma in Social Work/Certificate of Qualification in Social Work, full time – possible entry concessions for those aged 25-plus with some practical experience in social work (paid or voluntary). BTEC HND Physical Science, full time – enquiries welcomed from mature students, including those with limited entry qualifications or appropriate industrial experience.

Coventry Polytechnic: School of Occupational Therapy,
Full-time 3-year course leading to Diploma of the College of Occupational Therapists. School states: 'We do accept mature students. Admission over the age of 40 is exceptional. Mature students are considered on an individual

basis. However they need to be able to demonstrate evidence of recent academic achievement through the satisfactory completion, within the last two years, of a recognised course of study, in order to get a place on the course.'

Coventry Polyechnic: School of Physiotherapy
Full-time three-year course leading to Graduate Diploma in Physiotherapy (currently undergoing changes to convert it into a BSc (Hons) degree in Physiotherapy). School states: 'No formal upper age limit for mature candidate but acceptance is related to physical fitness.' The entry regulations specify that applicants holding qualifications from Access and Open University courses are considered on merit. *Important Note*: All applicants are expected to have had a total of 5 days observing physiotherapy in action in their local hospitals. These days need not be consecutive and need not be in the same department, but written confirmation of attendance is required from the Superintendent of all departments visited.

Coventry School of Nursing
Full-time 3-year courses leading to qualification as Registered General Nurse or Registered Mental Nurse. Candidates without statutory academic qualifications may take the UKCC entry test (held approximately every two months). Upper age limit for entry to training is 45 years.

Coventry School of Radiography
Full-time 3-year course leading to Diploma of the College of Radiographers (Diagnostic). Entry concessions possible for mature students who are considered by a special panel of the College of Radiographers. School states: 'The Coventry School of Radiography encourages mature applicants for its Radiography course. There is no upper age limit, and each applicant is considered in terms of their personal qualities and aptitude.' With regard to possible entry concessions, the School adds: 'There are no hard and fast guidelines to this and each case is considered on its own merits by a special panel set up for the purpose. As a general guideline, applicants should have the equivalent of a GCSE O-level in at least English, mathematics and one science subject, and preferably some experience of radiography as a profession.'

Coventry Technical College
(1988) BTEC Continuing Education in Software Engineering. HNC in Instrumentation and Control. HND in Mechanical and Information Engineering. All suggested by the college for people changing direction. Modes not specified – please ask college.

Derby School of Nursing
Full-time 3-year courses leading to qualification of Registered General Nurse or Registered Mental Nurse or Registered Nurse for the Mentally Handicapped. Candidates without statutory academic entry requirements may

take the UKCC entry test. School states: 'We do consider mature students for nurse training and we have no set upper age limit and consider each individual on their merit.'

Derbyshire College of Higher Education
BTEC HND Business Studies, full time, over-21s may be admitted without usual entry qualifications if they have commercial experience and relevant academic background. BTEC HND Design (Crafts, Studio Ceramics), full time, mature students with a high level of portfolio work may be admitted without usual entry requirements. BTEC HND Engineering (Mechanical/ Manufacturing and Electrical/Electronic), over-21s admitted without usual entry qualifications if they have commercial experience and relevant academic background. BTEC National Certificate and Higher National Certificate, sandwich, in Narrow Fabric Manufacture (UK centre for tuition in this field). Mature applicants must satisfy the college of their ability to benefit from the course. Certificate in Community and Youth Work, full time, applications welcome from over-23s without the usual academic requirements who can demonstrate appropriate experience. BTEC Higher National Diploma in Computer Studies,full time. 'The over-riding consideration in admitting you to the course will be evidence that you are likely to be able to complete the course satisfactorily'. Part-time courses include Institute of Personnel Management, Institute of Industrial Managers, Certificate in Supervisory Management (NEBSS), Design for Printing. Part-time and evening classes with earning potential include Lettering, Enamelling, Silversmithing, Jewellery-Making.

Derby: Derbyshire Royal Infirmary School of Radiography
Full-time 3-year course leading to Diploma of the College of Radiographers (Diagnostic). Entry concessions possible for mature students who are considered by a special panel of the College of Radiographers. School states: 'We are always pleased to hear from mature applicants' (no age limit specified).

Dudley College of Technology
(1988, excluding courses formerly sponsored by the MSC) Cookery, part time, for City and Guilds award. Soft Furnishing, part time, for City and Guilds award. Union of Educational Institutions Certificate in Dress (beginners or returners), part time. Fashion, for City and Guilds award, part time. Basic Hairdressing for mature students, for City and Guilds award, under 21-hour rule. Glass Making and Decoration, full time, part time, evenings or under 21-hour rule. RSA Diploma in the Teaching of Community Languages, part time or evenings, for students who are teaching community languages – e.g. Urdu, Punjabi, Gujerati – or are eligible for such work. BTEC Certificate in Business Administration, full time, and possibly under 21-hour rule, entry at tutor's discretion. Also similar opportunities to

study Production Control, Supervisory Management and Industrial Management. BTEC National/Higher National Business Studies, flexible entry requirement for mature students with suitable experience. Association of Accounting Technicians' course, part time, entry requirements flexible for over-21s. Book-keeping and Clerical work, 10 a.m. – 3 p.m. daily. Mature students may also apply for Medical Reception, full time (2 O-level/GCSE entry). Legal Secretaries, 10 a.m. – 3 p.m. daily (O-level/GCSE English Language required) and Intensive Secretarial, 10 a.m. – 3 p.m. daily (O-level/GCSE English Language required). Wide range of Office Skills part time, e.g. Word Processing, Audio typing, RSA, Pitman and Teeline Sorthand. Motor Vehicle Craft Studies (includes Welding, Fabrication and Vehicle Engineering), evenings, for mature, motivated students, for City and Guilds awards. Computing for Women 10 a.m. – 3 p.m. (four O-levels/GCSEs needed, including Maths and preferably English). Wide range of part time and evening Computer and Information Technology, NC/CNC Part Programming and similar updating courses. Flexistudy (see 'Open and Distance Learning Courses').

Grantham College of Further Education
10-week intensive Secretarial course (attendance 3 days per week on a modular basis) leads to RSA/Pitman examinations in Typewriting, Audio Typewriting, Information Technology, Word Processing and Teeline Shorthand. 18-week Office Technology coures (attendance 1 day a week on a modular basis) leads to RSA/Pitman examinations in Word Processing and Information Technology. 36-week 1 day per week courses lead to qualifications in Secretarial/Office Skills; Accountancy; Art, Design and Fashion; Building Crafts; Catering; Construction Technology; Electrical/Electronic and Mechanical and Production Engineering; Hairdressing; GCSE/GCE A-levels and Social Care. Adult students are also welcomed on full-time courses.

Hinkley College of Further Education
(1988) Alternative Programme for unemployed people, under 21-hour rule. Students may join or leave at any time and take as many subjects as they like, as long as they do not exceed 21 hours college time per week. Options include Typing (Beginners, Advanced and Word Processing); Cookery for the Catering Industry - for City and Guilds award; Computer Studies, Soft Furnishing and Upholstery; Motor Vehicle Maintenance; Photography/Video; Antique Restoration; Woodwork; Community Care Practice – for City and Guilds award; Shorthand; Creative Writing; Reprographics. Open Learning (see 'Open and Distance Learning Courses').

Kettering: Tresham College
(1988, excluding courses formerly sponsored by the MSC.) Site also at Corby. 50-50 retraining in Construction and Engineering under 21-hour

rule. Office Systems Procedures, clerical updating, afternoons. Electronic Servicing for City and Guilds award, evenings, to suit mature students. Supervisory Studies for NEBSS Certificate, for potential supervisors over 20. Playgroup Foundation, part time, school hours only. Non-vocational courses with earning potential, e.g. Furniture Restoration, Tailoring,Clothing Craft – may lead to City and Guilds award. New Technology updating courses, part time, also Open Learning (see 'Open and Distance Learning Courses'). Mature students welcomed on infill basis. Choices are: 'too numerous to mention. We respond to requests'.

Kidderminster College
Replan for unwaged adults, based on 21-hour rule. Students may take any number of options as long as combined hours do not exceed 21 hours a week. Options include: Supervisory Management, Selling, Retailing, Hairdressing and Cosmetology (Unisex), Business Accounting and the Use of Computers, Car Maintenance, Carpentry and Joinery, Introduction to Electronics, Hairdressing for the City and Guilds award, for mature students during school hours only. Mature students also welcome on full-time Hairdressing and Cosmetology. People with work experience welcome on Intensive Secretarial, full time.

Leamington Spa: Mid Warwickshire College
(1988) Replan for unemployed adults – start any time, no qualifications needed. Options include: Computing/Computer Literacy; Shorthand and Tping; Office Skills; Word processing; Welding; Painting and Decorating; Building Skills; Community Care; Leisure and Recreation, Intensive Secretarial Studies, 10 a.m. – 3 p.m., under 21-hour rule for people with home responsibilities. Community Care, full time, for Certificate in Welfare Studies,or Practical Caring Skills, part time, for City and Guilds award. Food and Management Studies, part time, for City and Guilds award. Flexistudy. Open College planned (see 'Open and Distance Learning').

Leicester: Charles Frears School of Nursing
Full-time three-year courses leading to qualification as a Registered General Nurse or Registered Mental Nurse or Registered Nurse for the Mentally Handicapped. School states: 'There is now no formal upper age limit, but candidates over age 40 years are considered on an individual basis: our oldest student nurse at present is aged 49. Mature applicants who do not hold the normal five subject passes at GCSE grades 1, 2 or 3 are likely to be offered the alternative entrance test.'

Leicester Royal Infirmary Schools of Radiography
Full-time 3-year courses leading to Diploma of the College of Radiographers (Diagnostic or Therapeutic). School states: 'Mature students are accepted by this school and there is no upper age limit. The College of Radiographers do

now allow some flexibility for mature students in their entry requirements and mature students without conventional academic entry qualifications may be considered by a special panel. Any type of degree from a British or Irish University or a CNAA degree will be accepted in lieu of the normal minimum entry requirements. A mature student must seek advice at an early stage from individual schools of radiography via whom special application must be made to the College of Radiographers.'

Lichfield College
This college plans considerable expansion of adult and continuing education. Currently has many part-time day and evening courses with earning potential – e.g. Dressmaking; Pottery; Upholstery; Cabinet-Making; Cookery; Creative Studies in Embroidery and Pottery for City and Guilds award. Photography for City and Guilds award, mode not specified – ask college. Open Learning (see 'Open and Distance Learning Courses').

Lincoln: Lincolnshire School of Radiography
Full-time 3-year course leading to Diploma of the College of Radiographers (Diagnostic). Entry concessions may be possible for mature students who are considered by a special panel of the College of Radiographers. School states: 'We do accept mature students. There is no set age limit.'

Mansfield: Mansfield and Worksop School of Nursing
Full-time 3-year course leading to the qualifications of Registered General Nurse or Registered Nurse for the Mentally Handicapped. School states: 'We accept mature students for nurse training leading to the General part of the Register and also to the Mental Handicap part of the Register. Our upper age limit to date is 50 years of age. Although entry to nurse training requires five O-level passes or their equivalent, we accept the UKCC entrance test and within the last month have commenced test sessions within the School of Nursing.'

Newark Technical College
Individually planned mature students' Secretarial course/mature students' Clerical course – may be fulltime, part time or under 21-hour rule. Can lead to awards of LCCI, RSA, BTEC, EMFEC, Pitman and/or GCSE. Wide range of Computer and Information Technology courses, evenings. Recreational Studies, full time, for potential supervisors in leisure industry – age limits 20–37, with good sporting and academic attainments. BTEC First Diploma in Design. BTEC National Diploma in Media Studies. Preliminary Certificate in Social Care (open to mature students). Playgroup Leaders' Basic course, evenings. Creative Studies (Fashion and Design, Embroidery,Ceramics, Cookery), full time or part time, can lead to City and Guilds award. Music Preparatory course, full time, admission by audition and interview. Musical Instrument Electronics course, full time, leads to BTEC National Diploma.

Candidates need GCSE/O-level/CSE Grade 1 Maths, Physics and English and ability in Music. Piano Tuning, Maintenance and Repairs, full time – mature students accepted aged up to 35. No academic or musical qualifications demanded, but GCEs helpful. Violin Making and Repairing, full time – mature students accepted up to age 35, knowledge of practical woodwork and technical drawing desired. Selection by interview. Woodwind Making and Repairing, full time – open to mature students aged up to 35, selection by interview and practical test. Musical Industry Studies and Music Industry Management, both full-time courses, are also suitable for mature students. Applications are also welcomed from mature students for BTEC National Diploma in Engineering and BTEC First Diploma in Caring, both full-time courses. Computer-Aided Engineering is available as a vehicle for updating in the new areas of technology.

Newcastle-under-Lyme College
Participates in Staffordshire Replan scheme. Employment Training submission with Training Agency – contact college for details. Centre for the Open University and for Staffordshire Basic Education Unit.

Northampton: Nene College
BTEC HND Business and Finance, full time – over-21s may be admitted with less than the usual entry qualifications. BTEC HND Graphic Design, full time – students without usual entry qualifications should have at least three years' relevant experience; exceptionally, those with considerable aptitude and potential considered. Advanced Diploma in Fashion, full time – mature students with relevant industrial experience or unusual aptitude and potential may be considered. Certificate of Qualification in Social Work (CQSW) full time – emphasis on recruitment of mature students with relevant experience. Over-25s may be exempted from academic entry requirements.

Northampton: Nene College/Northampton School of Chiropody
Full-time 3-year course leading to Diploma in Chiropody and State Registration. School states: 'We do accept mature students on to the course. There is no laid down upper age limit although we do tend not to accept students 42-plus at the time of starting the course. As regards entry requirements for mature candidates, these are assessed on an individual basis. We have in the past accepted mature students who do not have the traditional entry qualifications onto the course. As a school we organise "Taster Days". These days allow mature students to meet staff and students informally and discuss any problems they may have as well as giving them an insight into the type of course we offer.'

Northampton: Northampton Adult Education Centre
Refresher courses for 'returners' to office work offered on a sessional basis. Typically, a 9-week course combining Typing Refresher and Computers in

the Office would be offered on a mornings-only basis with no sessions during half-term. A crèche is available for children of 18 months plus.

Northampton: School of Radiography
Full-time 3-year course leading to Diploma of the College of Radiographers (Diagnostic). Entry concessions possible for mature students who are considered by a special panel of the College of Radiographers. School states: 'At this training establishment, we do encourage applications from mature students although the take up rate is very low. Applicants in excess of 35 years of age certainly require careful counselling before being encouraged to pursue their application.' *Important Note*: The school's prospectus gives 'Pre Training Advice' which includes: 'One should aim to visit an X-Ray Department for at least one whole day to gain some insight into the work of Radiographers and talk with them about the job, career prospects etc.'

Northampton: St. Andrew's School of Occupational Therapy
Full-time 3-year course leading to the Diploma of the College of Occupational Therapists. Entry concessions may be possible for mature students without the usual academic entry requirements. School states: 'Yes, we take mature students. There is no upper age limit, *per se*. It depends, as with all students, on their disposition and openness to learning, which is one of the factors we consider in our selection procedure. We ask for evidence of recent study, e.g. an A-level, an Open University credit.'

Nottingham: The Hogarth School of Radiotherapy
Full-time 3-year course leading to the Diploma of the College of Radiographers (Radiotherapy). Entry concessions possible for mature students who are considered by a special panel of the College of Radiographers. School states: 'We do accept mature students and there is no upper age limit.'

Nottingham School of Physiotherapy
Full-time 3-year course leading to Membership of the Chartered Society of Physiotherapy. School states: 'We accept mature students at this school with an upper age limit between 33 and 36. We do look at professional qualifications in lieu of A-levels and would expect some evidence of recent academic study.'

Nottingham: Nottingham School of Radiography
Full-time 3-year course leading to Diploma of the College of Radiographers (Diagnostic). Entry concessions possible for mature candidates who are considered by a special panel of the College of Radiographers. School states: 'We do accept mature students. No upper age limit is specified.'

Nottingham: South Nottinghamshire College of Further Education
Women Only courses in Information Technology, Community Care Practice and Management. Details from college. Open Learning proposed (see 'Open and Distance Learning Courses').

Nottingham: Trent Polytechnic
Applications are welcomed from mature candidates for the following full-time BTEC HNDs: Building Studies; Building Studies (Quantity Surveying); Business and Finance; Civil Engineering Studies; Computer Studies: Distribution Studies; Electrical and Electronic Engineering; Engineering (Manufacturing Systems); Engineering (Mechanical); Engineering (Surveying); Hotel, Catering and Institutional Management; Land Administration (Estate Management), (Housing); Mining Engineering; Printing; Science (Applied Biology); Science (Chemistry); Textiles. Part-time courses may also be available: contact the polytechnic for the part-time prospectus. For the courses in Computing and Engineering, a Foundation Year is available for applicants not possessing the normal entry qualifications. A Foundation course in Accounting and Foundation Studies in Art and Design are also available. Other advanced courses include Diploma Higher Education Social Sciences; Diploma in Environmental Health; Certificate of Qualification in Social Work (CQSW). In addition, the polytechnic provides a range of career updating and career change courses which include PICKUP courses (Professional, Industrial and Commercial Updating) and INSET (In-Service Education for Teachers).

Oswestry College
Managerial Skills, Office Skills, Science, Technology (Computing, Engineering, Performing Arts), Language.

Oswestry: Oswestry and North Staffordshire School of Physiotherapy
Full-time 3-year course leading to Membership of the Chartered Society of Physiotherapy. School states: 'We can confirm that mature students are accepted in this school and the normal pre-entry requirements of 7 points at A-level are normally waived for these applicants. The majority of our mature students are between 25 and 35 but under special circumstances, we may accept a person of 40 years. This is an unusual circumstance and acceptance is subject to rigorous medical examination and indepth interviewing. Each mature student is considered on merit and there may be alternatives to these arrangements identified.' NB: prospectus states that 'all candidates must be able to swim'.

Oxford: Dorset House School of Occupational Therapy
Full-time 3-year course leading to the Diploma of the College of Occupational Therapists. School states: 'We do accept mature students and at present have no firm upper age limit, although it is doubtful whether we would accept anyone over 45 years.' School prospectus suggests entry concessions may be possible for mature students, though they must be able to produce evidence of recent academic study.

Oxford Polytechnic
HND Business Studies, full time – over-21s with relevant work experience and suitable academic background may be admitted without usual entry

qualifications. Certificate of Qualification in Social Work (CQSW) full time, preferred age range 23–45 with some relevant experience; entry concessions for over-25s.

Oxford Regional School of Radiography
Full-time 3-year courses leading to the Diploma of the College of Radiographers (Diagnostic or Therapy). Possible entry requirement concessions for mature candidates who are considered on an individual basis by a special panel of the College of Radiographers. School states: 'We at the Oxford Schools are quite happy to accept mature applicants. Like all schools, we consider each mature candidate on an individual basis. We have no standard upper age limit, although we do consider the likely length of service by the applicant, post-qualification.'

Redditch College
It is proposed that this college should merge with North Worcestershire College to become North East Worcestershire College, so the range of courses may be affected when this happens. (1988) Design for Print, part time, for unemployed adults. BTEC National Diplomas in Business Studies or Distribution, full time, entry concessions for over-19s at Principal's discretion. Pre-Nursing and Caring Services, full time, for young students but over-19s admitted at Principal's discretion. Pre-Social Work, full time, mature students welcome. BTEC HND Computer Studies, full time, over-19s admitted on the basis of experience and/or aptitude. BTEC HND in Business Studies (Travel and Tourism), full time, over-19s. admitted at Principal's discretion. Office Skills (Beginner/Refresher) under 21-hour rule, for RSA/TVEI qualifications. Clerical Skills, under 21-hour rule, for unemployed adults aged up to 25 for RSA awards. Pre-School Playgroup Introductory Course and Leadership Course, part time. Sales and Selling, evenings, for those wishing to enter the full-time selling course. Wide range of part-time courses in fields as diverse as Computers and Export. Leisure courses with earning potential, e.g. Book Illustration, Creative Writing, Dressmaking, Woodwork. Flexistudy (see 'Open and Distance Learning Courses').

Retford: Eaton Hall International
Combines distance learning and residential block study methods. Certificate in Teaching English to Speakers of Other Languages – preliminary course; combines distance learning and residential block. Licentiate Diploma in Teaching English as a Foreign Language: 30-week Distance Learning Programme, four-week residential block, for Trinity College London Diploma. Diploma in Teaching English for Specific Purposes: six-month Distance Learning Programme, four-week residential block, for Eaton Hall Diploma (being validated by RSA).

TEFL/TESL Courses; viewpoints

'I've come from university. I graduated in July, spent eight or nine months unemployed, couldn't find anything for a Geography graduate, and then saw this advertised in the paper and was able to arrange a loan from the bank. One of the fascinating things about TEFL is that you can really go anywhere to work when you are qualified. You just take your pick – the world's your oyster.'

'I thought "I can't go on this course. I'm not a graduate. I'm not a teacher." But I wrote a letter, and very kindly I was accepted, and it shows that everyone has a chance if they try hard enough. My own early life was spent as an officer in the Merchant Navy. From that I graduated into handling ships as a ships' agent, and that's my job now, in Singapore, the second busiest port in the world. I hope to set up a language school in Japan with my wife and brother-in-law when I retire.'

'I'm an industrial chemist and hopefully I shall be getting involved in the field of specialised English teaching. I applied for a job abroad as an English teacher before I even enrolled on the course. I was luckily accepted. Then I decided I should get some qualifications behind me so that I would be a better teacher. I have now finished and leave for Japan next Tuesday.'

(Students: TEFL/TESL courses, Eaton Hall International)

'Most courses – 5 a year – contain a mixture of young people fresh from full-time education and mature students in their late 40s and 50s. The oldest TEFL student to date has been 69! The demand for teachers stems from the world's thirst for English. It is now indisputably the world language. The last figure I saw was that six hundred million people were using the English language every day as part of their programmes. On top of that you've got English pop records, English TV and radio programmes, American and British films all over the world – so access to English is something everybody's familiar with and people in most countries want. We have a never-ending stream of requests for teachers who have completed our course to go overseas.'

(Spokesperson, Eaton Hall International)

Retford: Rampton Hospital School of Nursing
Full-time 3-year course leading to qualification of Registered Mental Nurse (with Nottingham School of Nursing) or Registered Nurse for the Mentally Handicapped (with Hull School of Nursing). Candidates without statutory academic entry requirements may take the UKCC entry test. School states: 'We accept mature students up to the age of 50 years.'

Shrewsbury: Royal Shrewsbury Hospital School of Nursing
Full-time 3-year course leading to qualifications of Registered General Nurse or Registered Mental Nurse. NB: a part-time course leading to RGN for those who are unable to undertake the three-year course is in the planning stage

and it is hoped to commence in 1990. Candidates without the statutory academic entrance requirements may take the UKCC entry test. The upper age limit for entry to courses at this school is 45 years.

Solihull College of Technology
(l988, excluding courses formerly sponsored by the MSC.) Hairdressing, Floristry, Horticulture, Information Technology, all under 21-hour rule, for City and Guilds awards. Graphic Design for Print/Video Media, Commercial Photography, Commercial Photography/ Graphics, Fashion/Knit, all under 21-hour rule. Computer Programming for City and Guilds award, evenings (beginners). Basic Fabrication and Welding, Refrigeration Engineering, Motor Vehicle Maintenance, CNC Machining, Introduction to Basic Electronics and Computing, all under 21-hour rule, for City and Guilds awards. General and Specialised Secretarial training for beginners and those needing up-dating, under 21-hour rule. Wide range of Languages, part time and evenings, including French, German, Spanish, Arabic, Chinese and Japanese. Language Laboratory of tapes (see 'Open and Distance Learning Courses').

Conversational Japanese: viewpoints
'I spent some time in Japan and I've an interest in the country. The object, though, is to get a basic knowledge of Japanese to use in business, to try and get a better job. Communicating between a firm here and Japan – interpreter, possibly – depending on how good my Japanese becomes.'
    'I would like to learn the language so that I could go out there and live. I'd like to set up a job, stay there and work for a year and then come back and get my degree in Japanese.'
    'It's certainly easier than French – we're only speaking it phonetically and not learning the written language, so it's easier than you might think.'
(Students, Solihull College of Technology)

'We noticed there was a demand for Arabic, so we started courses in that, and following the success of that, we decided to offer Japanese, particularly in view of the Japanese interest in British Leyland and other quite large companies in this area. We find that often students have some connection with the country – they've got Japanese wives, or they've been abroad to Japan. Some businessmen are involved in meeting Japanese people so we know they'll need their Japanese phrases. One former student told me "I've got the best company I could have in terms of colleagues at work because most of them are Japanese".
(Spokesperson, Solihull College of Technology)

Stafford College of Further Education
(1988) BTEC HNC Typographic Design, sandwich. Adults with relevant work experience and good portfolio may be accepted without formal academic qualifications.

Stafford: Mid Staffordshire School of Nursing
Full-time 3-year courses leading to the qualification of Registered General
Nurse or Registered Mental Nurse. Full-time 2-year courses leading to the
qualification of Enrolled Nurse (General) or Enrolled Nurse (Mental).
Candiates for Registration courses without the statutory GCSE/GCE entry
requirements may take the UKCC entry test. Candidates for Enrolled
courses who are aged 27-plus may be exempted from the 2 O-level/GCSE/
CSE Grade I entry requirement. School states: 'This school does not specify
an upper age limit, since it is considered that mature candidates, both male
and female, can contribute significantly to the nursing profession. We
consider each application on its merits. Enquiries from mature candidates
will be welcome.'

Stoke-on-Trent: Cauldon College of Further and Higher Education
Retraining/Updating courses under 21-hour rule in: Catering; Hairdressing;
Beauty; Leisure; Performing Arts; Display; Exhibition Design; Fashion.
Most Construction crafts are also offered to City and Guilds level. (See also
'Open and Distance Learning Courses'.)

Stoke-on-Trent: North Staffordshire School of Nursing and Midwifery
Full-time 3-year courses leading to qualifications of Registered General
Nurse or Registered Mental Nurse or Registered Nurse for the Mentally
Handicapped. Candidates without statutory academic entrance requirements may take the UKCC entry test. *Note:* New 'Project 2000' nurse training
courses provided in association with the University of Keele are expected to
be offered from October 1989. School states: 'We do encourage mature
entrants into our school. Currently over-26 year-olds constitute 25% of our
students. We also take positive actions to encourage mature men into the
profession. The upper age limit we operate is 47 years – in particular
instances it may be slightly higher. People who have followed part of a
nursing course and wish to restart should be referred to the UKCC in case
any part can be credited when they recommence. Qualified nurses who
have had a break in nursing are catered for in this college with a well-
developed "Back to Nursing" course, tailored to the returners' needs.'

Stoke-on-Trent : Staffordshire Polytechnic
(1988) BTEC HND Design (Ceramics) full time. Mature students without
usual academic qualifications but with industrial experience may be
accepted. BTEc HND/HNC Business and Finance, full time or part time.
Over-21s may be accepted without usual academic qualifications. BTEC
National Certificate Ceramic Technology, full time, unqualified students
accepted at Polytechnic's discretion. BTEc HNC/HND Ceramic Technology,
full time or part time, unqualified students with considerable appropriate
experience accepted at Polytechnic's discretion. Institute of Personnel
Management, part time, candidates 23-plus with at least two years'

appropriate experience and who satisfy the IPM for student membership may be accepted without usual qualifications. Institute of Purchasing and Supply, part time, potential managers, supplies controllers, senior store-keepers etc. who satisfy the IPS may be accepted without usual qualifications. Institute of Industrial Managers, part time – over-27s with at least four years' experience who hold/have held a post of responsibility may be accepted without usual qualifications. Supervisory Studies for NEBSS Certificate, for potential managers over 21.

Stourbridge College of Technology and Art
(1988) BTEC HND Graphic Design, full time; those with at least two years in the graphic communications industry considered without usual qualifications. Preparatory Caring and Health Service course, full time, for young students, but mature students considered. Association of Accounting Technicians, full time, for young students, but others considered.

Sutton Coldfield College of Further Education
(1988) Mature students accepted on an infill basis to general courses. No details supplied – please contact college.

Tamworth College of Further Education
(1988) BTEC HNC Business and Finance, part time, over-21s without formal qualifications but with suitable experience may be admitted. (The college says: 'Many of the most successful candidates have been older people returning to college for refresher or retraining courses.') BTEC National Diploma Business and Finance, full time and National Certificate Business and Finance, part time, flexible entry requirements. RSA Diploma for Personal Assistants, full time. Mature students without formal qualifications but with relevant experience may be admitted. Beginners' Shorthand and Typing for mature students – school hours only. Wide range of Secretarial evening classes. Institution of Industrial Managers Certificate, evenings, over-27s with at least four years' industrial experience and employment in a post of responsibility may be accepted without formal qualifications.

Thame: Rycotewood College
(1988) BTEC Continuing Education Certificate in Design (Crafts). This course concentrates on the design and making of Fine Bespoke Furniture. Applications are invited from mature students (above the age of 25) and with a minimum of three years' work experience. BTEC HNC Service Engineering Management, full time, suited to technicians with experience in Agricultural Engineering; mature students may be accepted without usual entry qualifications.

Walsall: Sister Dora School of Nursing
Full-time 3-year course leading to qualification of Registered General Nurse or Registered Nurse for the Mentally Handicapped. School states: 'I am

pleased to confirm that we do accept mature students to undertake the full three-year courses for RNMH and RGN training. When deciding the upper age limit, consideration is given on whether or not they would be able to give the nursing profession ten years service upon qualifying.'

Warley and West Bromwich: Sandwell College
(1988, excluding courses formerly sponsored by the MSC.) Amalgamation of the former Warley College of Technology and West Bromwich College of Commerce and Technology. (1) Warley Campus: Construction, Electrical and Electronic Engineering, Fabrication Engineering, Vehicle Work – selected classes under 21-hour rule. Non-vocational evening classes with earning potential include Wood-Turning, Car Maintenance, Dressmaking, Cookery, Tailoring, Soft Furnishing, Community Care, full time or 21-hour rule, mature students welcome. Child-minders, evenings. Mechanical Engineering Craft Studies, under 21-hour rule. (2) West Bromwich Campus: BTEC HNC Business Studies, sympathetic consideration for those aged 21-plus with suitable work experience but without usual entry requirements. General Office Skills (Beginners or Updating), under 21-hour rule. Institute of Chartered Secretaries and Administrators, part time or evenings, candidates aged 23-plus without usual qualifications may be considered. BTEC National Diploma/National Certificate Hotel, Catering and Institutional Operations, full time, mature students with appropriate experience may be accepted without usual entry qualifications. International Health and Beauty Council courses, full time, entry requirements may be relaxed for more mature candidates. Furniture Craft, full time, for adults who wish to change careers. Speech and Drama Teachers' Diploma, evenings, mainly for mature students. Performing Arts, under 21-hour rule. Introduction to Journalism, under 21-hour rule. Counselling, part time or evenings, mature students especially welcome. Institute of Marketing Certificate, evenings, over-25s with at least three years' marketing experience may be accepted without usual entry reqirements. Institute of Industrial Managers' Certificate, part time, over-27s with at least four years' appropriate experience may be accepted without usual entry requirements. Institute of Purchasing and Supply Foundation, part time, over-26s with relevant experience need no formal qualifications. Institute of Management Services Certificate, part time, over-25s without formal qualifications accepted if they satisfy selectors they will benefit. Supervisory Studies for NEBSS Certificate, part time, for over-21s who are potential supervisors. Computing and Information Technology, full time or part time, from Beginners to Advanced. Evening classes with earning potential, e.g. Photography Assistant, Creative Radio, Radio Drama, Pottery, Millinery, Soft Furnishing, Dressmaking.

Warwick: Warwickshire School of Nursing
Full-time 3-year courses leading to qualifications of Registered General Nurse or Registered Mental Nurse or Registered Nurse for the Mentally

Handicapped. Full-time 2-year courses leading to qualifications of Enrolled
Nurse (General) or Enrolled Nurse (Mental Handicap). Candidates without
statutory academic entry requirements for Registration courses may take the
UKCC entry test. Candidates without statutory academic entry requirements for Enrollled Nurse courses may take the school's entry test. School
states: 'We do accept mature students for nurse training. The upper age limit
is 45 years.'

Wellingborough College
Automobile Engineering (three evenings a week) for City and Guilds award
for More Mature Students. Computer courses, from Beginners to
Advanced, part time. Introduction to Social Work, part time. BTEC Diploma
in Caring, under 21-hour rule. Shorthand and/or Typewriting, part time.
Skills Workshop (for office staff who feel out of touch with the modern office
world) school hours only. Sight and Sound keyboard training, part time.
Receptionist/Telephonist Skills, part time. Further Education Teacher Training, evenings, for over-23s, qualified in the subject they want to teach. Many
leisure courses with earning potential, e.g. Picture Frame Making, Dressmaking, Photography, Bee-keeping, Writing. Electronics courses, from
Beginners to Advanced, part time and evening. Electronic and Microelectronic Systems, TV and Video, Electronic Measurement and Control.
NEBSS General, for industry and commerce. NEBSS Recreational
Management.

Witney: West Oxfordshire Technical College
'Mature students are welcome on all courses and can be helped by
Employment Training arrangements.' Women into Manufacture. A day
course supported by a day nursery between 9.30 a.m. and 2.30 p.m. for
those with young children who may wish to return to a job in the
manufacturing industry. Evening course for City and Guilds 381 Part 1 in
Motor Vehicle mechanics work, attendance on Tuesday and Thursday
evenings 6.30 p.m. – 9.00 p.m. Basic Precision Machining, Wednesday
evenings 6.00 p.m. – 9.00 p.m. A course for people desiring to learn to use
centre lathes, milling machines, grinders and the use of precision instruments. Computers and Computing – a complete range of courses leading to
units of City and Guilds 726 in Information Technology. Agriculture: Stud
and Stable Husbandry – Thoroughbred Industry. Courses for those with
experience in stud work, Pony Club 'B', agricultural experience, farm
management. BTEC HND for stud administration – entry concessions: OND
Stud & Stable, agricultural degree, Certificate Stud & Stable plus A-levels.

Wolverhampton: Bilston Community College
Soft Furnishing and Upholstery, for City and Guilds award, evenings,
practical sewing ability needed. Catering and Food Service, for City and
Guilds awards, part time, day and evening, for mature unemployed people.

Licensed Trade Catering, part time, for established licensees, also suitable for those joining the trade. Design and Decoration of Flour Confectionery, for City and Guilds award, evenings. Diploma in Play Leadership, part time. Foundation course for Playgroup Supervisors, part time. Computer Programming and Information Processing; Information Technology; for City and Guilds awards, full time or part time. Adult Skills, Manufacturing, part time: choose from Welding, Electrical Installation and Maintenance, Domestic Electrics, Microelectronics, Turning, Milling, Grinding, Car Body Repair, Trailer Making, Vehicle Electrics, Car Maintenance, Engine Reconditioning, Engine Auxiliary Reconditioning, Computer Controlled Machining (CNC,CAM), Computer Aided Design (CAD), Computer Programming, Brass Decorative Sheet Metal Work, Small Portabuildings Manufacture, Activity Toys Design and Manufacture, Domestic Appliance Repair, Decorative Metalwork. Fashion for City and Guilds award, part time. Hairdressing for City and Guilds awards, full time or part time, Nursing and Caring Skills (for home nursing), part time or evenings. Hospital Play Specialist's course, part time, Office Studies, full time or part time, Secretarial skills, wide range, part time. Preliminary Certificate in Welfare Studies, part time, can lead to more advanced courses. Social and Community Service, part time. RSA Diploma in the Teaching of Community Languages, part time, for those with an A-level in the target language, or who have reached the level of a full secondary education in it. Wide range of language courses, part time. ESF-sponsored training for Women: Women Re-Entrants, Vocational and Language Training for Women, Women and New Technology, Women in Science and Engineering, Women in Supervision and Management, Women and Self-Employment, Women and Craft, Design Technology – all full time, but only 20 hours a week. Many evening courses with earning potential, e.g. Vehicle Painting and Customising, Renovating Furniture. Open Learning and Flexistudy (see 'Open and Distance Learning Courses'). Most of these vocational areas can be offered on a flexible roll-on, roll-off basis for participants in Training Agency schemes.

Hospital Play Therapy: viewpoint
'Candidates should usually be 20-plus and have substantial experience with children – for example, previous training in nursery nursing, nursing, teacher training, play leadership, or perhaps the Diploma in Residential Care. It is not essential to be employed by a hospital, though courses provide both day-release training for therapists in post and initial training for would-be play therapists. Their work in encouraging play helps children adjust to a strange and sometimes frightening environment and familiarise themselves with hospital apparatus and procedures, as well as advising the hospital on the selection of play materials, liaising with nursing and medical staff and encouraging parents and volunteers to participate in play.'
                    (Spokesperson, National Association of Hospital Play Staff)

Wolverhampton School of Nursing
Full-time 3-year courses leading to qualifications of Registered General Nurse or Registered Mental Nurse. Candidates without the statutory academic entry requirement may take the UKCC entry test. School also mentions that a pass in a validated Access course for entry to higher education may be acceptable to the UKCC. School states: 'Obviously other factors also are considered, such as health, attitudes, leadership potential etc.,the assessment of which would be at formal interview. Mature students accepted up to an age limit of 47 years.'

Wolverhampton: Wulfrun College of Further Education
(1988) ESF-sponsored Kitchen Design (Women Only) and Media Technicians (Women Only), both full time. Computer-Aided Design, Desk Top Publishing – mode not specified. Mature students welcome on infill basis on all courses. Homestudy (see 'Open and Distance Learning').

Worcester District School of Nursing
Full-time 3-year course leading to qualifications of Registered General Nurse or Registered Mental Nurse. Candidates without statutory entry requirements may take the UKCC entry test. School states: 'Mature candidates are considered individually and the upper age limit is 50. Evidence of recent study is advisable and if candidates do not have the necessary requirement they would be required to take the UKCC educational test.'

Northern England

Altrincham: South Trafford College of Further Education
BTEC Certificate in Business Administration – modular, combining college and home study for people over 21, or those with at least three years' experience in a responsible position in industry or commerce. BTEC National Certificate in Business and Finance, under 21-hour rule. Secretarial skills, part time and evenings, under 21-hour rule. Typewriting for Beginners and Refresher students. Shorthand, Word Processing, Audiotyping – daytime and evenings and 'roll on – roll off' flexible programme (daytime). Photography, evenings, for City and Guilds award. Embroidery, part time, for City and Guilds award. Jewellery, part time, for City and Guilds award. Languages: French, German, Spanish, Portuguese, Welsh, Japanese, Italian, Modern Greek, Russian – evenings. Leisure courses with earning potential include Dressmaking, Furniture Restoring. Courses under 21-hour rule in Catering for City and Guilds craft awards, also City and Guilds Hairdressing, City and Guilds Beauty Therapy, Foundation Art. Also daytime Employment Training in several areas including Computing and Caring Skills. Wider Opportunities for Women courses for women wishing to return to paid employment or change career (daytimes).

Ashington: Northumberland College of Arts and Technology
Employment Training/Directed Training – many skill areas available; access for Training Manager requests – any time. Full range of BTEC Certificate and Diploma courses, City and Guilds and RSA courses available – Construction, Engineering, Business Studies, Computer Studies, Catering and Hotel Management, Beauty Therapy, Care etc. (ask college for further details). TA-sponsored course for Clerks of Works – Mechanical and Electrical Engineering, full-time. Word processing (half day per week). City and Guilds 730-1 Further Education Teacher's Certificate – entry September each year. BTEC HND in Design (Communication), a course for the Television industry, entry September each year.

Barrow in Furness College of Further Education
(1988, excluding courses formerly sponsored by the MSC.) Practical Woodwork/Practical Brickwork/Practical Painting and Decorating – evenings, open to all ages. Electronics and Mechanical Engineering, various

levels and modes, some open to all ages; includes updating, e.g. Robotics and Computer Numerical Control courses. Secretarial, Computing and Management courses, various levels and modes,some open to all ages. Certificate and Diploma in Industrial Management, mode not specified. Supervisory Studies for NEBSS Certificate, part time, for potential supervisors. City and Guilds Further Education Teachers' Certificate, part time, for those with technical or professional qualifications wishing to teach in further education. Courses to suit individual mature students can be devised for part time day or evening study. Many leisure courses with earning potential, e.g. Dressmaking, Millinery, Machine Knitting,Cookery, Pottery. Open Learning (see 'Open and Distance Learning Courses').

Barrow-in-Furness: South Cumbria School of Nursing
Full-time 3-year course leading to qualification as a Registered General Nurse. Candidates without statutory academic entrance requirements may take the UKCC entry test. School states: 'The South Cumbria School of Nursing does accept mature students and we have an upper age limit of 48 years, though we would look at each applicant on an individual basis.'

Bishop Auckland: County Durham School of Nursing
Full-time 3-year courses leading to qualifications of Registered General Nurse or Registered Mental Nurse or Registered Nurse for the Mentally Handicapped. Candidates without the statutory academic entrance requirements may take the UKCC entry test. School states: 'Mature students are very welcome at this school and we have a policy of actively encouraging the mature applicant for nurse training. Our upper age limit is 45, as following completion of the statutory 3-year training period (and bearing in mind that female nursing staff may retire at the age of 55 if they so wish) this could result in an approximate "working life" of only 7 years.'

Blackburn College
TA-sponsored Private Secretarial Course for mature students with O-levels or equivalent, full time. London Chamber of Commerce and Industry's Private and Executive Secretary's Diploma, full time – mature students accepted at college's discretion. Vocational Preparation for unemployed people, options include Engineering, Motor Vehicle crafts, Electrical Installation, Construction Trades, Computing, Motor Vehicle Painting, Clerical Skills and Office Practice, all under 21-hour rule. City and Guilds Further Education Teacher's Certificate, part time – for potential and practising adult education teachers/trainers with qualifications relevant to the subject they want to teach. Management Studies, part time and evenings – entry concessions for people aged 25-plus with appropriate experience. City and Guilds Certificate in Media Techniques (Press and Radio Skills) and Certificate with Urdu and/or Gujerati and/or Arabic Languages, full time or part time (candidates must have GCE O-level/GCSE or equivalent in at least

four subjects at grades A,B or C, and for Urdu/Gujerati/Arabic options, evidence of A-level equivalent studies in the appropriate language). Institute of Personnel Management, part time and evenings – entry concessions for people with relevant experience. Supervisory Studies for NEBSS Certificate, part time – no formal entry requirements. Institute of Marketing Certificate, evenings – entry concessions for mature students with relevant experience. Institute of Purchasing and Supply, part time and evenings, entry concessions for people aged 25 with relevant experience. Open Learning (see 'Open and Distance Learning Courses').

Bolton Institute of Higher Education
TA-sponsored BTEC HNC Computer Studies, full time. TA-sponsored Diploma in Systems Analysis, full time. TA-sponsored Diploma in Computer Programming, full time. Other fresh start possibilities include: College Diploma in the Care of the Mentally Handicapped Adult, full time; Certificate in the Further Education and Training of Mentally Handicapped People, full time; BTEC HND Business Studies, full time (over-21s with relevant experience and education may be admitted without the usual academic qualifications). The college says: 'On the basis of your previous experience, you may also be granted exemption from certain modules; this would be subject to approval by BTEC.' BTEC HND Graphic Design, full time (candidates with related industrial experience may be considered without the usual academic qualifications).

Bradford Hospitals School of Physiotherapy
Full-time 3-year course leading to Membership of the Chartered Society of Physiotherapy. School states: 'Mature students are accepted in Bradford and although there is no set age limit, very careful consideration is given to candidates over the age of 45. Mature students can be given exemption from the minimum entrance qualifications, although this depends on previous qualifications and experience and each case is considered individually.'

Bradford School of Nursing
Full-time 3-year course leading to qualification as a Registered General Nurse. Candidates without the statutory academic entrance requirements may take the UKCC entry test. Upper age limit for entry is 45 years. NB: prospectus states that the School is currently seeking approval of a separate RGN course specifically for mature students with family commitments.

Bradford and Ilkley Community College
(1988) BTEC HND Business and Finance/Secretarial Linguist/Public Administration, full time, entry concessions possible for mature students. Certificate in Youth and Community Work, full time, entry concessions possible for over-25s. BTEC National Diplomas, full time, entry concessions possible for mature students: Building, Business, Computer Studies,

Design, Leisure Studies. Family and Community Care, full time, for City and Guilds award, mature students particularly welcome, no formal entry requirements. Nursery Nursing, full time, for NNEB Certificate – over-21s may apply without formal qualifications. Intensive Office Studies, full time, particularly appropriate for mature men and women seeking clerical posts. Pre-Nursing, full time, special provision may be made to accept mature students without formal qualifications. Textile Merchants' Special Certificate, full time, entry concessions for mature students. Preliminary course in Art and Design, part time, applications invited from mature unemployed people. BTEC Certificate in Textiles, part time, special admission arrangements for mature students. Students accepted on infill basis on all Art and Design courses. Community Sports Leader's Award, part time, no pre-entry conditions, approved by Central Council of Physical Recreation. Short courses in Outdoor Pursuits for would-be leaders with relevant experience, part time. In-Service courses in Social Care, part time, for people with 6 months' experience in a caring job, or in voluntary work. City and Guilds Further Education Teacher's Certificate, part time, for intending/practising teachers in FE. Wide range of BTEC Engineering courses (various specialities) for candidates who can show that they expect to be successful. Basic Technology courses, part time, for Women, school terms only, no academic qualifications required. City and Guilds Engineering updating courses, e.g. CAD/CAM. Wide range of BTEC Business Studies courses for candidates who can show they can expect to be successful by virtue of other studies/work experience. Institution of Industrial Managers Certificate, part time, entry concessions possible for over-27s with four years' industrial experience. Supervisory Management, part time, for over-21s with management potential, leads to NEBSS Certificate. BTEC Certificate in Management Studies, part time, unit-based, suitable for potential managers, entry concessions for candidates 25-plus with three years' experience. Languages, part time – French, German, Italian, Polish, Russian, Spanish, all levels. Wide range of Secretarial Skills/Office Technology courses, part time, all levels.

Bridlington: East Yorkshire College of Further Education
(1988) ESF-sponsored Tourism, Leisure and Recreation, Catering and Hotel Management, Control Technology and Caring in Institutions courses (apply for details). Mature students' Electronic Engineering, full time. Mature students' Private Secretary's Update, full time. Art Education, under 21-hour rule. Open Learning (see 'Open and Distance Learning').

Burnley College
TA-sponsored Business Studies Secretarial (details from college). Projected Introduction to New Skills and Women into Technical Education courses (details from college). City and Guilds Advanced Certificate in Furniture Crafts. This course is open to adults considering retraining in Furniture

Crafts. It provides the opportunity to acquire basic skills in Cabinet Making, Upholstery and Wood Finishing and to specialise in one of these. Students are encouraged to sit the City and Guilds Advanced Craftexaminations in their chosen craft. BTEC National Diploma in Caring (Social Care) and BTEC National Diploma in Nursery Nursing (subject to approval). These courses, which are equivalent to 2 A-levels, provide entry to Certificate of Qualification in Social Work courses, Probation and Police training, Infant Teacher training and into Community Services posts. Assessment is on a continuous basis and the entry requirements of 4 GCSEs will be waived for appropriate mature entrants. Open College (see 'Open and Distance Learning Courses').

Chester District School of Nursing
Full-time 3-year course leading to qualification of Registered General Nurse. Candidates without statutory academic entrance requirements may take the UKCC entry test. School states: 'An upper age limit for entry has been set by the Chester District School of Nursing at approximately forty-five years of age.'

Consett – Derwentside College
Employment Training – a range of training opportunities available including Business Studies, Catering, Clerical, Community Care, Hairdressing, Engineering, Electronics, Secretarial, Recreation and Leisure. Electronics, full time. Information Technology, part time. Community Care Practice, part time – for mature people employed/hoping to be employed in the caring field. Office Skills for the Adult Unemployed, part time (Shorthand, Typewriting, Audio, Word-Processing, Office Practice, Business Communications). Art and Design Skills for the Unemployed, part time (Three-Dimensional Studies, Painting and Drawing, Screen Printing etc.). Workshops in Electronics, Computers, Maths, Literacy, Numeracy, Drama, Languages. Wider Opportunities for Women. CNC Machine Operation. Part-Programming. Access to Information Technology. Catering, Management and Supervisory Studies. Training the Trainers. (Modes not specified – ask college for details.)

Dewsbury College
Scope programme (includes skills sampling – Construction, Engineering, Clerical, Retailing, Computer Skills). Motor Vehicle Fabrication. under 21-hour rule. Industrial Sewing and Design, under 21-hour rule. Construction trades (various), under 21-hour rule. Catering and Caring Skills, under 21-hour rule. Electrical and Electronic Skills, under 21-hour rule. Open Learning (see 'Open and Distance Learning Courses').

Doncaster Health Authority Department of Nurse Education
Full-time 3-year courses leading to qualifications of Registered General Nurse or Registered Mental Nurse or Registered Nurse for the Mentally

Handicapped. Candidates without statutory academic entrance requirements may take the UKCC entry test. NB: there is an Access to Nursing
course at this centre (see 'Pre-Entry, Sample and Access Courses'). Centre
states: 'We do accept mature students in Doncaster with no upper age limit
applying, each applicant being assessed individually.'

Douglas, IoM – Noble's Isle of Man Hospital School of Nursing
Full-time 3-year course leading to qualification of Registered General Nurse.
Mature candidates welcomed (no age limit mentioned). Candidates without
the statutory academic entrance requirements may take the UKCC entry
test. School comments: 'Isle of Man Control of Employment Acts state that
any person who does not qualify as an Isle of Man worker requires a work
permit issued by the Employment Committee of the Isle of Man Board of
Social Security before taking up employment in the Isle of Man.'

Durham: New College Durham
The college states 'all college courses are open to all – ask for the prospectus'.
TA-sponsored Scope courses with 'tasters' of Computing, Word-Processing, Basic Office administration, Typing, Book-Keeping, Social and Community Care, Construction crafts, Motor Vehicles. TA-sponsored Robotics,
full time. TA-sponsored Microprocessor and Industrial Control Systems,
full time. TA-sponsored Secretarial skills, full time or part time. BTEC HND
in Accountancy and Finance, Leisure Administration (Music and Entertain-
ment Industries and Sport and Recreation streams), Tourism Management
and Travel Management; RSA Personal Assistants' course and Bilingual
Secretarial course. Mode is not specified for any of these – ask college.
Certificate in Marketing, evenings – those with three years' Marketing
experience may enter without exam qualifications. RSA Teacher's Diploma
in Typewriting, Shorthand, Office Procedures – over-25s with English
O-level and appropriate skills eligible without usual qualifications. Various
part-time and evening Shorthand, Typewriting, Word Processing, Office
Skills courses. Association of Accounting Technicians Certificate in
Accounting, open entry, possibility of progressing to full membership of
Association. Certificate in Industrial Management, part time, entry requirements relaxed for over-27s with four years' industrial experience. BTEC
Certificate in Management Studies, part time, entry requirements relaxed
for over-25s with 3 years' experience. Must have the potential to develop as a
manager. Supervisory Studies for NEBSS Certificate part time – no entry
qualification but students must be over 21 and able to benefit from the
course. Institute of Management Services Certificate, part time – over-21s
admitted by discussion with course tutor. Adult Education Teachers' course
– candidates must have subject qualifications and an interest in teaching
adults. City and Guilds Further Education Teachers' Certificate – candidates
must have subject qualifications and intend to teach or train personnel in
commerce, industry or public service. BTEC Computer Studies, evenings,

and Information Technology for managers, evenings – for people with three years' experience in responsible position in industry/commerce and able to cope with course work. The Cookery Certificate (can lead on to the Cook's Professional Certificate) evenings – no formal entry requirements. City and Guilds Fashion award, evenings – candidates need a good grasp of dressmaking skills. Updating in Computing, Electronics, Robotics and New Technology, part time, to suit individual career plans. Open Learning (see 'Open and Distance Learning Courses').

Gateshead Technical College
Conservation of Fine Art, full time – open to people with previous conservation experience, or degree, or certain A-level qualifications. Computer-Aided Engineering, Computer-Aided Draughting, Computer Numerical Control, Computer-Aided Production Management, Robotics, Digital Electronics, Word-Processing, Computerised Business Systems – at various levels and in various study modes. TA-sponsored Selling courses, part time (evening version available) – suitable for beginners. Industrial Electronics, evenings, for mature students. Machine Tool Setting and Operation, leads to City and Guilds award – mature students without usual qualifications but with appropriate experience may apply. Leisure classes with earning potential; subjects include Dressmaking, Cordon Bleu Cooking, Machine Knitting. Open Learning (see 'Open and Distance Learning Courses').

Grimsby – Humberside College (see under Hull)

Halifax – Calderdale College
Adult Guidance Unit attached to Student Services. Staff talk to individuals and design a learning programme around their needs and commitments. No details of subjects or courses provided, but see also 'Open and Distance Learning Courses.'

Huddersfield Health Authority School of Nursing
Full-time 3-year courses leading to the qualifications of Registered General Nurse or Registered Mental Nurse. Candidates aged over 25 without the statutory academic entrance requirements may take the UKCC entry test. School states: 'Huddersfield School of Nursing accepts students, upper age limits 40 years for the Registered General Nurse course and 45 years for the Registered Mental Nurse course.'

Huddersfield Polytechnic
ESF-sponsored Women into Technology, school hours only, includes Design and Materials, Computing, Electronics, Chemical Science. BTEC HND Business and Finance, full time (opportunities for students without academic qualifications if their experience is very relevant). BTEC HND

Science (Chemistry) full time. Mature students encouraged but must offer usual entry qualifications. Foundation course in Accountancy, full time, mature students without usual entry qualifications may be admitted. Diploma in Careers Guidance, full time, over-25s with valuable employment experience may be considered with less than usual entry requirements. DipHE (Engineering) full time, mature students may be admitted with less than usual entry requirements. Diploma in Social Work/Certificate of Qualification in Social Work (CQSW), minimum age of entry 25, formal entry requirements not specified. An extended part-time CQSW is also available for people with home commitments. City and Guilds Further Education Teacher's Certificate, part time, for potential FE teachers and trainers, with qualifications relevant to their subject(s). Institute of Linguists' course, part time, for those who have studied French beyond A-level or similar level. Institution of Industrial Managers Certificate, part time, entry concession for over-27s with four years' experience. BTEC Certificate in Management Studies, part time, entry concessions for over-25s with three years' experience. Supervisory Studies for NEBSS Certificate, for candidates over 21 with supervisory potential, no formal entry requirement. BTEC HNC Business Studies, entry concessions possible for over-21s.

Huddersfield Polytechnic School of Chiropody
Full-time 3-year course leading to the Diploma of the Society of Chiropodists. School states: 'We do accept mature students and there are no definite upper age limits for application to the course. We interview each potential candidate and as our course runs for three years, after a certain age it may not be advisable for a person to train – but each case is assessed separately. Our current minimum entry requirement for mature students is A-level Biology or Human Biology, Grade C or above. Alternatively a Merit in a minimum of three Level 3 Biological/Physiological subjects in the BTEC National Diploma in Science (Health Studies) will be considered equivalent to the minimum A-level requirement.'

Hull: Hull District School of Nursing
Full-time 3-year courses leading to qualifications of Registered General Nurse or Registered Mental Nurse or Registered Nurse for the Mentally Handicapped. Candidates without statutory academic entrance qualifications may take the UKCC entry test. Full-time 2-year course leading to qualifications of Enrolled Nurse (General) and Enrolled Nurse (Mental Handicap). Upper age limit for entry to training is 45 years.

Hull School of Radiography
Full-time 3-year course leading to the Diploma of the College of Radiographers (Diagnostic). Entry concessions possible in accordance with the regulations of the College of Radiographers which has a special panel to consider applications from mature students. School states: 'At present each

mature student receives individual assessment and no upper age limit is applied.'

Hull: Humberside College of Higher Education
(1988, excluding courses formerly sponsored by the MSC.) BTEC Diploma in Exhibition and Museum Design, full time, mature students who do not meet academic entry standards considered on the basis of a portfolio of work. BTEC HND Business Studies (Private Secretarial, Accounting, Business Administration, Industrial Administration, Leisure Studies and European Marketing options), full time or sandwich, mature students who do not meet academic entry standards considered; French essential for European Marketing option. BTEC HND in the Science and Technology of Food, candidates with less than the usual entry requirements considered. DipHE, full time (can lead to a degree), over-21s considered without formal qualifications. Certificate of Qualification in Social Work, full time, over-25s need not have formal entry qualifications but should have some appropriate experience. Certificate in the Further Education and Training of Mentally Handicapped People, full time, over-21s need not have formal qualifications but must have had some appropriate experience. Open Learning (see 'Open and Distance Learning').

Kirkby College of Further Education
'We welcome mature students on all of our courses.' Motor Vehicle Maintenance, part time. BTEC National Diploma in Engineering (Mechanical/Manufacturing) full time. BTEC National Certificate in Engineering (Electronic) part time. BTEC First Certificate in Engineering, part time. BTEC First Diploma in Engineering, full time. Security and Emergency Alarms Systems for City and Guilds 185 award, part time. Microcomputer Technology for City and Guilds 223 award, part time. Electrical Installation Work for City and Guilds 236 award, part time. Basic Engineering Competencies for City and Guilds 201 award, part time. Mechanical Production Occupational Competences for City and Guilds 228 award, part time. Machine Woodworking for City and Guilds 606 award, part time. Construction Crafts for City and Guilds 585/588/594 awards, full time. Carpentry and Joinery for City and Guilds 585 award, part time. Brickwork for City and Guilds 588 award, part time. Painting and Decorating for City and Guilds 594 award, part time. Electronic Servicing for City and Guilds 224 award, part time. Computer Aided Engineering for City and Guilds 230 award, part time. BTEC First Diploma in Business and Finance, full time. BTEC National Diploma in Business Studies, full time. BTEC National Diploma in Leisure Studies, full time. BTEC First Certificate in Business and Finance, part time. BTEC National Certificate in Business and Finance, part time. Bankers' courses, part time. Audio-typing, full time. Secretarial studies, full time and part time. Medical Secretaries' course, full time. Hotel Reception, full time. Word Processing, part time. BTEC First Certificate in Distribution, part time.

Retailing Studies for City and Guilds award, part time. Data Processing and Applications Programming for City and Guilds award, full time. Nursery Nursing for NNEB qualification, full time. CCETSW Preliminary Social Care, full time. Home Economics for Family and Community Care, full time. BTEc First Diploma in Caring, full time. Community Care Practice for City and Guilds 325 award, part time. Open College – (see 'Open and Distance Learning').

Lancaster: North West Lancashire School of Radiography
Full-time 3-year course leading to Diploma of the College of Radiographers (Diagnostic). School states: 'Regarding mature students, we do consider them and there are entry concessions. Mature students do not have to meet the normal entry requirements. I would expect all mature students to start a course at this school to have done at some time, foundation courses, or to have GCEs in English and a Science subject.' Age limits are not specified.

Lancaster School of Nursing
Full-time 3-year courses leading to qualifications of Registered General Nurse or Registered Mental Nurse or Registered Nurse for the Mentally Handicapped. Normal statutory academic entrance requirements. School states: 'At this school of nursing, we have always made a practice of accepting mature students. Currently approximately 25% of our students are over the age of 25. We have an upper age limit of 45.'

Leeds: East Leeds School of Radiography
Full-time 3-year course leading to Diploma of the College of Radiographers (Diagnostic). Entry concessions possible in accordance with regulations of the College of Radiographers which has a special panel to consider mature applicants. School states: 'We consider each mature student on individual merit, but the following points should be borne in mind. (1) Radiography can be a physically stressful career and mature students should be physically fit with no history of back trouble. We would normally prefer students to be under 35 years of age. (2) These applicants should be able to demonstrate some level of academic ability which would enable them to tackle the theoretical aspect of the course. (3) The applicant would have to demonstrate strong motivation to undertake Radiography. We do accept mature students who generally meet these criteria and currently have three mature students in training.'

Leeds: Jacob Kramer College
(1988) Vocational Fine Art/Crafts, part time, for mature students unable (for reasons of age, qualifications, family commitments) to pursue full-time education within the HE sector. Unemployed students accepted under 21-hour rule.

Leeds: Park Lane College of Further Education
Secretarial Training/Retraining, part time and under 21-hour rule, including Shorthand, Typewriting, Word-Processing, Office Practice. Secretarial Duties, Medical Reception. Mature students also accepted on full-time Medical Reception and Private Secretarial courses. Access to Information Technology, evenings. RSA Computer Literacy and Information Technology, modular, part time and evenings. Word-Processing for beginners, part time and evenings. Modular Wider Opportunities course includes Wages/ Salaries, Computerised Record-Keeping, Book-keeping, Keyboarding, Typing, Word-Processing, Telephone Reception Skills, Office Skills, Job-Seeking Skills. The college is a regional centre for Travel and Tourism and has full-time and part-time courses for late entrants to this type of work. 40 GCSE subjects, part time day or evening, many with vocational bias, e.g. Accountancy, Graphic Art, Electronics, Health Studies, Science (modular), Science (environmental), Foreign Languages, Information Technology. Science Resource area. Computer Workshop. Mathematics Workshop for self-programmed courses.

Leeds Polytechnic
(1988) Skills Training and Career Development – over-25s who have been unemployed for six months, part time. Can lead to one-year full-time courses, e.g. Diploma in Administration Studies; Diploma/MSc in Health Education; Diploma in Institutional Management; Hotel and Tourism Studies; Diploma in Management Studies; Diploma in Personnel Management. Certificate of Qualification in Social Work for Graduates. Certificate in Teaching of Typewriting and Word Processing, part time. Postgraduate Diploma in Office Systems. Bilingual Diploma in Information Administration. Business Automation for unemployed 18–25-year-olds, under 21-hour rule. BTEC HND Finance and Accounting/Business Studies, full time, exceptionally, mature students without formal qualifications but with relevant work experience may be accepted. Polytechnic Diploma/Certificate in Sports Coaching Studies, full time, for those with recognised ability in the field of coaching/performance, and/or who have been recommended by the respective coaching body of the sport. Certificate in Education for intending teachers of Craft, Design and Technology, full time (for craftsmen/women with experience in industry. English and Maths O-level and the Full Technological Certificate of the City and Guilds of London Institute in an appropriate woodworking/metalworking trade, or BTEC HND/HNC equivalent; candidates must be 23 by 1 October in the year when their course begins). BTEC HND Hotel, Catering and Institutional Management, full time, exceptionally, mature applicants with a sound general education and/ or good relevant experience may be considered. Polytechnic Diploma in Modern Languages and Business Studies, full time, mature students with alternatives to the usual qualifications, and French or German equivalent to A-level standard, are considered. Certificate of Qualification in Social Work,

full time, candidates without formal qualifications will be required to take an educational attainment test.

Leeds: Western Health Authority School of Physiotherapy
Full-time 3-year course leading to Graduate Diploma in Physiotherapy and Membership of the Chartered Society of Physiotherapy. School states: 'Mature students are welcomed; normally the upper age limit is approximately 35. Must be fit enough to cope with rigours of the course and with patient care. Mature applicants are expected to show evidence of recent academic achievement to A-level standard or equivalent.'

Leeds: Western Health Authority School of Radiography
Full-time 3-year course leading to Diploma of the College of Radiographers (Diagnostic). Entry concessions for mature students possible in accordance with the regulations of the College of 'Radiographers' special panel which considers applications from mature students. School states: 'We certainly accept mature students but do not have an upper age limit as such; much would depend on whether or not we feel at interview whether or not the candidate can cope with the three-year course and serve a useful period of time after training.'

Leeds: Western Health Authority School of Radiotherapy
Full-time 3-year course leading to the Diploma of the College of Radiographers (Therapy). Entry concessions for mature students may be possible in accordance with the regulations of the College of Radiographers' special panel which considers applications from mature students. School states: 'We do accept mature students; there is no specified age limit.'

Leigh College
'All our courses are open to everyone in the community and outside who can benefit from them', says the Principal. Mature students are welcomed and present on almost all vocational courses. Special concessions for the unemployed. Full-time – Craft and BTEC courses leading to awards in: Catering, Hotel Administration, Accommodation Services, Reception; Hairdressing, Beauty Therapy, Business and Finance, Leisure, Light Music (Diploma), Secretarial skills, Clerical skills, Engineering (Mechanical/Production, Electrical, Automotive), Art and Design, Performing Arts, Computing, Caring Science, Health Studies. City and Guilds or equivalent: Automobile Engineering, Information Technology, Carpentry and Joinery: Part time – Hairdressing and Beauty Therapy leading to City and Guilds award, Catering – including specialised Pastry and Confectionery, Alcoholic Beverages. Office Skills, Secretarial and Secretarial Refresher; BTEC Business and Finance; Banking Certificate (Preliminary and Certificate); BTEC Mechanical and Production, Electrical and Electronic. Robot Technology, Machine Tool Setting, Robot Technological Control, NC/CNC Machine

Programming, Mechanical Engineering Craft – to Part III; Building Studies, Security Alarms; Electrical and Electronic Servicing to Carpentry and Joinery (including Advanced Craft), Electrical Installations; IEE Wiring Regulations; Automotive Electrical, Heavy Vehicles, Vehicle Body Craft, Motor Vehicle Technicians, Vehicle Parts; RTITB Instructions: Welding Craft, Fabrication and Welding. Light Music, Teacher Training (Regional Scheme): City and Guilds Further Education Teaching Certificate, Teaching Students with Special Needs; Teaching Mentally Disordered People; RSA Certificate in Continuing Education; Family and Community Care; Community Care Practice. Information Technology hard and software is available to all students. All BTEC courses mentioned are at First and National Level; some Engineering courses are at Higher National as well. Open Learning (see 'Open and Distance Learning Courses').

Lincoln, Gainsborough, Louth: North Lincolnshire College
TA-sponsored full-time courses for Building Site Managers and Estimators, for Electro-Mechanical engineers (HNC in dual engineering), for Software Engineers (IEE certificate in Software Engineering). Engineering Industry Training Board sponsored course for Women to enter Electronic Engineering (minimum age 18 and with some scientific/engineering experience preferred) which leads to an HNC in Electronics.

Liverpool Institute of Higher Education
Diploma in Occupational Therapy, full time. Students over 26 considered on merit (usual entry requirement five O-levels and two A-levels, plus First Aid Certificate).

Liverpool: Merseyside School of Radiography
Full-time 3-year course leading to the Diploma of the College of Radiographers (Diagnostic or Therapy). Entry concessions possible in accordance with the regulations of the College of Radiographers which has a special panel to consider applications from mature students. School states: 'This School usually considers applicants up to the age of approximately 35.'

Liverpool School of Nursing
Full-time 3-year course leading to qualification as a Registered General Nurse. The school has a special leaflet for would-be mature entrants which draws attention to Nursing Access courses offered at South Mersey College and Sandown College as a posssible choice for candidates who do not have the statutory academic entrance requirements for nurse training. School states: 'Liverpool School of Nursing accepts mature students to the age of 45. Above this age, they are given individual consideration.'

Liverpool: Sefton School of Nursing
Full-time 3-year courses leading to qualification as a Registered General Nurse or Registered Nurse for the Mentally Handicapped. Candidates

without the statutory academic entrance requirement may take the UKCC
entry test. School states: 'We do accept mature students and our upper age
limit is 48 years.'

Liverpool – South Mersey College
Marine engineering, navigation, yachting and industrial courses for careers
in Merchant Navy and for leisure. NB – mature entrants considering courses
related to Merchant Navy careers should query age limits and eligibility with
shipping lines. Automobile engineering courses leading to careers at
technican or management level. Construction courses at craft, technician
and professional level. Media Studies, for those wishing to enter the film
and television industry. Leisure & Recreation Management courses, including BTEC Leisure Studies.

Manchester Polytechnic
(1988) Mature students very welcome (send for free *Mature Students
Handbook*). Foundation course leading to Polytechnic Certificate in Visual
Studies, full time, entry concessions for mature students and those of
exceptional merit. Polytechnic Certificate in Recreational Arts for the
Community, full time, no entry requirements for mature students other
than commitment and ability to work in at least one art form. Diploma in
Careers Guidance, full time, various entry qualifications. Certificate of
Qualification in Social Work (CQSW) full time, entry concessions for
over-25s, paid or voluntary social work experience needed. Polytechnic
Certificate in Youth and Community Work, full time, entry concessions for
over-25s with relevant practical experience. BTEC Diploma in Clothing
Machine Technology, full time, entry test for mature students. BTEC HND
Technology of Food, full time, entry concessions for mature students.
Polytechnic Certificate in Meat Technology and Inspection, full time, entry
concessions for mature students with approved industrial experience. BTEC
HND Hotel, Catering and Institutional Management, sandwich, entry
concessions for mature students with appropriate industrial experience.
DipHE, full time, can lead to degree, entry concessions for mature students,
from whom applications are especially welcome. BTEC HND Science
(Chemistry), full time, sympathetic consideration to candidates with
alternatives to usual entry qualifications. BTEC HND Computer Studies, full
time or sandwich, entry requirement concessions for mature students with
relevant work experience; aptitude test possible. BTEC National Certificate
in Polymer Technology, entrance examination for candidates without
conventional qualifications. Extensive range of part-time courses welcoming mature students, which can be used as a bridge into full-time courses.

Science Laboratory Technology: viewpoints
'I took a laboratory technician's apprenticeship with Rolls-Royce at Crewe
and found myself stationed in the plastics and rubber laboratory, so

naturally I was doing polymer science at college, part time. First I did the TEC (now BTEC) sciences courses, then I came to Manchester to do the Higher BTEC and went into polymer science and technology. At the end of that course I was made redundant from Rolls-Royce – but my combination of work experience and college study made it possible to join degree students and get a degree in two years instead of four years.'

'People don't expect middle-aged Mums like me to want day release, but having started out as a medical laboratory technician and gained ONC before I left to marry and have a family, I was determined to pick up where I left off. I found I got quite a lot of opposition. When I first applied for the job I think they wanted somebody who'd just be an extra pair of hands, but I wanted to make a career, so after a lot of persuasion, I managed to get day release for the Institute of Medical Laboratory Sciences course.'

(Students, Faculty of Science and Engineering,
Manchester Polytechnic)

'Mature students bring their own experience in. It may sometimes happen that in a class, the group will be studying a particular topic and when the lecturer asks if there are any questions or comments, a mature student will say 'Oh, we don't do it at work that way now, we do it this way' – in which case the lecturer will be able to make use of that particular student's experience for the benefit of the class as a whole.'

(Spokesperson, Faculty of Science and Engineering,
Manchester Polytechnic)

Manchester Royal Infirmary School of Physiotherapy
Full-time 3-year course leading to a BSc (Hons.) Physiotherapy. Entry requirement concessions possible for mature students. School states: 'We regularly accept mature students. The upper age limit is very much dependent upon their physical fitness but it is unlikely that we would consider anyone who would be over the age of 40 years on or before graduation. Each mature applicant is considered as an individual but the school must be satisfied that they have (1) proven academic ability with a bias towards the Sciences (2) evidence of recent study ideally to A-level (3) no personal responsibilities which could prevent them from devoting themselves fully to the course.'

Manchester: North Manchester School of Nursing
Full-time 3-year courses leading to qualifications as a Registered General Nurse or Registered Mental Nurse or Registered Nurse for the Mentally Handicapped. Candidates without the statutory academic entrance requirements may take the UKCC entry test. School states: 'Applications from mature candidates are encouraged – there is no upper age limit.'

Manchester: School of Therapy Radiography, Christie and Clatterbridge Hospitals
Full-time 3-year course leading to Diploma of the College of Radiographers (Therapy). Entry concessions possible in accordancewith the regulations of the Society of Radiographers which has a special panel to consider applications from mature candidates. School states: 'We would have to think very carefully about accepting anyone over 45 years of age because of the high cost of the training and the candidate's potential lifetime as a radiographer then being only a maximum of 17 years.'

Manchester: South Manchester School of Nursing
Full-time 3-year course leading to qualification as a Registered General Nurse. Candidates without the statutory academic entrance requirements may take the UKCC test. School states: 'We are always keen to encourage mature students to consider the nursing profession, and individual advice and information is extended to any interested person. Advice is also given regarding Return to Study courses and Pre-Nursing courses with GCSEs etc. both on a full- and part-time basis. We have several mature students in training at the present time and prospective candidates are considered on an individual basis regarding an upper age limit.'

Manchester: South Manchester School of Physiotherapy
Full-time 3-year course leading to Membership of the Chartered Society of Physiotherapy. School states: 'We do accept mature students, but have an upper age limit of approximately 35. It is considered that a physiotherapy course, with its emphasis on physical as well as mental work, makes it difficult for anyone over the age of 35 to cope with the intensity. There are no particular entry concessions for mature students although they may not be required to have achieved the O- and A-levels required of 18-year-olds. Mature entrants are expected to provide evidence of recent study up to a high standard.'

Manchester: University of Manchester
Extra-Mural Department: Career Studies Unit with TA-sponsored pro-gramme of short courses – e.g. Foundation (Job-Hunting) Skills, Personal Evaluation and Presentation, Small Business Suitability, Computer Work-shop, Understanding Management, Effective Management, Executive Recruitment.

Manchester: UMIST (University of Manchester Institute of Science and Technology)
Conversion course in Computation/Computation and Optics, full time, leads to MSc, attracts some late starters.

Manchester: Withington Centre for Community Education
(note change of address – see address list at end of book)
Modern Office Skills Retraining, Garment Manufacturing (could attract TA

sponsorship). Open Workshops in Modern Office Skills, Maths, English, Book-Keeping, Basic Skills, English as a Second Language, Business English. Leisure courses with earning potential include Floristry for City & Guilds Certificate, Dressmaking, Tailoring, China Painting, Cookery and Cake Decoration, Information Technology. Flexistudy (see 'Open and Distance Learning Courses').

Middlesborough: Cleveland School of Radiography
Full-time 3-year course leading to Diploma of the College of Radiographers (Diagnostic). Entry concessions possible in accordance with the regulations of the College of Radiographers which has a special panel to consider applications from mature students. School states: 'We do not stipulate an upper age limit as such. All applicants would be invited to the school to talk over the career prospects, after which it would be at the discretion of the Principal.'

Middlesborough: Longlands College of Further Education
(1988, excluding courses formerly sponsored by the MSC.) College has ESF funded courses but did not give details. Also states that mature students are welcome on an infill basis to its regular courses. Open Learning (see 'Open and Distance Learning Courses').

Middlesborough: Teesside Polytechnic
Computer-Aided Engineering, full time. Management, full time.

Morpeth: Northumbria College of Nursing Studies
Full-time 3-year courses leading to qualifications of Registered General Nurse or Registered Mental Nurse or Registered Nurse for the Mentally Handicapped. Candidates without statutory academic entrance requirements may take the UKCC entry test. College states: 'Mature entrants are actively sought by this college as it is felt their greater life experience is of benefit, not only to the individual, but to the patients and clients with whom they come into contact. No hard and fast upper age limit is applied. However, candidates from the age of 50 should be able to demonstrate not only those attributes required for successful course completion, but also the intention of continuing in practice for a reasonable time on course completion.'

Nelson and Colne College
Courses in Secretarial skills and Technology are available. Some of these are exclusively for adults; for other courses it would be necessary to attend on an infill basis. The college also sponsors a 'Drop-In Skills Centre' where adults can retrain in Computing, Electronics or Modern Office Skills on a drop-in 'pay as you learn' basis.

Newcastle-upon-Tyne Polytechnic
Full-time 3-year course leading to the Diploma of the College of Occupational Therapists. College states: 'We do accept mature students on the Diploma in Occupational Therapy course. The age of maturity is considered 25 years and over. There is in fact no stated upper age limit. There are some concessions regarding entry for mature students although all are expected to have qualifications in English Language and a Science, e.g. Human Biology, mainly to ensure that they are prepared for the demands of the course ... we expect mature students to show evidence of recent successful study, i.e. within the last two and a half years prior to entry. We take into consideration Higher Certificate Foundation courses, BTEC courses, Open University Foundation courses, etc.'

Full-time 3-year course leading to Graduate Diploma in Physiotherapy of the Chartered Society of Physiotherapy. NB: Polytechnic is in the process of converting the Diploma to a Degree. No upper age limit specified but prospectus states: *Mature Students* (25+ years). Mature students will be expected to provide evidence of ability to cope with the academic and practical aspects of the course in lieu of the normal pre-entry qualifications.

Newcastle-upon-Tyne School of Nursing
Full-time 3-year courses leading to qualifications of Registered General Nurse or Registered Mental Nurse. Candidates without statutory academic entrance requirements may take the UKCC test. School states: 'The upper age limit is normally 47 years, but consideration may be given to older applicants.'

Newcastle-upon-Tyne Schools of Radiography
Full-time 3-year courses leading to Diploma of the College of Radiographers (Diagnostic or Therapy). Entry concessions may be possible in accordance with the regulations of the College of Radiographers which has a special panel to consider mature applicants. Schools state: 'We do accept mature students and there is no upper age limit.'

Northallerton: Friarage Hospital Nurse Education Department
Full-time 3-year course leading to qualification as a Registered General Nurse. Candidates without the statutory academic entrance requirement may take the UKCC entry test. Hospital states: 'We accept suitable mature students up to the age of 50.'

Ormskirk: West Lancashire Nurse Education Centre
Full-time 3-year course leading to qualification as a Registered General Nurse. Candidates without statutory academic entrance requirements may take the UKCC entry test. Mature students are accepted up to the age of 45 years.

Peterlee College
Business Development Unit and Employment Training programme provide
opportunities via: Practical Secretarial Skills, Engineering – short updating
courses including Robotics, CAD/CAM, Welding, Electronics, Motor Vehi-
cle Engineering. Employment Training provision in Painting and Decorat-
ing, Motor Vehicle Maintenance, Plastering, Bricklaying, Carpentry and
Joinery, Welding, Community Care, Care of the Elderly and Handicapped,
First Aid etc. Computing Workshop, day and evening – can lead to City and
Guilds Information Technology award. Flexistudy and Open Learning (see
'Open and Distance Learning Courses').

Preston College
CAD/CAM for Women; Painting and Decorating for Women; Electronics for
Women – funded by a variety of agencies. Periodic starts throughout the
year. Vocational training in new job skills, e.g. VDU operator, Telesales etc.
City and Guilds 730 series to enable skilled/professional people to undertake
teacher/counsellor training. City and Guilds 924/2 Youth Trainers Award.
City and Guilds 926/2 Adult Trainers Award. City and Guilds 725 Direct
Trainers Award. NWRAC Certificate in Further Education (Mentorship).
RSA Certificate in Counselling.

Preston: Lancashire Polytechnic
Opportunities for mature students on most courses, mainly at higher level
(see 'Degree and Advanced Courses'). Foundation/Introductory courses
include Accountancy, Management, Mathematics and Statistics, and there
are pre-degree courses (see 'Pre-Entry, Sample and Access Courses') and
Open College courses (see 'Open and Distance Learning Courses'). Polytechnic Diploma in Social Work/Certificate of Qualification in Social Work
(CQSW) - few formal entry requirements for over-25s; evidence of recent
study advantageous. TA-sponsored Conversion course to Microbiology.
Associate Student access to all courses (see 'Degree and Advanced Courses')
provides a useful means of retraining. ACOL Analytical Chemistry course
for updating.

Rotherham: Rockingham College of Further Education
Department of Industry-funded courses for redundant employees: options
include Microtechnology, Community Care, Sign Writing, Horticulture,
Jobbing Building, Painting and Decorating, Catering – full time, all for City
& Guilds awards. ESF-sponsored Basic Catering and Book-keeping (unemployed people over 25) under 21-hour rule. ESF-sponsored Community
Service (unemployed people 25-plus) under 21-hour rule. ESF-sponsored
New Office Technology Skills (minimum age limit 18-plus), under 21-hour
rule. ESF-sponsored Electronics (minimum age limit 18-plus). ESF-sponsored Computing (minimum age limit 18-plus). ESF-sponsored Construction (minimum age limit 18-plus). Wide range of leisure courses with

earning potential, e.g. Cake Decoration, Cookery, Fashion, Toymaking, Upholstery, Creative Writing etc.

Retraining After Redundancy: viewpoints
'Before I started on this Microelectronics course, I was a crane driver. I'd thought of doing Heavy Goods Vehicle driving, but I'd done a little bit inside CB Radio and I wanted to take a Radio and TV course, but there wasn't one available, so I chose this instead. It's proved to be a little bit heavy going but very interesting, and there's another stage of the course where we might be able to think about setting up on our own. I'd thought of doing the small jobs, like repairing home computers.'

'After being made redundant after 30 years, I took a Hairdressing course, but I haven't been able to find any work in that line. I think they're looking for more experience. I saw the Community Service course advertised and I thought 'Well, you can't know too much,' so I decided to come along. We've had a lot of visits – to the courts, the prison, the youth detention centre – and we're learning first aid and home nursing and going out on work experience. I've gained a lot of knowledge. I'd like a part-time job, but I'm quite happy to go and do something voluntary and get my satisfaction that way. If I got into the hospital scheme, perhaps I could start by helping the hairdresser.'

(Students retraining at Rockingham College)

Rotherham College of Arts and Technology
(1988) Workshop for the Unemployed, part time, with opportunities to learn a wide range of skills, from Woodwork to Industrial Sewing and from Light Crafts to Welding. Special Workshop, one day a week, with English Language support for students whose first spoken language is Mirpur Punjabi. Women's Workshop, one day a week, from 12.30 – 3.30 p.m. sampling Joinery, Painting and Decorating, Motor Vehicle Maintenance, Welding, Domestic Appliance Repairs, Electronics and Wood and Metal Turning with a woman teacher. PHIT (Physically Handicapped into Information Technology) under 21-hour rule, to prepare for training in Computer Studies and Information Technology. Industrial Electronics, under 21-hour rule, leads to City and Guilds award. Electrical Engineering, under 21-hour rule, leads to BTEC National award. Electronic Servicing, part time, day and evening, leads to City and Guilds award. Security and Emergency Alarms Systems, part time, day and evening, leads to City and Guilds award, very suitable for people wishing to retrain for a new career. Cleaning Science, part time, leads to City and Guilds award, can lead to work in hotel housekeeping, as warden of sheltered accommodation, in hospital domestic supervision etc. Computer-Aided Engineering, various levels, evenings – to update engineering tradespeople and technicians. Microelectronics, various levels, evenings, to update electrical/electronic tradespeople and technicians. Ceramic Technician's Certificate, part time,

mature students accepted at discretion of Head of Department. Construction courses, part time: Brickwork, Carpentry and Joinery, Plumbing, all leading to City and Guilds awards, mature students accepted at discretion of Principal. Basic course in Youth and Community Work, evenings, for people 21-plus with at least six months' experience of voluntary youth work. Further Education Teacher's Certificate, for people aged 22-plus who are intending to teach in FE or are engaged in training, leads to City and Guilds award. Teaching and Training People with Mental Disorders, evenings, with seven 1-day visits, leads to City and Guilds award. Community Care Practice, part time, for people, 21-plus, who wish to obtain employment in the Caring field, leads to City and Guilds award. Playgroup Leaders and Assistants, part time, for people wishing to work in that field. Social Care Preparation, full time, includes A-levels and City and Guilds award.

Salford College of Technology
Certificate in Residential and Day Care, full time – entry concessions for over-23s with relevant work experience. Pre-employment Common Unit of the Certificate in Social Service, full time – entry concessions for over-25s with relevant experience. Association of Accounting Technicians, full time – exceptionally, entry concessions for candidates over 21. BTEC HNC Business and Finance, part time – exceptionally entry concessions for over-21s. BTEC HND/HNC Business and Finance or Public Administration, full time or part time - exceptionally, entry concessions for over-19s with relevant experience. College course in Conveyancing, full time, O- and A-level entry, for students of 21 and over. BTEC Post Experience Certificate of Business Administration, part time, for Professional Footballers aged 21 and over entering business. Certificate in Accountancy, part time - entry concession for mature students. Accounting Technician's Certificate, part time – for students 21 and over with good command of English. Institution of Industrial Managers Certificate, part time – entry concessions for over-27s. Institute of Purchasing and Supply Foundation, part time – entry concessions for over-25s. Certificate in Production and Inventory Control, part time – entry concessions for over-25s. Institute of Health Service Administrators, part time – for people with professional health service qualifications (medicine, nursing, paramedical, ambulance); or entry concessions if over 30 and working in health service administration. Certificate in Business Management, part time – entry concessions for over-25s at discretion of Principal. Institute of Personnel Management, part time – various entry requirements, including two years' personnel experience in a post of responsibility. Diploma in Training Management, part time – various entry requirements including relevant training experience. Institute of Marketing Certificate, part time – various entry requirements, including three years' experience. Preparation for Professional Social and Community work, part time or evenings. Languages: French, German, Spanish, all

levels, part time. Computing, all levels, part time. Microprocessors and Microelectronics: various short courses, open to anyone needing retraining. TA-sponsored 'Step Up' retraining opportunities, full time, for unemployed people:options are Computer Numerical Control, Computer-Aided Design, Quality Assurance, Robotics, Electronics, Microcomputer Applications; when combined with appropriate industrial experience, scheme leads to BTEC HNC Engineering. BTEC Post Experience Units in Computing and its applications – open to over-21s with significant work experience. See also paramedical courses, below.

Salford College of Technology: Manchester School of Radiography
Full-time 3-year course leading to the Diploma of the College of Radiographers (Diagnostic or Therapy). Mature students are accepted in line with the entry regulations of the College of Radiographers – see introduction to this section. No age limit is mentioned by this School.

Salford College of Technology: Northern College of Chiropody
Full-time 3-year course leading to Diploma of the Society of Chiropodists. College states: 'We have no upper age limit for students, but point out the potential employment problems for people who will be 50+ on qualification. All applications are treated individually. We are looking for a background which shows some familiarity with and understanding of biology and its principles. We frequently advise prospective students to obtain an A-level pass in one of the biology syllabi. Experience shows that entrants without that background have a poor chance of passing the first-year examinations. We regularly have one third of our students over the age of 21 and are happy to have mature students on the course.' (An Access course is under consideration as this book goes to press.)

Salford College of Technology: School of Occupational Therapy
Full-time 3-year course leading to the Diploma of the College of Occupational Therapists. School states: 'We encourage mature students. Over the last two years the average age of students at entry has been 25, 48% and 42% respectively being 25 or over on enrolment. There is no upper age limit, although we would not seriously consider training someone who will have reached retirement age on qualification. There are entry concessions for mature candidates negotiated in individual cases and at the discretion of the Head of School. We would normally regard evidence of recent study as being of particular importance.' NB – with regard to graduate entrants, the school states that 'in considering their applications, we prefer them to have been self-supporting for two years since last receiving public funding.'

Salford College of Technology: School of Physiotherapy
Full-time 3-year course leading to Graduate Diploma in Physiotherapy and Membership of the Chartered Society of Physiotherapy. School states: 'This

school has a positive attitude to mature students and welcomes their application for physiotherapy training. Any applicant over the age of 21 and under the age of 40 is eligible to be considered as a mature student. Entry to training is at the discretion of the Head of School, but experiential learning is taken into account at interview. Academic requirements must include evidence of recent study in order that the School and applicant are satisfied that the applicant will be able to cope with the academic rigour of the physiotherapy training course.'

Salford: University of Salford
Information Technology in Modern Management, full time.

Scarborough: York and Scarborough School of Nursing
Full-time 3-year course leading to the qualification of Registered General Nurse. Candidates without the statutory academic entrance requirements may take the UKCC entry test. School states: 'We do accept mature entrants with an upper age limit of 45.'

Scunthorpe: Scunthorpe and Goole School of Nursing
Full-time 3-year course leading to qualification as a Registered General Nurse. Candidates (aged 22 or over) without statutory academic entrance requirements may take the UKCC entry test – selection for the test by informal interview. The school welcomes applications from mature candidates, age limits 18–43 years.

Sheffield: Loxley College
HITECC engineering conversion course – see 'Pre-Entry, Sample and Access Courses'.

Sheffield: North Trent Schools of Radiography
Full-time 3-year courses leading to Diploma of the College of Radiographers (Diagnostic or Therapy). Entry concessions possible in accordance with regulations of the College of Radiographers which considers applications from mature students. School states: 'We are pleased to inform you that we accept mature students up to the age of 40.'

Sheffield: Parkwood College
(1988) 'All our courses are open to mature entrants.' Diploma in Community Care, full time, specifically designed for mature students. Diploma in Signwork, full time, leading to City and Guilds Certificates, entry at discretion of college after aptitude test and interview. Diploma in Furniture, full time, entry at discretion of the college. Courses under 21-hour rule in Brickwork, Carpentry and Joinery, Machine Woodworking, Painting and Decorating, Plastering, Mechanical Services, Welding, Maintenance of Building Services Equipment and Gas Installation Technology. Supervisory

Studies for NEBSS Certificate, part time, open to potential supervisors. Computer Studies through Access to Information Technology scheme, plus exam courses leading to City and Guilds and BTEC awards.

Sheffield: Rother Valley College of Further Education
(1988, excluding courses formerly sponsored by the MSC.) ESF-funded Information Technology, full time. Non-Metallic Moulding and Casting, full time. Motor Vehicle Craft Studies, full time. Courses under 21-hour rule include: Bricklaying and Woodwork, Catering and Food Studies, Art, Craft and Photography, Agriculture, Horticulture (including greenhouse work), Recreation and Leisure Studies (leads to City and Guilds award), Modern Office Skills, Motor Vehicle Craft Studies Part II, Fibrous Plaster and Fibreglass work, BTEC Commercial Computing Certificate, BTEC Electronics/Computing Certificate, BTEC Continuing Education units (e.g. Using Word Processors, Working with People). Mature students accepted on infill basis on wide range of full-time courses. Many part-time day and evening leisure courses with earning potential, e.g. Welding, Photography, Woodwork, Catering, Horticulture, Stained Glass Work.

Sheffield: Stradbroke College
Mature students welcomed on all the following courses. Entry concessions possible in many cases. BTEC National Diploma/Certificate in Business and Finance. BTEC National Certificate in Public Administration. BTEC Higher Conversion course, various modes. Range of Secretarial courses including Private Secretary's course with A-level Business Studies; Linguistic Secretarial, for students with a mother tongue other than English who are also competent in English; evening and day-release single subject courses, e.g. Shorthand, Teeline, Typewriting, Audio-Typewriting, Word Processing (typing skill desirable) and Office Practice). Available also as an integrated package. Applications invited from both men and women. Part time Teachers' Certificate and Diploma courses leading to qualifications by the RSA and/or JEB and/or Faculty of Teachers in Commerce. Library Assistants course, leading to City and Guilds 737 award. BTEC National Diploma/ Certificate in Science; BTEC National Diploma in Dental Technology; BTEC National Certificate and Higher National Certificate in Medical Physics and Physiological Measurement; BTEC National Certificate in Pharmaceutical Sciences. Iron and Steel Production leading to City and Guilds 067 award. Dental Surgery Assistants course, full time. Photography, leading to City and Guilds 745 in Scientific and Technical Photography. Intensive Bilingual Administrative course, 1 year, full time or part time, leading to University of Sheffield Certificate in Bilingual Business Administration and RSA Diploma for Bilingual Secretataries. Although a degree or good A-level pass is the usual requirement, mature candidates who can demonstrate equivalent experience in a foreign language will be considered for acceptance. See also Journalism (in 'Pre-Entry, Sample and Access courses').

Shipley College
Send for free 'Tickets to Employment' leaflet with details of full- and part-time courses for qualifications such as RSA, BTEC, City and Guilds, Royal Horticultural Society. Teacher-training, part time, leads to City & Guilds Part-time Teachers in Further Education Certificate (730) evenings and occasional Saturdays. BTEC Caring, part time, BTEC Business Studies, part time, day or evenings, City & Guilds Professional Cook's Certificate, part time; all these can enable 'returners' to get qualifications in their work area without giving up a job.

Southport College of Art and Technology
Courses available to adults include: Introduction to Information Technology, Catering, Reception Skills, Typing for Beginners, Word-Processing, Audiotyping, Shorthand, Book-keeping, Electronic Office, Photography, Design Skills, Hairdressing, Looking After People, Housekeeping, Crafts, Horticulture/Gardening, Electronics/Electrical Systems, Building, Painting and Decorating, Household Repairs, Small Appliance Maintenance, Basic Engineering Skills, Fabrication and Welding, Motor Vehicle Maintenance. Access to Information Technology and a wide range of Computer courses. Older students and those with industrial experience welcome on most full-time couress, e.g. BTEC National Diploma in General Art and Design, full time; Nursery Nursing Examination Boad, full time; City and Guilds Certificate of Travel Agency Competence, evenings; adult job seekers welcome. Leisure courses with earning potential include Vehicle Restoration, Dressmaking, Creative Writing, Machine Knitting, Welding. Open Learning (see 'Open and Distance Learning Courses'). The college offers a range of 'Train the Trainers' courses including City and Guilds 730 and 725 to those wishing to qualify to teach in Further Education or other training organisations.

Stockport: Stockport Department of Nurse Education
Full-time 3-year courses leading to qualifications of Registered General Nurse or Registered Mental Nurse. Prospectus states that candidates without statutory academic requirements 'may be offered the opportunity to sit the UKCC approved entry test. This will depend on the age, and the educational and work background of the candidate.' School did not send information on age limits.

Sunderland Polytechnic
Applications from 'late starters' are welcomed on all courses – for a complete list, send for the Polytechnic prospectus (see address list). For the following courses, mature students without formal entry requirements are considered, especially those with relevant experience: Diploma in Training Management, part time. Diploma in Personnel Management, part time. Institute of Personnel Management Stage II, part time. NEBSS Certificate in

Supervisory Management, part time (students must be aged 21-plus). BTEC HND Design, full time. Certificate in Youth and Community work, full time and part time. Diploma in Social Work (CQSW), full time (minimum age 30 years). BTEC HND Business and Finance, full time. BTEC HND Business Studies, part time. BTEC HND Applied Biology, full time and sandwich. BTEC HNC Applied Biology, part time. BTEC HND Computer Studies, full time, sandwich and part time. BTEC National Diploma Pharmaceutical Sciences, part time. Diploma of the Gemmological Association, part time, Diploma in Music, part time. (See also 'Degree and Advanced Courses'.)

Wakefield: Pinderfields College of Physiotherapy
Full-time 3-year course leading to Membership of the Chartered Society of Physiotherapy. College states: 'We do accept mature students (the prospectus states up to 35 years, but it might now be to 40 years), without the normal entry requirements. They should, however, give evidence of their ability to undertake the course.'

Warrington: North Cheshire College
(Amalgamation of former Padgate College of Higher Education, Warrington College of Art and Design, Warrington Technical College and local Adult Education Centres.) 'All our full-time courses are open to mature students.' Options include Medical Secretarial, Executive Secretarial, BTEC National Diploma in Computer Studies, BTEC National Certificate/Diploma in Leisure Studies, BTEC Certificate in Science, BTEC National Diploma in Engineering, Nursery Nursing for NNEB, Family and Community Care, BTEC National Diploma in Health Studies, City and Guilds in Hairdressing. (See also 'Degree and Advanced Courses'.)

Widnes: Halton College of Further Education
'We accept mature students on all our courses.' The college has indicated the following courses as attracting mature students: BTEC HND in Chemistry (sandwich); BTEC National Diploma in General Art and Design, Business Studies, Computing, Engineering, Health Studies, Hotel & Catering, Leisure Studies, Science. Mature students are accepted on Secretarial coures and for NNEB (Nursery Nursing), Preliminary Certificate in Social Care, Hairdressing, Hotel Reception and City & Guilds catering courses. Those with suitable experience are welcome on a wide range of part-time courses including Accounting Technicians, Institute of Supervisory Management, Institute of Administrative Management.

Wirral School of Nursing
Full-time 3-year course leading to qualification as a Registered General Nurse. Candidates without the statutory academic entrance requirements may take the UKCC entry test. School states: 'We certainly do encourage mature entrants, both male and female, to come into a career in nursing and

we do not have an upper age limit. We offer counselling prior to application for training every Wednesday beween 3 and 4 p.m. so that prospective candidates can discuss their individual needs.'

York: College of Ripon and York St John
Full-time 3-year course leading to Diploma in Occupational Therapy moderated by the College of Occupational Therapists. College states: 'We have a very high proportion of mature students; approximately two thirds of an intake of 60 are over the age of 21, though as you will see from our prospectus, the academic qualifications cannot be waived until candidates reach the age of 24 years. In regard to the latter, candidates do not have to fulfil the range of minimum entry requirements, but do need to have followed a recent successful course of academic study equivalent to GCSE or above in order to prove their educability. Some of these candidates undertake Open University courses to gain particular unit credits, while others embark upon attendance or correspondence courses at A-level. Access courses may also be considered.

It may also be of interest to you that approximately a quarter of our intake is male and many of these are persons over the age of 25. We do not have a specific upper age limit and currently have accepted students aged 50 and 51 into our current first year. The obvious criteria are that they have ability to complete the course and the capacity to spend some time working before retirement.'

Wales and Western England

Aberystwyth: Ceredigion Further Education College
(1988) Amalgamation of Aberystwyth College of Further Education, Cardigan College of Further Education and Felinfach College of Further Education. BTEC First Diploma in Business and Finance, full time, National Diploma in Business and Finance (Business, Secretarial, or Media Studies – Bilingual Options), full time. Mature students on all these courses accepted at Principal's discretion. Royal Society of Arts Diploma for Personal Assistants, full time, mature students with relevant business/secretarial experience accepted at Principal's discretion. Postgraduate and A-level Bilingual Secretarial course, full time, unqualified mature students accepted at Head of Department's discretion. Intensive Secretarial course, fulltime, suitable for students who wish to train/retrain for a secretarial career. Private Secretarial course, part time, suitable for those with some knowledge of office skills who wish to resume a career. Signwork, for City and Guilds award, full time, no entry qualifications other than natural aptitude and interest.

Bangor: Gwynedd School of Nursing
Full-time 3-year course leading to qualification of Registered General Nurse or Registered Nurse for the Mentally Handicapped. Candidates without the statutory academic entrance requirements may take the UKCC entry test. School states: 'Each candidate is assessed individually regarding an upper age limit. Generally speaking, it is approximately forty-five years of age.'

Barnstaple: North Devon College
The college says: 'We welcome mature students to all of our full-time courses. Already mature students have been offered places on Art and Design, Catering, Hairdressing, Nursery Nursing courses.'Foundation Art Course, full time – mature students welcome to apply for the one- or two-year General Art and Design course. Other opportunities include City and Guilds BTEC and NNEB courses.

Bath: Norton Radstock College
Courses for unemployed adults and those on Employment Training programmes. Options include Hairdressing, Health and Community Care,

Computerised Office and Information Technology, Commercial/Clerical Skills, Secretarial and Business Studies, Agriculture, Engineering, Computer Use, Horticulture, Crafts. Basic Engineering Competence, full time, leads to City and Guilds qualifications, suitable for those who wish to update skills. Welding Craft Practice, evenings, leads to City and Guilds 165, suitable for people with no previous welding knowledge. Horticulture, part time, leads to City and Guilds awards in various subjects – e.g. Amenity Horticulture, Decorative Horticulture, suitable for unemployed adults. Car Maintenance for the Owner-Driver, part time, includes servicing and preparation for MOT – could have earning potential. TA-sponsored ITEC unit – free courses for unemployed in subjects like Industrial Control by Computers, Introduction to Information Technology, Print Your Own Magazine (desktop publishing). Leisure courses with earning potential include Creative Writing, Painting and Drawing. Flexistudy courses (see 'Open and Distance learning'). An Educational and Career Guidance service can provide further guidance on entry criteria, and support is also available on basic skills such as confidence building, literacy and numeracy. Retraining for adults in employment also available through the college's own training company.

Bath School of Physiotherapy
Full-time 3-year course leading to Membership of the Chartered Society of Physiotherapy. School states: 'We do take mature students. The upper age limit is usually 35 years, although exceptions have been made up to the age of 40 years. Applicants are required to have the five O-levels as detailed in the prospectus, but only one academic A-level, preferably in a biological subject. Health related professional qualifications may be considered in lieu of the A-level.'

Bath School of Radiography
Full-time 3-year course leading to Diploma of the College of Radiographers (Diagnostic). Entry concessions possible in accordance with the regulations of the College of Radiographers which has a special panel to consider mature candidates. School states: 'We do consider mature students, and have no restrictions up to age 30 years. Between 30–40 years, we would like to be able to establish an applicant's likelihood of settling back to formal study and mobility for employment after qualification. We would consider applicants beyond 40 years of age only in exceptional cases.'

Bridgewater College
(1988, excluding courses formerly sponsored by the MSC.) Caring and Services, full time, for those wishing to work in the Social Services. RSA Counselling Skills course, mode unspecified. Open Learning, (see 'Open and Distance Learning Courses').

Bristol: Avon School of Nursing
Part-time 3 years 8 months course leading to the qualification of Registered General Nurse. Candidates without statutory academic entrance requirements may take the UKCC entry test. Prospectus states: 'This course is based on three periods of experience in each year, planned to run concurrently with the school terms of Avon County Education Committee. A 60-hour fortnight (30-hour week) will be a requirement of the course with fixed holidays at Christmas, Easter and in the Summer.'

Bristol: Brunel Technical College
HCIMA catering courses, part time, suitable for adult job-changers or 'women returners'. Beauty Therapy, full time, open to anyone over 18, leads to five City and Guilds awards. Hotel Reception, full time, open to anyone over 18. CAA-approved Aero Electronics, full time, leads to Category 'R' (Radio) Licence; mature student entry by interview, practical aircraft maintenance engineering experience often accepted in lieu of formal qualifications or advice given on suitable preliminary courses. CAA-approved Airframes and Engines, full time, leads to Category 'A' and 'C' Licence, for prospective aircraft maintenance engineers in civil aviation. BTEC Electronics and Communications Engineering courses for National/ Higher National awards, mature students may be accepted on the basis of an interview (no age restrictions). Fundamental Electronics, part time, for those who use electronic equipment and want to know how it works, no entry qualification. Links with St Paul's Outreach Centre (Inner City Project) – two former students of this centre are now on full-time Electronics Servicing courses. Courses in Essential Electricity, part time, for City and Guilds award, open to anyone in 16–50 age range, no formal entry qualifications.

Aeronautical Engineering for Mature Students
'One of our students, a woman in her late 20s, said she always wanted to work on and with aircraft, but was persuaded at school into a more ladylike career. She became a State Registered Nurse and a Ward Sister. Nevertheless, she felt this was not her true vocation and decided life was passing her by. She came to the college, obtained her CAA Airframes and Engines Licence (not without a little struggle because she was not a 'natural') and then emigrated to Australia. Another male student finally achieved his CAA-approved Aircraft Maintenance Licence when he was 41. He was originally rejected for the course because he lacked the minimum entry requirements, but we advised him to take a part-time course for some BTEC Level 1 units. These gained him entry to the CAA course. As his LEA would not give him a grant, he supported himself by working in the evenings and at weekends. He did so well that he was awarded the Society of Licensed

Aircraft Engineers and Technologists prize, and subsequently obtained work with Birmingham Executive Airways.'

(Spokesperson, Brunel Technical College)

Bristol: Diagnostic and Regional School of Therapeutic Radiography
Full-time 3-year courses leading to Diploma of the College of Radiographers (Diagnostic or Therapy). Entry concessions possible for candidates 24 years and over – they must offer five passes at GCSE Grades A–C to include Mathematics and Physics; a written English subject and one other science subject. The four points at GCE Advanced level required for students under 24 are not essential. NB: Other qualifications such as BTEC National Certificates/Diplomas or Higher National Certificates/Diplomas may be accepted as meeting the A-level requirement. School has not specified an upper age limit.

Bristol: Filton Technical College
TA-sponsored Export/Marketing, full time. BTEC National Certificate, part time or evenings, (options in Business Studies, Banking, Accountancy Technician's work). Entry concessions possible for mature students. BTEC Pre Higher National Certificate Conversion course, part time or evenings. Entry concessions possible for over-21s with GCE O-level English Language. Access to Information Technology 20-hour intensive courses, weekends/evenings. Supervisory Studies for NEBSS Certificate, part time/ evenings, no formal entry requirements for potential supervisors. Trade Union Studies, part time, for workplace representatives. Association of Accounting Technicians, part time or evenings, entry concessions for over-21s with two years' accounting experience. Finance Houses Association, evenings. Entry concessions for mature students. Wide range of Secretarial and Professional Institute courses – possible entry concessions for mature students. Flexistudy (see 'Open and Distance Learning Courses').

Cardiff: South East Wales School of Radiography
Full-time 3-year course leading to Diploma of the College of Radiographers (Diagnostic). Entry concessions possible in accordance with the regulations of the College of Radiographers which has a special panel to consider mature applicants. School states: 'Yes, we do accept mature students up to the age of about 40 years. The entry qualifications are usually flexible, depending on the educational background and experience if the candidates are 24 years old or over. These qualifications have to be approved by the College of Radiographers prior to registration.'

Cardiff:South Glamorgan Health Authority School of Physiotherapy
Full-time 3-year course leading to Membership of the Chartered Society of Physiotherapy. School states: 'Cardiff School of Physiotherapy has a fairly

large proportion of "mature" students, i.e. over 24. As far as entry requirements are concerned, many have a degree, but a considerable number has no formal qualifications. With this latter group we might offer a place on the proviso that they produce some evidence of recent academic work – an Open University Credit, some O- or A-levels etc. As far as age limits are concerned, we have had students of 40. Any prospective mature student should visit the school to which they apply to discuss their position.'

Cardiff: South Glamorgan Institute of Higher Education

(1988) 'We accept mature students on all our courses.' The college has indicated the following courses as attracting mature students: BTEC HND Design, full time. BTEC HND Business Studies and ND Business Studies, full time. BTEC HND Catering and ND Catering, BTEC HND Science (Medical Laboratory Sciences, full time. BTEC ND Dental Technology, full time. BTEC HND Science (Applied Biology) full time. BTEC ND Science, full time. BTEC HND Technology of Food, full time. BTEC ND Food Technology, full time. BTEC HND Hotel, Catering and Institutional Management, full time. BTEC ND Hotel, Catering and Institutional Operations, Diploma in General Catering, full time. Diploma in Baking (Technician) full time. Diploma in Baking (Craft) full time. BTEC ND Construction, full time. BTEC HNC/HND Engineering (Electronics and Communications) full time. BTEC HND Engineering (Electronic Products: Manufacture and Test) full time. BTEC ND Engineering (Electronics and Communications), full time. BTEC NC Engineering (Electronics) part time. BTEC HND Engineering (Plant and Engineering Services) full time. BTEC Diploma in Technology (Engineering) full time. City and Guilds Electronics Servicing, full time. Diploma in Social Work/Certificate of Qualification in Social Work (CQSW) full time, entry concessions for the over-25s. Certificate in the Education and Training of Mentally Handicapped People, full time, entry concession for over-23s but one year's paid or voluntary work experience essential. Working Together with people who have a Mental Handicap, sandwich. Candidates must be over 25 with five O-levels or equivalent and at least two years' work experience with mentally handicapped people. Chiropody, full time, see below. Ladies' Hairdressing/Beauty, full time, leads to IHBC and City and Guilds awards, entry by interview and test. Beauty Therapy and Hairdressing, full time, leads to seven awards including Remedial Cosmetology and Theatrical Make-up; candidates need three O-levels or equivalent and success in test and interview. Certificate in Printed Communication, full time; candidates normally need equivalent of CSE Grade 3 in three subjects; courses can lead into BTEC course or employment in Reprographics (see also 'Degree and Advanced Courses').

Cardiff: South Glamorgan Institute of Higher Education School of Chiropody

Full-time 3-year course based on the syllabus of the Society of Chiropodists and leading to State Registration in Chiropody. School states: 'Applications from mature students will be judged on their particular merits. What this means in practice is that we tend to offer all mature students an interview on the basis of their existing qualifications and relevant experience, i.e. nursing or some form of health care, laboratory or other scientific work. In our present first-year cohort we have a dental technologist, a dental assistant and a student with a graduate certificate in nursing. Our second year has a State Enrolled Nurse. Generally speaking, we have an upper age limit of 35 years. This tends in practice to be flexible up to another four years or so. Again, previous experience is sometimes a useful guide. People who have been used to manipulating small instruments or who had modelling or sensory skills may adapt to our practical techniques more readily.'

Cardiff: South Glamorgan School of Nursing
Full-time 3-year courses leading to qualification as a Registered General Nurse or Registered Mental Nurse or Registered Nurse for the Mentally Handicapped. Full-time two-year course leading to qualification as an Enrolled Nurse (General). Candidates without the statutory academic entrance requirements for Registration courses may take the UKCC entry test. Candidates for the Enrolled Nurse (General) course must have at least 2 academic O-levels at Grade C or above or two CSE Grade 1 passes, one of which must be English Language or History. No age limit is mentioned in this school's literature.

Cardiff: South Wales School for Therapeutic Radiography
Full-time 3-year course leading to Diploma of the College of Radiographers (Therapy). Entry concessions possible for mature candidates in accordance with the regulations of the College of Radiographers which has a special panel to consider mature applicants. This school did not mention an upper age limit.

Cheltenham: The College of St Paul and St Mary
(1988) Teaching English as a Foreign Language, full time, leading to RSA Preparatory Certificate, or Licentiate of Trinity College, London. Teaching English as a Foreign or Second Language; RSA Further Education Certificate (graduate, or graduate-equivalent, or teacher entrants). (See also 'Degree and Advanced Courses'.)

Chippenham Technical College
(1988, excluding courses formerly sponsored by the MSC.) Modular Office Skills, to suit students, part time. Publicity Production, full time and under 21-hour rule. Caring Skills, full time and part time. Managing the Office, part time, can lead to BTEC award. Making Numbers Work For You, part time, can lead to BTEC award. Improve Your Financial Decision-Making, part time, can lead to BTEC award. Mature Students' Typewriting, part time. Word Processing, part time. Advanced Hairdressing, full time or part

time. Supervisory Management, part time. ESF-sponsored Welding and Sheet Metalwork, full time. Mature students accepted on infill basis on many of the college's courses – unusual options include Horse Management and Training, full time, and Equestrian Studies for BTEC award, full time. Wide range of part-time courses with earning potential in and around Chippenham includes: Computing, Cookery, Copper Enamelling, Dress-making, Machine Knitting, Photography, Picture Framing, Pottery, Sewing Machine Techniques, Silversmithing, Upholstery, Writing for Profit, Book-Keeping, Business Studies, Electronics, Shorthand, Typewriting. Also Flexistudy (see 'Open and Distance Learning Courses').

Exeter College
Courses under the 21-hour rule: Leisure and Recreation, Catering, Manage-ment Training. Concessions for mature students without usual entrance qualifications on many courses. 'The main condition is *evidence* that the person in question is likely to succeed.'

Exeter: Devonshire College of Nursing and Midwifery
(Includes the former Exeter School of Nursing, Torbay School of Nursing and North Devon School of Nursing.) Full-time 3-year courses leading to qualification of Registered General Nurse or Registered Mental Nurse or Registered Nurse for the Mentally Handicapped. Candidates aged over 25 without statutory academic entrance requirements may be able to take the UKCC entry test. College states: 'All sections of the College accept mature entrants. There are no firm upper age limits as applications are treated on an individual basis.'

Exeter: The University of Exeter
Retraining for Women. The University is to run a part-time 9-week TA-sponsored Professional Updating Course for Women. All student fees will be paid.

Gloucester: Gloucester Health Authority School of Radiography
Full-time 3-year course leading to Diploma of the College of Radiographers (Diagnostic). Entry concessions possible for mature candidates in accord-ance with the regulations of the College of Radiographers which has a special panel to consider mature applicants. School states: 'Regarding upper age limit – considered on each individual case.'

Gloucester: The Gloucestershire School of Nursing
(Also at Cheltenham.) Full-time 3-year courses leading to qualification as a Registered General Nurse or Registered Mental Nurse or Registered Nurse for the Mentally Handicapped. Candidates without the statutory academic entrance qualifications for Registration courses aged 21 or over may take the UKCC entry test (see 'Introduction'). School states: 'We accept candidates

between the ages of 18 years and 50 years subject to the usual employment practices in respect to interview and health screening. We feel older candidates bring a wealth of experience into nursing which is essential in the caring relationship.' NB: This School of Nursing is looking at the possibility of part-time nurse training courses with mature students in mind.

Haverfordwest and Neyland: Pembrokeshire College
Extensive Employment Training (ET) provision. A wide range of professional, industrial, commercial (PICKUP) and retraining programmes in Catering, Business and Finance, Agriculture, Construction, Engineering, Hairdressing, Office Skills, Health Care and Computing.

Llanelli: Carmarthenshire College of Technology and Art
(1988, excluding courses formerly sponsored by the MSC.) ESF-sponsored Business Technology, full time. Open Learning (see 'Open and Distance Learning Courses').

Newtown: Montgomery College of Further Education
'The college accepts mature people on all courses and has done so for years.' TA-sponsored Employment Training courses are now becoming established at the college in Modern Office Technology, Electronics, Secretarial/Clerical and Caring. Other main areas of interest to mature entrants are a range of BTEC National Diplomas (Business Studies, Computing, Textiles, Catering and Hotel Management, Engineering, Nursery Nursing and Construction), Secretarial and Clerical courses and a wide range of First award and Craft courses. BTEC National Certificates can be arranged within Diploma programmes and in the past this has been a particularly attractive method for 'returners'. Short courses are available in Computing, Word and Information Processing, Desk Top Publishing and a range of areas in Electronics & Engineering and day-release facilities are also well established.

Plymouth College of Further Education
Nursery Nursing, full time, for NNEB award. Human Development, Child Care & Social Responsibility, full time, for NAMCW award. Family and Community, full time, for City and Guilds award. Recreation and Leisure Studies, full time for City & Guilds award. Community Care Practice, part time (Employment Training course) for City and Guilds award. In-Service course in Social work, part time, for CCETSW award. Further Education Teacher's Certificate, part time, for City and Guilds award. Teachers of Special Needs, part time, for City and Guilds award. Hairdressing, full time and part time, for City and Guilds award. Beauty Therapy, full time, for CIBTAC/CIDESCO awards. Beauty Therapy, full time, for City and Guilds award. Floristry, full time and part time. Flower Arranging. Floristry Refresher. Hairdressing Refresher. Hairdressing for City and Guilds award

(Employment Training course). Floristry for City and Guilds award (Employment Training course). Evening, day-release and block-release courses for NEBSM Supervisory Management awards. Introductory Certificate and Diploma awards in Operations Management; Retail: Personnel; Hotel and Catering; Safety; Security; Administrative Management and Computing Systems; Financial Services Management. Institution of Industrial Managers Certificate Course. Institute of Marketing Certificate courses. Association of Supervisors in Purchasing and Supply Certificate courses. Certified Diploma in Accounting and Finance course. College adds: 'Mature students form about 25% of our courses leading to BTEC National Diploma in Computer Studies and the City and Guilds Microcomputer Technology course. In addition, specialist 12-week courses leading to a BTEC Continuing Education Certificate are available for adults who wish to retrain quickly in the latest microelectronic techniques.' This college has also supplied details of all the courses in its School of Engineering Technology in a leaflet aimed at those preparing to leave school, and presumably also open to mature students. These include BTEC First, National and Higher Awards in various branches of the BTEC First Diploma in Construction and certain Marine Radio and Radar qualifications integrated within BTEC courses in Electronics and Communications Engineering.

Plymouth College of Further Education School of Chiropody
Full-time 3-year course leading to Membership of the Society of Chiropodists. Upper age limit normally 45 years of age. Entry concessions possible for mature students without the usual academic entry requirements. The school lists possible alternatives as: (i) an Open University Foundation Course in Science (S1O1) or Technology (T1O1); (ii) an Access course for students wishing to enter Higher Education to study a biology-based subject (available at the college); (iii) A Biology A-level plus a small range of GCSEs usually chosen after an informal interview with the prospective student.

Plymouth: Cornwall and Plymouth Schools of Nursing and Midwifery
The Cornwall base for this school is at the Royal Cornwall hospital (Treliske), Truro. Full-time 3-year course leading to qualification as a Registered General Nurse. Candidates without the statutory academic entrance requirements who are aged over 19 may take the UKCC entry test. Schools state: 'We do accept mature students and we do not have an upper age limit but consider candidates individually on their merit.'

Plymouth School of Radiography
Full-time 3-year courses leading to the Diploma of the College of Radiographers (Diagnostic or Therapy). Entry concessions possible for mature students in accordance with the regulations of the College of Radiographers which has a special panel to consider mature applicants. This school did not specify an upper age limit.

Pontyclun: Mid Glamorgan Health Authority School of Nursing
Full-time 3-year courses leading to qualification as a Registered General Nurse or Registered Mental Nurse or Registered Nurse for the Mentally Handicapped. Part-time 4-year course leading to qualification as a Registered General Nurse for mature students; 30-hour week, mainly school hours and terms. Candidates without statutory academic entrance requirements for Registered Nurse training may take the UKCC entry test (see 'Introduction'). School states: 'The Mid-Glamorgan School of Nursing has no upper age limit for mature students, and we have many students in their 50s currently training with us. Our part-time RGN course for men and women with children at school is currently over-subscribed.'

Pontypool College
Employment Training courses available. Mature students are also accepted on an infill basis to the following courses: BTEC National Diploma in General Art and Design; BTEC National Diploma in Business Studies (also with Secretarial options); BTEC First Diploma in Business and Finance; BTEC National Diploma in Science; BTEC National Diploma in Computer Studies; BTEC National Diploma in Construction; BTEC First Diploma in Construction; BTEC National Diploma in Electronic/General Engineering; BTEC National Diploma in Leisure; BTEC First Diploma in Leisure. Family and Community Care for City and Guilds 331 award. Catering for City and Guilds 706, 706/1, 706/2 awards. Nursery Nursing for NNEB qualification. Diploma in Hotel Reception and Front Office Practice. Hairdressing. Secretarial and Word Processing Studies. All the above are full-time courses. In addition, the college offers a range of part-time coures which can be studied as evening-only classes, day-release classes and block-release classes. (See also 'Pre-Entry, Sample and Access Courses' and 'Open and Distance Learning Courses'.)

Pontypridd: The Polytechnic of Wales
(1988, excluding courses formerly sponsored by the MSC.) Mature students without conventional entry requirements may be considered for many BTEC (and degree) courses at the discretion of the Polytechnic, and are advised to seek advice from the appropriate Course Leader before applying.

Poole: Dorset Institute of Higher Education
(1988) BTEC HND Business and Finance, full time. BTEC HND Business and Finance (Tourism) full time. BTEC HND Business Information Technology, full time. BTEC HND Hotel, Catering and Institutional Management, full time. BTEC HND Computer-Aided Engineering, full time. BTEC HND Practical Archaeology, full time. BTEC HNC in Electronics, full time. Most full-time courses are open to those mature students without formal qualifications who can present evidence that convinces admissions staff that they have the capacity and ability to succeed in and benefit from the course.

Rhyl: Clwyd School of Nursing
Full-time 3-year course leading to qualification of Registered General Nurse available at Clwyd North School of Nursing, Bodelwyddan and at Wrexham School of Nursing. Full-time 3-year course leading to qualification of Registered Mental Nurse available at North Wales Psychiatric School of Nursing, Denbigh. Upper age limit for all courses is 45 years. *Note*: These schools do not mention that the UKCC entry test is available to candidates without the statutory entrance requirements, so applicants are advised to offer GCE/GCSE in five academic subjects including English or Welsh or History (Grades A–C).

Salisbury College of Technology
(1988, excluding courses formerly sponsored by the MSC). Modern Technology; opportunities to learn or re-learn skills in Computer-Aided Engineering, short courses in Computer-Aided Draughting and Design (CAD), Introduction to Numerical Control (CNC), Further Numerical Control (CNC). Quality Assurance (QC). City and Guilds Further Education Teacher's Certificate, for practising or potential teachers/trainers in colleges, commerce, industry, public service, part time or evenings. Call Order Cookery, under 21-hour rule. Mature students welcome on infill basis to all part-time courses (send for part-time prospectus). BTEC Continuing Education Units in Business Administration and Management. Many leisure courses with earning potential, part time or evenings – examples: Picture Frame Restoration, Modern Furniture Repair and General Woodwork, Dressmaking, China Repair, Tailoring, Typing Skills, Machine Knitting, Small Outboard Engine Maintenance, Creative Writing, Bookbinding, Better Driving.

Salisbury School of Nursing
Full-time 3-year courses leading to qualification as a RegisteredGeneral Nurse or Registered Mental Nurse. Candidates without the statutory academic entrance requirements may take the UKCC entry test. School states: 'We accept mature students for nurse training, there is no upper age limit and all applications are considered individually.'

Street: Strode College
Mature students accepted on infill basis: possible subjects include Typewriting, Shorthand, Word-Processing, Hairdressing, Beauty Consultants etc. Pre-School Playgroup Foundation course, part time. Wide range of leisure courses with earning potential e.g. Cookery, Dressmaking, Machine Knitting, Quilting, Poultry-Keeping, Upholstery, Woodwork etc. Business Skills Workshop available for work with full range of Information Technology.

Swansea: South West Wales School of Radiography
Full-time 3-year course leading to Diploma of the College of Radiographers
(Diagnostic). Entry concessions possible for mature candidates in accordance with the regulations of the College of Radiographers which has a
special panel to consider mature applicants. School states: 'We do accept
mature candidates, from 24 to about 40 years of age.'

Swansea: West Glamorgan School of Nursing
Full-time 3-year course leading to qualification as a Registered General
Nurse or Registered Mental Nurse. Full-time 2-year course leading to
qualification as an Enrolled Nurse (General) or Enrolled Nurse (Mental).
Candidates without statutory academic entrance qualifications may take the
UKCC entry test. School states: 'We accept mature students, the upper age
limit being 47 years of age.'

Swindon School of Nursing
Full-time 3-year courses leading to qualifications of Registered General
Nurse or Registered Nurse for the Mentally Handicapped. Part-time 3 years
and 8 months course leading to qualification of Registered General Nurse
designed for mature entrants who because of domestic circumstances are
unable to undertake the existing full-time RGN course. Candidates without
statutory academic entry requirements for these courses may take the UKCC
entry test. The upper age limit for all three courses is 45, and for the part-
time RGN course, candidates should be aged between 25 and 45 and be
within easy travelling distance and have satisfactory transport from their
home to their place of work.

Taunton: Somerset College of Arts and Technology
TA-sponsored Modern Office Practice, full time. Sponsored Secretarial
Refresher/Upgrading, full time. Sponsored Accounting Technicians'
course, full time, leads to BTEC Certificate. Consideration given to mature
students for all courses; they find BTEC HND Graphic Design, full time, and
BTEC HND Textile and Surface Pattern Design, full time, attractive choices.
Selection by interview and portfolio work. Open Learning (see 'Open and
Distance Learning Courses').

Graphic Art Design for Mature Students: viewpoint
'I was a draughtsman in the Portsmouth area, and I left my job and got a
postman's job in Somerset so that I could find the time during the day to
develop my art. I'd been working alone, mainly in cartooning, but about
four years ago, I decided to try and get into art college, to just find out what I
wanted to do, and develop various styles. It was the best thing I could have
done and at the right time. If I'd left school and gone into art as my friends
did – well, most of them wasted it totally, and none of them are in art now. I
know exactly what I want to do and I'm totally committed to it. I've also

found the business studies side of my course very interesting; there are a few things that never crossed my mind. My plan is to buy my way into a group of established artists in a London agency, and I've discussed it with the business studies chap here and he gave me advice on it.'

(Student on HND Art course, Somerset College of Art and Technology)

'When we are choosing mature students for Art and Design courses, the main factor we look for is commitment. To decide to give up your job and take a minimum of three years' training is a pretty big decision for anybody. Certainly the first (Foundation) year is not likely to be very easy from the financial point of view, though the HND course will be supported by a mandatory award. Mature students, too, need to be able to see the career prospects ahead. Having made their decision, they have to be very sure about what they want. Provided they can produce evidence of really good work, it wouldn't matter that they were say 36 with no O-levels, even for a grant, when it came to the Higher National Diploma.'

(Spoksesperson, Somerset College of Art and Technology)

Taunton: Somerset School of Nursing
Full-time 3-year course leading to the qualification of Registered General Nurse or Registered Mental Nurse. Full-time 2-year course leading to the qualification of Enrolled Nurse (General) or Enrolled Nurse (Mental). Candidates for Registration courses without the statutory academic entrance requirements *may* be offered the opportunity to take the UKCC entry test. Candidates for Enrolled Nurse training should have 3 O-levels/ GCSEs at grades A, B or C, or CSE Grade 1 or a *minimum* of no less than 4 subjects at grade D or CSE grade 2. There is no entrance test for the Enrolled nurse courses and applicants not having an educational qualification in Mathematics or Arithmetic may be asked to demonstrate their ability to calculate using the metric system. School states: 'We certainly welcome mature applicants into nurse training, up to the age of 45. We cannot, however, make concessions for older candidates who do not meet our normal entry requirements.'

Tiverton: East Devon College of Further Education
(1988, excluding courses formerly sponsored by the MSC.) College specifies Technology, Engineering, Leisure and Recreation, Business Studies and Secretarial courses as attracting late starters.

Truro: Cornwall School of Radiography
Full-time 3-year course leading to Diploma of the College of Radiographers (Diagnostic). School states: 'We do accept mature students up to the age of 40 years. However, no special concessions are made to our educational qualifications for entry to our courses. Entry qualifications for all candidates to this school are as required by the College of Radiographers, i.e. 2 A-levels

and 5 O-levels. Other qualifications may be accepted in lieu of the two A-levels, e.g. suitable BTEC Diplomas.'

Weymouth College
(1988) Diploma in the Conservation of Stonework, full time, open to candidates with qualifications or experience necessary to benefit from the course; includes History of Sculpture, Carving, Stone Working and Building Technology, Conservation and Restoration. Open Learning (see 'Open and Distance Learning Courses').

Wrexham: North Wales School of Radiography
Full-time 3-year course leading to Diploma of the College of Radiographers (Diagnostic). Entry concessions possible for mature candidates in accordance with the regulations of the College of Radiographers which has a special panel to consider mature applicants. School states: 'We have suggested that probably the maximum intake age would be 37 years. Although the College of Radiographers states that mature students can enter the profession regardless of lack of qualifications if the person is deemed suitable by the School and Clinical Department, we would prefer these people to have a certain basic education, e.g. four or five O-levels or the equivalent, including English and Mathematics.'

Yeovil College
College states: 'The aim is to open up *all* courses from basic literacy to preparation for higher education and from basic numeracy to advanced engineering and business qualifications to mature people, and to give them appropriate support and tutorial help during their time at college. Plans are in hand to open a Women's Training Centre in Yeovil specifically to help women retrain in non-traditional skill areas where there are expected to be job opportunities, e.g. engineering, electronics, construction, motor vehicle etc.'

Scotland and Northern Ireland

Aberdeen College of Commerce
'We are keen to attract mature students to the college'. College offers full-time and part-time day and evening courses in the following subject areas: Accounting, Art and Design, Behavioural Studies, Computing, Communication, English as a Foreign Language, General Education, Languages, Legal Studies, Travel, Management and Marketing, Secretarial Studies. Students sit the examinations of: SCOTVEC, IPM, CAM, Trinity College London, Institute of Linguists etc.

Aberdeen:Grampian School of Occupational Therapy
Full-time 3-year course leading to Diploma of the College of Occupational Therapists. College states: 'The Grampian School of Occupational Therapy welcomes applicants, both men and women, who have had work experience since leaving school. The professional body advises that those over the age of 40 would find the course taxing, and it is therefore progressively more difficult to be selected over this age. Applicants under 21 must have the full academic entrance requirements ... Applicants over 21 will be considered on an individual basis. They must, however, show evidence of recent academic achievement and experience with the disadvantaged. The scope of this evidence must necessarily vary, but Higher National Diplomas, nursing qualifications for the Register, half credits with the Open University etc. would be acceptable as would successful study for Highers at evening or day classes. English is recommended and Biology and Anatomy, Physiology and Health have proved useful.' NB: This school's prospectus makes the point that due to economic cutbacks, the DHSS has decided not to award grants to English and Welsh students wishing to train in Scotland.

Aberdeen: Grampian School of Physiotherapy
Full-time 3-year course leading to Membership of the Chartered Society of Physiotherapy. School states: 'We do indeed accept mature students with a tentative upper age limit of 35, but this along with entry qualifications is considered on an individual basis for each mature candidate. We do expect candidates to have shown evidence of recent academic involvement so that they have experienced college life and studying prior to entry on the course.'

Alloa: Clackmannan College of Further Education
Full-time advanced courses in Accounting, Business Studies, Secretarial
Studies; full-time and part-time National Certificate programmes in Build-
ing and Horticultural Skills, Business Studies, Child Care, Health Care,
Carpentry and Joinery, Catering, Computer Studies, Construction, Design,
Distribution, Engineering, Hairdressing, Hotel Reception, Motor Vehicle
Engineering, Secretarial Studies.

Antrim: Northern Area College of Nursing
Full-time 3-year course leading to qualification as a Registered General
Nurse. College states: 'Mature applicants – aged 25 or over – are accepted
into nurse training. Because we have experienced no problems in recruiting
so far the UKCC Entrance Test is applied only to mature students.' NB: the
prospectus states that this test is only offered to people aged 25 and over.

Belfast College of Mental Health Nursing
Full-time 3-year course leading to the qualification of Registered Mental
Nurse. School states: 'Mature students are accepted with an upper age limit
of 45 (normally) but they are required to fulfil the minimum entry
requirements (see 'Introduction') and no special arrangements or entry
concessions apply with respect to mature students.'

Belfast College of Technology
(1988) Courses for unemployed adults, part time, include Computing Skills,
Word Processing, Programming in BASIC, Photography, Gardening, Motor
Vehicle Maintenance, Home Electrics, Brickwork, Plumbing, Decoration,
Woodwork, Garment Making, Domestic Machine Knitting, Contemporary
Affairs, Communication Skills.

Belfast College of Technology: Northern Ireland School of Chiropody
Full-time 3-year course leading to Diploma of the Society of Chiropodists.
School states: 'We do accept mature students and there exists no upper age
limit. Mature students, like A-level students, all have to attend for
interview. On the basis of the interview, which must be combined with
evidence from the student that he/she is capable of studying "to degree
level", a decision regarding a place will be made.'

Belfast Southern College of Nursing
Full-time 3-year course leading to qualification as a Registered General
Nurse. College states: 'We have defined "mature" as those aged 25 and over
on date of the commencement of training and not more than 45 years of age.
Those applicants over 25 years of age not in possession of (statutory
academic entrance requirements) may take an approved Entrance Test
measuring numeracy and literacy.'

Clydebank College
TA-sponsored programmes (subjects not specified). SCOTVEC National Certificate modular courses; you can choose your own modules and make up a 21-hour course of study.

Dumfries and Galloway College of Technology
TA-sponsored Catering Crafts, full time. TA-sponsored Catering, full time. Mature students over 21 may be granted entry concessions on SCOTVEC HND/HNC full-time courses – popular options are Business Studies, Computer Studies, Information Studies and Secretarial Studies. Courses that may be of additional interest are: the SCOTVEC NC programme for Medical Secretaries, full time, over-21s may be granted entry concessions; and the Institute of Clerks of Works Mature Candidates' Course – evenings, for people over 40 with at least five years' relevant experience. There are 21-hour opportunities in Engineering and Science. Skills Training Programme for unemployed people, shift workers, housewives, retired people in a wide range of options, such as Brickwork, Carpentry and Joinery, Painting and Decorating, Interior Design, Screen Printing, Upholstery etc.

Dundee: Duncan of Jordanstone College of Art
Up to 10% of admissions to First Year General Course in Art and Design may be without formal qualification, on the basis of outstanding portfolio of work and by satisfying selectors of the candidate's ability to complete the course. Diploma in Home Economics, full time, welcomes mature students, as does SCOTVEC HND Catering, Hotel and Institutional Management, full time.

Edinburgh: The British Isles Study Programme
Part-time Tour Management training course with lectures all day Saturday, including an eight-day training tour. Applicants must be at least 25 and preference is given to people with foreign language qualifications. Course is approved by the Association of British Travel Agents (ABTA) and leads to City and Guilds Certificate in Tour Management. (For more details, see under 'London and Middlesex' in this section.)

Edinburgh College of Art
Up to 10% of exceptionally gifted students may be admitted to courses without formal entry qualifications, on the basis of portfolio suitability, essy and/or interview. The college states that: 'The Central (Art) Institutions are empowered to admit a very small number of students annually who do not hold the requisite academic qualifications but whose portfolios of work are of an exceptionally high standard. In support of applications for courses in Art, candidates are required to submit a portfolio of their own unaided work. The College's assessment of the standard and promise indicated by the portfolio of work is of great importance in arriving at the final selection of candidates.'

Edinburgh: Napier Polytechnic of Edinburgh
HND Legal Studies, full time – those aged 21-plus may be granted entry concessions. Diploma in Careers Guidance, full time – those aged 25-plus with at least five years' relevant work experience may be granted entry concessions. SCOTVEC HND Business Studies, full time – those aged 21-plus may be granted entry concessions. College Diploma and Membership of the British Institute of Interior Decorators, full time – candidates must have two A-levels or three H-grades. SCOTVEC HND Printing (Administrative and Production), full time, candidates must have two H-grades.

Edinburgh: Queen Margaret College School of Chiropody
Full-time 3-year course leading to Diploma of the Society of Chiropodists. No upper age limit is specified and SCE, GCE or SCOTVEC qualifications may be accepted to satisfy academic entry requirements.

Edinburgh: Queen Margaret College Department of Physiotherapy
Full-time 3-year course leading to BSc in Physiotherapy. College states: 'We do accept mature students with an upper age limit of mid-30s. Candidates must have the minimum qualifications for entry to a degree course.' (See 'Introduction'.)

Edinburgh School of Diagnostic Radiography
Full-time 3-year course leading to Diploma of the College of Radiographers (Diagnostic). Entry concessions possible for mature candidates in accordance with the regulations of the College of Radiographers which has a special panel to consider mature applicants. No upper age limit mentioned by this School.

Edinburgh: Telford College of Further Education
Wide range of Open Learning opportunities (see 'Open and Distance Learning').

Fermanagh College of Further Education
'Fermanagh College aims to provide open access for handicapped and able-bodied mature students to the full range of full-time and part-time courses on the Eniskillen campus and in the large number of Outcentres throughout the County.' Courses include: BTEC First and National courses in Building Studies, Business and Finance, Computer Studies, Construction, Distribution, Engineering and Leisure Studies, and Higher BTEC in Business and Related Studies (including Tourism). City and Guilds Craft, Advanced Craft and Supplementary Studies in Building, Caring, Catering, Distribution, Engineering, Hairdressing and Recreational and Leisure Studies. RSA Higher Diploma in Administration. LCC1 programmes in Secretarial Studies and NEBSS awards in Supervisory Studies.

Glasgow: Anniesland College
'We welcome mature students on all our courses.' Candidates over the age of 21 who do not possess the normal entry requirements may be admitted at

the Principal's discretion. Full-time courses leading to the award of the SCOTVEC National Certificate include Business Studies, CAD/CAM, Computer Studies, Electronics, Leisure and Recreation, Marine Engineering for Small Boat Builders, Medical Secretaryship, Secretarial Studies, Stringed Instrument Repair and Travel and Tourism. Full-time SCOTVEC Higher National Diploma courses in Business Studies, Computing and Secretarial Studies are offered. Part-time courses include day release and evening, and unemployed adults can attend for up to 21 hours per week. A wide range of subjects is available including Art, Catering, Computing, Construction, EFL, Engineering, Fashion and Secretarial. Candidates for non-advanced and advanced courses may be eligible for bursaries or awards respectively.

Glasgow Northern College of Nursing and Midwifery
Full-time 3-year courses leading to the qualifications of Registered General Nurse or Registered Mental Nurse or Registered Nurse for the Mentally Handicapped. Candidates without the statutory academic entrance requirements may take the UKCC entry test. College states: 'We are more than willing to consider mature candidates, and while we have no fixed upper age limit, this appears to be self-limiting beween the age of 45 and 50 years.'

Glasgow: The Queen's College School of Physiotherapy
Full-time 3-year degree course leading to BSc in Physiotherapy. College states: 'We do consider mature applicants for the BSc in Physiotherapy. Age limits are nomally from 21–35, although the upper age limit is not laid down as sometimes applicants with exceptional qualifications may be accepted. Mature applicants are considered individually on their work experience and the qualifications they already hold. They are not expected to achieve the qualifications required of a school-leaver. Usually some evidence of recent study is required and we do prefer applicants who have studied science subjects. Our annual intake is 82 and we currently can only accept around 10% of that number as mature applicants.'

Glasgow: The Queen's College School of Radiography
Full-time 3-year course leading to Diploma of the College of Radiographers (Diagnostic). Entry concessions possible for mature candidates in accordance with the regulations of the College of Radiographers which has a special panel to consider mature applicants. This School does not mention an upper age limit.

Glasgow School of Chiropody
Full-time 3-year course leading to Diploma of the Society of Chiropodists. College states: 'Normal upper age limit – 45 years. Entry qualifications are either two Higher (Scottish) or Access Course with relevant SCOTVEC modules.'

Glasgow: The University of Strathclyde
Effective Management Programme – seven separate but interrelated modules, which may be taken separately or built into a comprehensive management development programme. Effective Supervision – 3-day course, repeated during the year. Both these are organised by the Strathclyde Business School of the University.

Inverness College of Further and Higher Education
(1988) Study programmes are organised on a modular basis; in theory, therefore, anyone can take any module. Assessment is by continuous monitoring (no exams). You select modules to make up your own study programme, and unemployed people can take up to six half-day modules under the 21-hour rule without losing benefit. Study areas specifically recommended for unemployed/mature people are in Hotel and Catering Administration, Food Trades, Home Crafts, Mechanical and Petroleum Engineering. Open Learning (see 'Open and Distance Learning Courses').

Kilmarnock: Ayrshire and Arran College of Nursing and Midwifery
Full-time 3-year courses leading to qualification as a Registered General Nurse or Registered Mental Nurse. Training leading to the qualification of Registered Nurse for the Mentally Handicapped is not undertaken in Ayrshire but secondment to other Health Boards may be arranged. No upper age limit is specified. College states:'There are limited opportunities for mature candidates over the age of 23 to sit an entrance test.'

Kirkcaldy: Fife College of Nursing and Midwifery
Full-time 3-year courses leading to qualifications of Registered General Nurse or Registered Mental Nurse or Registered Nurse for the Mentally Handicapped. Full-time 2-year courses leading to qualifications of Enrolled Nurse (General), Enrolled Nurse (Mental) or Enrolled Nurse (Mental Handicap). College states: 'We use the University definition of maturity, i.e. 23 years of age and above. Our upper age limit would be 50 years. Requirements are as stated for entrance to nurse education by the UKCC regulation. We are as flexible as possible under these regulations, e.g. (1) Minimum is 5 O-grades in SCE at 1, 2 or 3 banding. English must be one of the subjects. (2) The equivalent of 5 O-grades using a pointage system of (a) 1 point for an O-grade, 2 points for an H-grade, two and a half points for a full Open University Credit (b) SCOTVEC modules accepted by the UKCC. (3) UKCC entrance test.'

Melrose: Scottish Borders College of Nursing
Full-time 3-year course leading to qualification as a Registered General Nurse. Candidates without statutory academic entrance requirements who are aged over 23 may take the UKCC entry test. College states: 'The age limit for mature entrants is based on individual candidates, up to the age of 48 years.'

Motherwell College
Mature students are accepted on all full-time courses (1 year unless stated) leading to SCOTVEC National Certificate awards, e.g. Foundation Courses in Automobile Engineering, Mechanical and Production Engineering, Fabrication and Welding, Electrical and Electronic Engineering, Business Studies, Marketing, Office Skills, Catering Craft, Hotel Reception, Bakery and Confectionery, Catering Technician (2 years), Diploma in Building (2 years), Nursery Nursing, Pre-Nursing, Clothing Studies, Leisure and Recreation, Travel and Tourism, Social Care, Media Studies, Computing. SCOTVEC Higher National Certificate courses (full-time and part-time): Business Studies, Secretarial Studies, Travel and Tourism, Distribution Studies, Computing, Motor Vehicle Engineering, Multi-Disciplinary Engineering, Fabrication and Welding. Students with disabilities can be accepted on to most courses and are supported in their studies by the considerable resources of the Special Needs Department.

Newry: Newcastle College of Further Education
(1988) Pre-School Playgroups, part time, for City and Guilds award. Open Learning under consideration.

Newtownabbey College of Further Education
Adults are welcome to enrol for any course in the college, full time or part time, and there is no upper age limit. Adult Unemployed Initiative, part time – options in Vehicle Maintenance, Welding, Metalwork Skills, BTEC First and National Diplomas, full time, and Certificates, part time, in Business and Finance, Engineering and Construction. Over-19s without minimum qualifications admitted at Principal's discretion. Wide range of part-time courses leading to RSA (Certificate of Continuing Education) and City and Guilds awards, e.g. Computer Programming, Welding, Engineering, Motor Vehicle Crafts, Plumbing, Heating and Ventilating, Radio and Television Electronics etc. – for school-leavers but open to adults on an infill basis. Office Skills/Secretarial subjects, part time and evenings, in Shorthand, Typewriting, Audio Typing, Word-Processing etc. Leisure courses with earning potential, part time, include Creative Embroidery, Dressmaking, Recreational Metalwork, Recreational Brickwork, Recreational Woodwork, Recreational Car Maintenance, Video Techniques. Many of the above can be taken through Open Learning courses (see 'Open and Distance Learning Courses').

Perth College of Further Education
Directed training for Employment Training available across the range of college subjects. SCOTVEC modular courses in a range of subject areas including Business Studies, Secretarial Studies, Computing, Rock Music, Media Studies, Catering, Hairdressing, Retail, all aspects of Building and Construction, Engineering, Motor Vehicle Engineering, Land-Based Industries, Sport and Recreation, Drama, Art and Design, Hotel Reception,

Beauty Care, Nursery Nursing, Social Care, Pre-Nursing, Care of the Elderly.SCOTVEC HND/HNC in Computing, HNC in Media Studies, HNC in Rock Music, HND/HNC in Accounting, HND/HNC in Business Studies (with or without languages), HND/HNC in Secretarial Studies (with or without languages).

SMALL BUSINESS AND SELF-EMPLOYMENT COURSES

Ideas and courses that teach marketable skills and profitable ways of using them

Introduction

Working for yourself is very tempting to anyone who gets tired of the 'work-mortgage-work' lifestyle described so aptly by someone I once interviewed. But it can disintegrate into a 'work-no mortgage-work' lifestyle that is even tougher than punching a time clock unless you are very careful about the kind of business you are going to set up and how you are going to make a profit.

The temptation to go it alone beckons even more seductively when redundancy not only makes a nonsense of career plans, qualifications, overtime and all that, but presents you with a lump sum you can invest in yourself. This is when the 'How can I fail?' syndrome takes over. 'If I employed myself...' the argument goes 'I wouldn't have to rely on whether the marketing department was efficient. I wouldn't have to price my products so highly that they couldn't compete. I could even offer extra services (delivery/gift-wrapping, late-night opening).'

At this stage it's very wise for the would-be entrepreneur to take a small business course. You do need to be enthusiastic to be self-employed but you also need to be able to bounce your ideas off someone who is strictly practical – the sort of person who will say 'Yes, but what's the profit margin?' when you suggest a delivery service, or 'Yes, but what will it cost you?' when you propose staying open until eight in the evening.

Often the lecturers at small business and self-employment courses have themselves been self-employed. They know the demands and the long hours involved in simply getting a business to tick over. It may be true as TV advertisements tell us that 'Inside every employed person is a self-employed one'. But before taking the plunge, you need to consider if you are the sort of person willing to accept the unsocial hours of self-employment, and having to work without sick pay or holiday pay. You also need to be capable of coping, in the same week, with the challenge of getting extra credit from the bank, quoting for a vital long-term order and getting the VAT return in on time. These are the aspects of self-employment that take their toll of enthusiasm, rather than matters like under-cutting the competition or thinking up new publicity stunts.

Any skills you can learn in advance, from how to keep books in a way that satisfies the Income Tax authority to using a computer for stock control records, will save your time and temper when you are actually in business. These may seem rather dull subjects to study when you are longing to get your enterprise off the ground, but the time will come when, wishing there were 60 hours in the day or 12 days in the week, you'll be glad to be able to whisk through your essential 'business housekeeping' and concentrate on turning out your products or promoting your service.

Helping Hands

Apart from benefitting from expert advice on a small business course, it is constructive to think ahead and ask yourself where you can get further help if you need it. Not having a boss has its compensations, but you will also have no-one around to say 'How awful!' when you have a problem or a tragedy and need to take a few days off. Good friends, who will step in when you are carted off to hospital with appendicitis, are worth their weight in gold, for, sympathy or no sympathy, your clients will be depending on you and you'll lose them if you let them down. (Incidentally, though the NHS will whip out your appendix with instant and splendid efficiency, you will find you can't even direct your business by phone from a hospital bed in a general ward, so private medical insurance has especial value for the small businessman/woman. It's not so much the speed of treatment but facilities like a phone, the ability to instruct your helper(s) or even see your most valued customer while you're recovering.)

Insurance is a word to keep closely in mind when you are thinking of going self-employed, and I don't only mean the kind of official policy you take out to protect you against employers' liability, accident or illness. You need to consider the kind of business you are in, and imagine what kind of trouble might lose you an important customer. How can you provide yourself with a safety net?

For instance, suppose your business activity includes delivery of a large number of heavy packages of brochures by road as soon as they are printed, and your van breaks down. Have you a network of good friends who will lend you transport, or a contact in the local car hire firm who will rent you a van instantly? Do you really understand how the Red Star parcels systems works? (Red Star once saved *my* neck when I left a vital tape-recording needed for the next day's radio programme up in Derby; the interviewer found it and despatched it instantly to my home railway station.)

COLLEGE EXPERTISE

It's this kind of tip that you're likely to be given on a small business course, along with advice on costing, on record-keeping, on advertising and promotion and on legal,insurance and tax problems. If you want to be able to concentrate on making a success of your business, you owe it to yourself to learn the basics of management first, so that the everyday business procedures become a matter of routine, leaving your 'fine tuning' to be given to the product or the service you offer. You can't afford to waste time worrying whether you've set aside the right percentage of sales for VAT, or ordered enough invoice forms to see the quarter through.

On college small business courses, you can, for example, learn about computers, using *their* computers and *their* discs, rather than trying to teach yourself on your own new and very expensive equipment at home after a day's work. If your business happens to rely on regular supplies of materials from outside suppliers, a business course leader can help you devise an ordering and stock control system that will ensure items are automatically re-ordered before you run out. That's when you'll be advised about setting up a back-up provision, for getting materials when there is a rail, road or postal strike.

Some of the courses listed in this section are provided by colleges with the support of the Training Agency – they'll be identified by 'TA-sponsored', or by a mention of Employment Training. For people who satisfy the entry conditions, they're free. But even for non-sponsored courses, costs are moderate, e.g. an evening course called 'Mind Your Own Business' at Sutton College of Liberal Arts costs £16 for one session a week for ten weeks.

ENTERPRISE TRAINING

If you are unemployed, aged between 18 and 60 and want to start a business, you are eligible to enter Enterprise Training in Employment Training. (For this training, there is no requirement to have been unemployed for any set length of time.)

There are various components to Enterprise Training which can include several elements. Here's how the Training Agency describes them:

1. *Formal start up training* (e.g. Business Development Programme (BEP) courses).
2. *Assignments* in which trainees are given enterprise-related tasks (market research, visits to banks to discuss loans) and then report and discuss their findings.
3. *Occupational Training*, where trainees need to develop particular skills and knowledge to carry out their business idea.
4. *Counselling sessions* where the trainees can discuss the problems and progress of their business plans. These may be arranged individually or for a group; and
5. *Enterprise Rehearsal* in which trainees can try out their business idea under the control of the (locally appointed) Training Manager. Trainees continue to receive their training allowance, and money generated by the trading is controlled by the Training Manager, although any profits are made over to the trainee when they leave the programme. Enterprise Rehearsal will normally be taken to the final part of a trainee's time on the programme and is subject to a maximum of six months (trainees eligible for the Enterprise Allowance Scheme should restrict their time on Enterprise Rehearsal to three months).

ENTERPRISE ALLOWANCE

This is one of the most successful government projects to help individuals get a business off the ground. You can claim £40 per week for up to 52 weeks to help you get your business started. There are rules to abide by; you must have been unemployed for 8 weeks on the date you apply, you must apply *before* you start the business and you must have access to £1000 capital (which may be in the form of a loan from a bank). Any Jobcentre has a leaflet with details.

BUSINESS ENTERPRISE PROGRAMME (BEP)

This offers classroom sessions spread over a 5-week period and covers topics such as marketing, market research and book-keeping. *It is open to employed and self-employed people*. The training is free. Participants on BEP who are not eligible for Employment Training may not undertake any of the other elements of the Enterprise Training Programme listed above and do not receive a Training Agency allowance.

GRADUATE ENTERPRISE PROGRAMME (GEP)

This is designed for recently qualified graduates who want to set up their own business. It offers initial Briefing Sessions and Business Workshops to students in their final year considering self-employment, followed by 20 days of intensive business management training at a Business School for a selection of those committed to starting up. (The Careers Advice Service in Higher Education institutions can provide further details.)

BUSINESS GROWTH TRAINING – INCLUDING PEP

For those already established in business, the Training Agency has recently launched Business Growth Training, which includes five options to help tackle a wide range of training requirements of employers and owner/managers. Option 2 is PEP – the Private Enterprise Programme – especially for small firms. PEP offers a range of one-day seminars in a range of business topics such as Marketing, Selling Skills and Computing in small business. There is a charge of £35 for attendance at each day, which includes a workbook on the subject which can be taken away for reference.

FIRMSTART

For new businesses in their first three years of trading and with a realistic potential to expand, Firmstart offers part-time training over a 6-month period in the evenings and at weekends, which allows participants to meet their existing business commitments. Leading Business Schools around the country provide Firmstart and entry is competitive. There is a charge of about £200 to participants on Firmstart.

More details of Enterprise Training are readily available from the Training Agency, which is based at Moorfoot, Shefield, Sl 4PQ. But a quicker way of getting details of what's offered in your particular area might be to ask your

Jobcentre where you can contact your locally-appointed Enterprise Training Manager.

BACKGROUND READING
As well as taking a course – perhaps even before you take a course – it will help to read about self-employment and small business, and to get an idea of how other people have coped. Two very useful handbooks, both by Godfrey Golzen, who has made something of a speciality of advising future entrepreneurs, are *Going Freelance* – particularly strong on ideas for second incomes, and *Working for Yourself* – explaining how to set up a business and keep it running efficiently. Both books are published by Kogan Page who published this book.

COURSE LISTS
The courses listed in the sections which follow mostly concentrate on the nuts and bolts of setting up and running a business, e.g. raising finance, keeping books, selling, dealing with tax and insurance and so on. There are also a few courses on particular kinds of business, e.g. Running a Retirement Home or Heavy Goods Vehicle Driving. Some people have chosen to set up on their own after taking some of the courses in the 'Retraining and New Skills Courses' section. If you think you are the right sort of person to manage a business, but you need an idea on which to base it, take a look through the subjects in that section which colleges have suggested have 'earning potential' and you may find there is a skill you can learn and then market as a small business service or product.

DON'T MISS OUT
Always check with your Jobcentre on the latest government initiatives to help people set up in business for themselves. As new schemes are announced and colleges get involved in them, course titles may change, but the Jobcentre should know not only what's on offer, but what may be planned for next term as part of the area's Enterprise Training provision.

London and Middlesex

College for the Distributive Trades
'Your Own Shop', part time, evenings. Certificate of Travel Agency Competence, part time, evenings.

East London Polytechnic
Short courses in Small Business Management – content and mode to suit individual needs.

London College of Printing
Diploma in Publishing Production, full time, for people who want to set up in book or magazine production.

Middlesex Polytechnic
Business Enterprise Programme, part time.

Morley College
(1988) Running a Workers' Co-operative, evenings. How to Survive Information and Work Overload, evenings. Many leisure courses with earning potential (see 'Retraining and New Skills Courses').

North London College
A range of part-time and evening short courses in Business Skills, Media and Computing is available.

North London Polytechnic
Short courses in Business Management.

Paddington College
Computing for Small Businesses is offered as part of BTEC National Certificate/Diploma in Computer Studies. Short course in Book-keeping may also be available.

South East London College
(1988) Guest House and Small Establishment Management, part time, for City and Guilds award. Cooks' Professional course, part time or evenings,

for City and Guilds award – suitable for those planning to set up their own catering service.

South West London College
(1988) Community Entrepreneurs' Training Programme, part time, for people involved in organisational or management role in community-based employment project; specially useful for people from ethnic minority self-help projects.

Thames Polytechnic
Courses in running small businesses are offered by the Small Business Unit.

Uxbridge College
Employment Department Training Agency Enterprise Programme. Enterprise Awareness Days (one-day). Business Enterprise Programme (six-seven days) and Private Enterprise programme (day-long modules) for those setting up or developing their own business.

Southern and Eastern England

Aylesbury College
(1988) At their Hampden Hall, Stoke Mandeville Centre, the college's short course unit offers a variety of intensive courses lasting from one to five days. Subjects include: Starting Your Own Smallholding; Taking a Small Farm; Going Self-Employed in Rural Enterprises; Flower Arranging for Restaurants, Shops and Offices; Producing Food Organically; Garden Design and Planning; Principles of Vegetable Growing. There is a 'back to nature' approach to Pig-Keeping, Goat-Keeping and many other subjects.

An Income from the Land: viewpoints
'My husband and I plan to have a small amount of land and keep chickens, bees and a couple of sheep, and also grow vegetables, but mostly we'll sell free-range eggs. Our idea is to sell our house and get something a bit run down to do up, which means we would have a bit of money left over to do what we want. But my husband still wants to commute to London, so we can't go too far.'

'From this course, I've sorted out the animals we want. I was quite keen on having a house cow, but I've changed my mind about that. I didn't like the idea of the calf every year that you have to do something with. I would perhaps have gone in for the wrong things without this course.'

'I'm a barrister, but I've wanted to be a farmer ever since I was five, and I was very surprised to find you could learn about farming in "dribs and drabs" of a few days here and there. I had always imagined that you'd have to do a full-time course, which would take you away from what you were already doing. At the moment I'm in the marvellous position of being able to carry on with my current employment while I learn about something else. Hopefully, by the time I've spent a bit of time doing a few courses, I'll be in a position to move out of my current job and into something else without any fear that it's going to fail.'

(Starting Farming students, Aylesbury College)

Bracknell College
Business Enterprise Programme. 7 days' free government-sponsored training covering Business Planning, Marketing, Book-keeping and Accounts.

Bromley College of Technology
(1988, excluding courses formerly sponsored by the MSC.) BTEC Post-Experience courses (various options) teaching useful business/management skills, part time and under 21-hour rule. The college has a Small Business Club.

Cambridge: Cambridgeshire College of Arts and Technology
This college is merging with Essex Institute of Higher Education and no information about courses is available during this process.

Chichester: West Dean College
(1988) Independent College. West Dean/British Antique Dealers' Association courses in Restoration of Antique Clocks, full time; Restoration of Antique Ceramics and Porcelain, full time; Restoration of Antique Furniture, full time. NB: these are advanced courses. Also numerous short full-time courses in subjects with earning potential, like Upholstery, Cabinet-Making, Blacksmithing, Pottery, Cane Seating, Silversmithing etc. (See'Retraining and New Skills Courses'.)

Antique Clock Restoration
'I've always been interested in clocks, but there just isn't anybody doing the kind of course in Scotland where I live, so it seemed a good idea to come down here and study and then go back when I was reasonably accomplished and could set up in business. There are probably only one or two other people who would represent any competition to me and there are lots of nice clocks about to restore. If you are a good restorer, people will pay for it, because they know your work will last for a very long time.'
                    (Student, West Dean College, Chichester)

'Students don't need to have previous training in clock making, but they do need to be dextrous and demonstrate an aptitude for the intricate work. Clocks for restoration are supplied by antique dealers, museums and private owners. The West Dean/BADA Diploma in Clock Restoration is awarded to students on successful completion of the course. Final assessments are based on continous assessment of practical work, a written paper and a visual recognition test. Diplomas are awarded on satisfactory completion of the course.'
                    (Spokesperson, West Dean College, Chichester)

Epsom: North East Surrey College of Technology
(1988) Accounting for Small Businesses, evenings. Microcomputers in Business, part time or evenings. Thinking of Starting a Guest House? – occasional course. Management and Care Training Course for Proprietors and Managers of Voluntary and Private Residential Homes, part time.

Havering Technical College
(1988, excluding courses formerly sponsored by the MSC.) Book-keeping for the Small Businessman, part time. Start Your Own Business, part time. Word Processing, part time. Information Processing, part time.

Hemel Hempstead: Dacorum College
(1988) Start Your Own Business, short course. BTEC National Certificate in Business and Finance, modes not specified – please ask college.

Kingston Polytechnic
Variety of short courses – contact Kingston Regional Management Centre for up-to-date programme.

Mendlesham: RTT Training Services Ltd
(Independent college) Range of courses connected with Road Transport and Road Transport Management – in particular: courses for RSA Certificate of Professional Competence to run National/International Road Transport Operations and intensive courses for HGVI, II, III and PSV licences. Various short courses that might be combined with driving for self-employment, e.g. Prospecting for Sales, Distribution Management.

Heavy Goods Vehicle Driving
'The duration of HGV training is subject to an assessment of a candidate's ability, but it can last from about five to 15 days. I would expect an average ability candidate to pass the Class I HGV driving test in about 10–12 days. The course consists of 30% theory – the theory of driving, observation and planning, the Highway Code, safety regulations, mechanical conditions and the tachography – and the other 70% is on the road. Taking the test is all part of the training package.'
(Spokesperson, RTT Training Services, Mendlesham)

Morden: Merton College
Licensed Conveyancers, details on request. Starting Your Own Business, part time. Book-keeping for the Self-Employed, part time. Law for the Self-Employed/Taxation for the Self-Employed/Computer Uses in the Small Business – apply to the college for details. Wide range of evening computer courses for small business owners.

Norwich City College
Proprietors of Private and Voluntary Homes for the Elderly, evenings. Proprietors of Private Residential Homes for the Elderly and Handicapped, residential, one week full time.

Portsmouth Polytechnic
In addition to the extensive full-time and part-time course programme, a considerable number of short residential courses on various topics is offered by the Portsmouth Management Centre.

Slough: Langley College
Book-keeping for the Small Businessman, part time. Start Your Own Business, part time. Word-Processing, part time. Information Processing, part time.

Sutton College of Liberal Arts
Part-time courses in Computers, Typewriting, Mind Your Own Business, Tax and Accounts, Start Your Own Catering Business, Word Processing/Office Skills.

Watford: Cassio College
(1988) Short Course Unit runs a series of one-day and part-time evening courses including Book-keeping, Accountancy, Retail Customer Care, Consumer Law, Retail Security and Loss Prevention, Telephone Techniques. Small Business courses are also offered through Open Learning (see 'Open and Distance Learning Courses') including subjects like Pub Management, Running a Guest House etc. The Department of Adult Studies runs 'Starting and Running a Small Business' course, mode unspecified – please ask college.

Welwyn Garden City: De Havilland College
(1988) Starting and Running Your Own Business, evenings. Accounting for Small Businesses, evenings. Computer-based Accounting, evenings. Introduction to Salesmanship, evenings. Communication for Managers, evenings.

Central England

Bournville College of Further Education
Guest House Management.

Bridgnorth and South Shropshire College of Further Education
City and Guilds 491, Guest House Management.

Derbyshire College of Higher Education
The Business Enterprise Unit provides a tailormade service to individual and organisational needs, including small business and business update courses, in response to local need.

Dudley College of Technology
(1988, excluding courses formerly sponsored by the MSC.) Self-Employment, full time. Mini-Business, evenings. Management Extension programmes for redundant executives; include 3 weeks' intensive training in Small Business Management plus 23 weeks with a small business solving a particular problem.

Kettering: Tresham College
(1988) Wide range of Open Learning Small Business packages (see 'Open and Distance Learning Courses'). Also short courses, one and two days, in varied range of topics, including Accounting for the Non-Accountant, Marketing for the Small Business, Trading Opportunities Overseas.

Kidderminster College
Enterprise Skills for Self-Employment, under 21-hour rule – includes Raising Finance, Market Investigation, Selling, Advertising, Financial Control etc. Also support services for new enterprises, and Small Business Club.

Leamington Spa: Mid Warwickshire College of Further Education
(1988, excluding courses formerly sponsored by the MSC.) Food and Management Studies, for mature students, under 21-hour rule, suitable for those who want to set up their own food business, go into catering or run a private guest house.

Newark Technical College
Managing Your Own Business, evenings. Managing the Finances for Your Own Business, evenings. Management workshops for Small Businesses, mode unspecified. Computers for Small Businesses, mode unspecified.

Nottingham: Trent Polytechnic
Special programmes are available for those who are contemplating or have started a new business. Our Business Development Centre offers tailor-made programmes for updating and improving management skills, including the following: Increasing Sales, Improving Organisational Effectiveness, Controlling Costs, Improving Customer Relations, Improving Management Information and Control, Improving Management Skills, Solving Specific Problems, Preparing for Expansion, Identifying Training Needs, Improving Performance, Preparing for Promotion, Monitoring Performance. For information, please contact the Business Development Centre, tel: 0602 418418 ext 2488.

Oswestry College
A comprehensive small business programme including consultancy support.

Redditch College
It is proposed that this college should merge with North Worcestershire College to become North East Worcestershire College so the range of courses offered may be affected by this. Small Business Service: part-time courses to suit individual small firms. Retail Management, evenings, for independent retailers. DIY Credit Control course, to assist companies to reduce the amount of outstanding credit.

Solihull College of Technology
(1988) Starting and Running Your Own Business, evenings. Book-keeping for the Small Business, evenings. Marketing on a Small Budget, Marketing Workshops, Computing for Small Businesses, Business Law for Small Businesses – these are follow-up courses; details from the Small Business Unit.

Stoke-on-Trent: Staffs Polytechnic
(1988) Small Business Development programmes, mode varies.

Tamworth College
(1988) Range of small business courses – including: Self Employment, Small Businesses, Book-keeping for Small Businesses, Computerised Accounting for Small Businesses, Computerised Payroll for Small Businesses, Marketing and Advertising for Small Businesses, Salesmanship and Customer Relations.

Warley Campus: Sandwell College
(1988, excluding courses formerly sponsored by the MSC.) Be Your Own Boss, part time. BTEC Post Experience Units, part time, in different aspects of business management, e.g. working with People, Word Processing, Implementing Small Business Computer Systems etc. Small Business Club.

Wellingborough College
TA-sponsored Business Enterprise Programme, evenings and weekends. TA-sponsored Private Enterprise Programme, includes: Computers, Marketing, Accounting, Employing People. BTEC Small Business Units, part time, includes: Options in Financial Control, Costing and Pricing, Raising Finance. A Shoe Repair course is suitable for those considering setting up in business (not sponsored).

West Bromwich Campus: Sandwell College
(1988, excluding courses formerly sponsored by the MSC.) Small Business, afternoons or evenings. Selling for the Self-Employed, evenings. Bookkeeping for the Self-Employed, evenings. Employing Someone, evenings. Starting a Shop, evenings. Business Development Course, evenings. Introduction to Managing a Newsagency, evenings. Merchandise Course for the News Trade, evenings. Small Business Club.

Witney: West Oxfordshire Technical College
Small Business courses related to Stud and Stable Husbandry – Thoroughbred Industry: Financial management, secretarial control of stud or stable business. Records required for trainers' yards, familiarity with Wetherbys. Personnel management and organisation.

Wolverhampton: Bilston Community College
Self Employment course covers Book-keeping, Marketing, Finance, Communications, Law, Pricing and Costing. Co-operative Business Enterprise, part time, covering all aspects of a successful co-operative business start up. Skills Expansion, for the Prospective Self-Employed, part time. Many other short courses are run by the college's Business Development Centre (tel: 0902 43065) relevant to the training and updating needs of new and expanding businesses. Courses include Accounting, Marketing, Computing, Supervisory Skills etc. Much of this provision is now supported by Open Learning packages.

Wolverhampton Polytechnic
(1988, excluding courses formerly sponsored by the MSC.) Under the PICKUP programme, the college offers courses in Management Information Systems, Desk Top Publishing, Marketing for Small Business and Computer-Aided Design. Modes variable.

Wolverhampton: Wulfrun College of Further Education
(1988) Self-Employment and Small Business courses. Twelve-week courses
for unemployed wanting to start self-employment; basic skills.

Northern England

Altrincham: South Trafford College of Further Education
Start Your Own Small Business, evenings. Business Law for the Small Business, evenings. Marketing for the Small Business, evenings. Microcomputing in Business, evenings. Book-keeping and Taxation for the Small Business, evenings. Finance for the Small Business, evenings.

Ashington: Northumberland College of Arts and Technology
Small Business and Self-Employment courses.

Ashington: Northumberland Technical College
TA-sponsored Business Enterprise Programme and Private Enterprise Programme. Short courses in Small Business Computing Systems, database, spreadsheet and desk-top publishing.

Bradford and Ilkley Community College
(1988) Small Business Development Unit. General introductory course to Setting Up in Business, part time and evenings. Practical Accounting, part time, and evenings. Setting Up and Keeping Books, evenings. Purchasing and Stock Control in the Small Business, part time. The Use of Microcomputers in the Small Business, part time. Marketing and Selling in the Small Business, part time. Business Correspondence in the Small Business, part time.

Bridlington: East Yorkshire College of Further Education
(1988) ESF-sponsored Small Business Course, full time. Catering and Hotel Management, full time. Start Your Own Business. In-House audit and training in Business Systems and Use of Information Technology, mode unspecified.

Burnley College
Small Business courses available through Open Leaning (see 'Open and Distance Learning Courses').

Consett: Derwentside College
Series of short courses in Small Business Planning, Financial Management, Small Business Book-keeping, part time or evenings.

Dewsbury College
Small Business Unit, offers Self-Employment Programme, evenings, plus 'after care' service. Small Business Workshop – taster programme, part time. Small Business Development Programme (for businesses with three or more employees), part time. Book-keeping for the Small Business, evenings. Business Computing, part time. Marketing for the Small Firm, evenings. Finance for the Non-Accountant, part time. BTEC Continuing Education awards, part time. (See also 'Open and Distance Learning Courses'.)

Durham: New College Durham
Small Business Unit offers a range of courses, including: 'Business Enterprise Programme', comprehensive course of 7 days or 14 evenings, available free to business start-ups; 'Private Enterprise Programme' one-day follow-up courses in single subjects, e.g. Book-keeping, Marketing, Employing People: available free to businesses less than one year old. Also evening courses (6 evenings) 'Practical Book-keeping for Small Businesses'.

Gateshead Technical College
Self-Employment courses, part time and evenings, some TA-sponsored.

Halifax: Calderdale College
(At The Enterprise Campus, Dean Clough.) Enterprise Allowance Seminars, Wednesday, fortnightly, for all wishing to apply for the Enterprise Allowance Scheme. Part-time programme of Workshops for people exploring the possibility of self employment: Your Business Success Kit. Small Business Consultancy. Industrial Training (customised packages to meet client needs). See also 'Open and Distance Learning' section for small business packages.

Leeds: Park Lane College
Being your Own Boss, evenings. Being Your Own Book-keeper, evenings.

Leigh College
New Business courses – numerous in the evening and day.

Lincoln, Gainsborough, Louth: North Lincolnshire College
Small Business courses, many sponsored by the Training Agency, offered by Lincolnshire Enterprise, the Training Managership for Lincolnshire.

Liverpool: South Mersey College
Starting and running a Small Business for people interested in self-employment. Short management courses for industry and commerce, includes courses for supervisors, trade union officials and middle management.

Manchester: University of Manchester
Extra-Mural Studies Department, Career Studies Unit. Small Business Suitability, one-week full-time assessment course for self-employment.

Middlesborough: Longlands College of Further Education
(1988) BTEC Continuing Education Units, leading to Certificate in Business Administration. Operational Salesmanship.

Nelson and Colne College
Small Business: courses covering Introductory Skills and knowledge of Marketing etc. as well as courses dealing with Book-Keeping and Financial Management.

Newcastle-upon-Tyne Polytechnic
(1988) Small Business Unit. 'Various programmes available, both day and evening, for people who have just started or are contemplating their own businesses. Also programmes for people who are unemployed but have tranfersable skills, placing them (after short training courses) within small companies with potential for growth.'

Peterlee College
Variety of courses available through Business Development Unit. Open Learning programmes available for housebound on business development.

Rotherham: Rockingham College of Further Education
Running Your Own Business, evenings. Accounts for the Small Business, evenings. The Licensee's Complete Wine Course, part time, for people who wish to enter the Licensed Trade (offered when there is sufficient demand).

St Helen's School of Management Studies
Extensive range of short courses and block-release courses, *normally residential*. Among those likely to be of interest to potential or existing small business operators are Retail Management, Retail Food Management, An Introduction to Effective Storekeeping, Effective Salesmanship, Purchasing Management.

Salford College of Technology
Small Business Operations, full time, for people considering starting and operating small businesses. BTEC Post Experience Certificate of Business Administration, part time, day and evening, for Professional Footballers entering business.

Sheffield: Rother Valley College
(1988) Business Enterprise Programme and Private Enterprise Programme seminars, under 21-hour rule. BTEC Continuing Education courses, under 21-hour rule – select from Computer Studies, Improve your Financial Decision Making, Managing the Office, Using Word Processors, Working with People, Computer Programming, Methodology, Computer Systems. Run Your Own Guest House and Bed and Breakfast Business. Run Your

Own Dressmaking Business. Arts and Crafts (including Stained Glass Work) for self-employment – modes not specified.

Shipley College
Business Enterprise, Book-keeping, Basic Accountancy, Computers in Business, Computerised Accountancy, Employing People, Customer Care.

Southport College of Art and Technology
Managing a Residential Care Home, part time. Guest House owners course, part time. The college Short Course unit now offers 'tailor-made' courses for local commerce and industry, e.g. Supervisory Skills, Interpersonal Skills, First Aid, Counselling Skills etc.

Sunderland Polytechnic
Range of short courses in the Business School – options include Starting Your Own Business, Running a more Profitable Business, Finance for Non-Financial Managers, etc. other short courses suitable for the small business owner may be offered by the Micro Technology Centre. Ask college for details.

Warrington: North Cheshire College
Short course in Computing for Accountants.

Widnes: Halton College of Further Education
'Start Your Own Business' course for people contemplating self-employment or those newly started in business.

Wales and Western England

Barnstaple: North Devon College
Short courses in Small Business. The college has its own Small Business Club.

Bath: Norton Radstock College
Self-Employment and Enterprise Skills, part time or full time, within the county's Employment Training programme. Enterprise Unit at College with full-time Adviser on Self-Employment, plus seven-day Business Enterprise Programme, covering all aspects of setting up in business from Understanding Business Records, Income Tax, National Insurance and VAT to Costing and Pricing. Also Management Extension programme, whereby redundant executives are first trained in the techniques of Small Business Management, then seconded to a small business for up to three months.

Bristol: Brunel Technical College
(1988) Wide range of part-time and short courses which could be a foundation for self-employment (See also 'Retraining and New Skills Courses'.) Options include Painting and Decorating, Telephone Installation for Electrical Contractors, Commercial Cake Decorating and Finishing, Vegetarian Cooking, Licensed House Catering.

Bristol: Filton Technical College
BTEC Continuing Education Units in Small Business (include Computer Studies, Financial Decision Making, Marketing, Exporting) by Flexastudy (see 'Open and Distance Learning Courses').

Chippenham Technical College
(1988) Setting Up in Business, evenings. Cash Flow and VAT, part time. Salesmanship and Retailing Techniques, part time. Introduction to Microcomputers in Small Business, part time. Company Law and Finance, part time. Employment Law, part time.

Haverfordwest and Neyland: Pembrokeshire College
Pembrokeshire College Small Business Centre primarily operates on a supported home study basis. (See 'Open and Distance Learning Courses'.)

Llanelli: Carmarthenshire College of Technology
(1988) Business Information Technology Applications Packages for Self-Employment and Small Business, mode unspecified.

Salisbury College of Technology
(1988) Starting a Small Business. Business Enterprise Programme (BEP). Private Enterprise Programme (PEP). Small Business Finance and Development. Finance and Accounting for Non-Financial Managers. Guest House Management, for City and Guilds award, all evenings.

Street: Strode College
Be Your Own Boss, evenings. Book-keeping and Finance for the self-employed; Using Computers in a Small Business.

Taunton: Somerset College of Arts and Technology
Your Own Business, evenings.

Weymouth College
(1988) Starting Your Own Business, part time. The Business of Book-keeping, part time. Wages, PAYE and Employment, part time. Running Your Own Business, part time.

Scotland and Northern Ireland

Belfast College of Technology
(1988) Small Business Administration, part time. Starting a Business, evenings.

Dumfries and Galloway College of Technology
TA-sponsored one day course in Implications of Self Employment. Two Saturdays and evenings on TA-sponsored Self-Employment course.

Edinburgh: Queen Margaret College
(1988, excluding courses formerly sponsored by the MSC.) Business Development Centre. SCOTVEC Small Business Development (see 'Open and Distance Learning Courses'). Former trainees from this Centre have established businesses as diverse as retirement homes and knitwear manufacture, shipping, packing, and fish-farming.

Glasgow: Anniesland College
Evening Small Business Programme, includes 'Starting and Running a Small Business', Marketing and Business Accounting.

Glasgow: University of Glasgow
The Glasgow Business School offers a full time International Master of Business Administration degree, a part-time Executive Master of Business Administation degree, a Corporate Management Development Programme and an MSc in Information Technology. The School's Centre for Entrepreneurial Development has a complete portfolio of full-time and part-time programmes for people wishing to start, expand or rescue small and new businesses.

Inverness College
(1988) Starting and Running a Small Business, part time. Business Enterprise Programmes. Private Enterprise Programmes and College-Based Programmes. Employment and Payroll, part time. Financial Record-Keeping, part time. Costing, part time. Cash Handling, part time. Also Start-Up Support and Training in Health and Beauty, part time. Start-Up in Catering, part time.

Lisburn College of Further Education
Self-Employment and Small Business, evenings.

Motherwell College
TA-sponsored short courses, e.g. Business Enterprise, are provided regularly. Small Business (Enterprise elements are included in most full-time courses). Students with disabilities can be accepted on to most courses and are supported in their studies by the considerable resources of the Special Needs Department.

Newcastle College of Further Education
Enterprise Training and Into Business courses.

Perth College of Further Education
The college has an active 'Centre for Business Development'. Courses are available for those intending to start up in business and these courses are free. Courses on a short-term intensive basis are available for those established in business but who require further help, e.g. Marketing Overhaul, Sales Promotion, Training Needs Analysis, Time Management, Sources of Finance.

OPEN AND DISTANCE LEARNING COURSES

Ways of adding to your skills and qualifications 'At your own pace, in your own place'.

Introduction

Many people looking through *The Mature Student's Handbook* will be unaware of the opportunities that exist for them to change careers or update their knowledge through 'Open and Distance Learning Courses'. Most have heard of correspondence courses; the forerunner of 'Distance Learning', but the word 'Open' is new to them. Does it mean 'Open to anyone?' for example – meaning you need no qualifications to start a course? Or does it mean 'Open' in the way that the Open University and The Open College operate - meaning you can study at home, at your own pace?

OPEN OPPORTUNITIES: one description for *two* kinds of course

Open in the description of a course often means that you need no entry qualifications to start. It often (but not always) means that you can study at home, or use a self-directed study pack on your employer's premises or at a local college.

In this connection, you'll see, as you look through this section, some colleges say they are centres for The Open College (note the capital T for The – meaning the *national* Open College, which was at one time going to be called the Open College of the Air). Most readers will know that this provides home study packages – in the same way that the Open University does – but linked to vocational qualifications rather than degree courses. (A fuller description of what The Open College offers is given on page 237.)

Some colleges say that they offer *Open Learning*. This usually means that they offer study packages. (A fuller description of Open Learning methods is given on page 234.)

OPEN COLLEGE FEDERATIONS

Other colleges, though, say that they are centres for organisations like the 'Open College of the North West' or the 'Open College of South London'.

These have nothing to do with 'The Open College' – the national organisation. Nor do they provide home study packages.

'Open' in this sense means open to anyone, i.e. they provide courses that require no previous academic entrance qualifications, but where you attend college – normally part-time, say for one morning or one evening session a week – and take unit-based courses that can earn you 'credits' towards a diploma or degree. You don't have to commit yourself to more than one unit at a time, and you don't have to aim at a diploma or a degree unless you want to do so. You can break off your studies if necessary (for instance if you move jobs or home) and take up where you left off, when it's convenient.

(Take a look at the entry for Blackburn College, on page 255, to get an idea of this system.)

The name and address of an Open College Federation that covers your area (if there is one) can be obtained by writing to
National Open College Network
Mail Box
c/o Peter Wilson,
South Yorkshire Open College Federation,
Sheffield City Polytechnic,
36 Collegiate Crescent,
Sheffield S10 2BP

Each of these federations includes a range of colleges within the area it serves. Not every college will offer the same range of study units, but each one will offer some 'Open College' provision. In the 'Pre-Entry, Sample and Access Courses' section of this book, you will find details of a free book which describes all the London schemes. Otherwise, if you can't find a scheme of this kind near your own home listed in *The Mature Student's Handbook* it is worth writing to the National Open College Network, to see if they know of one that is starting up in the near future.

OPEN LEARNING: INDIVIDUAL SCHEMES *(for the Open University, see page 236 and for The Open College, see page 237)*.

Many further and higher education colleges identify themselves as providing 'Open Learning' opportunities. This means that they provide study packages that can be used at home, or on an employer's premises, or sometimes in a specially equipped room set aside at a college, for self-directed study.

If you think that 'self-directed study' sounds a bit like learning by correspondence course, you'd be right. Open Learning packages are often very much more sophisticated than many of the correspondence courses they have replaced (or compete with). But the basic idea is the same. The student is provided with learning materials, which today can include not just textbooks and workbooks but audio cassettes, video cassettes and computer tapes or discs. For science and technology courses, home experiment kits can also be among the teaching materials.

Many colleges which offer Open Learning facilities provide support for learners who need to visit their local college to use equipment like computers and video-recorders, or who take advantage of the opportunity to consult a tutor (face-to-face or by telephone).

You will find details of over 1500 courses and suppliers of open learning materials in *The Open Learning Directory* (COIC), a major reference book likely to be available through public libraries or jobcentres. The course ranges from beginner to advanced; many of the courses having been funded by the government's original 'Open Tech' project to extend the availability of technical and vocational self-study materials.

(Take a look at Watford College on page 244 to get an idea of the extent and variety of Open Learning packages available from a typical college access point.)

Open Learning facilities are particularly valuable for those who:

- have home responsibilities which prevent them going to college
- work shifts which mean they miss college classes
- are disabled and can't easily get to college
- live in the country, without transport to college
- are apprehensive about joining a class of strangers
- want to 'catch up' a bit before studying with a group

OPEN LEARNING: VARIATIONS

Some of the very first Open Learning courses to provide students with audio tapes and science experimental kits came from the National Extension College, a long-established and highly regarded provider of correspondence college materials. Many further education colleges who choose to offer Open Learning facilities base them on NEC materials and refer to them as *Flexistudy* courses (this being a title that belongs to the National Extension College). They combine NEC course materials with the availability of their own tutors to support students who work mainly at home.

Other colleges create their own Open Learning courses, using selected materials from the Open Learning Directory or other sources of distance learning, and specially appointed tutors. They may use their own titles for these courses, such as *Homestudy*.

Finally, there are the colleges which use Open Learning materials and their own tutors to provide for students who might otherwise have no tutorial support or technical facilities whilst studying mainly at home. Look out for the description *'Flexastudy'* which identifies these. The basic idea is that students bring their own Open Learning packages or correspondence college materials to the college for a study session, where tutors are willing to counsel students on a range of different courses within the same study period. They can also use college equipment where necessary to access computer programmes or watch videos.

(Take a look at Bristol: Filton Technical College, on page 263, for a description of this scheme.)

OPEN LEARNING: NATIONAL SCHEMES

The Open University and The Open College operate on a national basis, and provide different kinds of course for different kinds of learner. However, they have some things in common:

Anyone is eligible to start at a Foundation or Introductory level. You don't need qualifications. (But if you do have any exam qualifications, you may be able to start further on in a course, gaining exemptions from subjects you have already studied and passed.)

You do the work at home and you set the pace. You can stop and start, depending on your circumstances. No-one will badger you to spend more time studying than you can spare, but if you want extra help, there's a specially trained tutor to consult.

Course-work materials are provided though you may need a radio and/or cassette recorder, and/or TV and/or video recorder to use them (or access to this equipment – see 'College Links' below). They can include kits for science and other experiments, audio cassette tapes to listen to and TV programmes or videotapes to watch. As home computer ownership grows, some courses have materials on computer disc or tape that you can use – again 'College Links' can make it possible for people without computers to use these study materials.

College Links

I have mentioned access to tutors where you need face-to-face or telephone help with problems. As you look through the course lists that follow, you may see that certain colleges identify themselves as 'Gateway' centres for The Open College or say that they provide tutorial help for people on Open Learning courses. A variation on this theme is that some colleges have Open Learning Workshops, where you can book time to use their computer or their video recorder to study an item from your learning package.

THE OPEN UNIVERSITY

The Open University has undergraduate ('first degree') courses and postgraduate courses. Units of these can be taken as *Associate Student* courses if you only want to study one item in depth, or as a preparation or 'taster' for a full course. It also has an Open Business School, for managers and would-be managers, and in its Continuing Education Unit, it provides courses for people who want to build on to their existing education. There are many special-interest courses for particular needs (see the University's entry in 'Open and Distance Learning Courses').

Important: No A-levels or other exam passes are needed to enter undergraduate courses or associate student courses. Only for advanced courses are you likely to need work or study qualifications, but formal qualifications are not specified as a condition of entry.

Open University degrees are exactly the same as any other degrees when it comes to getting jobs that demand 'graduate status', or entering post-graduate courses of study or training, *except* that employers and college interviewers tend to give you extra consideration because you have shown you have self-discipline and staying power by getting a degree at home.

Learning packages sent to your home are backed up by audio and video cassettes and by television and radio programmes, and on many courses, there's a summer school each year, where students meet and attend seminars, lectures and discussions. (See also 'Degree and Advanced Courses'.)

For information, write to: The Open University, Walton Hall, PO Box 71, Milton Keynes, MK7 6AG and read the further entry in the Southern and Eastern England listing of 'Open and Distance Learning Courses' and 'Degree and Advanced Courses'.

THE OPEN COLLEGE

The newest national initiative is The Open College. It extends the range of courses available for home study into areas like craft skills, caring skills and personal skills. For example, one of the first courses to be offered was 'It's a Deal: An Introduction to Effective Selling'. Another was 'IT for the Terrified', which introduces you to Information Technology in commerce, retailing and as a basic office resource. 'IT for the Terrified' is aimed at school leavers and people changing careers or returning to work after a break. The full range of technology courses includes more advanced courses in Electronics and Computer-Aided Information Systems in Design. There are many courses connected with Business and Management, including Starting a New Business.

An interesting feature of The Open College is that it really does begin at the beginning; there is a course to teach you how to study, and another on basic arithmetic called 'Make It Count'.

With all the courses, you can assess your own progress, but some of them prepare students for the exams of national organisations like City and Guilds, BTEC and SCOTVEC. And you also have access at Open Access Centres, based in colleges throughout the country. You can also buy courses directly, with a credit card, by calling The Open College hotline (0235 555444).

Some of the courses are 'bought in' from other open-learning providers. The actual package you get depends on the course. For instance, in a course for women seeking a change of direction, called 'Women – the Way Ahead' you get a workbook, an audio tape, a paperback book and a videotape of case studies from the accompanying TV series. You're told that you need 30 hours of study to complete the course.

A total contrast, the 'Multi-Disciplinary Engineering' course is aimed at anyone operating, or wishing to operate plant in the process industries. The course covers the basic principles and concepts of Electrical Engineering, Mechanical Engineering and Instrumentation and Control. 'Multi-Disciplinary Engineering' is available in two formats, one leading to a City and Guilds Certificate, the other, which is for more experienced learners, to a BTEC

Higher National Certificate. Each course comes in the form of practical workbooks with set assignments and optional tutorial support. As with all Open College courses, the modules indicate clearly how much study time is likely to be needed and the number of books used.

For information, send for the (free) Open Book *guide to courses from The Open College, by post from The Open College, Freepost, PO Box 35, Abingdon OX14 34BR or phone The Open College hotline (number given above). The book contains many useful addresses as well as information about the range of courses offered.*

DISTANCE LEARNING

It's worth emphasising that correspondence colleges – which blazed the original trail for the many varieties of home study and open learning opportunities now available from further education colleges and training access points – still continue to flourish.

Some of the colleges are highly specialised, offering courses in subjects like salesmanship, kennels management, accountancy and freelance writing. Others offer a vast range of subjects, from commercial courses to university degree preparation.

You can expect that any college accredited by the Council for the Accreditation of Correspondence Colleges will conscientiously seek to offer value for money and a realistic appraisal of a student's work. Accreditation is subject to periodic review. With the same subject, teaching methods can vary, so if you have a subject in mind that is taught by several colleges, it is worth getting literature from each one; then you can compare what is offered and how well it suits your personality and circumstances.

For information, write to the Council for the Accreditation of Correspondence Colleges, 27 Marylebone Road, London, NW1 5JS. Their Secretary will be pleased to send you the list of approved colleges, with details of each college's range of subjects. Please enclose a stamped, self-addressed envelope when you send your enquiry.

In the course lists that follow, you may well find that some colleges offer their own, or a correspondence college's open learning package and that they are also Gateway centres for The Open College. Some may also be members of one of the Open College Federations described at the beginning of this Introduction. In such cases, tutors are likely to know the plus factors of each type of course, depending on the circumstances and starting point of each student, so take advantage of their experience when you are making your choice of course. Finding the right person may not be straightforward; colleges give different titles to people doing the same sort of job. But you could ask to be put in touch with an Open Learning tutor (if you want to study mainly at home) or the college representative of the appropriate Open College Federation (if you want to attend college and take individual course units to suit your own career plans).

London and Middlesex

College for the Distributive Trades
NEBSS Open Learning centre with tutorial support workshop.

London – University of London
The following entry is a shortened version of a leaflet available from the Secretary for External Students, University of London, Room 204, Senate House, Malet Street, London, WC1E 8HU:

'The University of London makes a number of its degrees available to External Students worldwide. Whereas an Internal Student studies at one of the Colleges in London and has available the teaching resources of the College, External Students study away from the University in their own time. There is no formal tuition as such for External Students, but the University provides a range of learning materials, short courses on particular topics, informal tutorial assessments and reading lists. Students may also take correspondence or tutorial courses offered by other colleges for the London degree.

Subjects: BSc (Econ) awarded in any one of the following: Economics; Economics & Management Studies; Accounting; Management Studies; Banking, Trade & Industry; Government & Politics; History; Geography; Sociology. LLB (includes the "core subjects" necssary for exemption from relevant parts of UK professional examinations). BA. Principal subjects include: English; Philosophy; Geography; French and other modern languages; Classical languages (European and Oriental). BD (the Bachelor's degree in Divinity) is non-denominational and of interest to both clergy and lay students. At postgraduate level there is a Diploma in Education, and there are also Master's degrees in Agricultural Development, Contemporary French Studies, Classics, and (for graduates of UK universities or of the CNAA) Law. In addition the research degrees of MPhil and PhD are available in all subjects to students who are already graduates of the University of London.

Paddington College
Paddington is a registered centre for The Open College, offering support for Open College programmes.

South London College
(1988) Part of the Open College of South London; works in association with the Polytechnic of the South Bank to provide courses for adults without conventional entry requirements, details from the college.

South West London College
(1988) Directed Private Study Unit, combines distance-learning materials with short periods of face-to-face tuition and telephone advice sessions. Options include: Institute of Chartered Secretaries and Administrators course; BTEC Higher National Certificate in Business Studies, British Ports Association Certificate. South West London College is a member of the Open College of South London, providing a range of courses for adults without conventional entry requirements; details from college.

Southern and Eastern England

Basingstoke Technical College
Flexistudy courses for GCSE/A-levels now available, and Open Learning Workshops in English, Maths and Languages.

Borehamwood: De Havilland College – see under Welwyn Garden City

Bromley College of Technology
(1988) Open Learning. Variety of distance-learning materials ranging from BTEC National Certificate in Telecommunications to Diploma in Engineering Management.

Canterbury College of Technology
Also at Maidstone and Rochester. (1988) Flexistudy: Fleximaths (preparatory), GCSE English Language or English Literature, French, German, History, Economic History, Human Biology, Sociology, Accounts, Mathematics, O/A Psychology – Child Development. GCE A-level Economics History, English Literature, French, History, Law, Sociology. Not all subjects available at all three centres. A full range of vocational open learning and courses from The Open College also available. Contact the Open Learning Unit on 0634 830688.

Colchester Institute
Flexistudy courses using National Extension College and other tutorial materials, plus college facilities where practical work is involved, plus tutorial help by phone or face-to-face. Options are: Return to Study, Literacy and Basic Mathematics, Basic Computing, COBOL and PASCAL programming; GCSE in Accounts, History, Chemistry, Economics, English Language, English Literature, Geography, Human Biology, French, Law, Mathematics, Psychology, Physics, Sociology and also most available at GCE A-level. Professional and Management subjects include ISCA, Institute of Legal Executives, NEBSS Supervisory Studies.

Crawley College of Technology
(1988) Open Learning: Management Development Programme; Management Update Programme.

Dunstable College
We offer 400 different Open Learning packages for people wanting more flexible studies.

Epsom: North East Surrey College of Technology
(1988) Flexilearning facilities in the Department of Community and General Education, with home-study packages plus tutorial support. Details from college. Open Learning courses in Managerial Studies offered by the Department of Management.

Hastings College of Arts and Technology
Full range of Open Learning packages from a wide variety of suppliers. Tutorial support provided. Special programmes devised for individuals and groups.

Hatfield: De Havilland College – see under Welwyn Garden City

Havering Technical College
(1988) Open Learning facilities with home study packages plus tutorial support by phone or face to face. A range of GCSE and GCE A-levels available; also Shorthand and Typing. 'We are an Open College Access Gateway Centre and provide pre-course counselling and tutorial support during the course. We also have Independent Learning Suites on every site.'

Hemel Hempstead: Dacorum College
(1988) Open Learning Drop-in facility, offering the chance to brush up your Maths and English.

Kingston Polytechnic
Distance-learning courses: DMS and MBA with Rapid Results College and BBP Holding respectively.

Luton College of Higher Education
(1988) Open Learning centre, providing the following courses in distance learning form with tutorial support: Institute of Road Transport Engineers examination subjects; Institute of the Motor Industry examination subjects; Writing and Presenting Reports; Presenting Information Visually; Managing Your Own Learning; *Laboratory Safety; *Electronics; *Everyday Forms of Energy; *Food and Drink – a Biochemical Recipe; *Everyday Chemistry; *The Garden – Studies in Plant Growth; *Health Choices; *Introduction to Computing – * indicates components of a conversion course for women moving from arts to sciences.

Morden: Merton College
Offers the full range of courses from The Open College, including learning skills, setting up your own business, management, computing, basic

electronics and many more. All available through open learning with the help of a tutor. Adult Basic Skills Programmes (improve your writing and number skills in an open learning workshop, with individual help available). Open Languages workshop – flexible study times at most levels in French, Spanish, German and Italian – Business courses, beginners' courses and academic courses. Community languages – Gujerati, Urdu.

The Open College: viewpoint
'At the interview (for a full-time course in higher education), I mentioned I had done the "Effective Learner" course and they seemed impressed that I had taken the time to do some private studying. I received a letter of acceptance this morning and I'm over the moon. The Open College has been a Godsend.'

Milton Keynes: The Open University
See description given in introductory chapter. Provides home study facilities with specially written tutorial materials, practical kits for experiments, broadcasts on radio and television, audio and video cassettes plus support from tutorialgroups and summer school. Undergraduate Programme for BA (Open) degree/degree with Honours; credit-based, with more than 130 courses, including the Open University Foundation courses with which students begin their studies. Open University Foundation course credits are accepted by many universities, polytechnics and colleges in lieu of A-levels for entry to their courses. Higher Degree Programme for taught masters' degrees and postgraduate degrees by research. Continuing Education Programme, incorporating the Open Business School (in which two-thirds of students are employer-sponsored), professional courses for teachers and health and social welfare workers, postgraduate-level courses in Manufacturing and the Industrial Applications of Computers. Community Education packs – subjects such as energy conservation, school governing, planning retirement. Personal Interest packs – in literature, music and art. (See 'Degree and Advanced Courses'.)

Norwich City College
Open Learning using distance-learning tutorial materials and, where appropriate, cassette tapes plus tutorials, by telephone and face to face. Current options are GCSE/A-level French, Beginners/GCSE German, Beginners/GCSE/A-level Spanish, GCSE English, How to Study Effectively, How to Write Essays, GCE A-level English, Sociology. Links with The Open College for wide range of courses.

Portsmouth College of Art, Design and Further Education
Centre for the Portsmouth Open Learning Programme, with distance-learning packages for both Return to Study and GCSE/GCE A-level subjects.

Portsmouth: Highbury College of Technology
(1988) Flexible/Open Learning Workshops; details from college. Flexistudy for adults; details from college.

Reading College of Technology
The College is a centre for The Open College and welcomes students studying via Open Learning across the whole spectrum of courses available.

Richmond Adult and Community College
Open Learning facilities in languages – French, Italian, Modern Greek, German, Spanish, Portuguese, Japanese and Russian. Other languages may be available on request. Computer-based training in Typing/Keyboarding, Computing for beginners, Word-processing, spreadsheets, MS-DOS and computer literacy. GCSE and A-level Study Packs – all subjects. This college is a centre for The Open College.

Southampton Technical College
Flexistudy, using tutorial material produced mainly by the National Extension College, with tutorial support from college by post, telephone or face-to-face. Options include GCSE or A-level Biology, Chemistry, Computing, Economics, English Literature, French, German, History, Human Biology, Mathematics, Physics, Politics and Government, Spanish, Statistics. Other options may be possible – ask for details from the college.

Southend College of Technology
Open Learning distance facilities in a wide range of subjects to suit individuals, including those interested in a 'minority' subject. Study materials for use at home plus tutorials at college to suit your circumstances. The college offers a Drop-In workshop for Numeracy, Literacy, English as a Second Language, Computing and Information Technology and is also a centre for The Open College.

Watford: Cassio College
(1988) 'A very wide range of Open Learning materials is available. Enquiries regarding open learning and short courses to Mrs. Sue Baker, Watford 248828.'

Watford College
Open Access Centre with distance-learning packages, use of equipment and tutorial help available to everyone – employed/unemployed, industrial, commercial and private clients, from 9.30 a.m.- 8.30 p.m. Monday to Friday, 9.30 a.m. – 4.30 p.m. Saturdays by appointment, 46 weeks a year. Areas of training are: Computer-Aided Engineering (13 study programmes, including Computer Programming and Electronics Servicing), IBM PC Business Systems (six study programmes, including Word processing and

Databases), Printing (four study programmes, including Lithography, Flexography, Screen Printing), Automotive Electronics (five study programmes, including Electronic Fuel Injection Systems). Also Open and Distance Learning provision, especially for the Printing, Publishing and Ink industries (also open to unemployed people). No entry qualifications: candidates can work for BTEC National Certificates on a unit-based system or in modules of training. Wide range of units and modules for self-study, ranging from Design and Print planning to Costing and Estimating, and Bookbinding and Print Finishing; plus special modules on Silk Screen Printing and Magazine and Book Publishing. Extensive range of GCSE/ A-level courses. Small Business Courses and Self-Management courses – send for Midtech Catalogue.

Welwyn Garden City: De Havilland College
Also at Borehamwood and Hatfield. (1988) Open Learning provision for most courses in general prospectus and some others; tutorial materials are designed for home study plus college tutorial support. Details from the college.

Central England

Abingdon College
Open Learning with distance-learning materials, including books, tapes and videos plus telephone or face-to-face tutorials at convenient times. Details of available subjects from college; start at any time of year.

Abingdon: The Open College
(See description given in Introduction.) Designed to provide vocationally related courses, linked to qualifications in many instances, for people to study in their own time at home. No pre-qualifications are needed to study a course. The Open College will offer courses leading to nationally-recognised qualifications and is working closely with the National Council for Vocational Qualifications (NCVQ) a body which is examining and accrediting work-related courses and the value of their qualifications. Students of The Open College use home study materials and practical kits, supported by radio and television programmes. The programmes began on Channel 4 in September 1987 and are now also shown on BBC. Future broadcasting is planned on independent TV and local radio. NB: Students of The Open College will work for the examinations of outside organisations, rather than the College's own awards. The address given is the one to which you write for *The Open Book*, which lists all the courses available (see page 238). You can, of course, study these courses anywhere in the UK.

Bournville College of Further Education
Funeral Directing (by distance learning). In addition, facilities are available for studying English, Maths, Sociology and Psychology on an Open Learning basis.

Bridgnorth and South Shropshire College of Further Education
Centre for The Open College – please contact for full details. Wide number of Homestudy courses available.

Chesterfield College of Technology and Arts
(1988) Open Learning facilities on demand; details from college.

Corby: Tresham College – see under Kettering

Coventry: Henley College
(1988) Homestudy courses for Pitman's Shorthand and Typewriting (Beginners and Advanced), Word Processing. Technical Training Packs: Mathematics, General and Communication Studies, Electronics and Electronic Principles, Physical Science, Line and Customer Apparatus, Telecoms Systems, Electrical Drawing, Business Development Courses in Tourism (65 units), Computing – Beginners, Advanced, Understanding Computers, Computer-Aided Design. Catering – Royal Institute of Public Health and Hygiene Certificate, Running and Establishing Small Guest Houses. Short courses in, e.g: Office Administration, Purchasing, Personnel (12 subjects altogether). Language packs (10 languages, including Indonesian and Malay). Export courses (languages plus cultural background courses). Catering courses (Basic Canteen to Executive Dining Room). Education Engineering (for people writing new training programmes). Public Speaking. Executive Fitness. Technical Authorship. GCSE (16 subjects), GCE A-level (11 subjects). Pre-entry courses. RSA Examination courses (12 Stage Two, seven Stage Three).

Dudley College of Technology
(1988) Flexistudy distance learning packages plus tutorial support. Options are: BTEC National, Institute of Bankers, GCSE and A-level Physics, Chemistry, Accounts, Mathematics, Law, Sociology, Geography, Economics, Psychology, Statistics, Government and Politics. GCSE only: Human Biology, English Language. GCE A-level only: English Literature. Fleximaths. RSA Book-keeping. Open Access Centre which students can attend by appointment during opening hours (12 hours a day, five days a week); uses training packages with tutorial help available if required. Programmes include Industrial Electronics, Control Engineering, CAD/CAM, Business Computer Applications, Microelectronics, Robotics, CNC Machine Tool Programming, Word Processing. Centre for The Open College.

Hinkley College of Further Education
(1988) Open Learning, using distance-learning packages plus tutorial support. Options are: Understanding Information Technology, Word Processing/Keyboard Skills, Basic Digital Electronics, Decoders and Combinational Logic Digital Devices, Microprocessor Appreciation in Business, Computer Applications in Business, Supervisory Studies (NEBSS), Book-keeping for the Small Business, Food-Handling for the Small Business, Fabric Analysis, Design Appreciation and all other materials originating from the Knitting Industry Open Tech project.

Kettering: Tresham College
Same distance-learning facilities available at Corby, where the contact is P.Hindley: Corby 203252. (1988) Distance-learning packages include Leadership, Pricing for Profit, This is Marketing, Typing Made Easy, Decision

Making, Time Management, CNC Appreciation, Basic Electrical Skills, Microelectronics Level l and Level II, Report Writing, Your Own Business, Food Handing, Book-keeping for a Small Business, Computers and Business, Understanding Information Technology, Introduction to Distribution, Looking After Children. Also Open Learning facilities for Preparatory Psychology, BASIC Programming, GCSE Chemistry, English Language, Human Biology, Mathematics, English Literature, Geography, History, World History. GCE A-level Biology, History, Sociology, English Literature, Mathematics, Geography. Inside Information (Information Technology) can lead to City and Guilds certificate. Centre for The Open College. College spokesperson says: 'In Open Learning, we can offer almost anything the customer requires – our free leaflet shows some of the courses available at both Kettering and Corby.'

Kidderminster College
Flexistudy – details from college. Also Open Office – a new flexible facility available for anyone who would like to learn new skills or update existing ones. Areas of study include Word-Processing, Audio typing, Typing and Shorthand; each may be followed at all levels.

Leamington Spa: Mid-Warwickshire College
(1988) Open Learning GCSE in English, Mathematics, Human Biology, Sociology, Child Psychology, Law. A-level in English Literature, Economics, Mathematics. Open BTEC awards in 'Management and Leadership within Small Firms'and 'Working with People'. Courses from The Open College, e.g. Electronics, Book-keeping and many othes. Study packages to use at home, plus tutorial support by post or telephone, or face-to-face.

Lichfield College
Open Learning provision in association with Staffordshire Polytechnic. At present Lichfield College can only support certain GCE A-level subjects, but candidates seeking other subjects are helped to contact the Staffordshire Polytechnic Open Learning Unit.

Loughborough Technical College
(1988) Open Access New Technology Learning Centre provides individual learning packages, backed up with computer and video-based training. Options include: Basic Electricity; Analogue Electronics; Digital Electronics; Microprocessors; Starting in Information Technology; Computer Literacy (can lead to City and Guilds certificate). Open Learning Basic Maths – no qualifications needed, suitable for people preparing for entry tests, pre-Nursing, pre-GCSE etc.

Nottingham: South Nottinghamshire College of Further Education
(1988) Open Learning unit with provision for CSE and GCE A-levels. Management courses, Information Technology courses, Office Skills, Typewriting, Word Processing Workshops.

Oswestry College
We are able to help clients towards 9000 separate courses of study.

Redditch College
It is proposed that this college should merge with North Worcestershire College to become North East Worcestershire College, so the range of courses may be affected when this happens. (1988) Flexastudy system, provides both for intensive full-time study at college, using distance-learning materials, and part time and evening facilities, using distance-learning materials, both with tutorial support and use of college facilities. Examination courses available include: Accountancy (several professional institutes), Institute of Chartered Secretaries and Administrators, Institute of Marketing, Institute of Export, Institute of Purchasing and Supply, Institute of Taxation, Overseas Trade, Institute of Personnel Management, Institute of Credit Management. Open Learning, part of the county's original Open Tech project which funded distance-learning packages for students to use at home, plus telephone advice service and group study sessions.

Flexastudy: viewpoint
'There's a lot of reading to start off with. Remember, you have to read everything that a lecturer would have researched and put into a lecture. You are given a scheme of work at the beginning, with the topics you have to cover to get through the part you are studying for, and then, within each topic, you are given suggested reading from recommended books. You are also given worksheets which contain printed examination questions, generally of the standard that you are at, and it's suggested that if you feel you understand the topic, you should go ahead and work through the questions.'

(Student, Flexastudy Accountancy course, Redditch College)

'At this college, we are prepared to take anybody who has reached the necessary standard to be able to register with a professional body. That is the only requirement in which we need to be satisfied. In any one year, you will find within the system students ranging from 18 up to the mid-50s. We find that the problems which arise in a correspondence course are very much more easily dealt with and comprehensibly dealt with on a face-to-face basis, and it is perhaps illuminating to take one of the major accountancy bodies, the Chartered Institute of Cost and Executive Accountants, where, in the last six years of examinations, the pass rate here has not dropped below 90%. When you compare this with the national average, somewhere in the region of 35%, it speaks volumes for the system.'

(Spokesperson, Flexastudy unit, Redditch College)

Retford: Eaton Hall International
Primarily distance-learning courses (some residential element) in Teaching English as a Foreign or Second Language (see 'Retraining and New Skills Courses').

Solihull College of Technology
(1988) Distributive Industry Open Learning (DIOL) support centre. Centre for The Open College, offering a full range of facilities and course advice. NEBSS Supervisory Studies by open training, and a full range of GCSE/A-level Flexistudy courses.

Stafford College of Further Education
(1988) Open College course in Twentieth Century Life. No entry requirements, but this is the kind of open learning course where you attend college (two evenings a week for the first year, one evening a week for the second). It can lead to a degree course at Staffordshire Polytechnic. Open learning Access courses are available in a variety of GCSE, GCE and Business Studies subjects.

Stoke-on-Trent: Cauldon College of Further and Higher Education
Range of Open Learning courses at GCSE and A-level, and Building Engineering Services.

Stoke-on-Trent: Staffordshire Polytechnic
(1988) Open Learning Unit in association with further education colleges, details from Polytechnic.

Stratford-upon-Avon: South Warwickshire College of Further Education
(1988) Homestudy distance-learning facilities for GCSE Mathematics, RSA Typing Stage I and Teeline Shorthand.

Tamworth College of Further Education
(1988) Distance-learning. All Languages, Distribution, Inn-Keeping, GCSE and A-level subjects. Details from college.

Wakefield: Bretton Hall College of Higher Education
Distance-learning packs can be provided for students wishing to take the Mature Matriculation examination.

Warley and West Bromwich: Sandwell College
(1988) Flexistudy GCSE English and Shorthand with distance-learning packages and tutorial classes at college. Courses originated from Open Tech project in Computer-Aided Engineering – distance-learning materials plus personal computer graphics workstation, plus telephone and face-to-face tutorials. Open Learning distance-learning plus tutorial facilities in various

subjects, including LCCI Private Secretary's Diploma. Shorthand and Association of Medical Secretaries and Practice Administrators' Diploma.

Warwick: University of Warwick

(1988) Distance-learning MBA. The university states: 'This is a flexible programme, normally completed in four years, though some students may complete in three years while others may take up to eight years. Should a student have to discontinue studying, he or she may be eligible for a Certificate or Diploma. The programme consists of examined courses, taken over three years at the rate of four courses per year, plus a dissertation based on a project agreed between the university and the student. The distance-learning scheme for the course work is administered by Wolsey Hall, Oxford (a leading distance-learning college for over 90 years), students being required to complete approximately three assignments per month. A compulsory eight-day seminar is held each September at the University of Warwick to review topics studied the previous year; course assessment is by examination (sometimes under an "open book" system). Applicants should either hold, or expect to obtain a first- or second-class honours degree, or the final qualification of an acceptable professional body, *or* a Higher National Diploma or equivalent qualification, provided that they are over 27 on the proposed date of entry to the programme, and have a minimum of four years' experience in an executive capacity in industry, commerce or the public sector; some candidates (especially those with non-UK qualifications) may be asked to take the Graduate Management Admission Test.'

Wellingborough College

This college is developing an Open Learning Centre. Initially the College is offering NEBSS by Open Learning, support to the courses funded by the original Footwear Open Learning Tech and a Maths Workshop. Workshops in Communications, Adult Literacy and Numeracy, Human Biology and Computing should follow.

Witney: West Oxfordshire Technical College

Agriculture – stud and stable husbandry – thoroughbred industry:Skills dialogue in isolated business management. Running of yard with phase learning materials backed up with tutorial support system.

Wolverhampton: Bilston Community College

Flexistudy: home study courses, tutorial support available or students may attend occasional classes. Options include the following courses (but similar arrangements may be possible for other subjects), and teaching is generally geared towards GCSE, though work may be undertaken at other levels: American Studies A-level; Britain, Europe and the World 1948-1950; Business Studies A-level; Classical Civilisation GCSE/A-level; Community Studies; Creative Writing; English; English Literature; General Studies

GCSE/A-level; History of Medicine with Social Aspects; Human Biology; Integrated Humanities GCSE; Latin GCSE/A-level; Maths; Religious Studies GCSE (Mark and Christian Responsibility); Religious Studies A-level (two chosen from The Old Testament, The New Testament and Aspects of Religious Belief); Social and Economic History of Britain since 1750; Sociology; Welfare and Society; Study Skills. In addition the College can provide flexible learning support in a range of vocational areas for employers wishing to retrain their staff. Contact the Open Learning Co-Ordinator on Wolverhampton 353877 for details.

Wolverhampton: Wulfrun College
(1988) Homestudy courses using specially prepared learning materials plus support from tutors at pre-arranged times (telephone tutorials or face-to-face tuition). Options are: Introductory English, Introductory Mathematics; How to Study; 30-hour course in BASIC; Shorthand; Typewriting; GCSE Accounts, Art, Biology, Commerce, Economics, English Language, English Literature, Geography, Human Biology, History, Law, Mathematics, Sociology, Local History, Religious Education. GCE A-levels in Economics, English Literature, History, Sociology. Open University Preparatory courses in Arts and Social Science.

Homestudy: viewpoints
'I did two O-levels at college last year and I decided I would like to do Maths – well, not that I would like to do it, but that I needed to do it if I was going to do anything else. A lot of employers ask you for both O-level English and O-level Maths or the equivalent. I did do the Pre O-level Maths course at college, but I decided that with the exam course, I would probably fall behind in a classroom full of younger students who had probably come straight in from school. I don't think I would have tackled Maths if there hadn't been this way of doing it, in my own time. At home, I can take all the time I need to get through any specific part that I find difficult.'
(Homestudy student, Wulfrun College of Further Education)

'The beginning of the course is crucial. As a tutor, you've got to be extremely supportive in the early stages, because you want the students to get into the course of study, to become familiar with their materials, and to enjoy the course. Then the aim is to try and keep the students motivated, and get them to study at fairly regular intervals, which can be a problem, given that many of them have other commitments, apart from studying. All the tutors involved in the Homestudy programme get together regularly to discuss how they are getting on, and share ideas and experiences. We find that one of the advantages is that students work at their own pace and some are able to progress quite rapidly – for instance, some who start in September are sitting an examination the following June. Other students are deferring their entry for another few months or for a year. We can cater very much for an individual student's needs, and if we have just one student who wants to do a particular subject, and one tutor who wants to teach it, that's perfectly possible in a way that it wouldn't been in a clasroom situation where we have to have at least 10 or 12 students for one tutor.'

(Spokesperson, Wulfrun College of Further Education)

Northern England

Accrington and Rossendale College
Centre for the Open College of the North West, providing part-time, unit-based courses open to people without qualifications. By building up units you can become eligible for entry to appropriate degree, diploma and equivalent courses at Lancaster University, Lancashire Polytechnic and their associated institutions. Many other universities, polytechnics and colleges have already admitted Open College students. A range of professional associations, including the Institute of Personnel Managers and the Social Work Council have also recognised Open College courses, which are available throughout the North West (see entries below), though not every college can offer every subject.

Altrincham: South Trafford College of Further Education
Flexistudy courses using distance-learning materials at home with tutorial support at college. Options are: English Language and Literature, Foreign Languages, Geography and History, Marketing and Economics, Sociology, Psychology and Child Devlopment, Human Biology, Physics, Art.

Ashington: Northumberland College of Arts and Technology
College is the major provider of flexible learning in Northumberland. This Gateway centre for The Open College offers a large range of training opportunities in Information Technology, Business Development, Caring Skills and many other subjects. Access – contact Norcat 0670 811516 or Access centres at Berwick and Alnwick at any time.

Barrow-in-Furness College of Further Education
(1988) Open learning facilities for students who cannot attend conventional classes – include tutorials and practical classes as required. Details from the college.

Blackburn College
Centre for Open College of the North West with courses validated by Lancaster University and Lancashire Polytechnic, no formal entry requirements. Unit-based part-time courses, available by day or evening. Options

include Study Techniques, Sociology, Electronics,Microprocessor Systems, Computing, Business Studies, Music, English Literature, Politics, Edwardian Britain, Art,German, Economics, Drama, Accounting, Philosophy, English Language, Economic and Social History, Psychology, Spanish, Women's Studies, Creative Writing, European Studies, Italian, Sociology, Mathematics, Industrial Relations, Classical Studies. Students do have to attend college one session a week for their part-time courses, though they can work at their own pace at home. 'A' units are introductory and 'B' units are widely recognised as A-level equivalents. Also Open Learning facilities are available in most areas of the college.

Blackpool and Fylde College of Further and Higher Education
Centre for Open College of the North West (see Accrington and Rossendale College for details).

Bradford and Ilkley Community College
(1988) Open Learning as part of the West Yorkshire Open Learning Federation. Courses at foundation, preliminary, intermediate, advanced and post-experience/higher education levels.

Bridlington: East Yorkshire College of Further Education
(1988) College acts as agent; it can offer guidance and obtain and sell Open Learning materials.

Burnley College
Centre for Open College of the North West (see Accrington and Rossendale College for details). Participates in Open Learning scheme, details from college.

Consett: Derwentside College
Is part of the Durham Access Centre.

Dewsbury College
Home-Based Study programmes with texts, practical kits, video or computer programmes (students can use them at the college) plus tutorial support by phone or face-to-face counselling, Options include How to Study, Accounting (GCSE/A-level), Biology (GCSE/A-level), Chemistry (A-level), Economics (A-level), English Language (GCSE), English Literature (GCSE/A-level), History (GCSE/A-level), Physics (A-level), Psychology and Child Development (A/O-level), French (Preliminary/GCSE), German (Preliminary/GCSE), Spanish (Preliminary/GCSE), Maths (GCSE/A-level – Pure, Applied, Pure and Applied), Sociology (GCSE/A-level). SciTech modules for use by laboratory technicians in schools, college or industry. Fabrication Engineering (for mature students with a working knowledge of plate, structural or sheet metal trades), leads to City and Guilds awards. Wide

range of open learning modules, development of which was originally funded by the government-sponsored Open Tech project. Students are usually employer-sponsored but individuals may purchase study packs. Options include Computing, Construction, Engineering, Health Professions, Management, Supervisory Skills, Maths and Statistics, Science, Service Industries, Training.

Durham: New College Durham
Open Learning Access Centre can provide open or flexible learning materials, with tutorial support if desired, on a wide range of topics. Will develop supervisory management courses with employers, to be offered 'in house' and using flexible learning materials and college/company tutorial support. Tutorial materials, audio tapes, video tapes, computer programmes and practical kits are supported by college tutorials, workshops and study groups. Wide range of options include Open BTEC courses, Open Learning for Small Businesses, Open Learning for Supervisory Management. Flexistudy using National Extension College materials with college tutorial support by telephone or face to face. GCSE options include English Language, English Literature, History, Human Biology, Mathematics, Statistics, Social Studies. GCE A-levels include English Literature, History, Sociology.

Gateshead Technical College
Has Open Learning Access Centre. Flexistudy programmes using National Extension College materials with college tutorial support – wide range of GCSE/GCE A-level subjects. Open University leisure packages with tutorial support. Open Learning packages for technician, supervisory and management studies, all levels from beginner to advanced, originally developed with funding from the government-sponsored Open Tech project.

Halifax: Calderdale College
Open Learning as part of the West Yorkshire Open Learning Federation – no entry requirements, attendance at College when possible for individual students. Options include literacy, numeracy, adult education and courses equivalent to GCSE and A-levels for higher education – details from College. Flexistudy for GCSE/A-levels and City and Guilds awards – home study packages and practical kits to use at home, plus telephone and face-to-face tutorials. Gateway centre for The Open College. Open and distance learning programmes include: Small Business Start-up, Business and Management Development, Languages for Work, Computing, Services Skills, Tourism, Catering.

Kirkby College of Further Education
Centre for Open College of the North West (see Accrington and Rossendale College for details). Wide range of subjects.

Lancaster and Morecambe College of Further Education
Centre for Open College of the North West (see Accrington and Rossendale College for details).

Lancaster College of Adult Education
Centre for Open College of the North West (see Accrington and Rossendale College for details).

Leeds: Park Lane College
Distance learning courses available in a wide range of GCSE, A-level and professional subjects, including English Language, Maths, Biology, Law, Chartered Insurance Institute, Chartered Institute of Bankers course, Association of Accounting Technicians course, Legal Secretaries course. Also Gateway centre for The Open College.

Leigh College
Open Learning. Gateway centre for The Open College. Drop-In centre: many learning packages. Flexistudy.

Lincoln, Gainsborough, Louth: North Lincolnshire College
Flexistudy and courses from The Open College in a wide range of subjects.

Liverpool: South Mersey College
Riversdale Open Technology Centre – ROTEC. National Training Award 1988. Provides flexible, practical training in Computer Applications and use of New Technology equipment for individuals and business. ROTEC is a Gateway centre for The Open College. There are no entry requirements for courses and programmes.

Manchester: University of Manchester
Distance-learning: Return to Study course, home-based study packages for 10 unit modules, plus postal and telephone contact with a tutor plus five Saturday group meetings. Based on six months' completion period but you can take longer. Also possible to study the course on a 'roll on – roll off' basis. Completion earns Preparatory Certificate in Higher Education.

Middlesborough: Longlands College of Further Education
(1988) Open Learning packages in all Engineering, Technology, Science and Computing courses, produced by the college itself and multi-disciplinary material available to HND level. Distance-learning courses in Process Plant Operation, Fabrication, Welding Inspection and Quality Control. Basic Mathematics. Flexistudy provision; wide range of subject options available. Drop-In centre facilities; wide range of subject options available.

Nelson and Colne College
Centre for Open College of the North West (see Accrington and Rossendale College for details). Wide range of subjects.

Newcastle-upon-Tyne Polytechnic
(1988) 'Teelang' Language Laboratory, using self-selected packages, working in the privacy of an individual booth and attending as often as you like. Tutorial help is available. There are 35 languages available at various levels: Afrikaans, Arabic, Chinese (Mandarin and Cantonese), Czech, Danish, Dutch, Finnish, French, Gaelic (Irish and Scottish), German, Greek, Hebrew, Hindi, Hungarian, Indonesian, Italian, Japanese, Malay, Mongolian, Norwegian, Persian, Polish, Portuguese, Punjabi, Romanian, Russian, Serbo-Croat, Spanish, Swahili, Swedish, Turkish, Urdu and Welsh. Contact Nigel Thomas, Department of Modern Languages, extension 3791.

Oldham Centres for Community Education
Centre for Open College of the North West (see Accrington and Rossendale College for details).

Peterlee College
Access Centre to Co. Durham Open Learning (see Durham – New College Durham, above). Mathematics Open Learning Workshop and Communication Workshop – all stages, using self-study packages with tutorial help available. Open Learning Computing Workshop with packages and tutorial help allowing study to be divided between home and college. Participants in Open Learning for unemployed and housebound.

Poulton-le-Fylde: Wyre District Adult Education Service
Centre for Open College of the North West (see Accrington and Rossendale).

Preston College
Centre for Open College of the North West (see Accrington and Rossington College for details). Open entry to a range of subjects providing an alternative to GCSE/A-levels. Home study available for some units.

Preston: Lancashire Polytechnic
Distance-learning provision for Analytical Chemistry (ACOL) and Criminology (in conjunction with Open College of the North West). Law degree in development. BTEC unit in Construction available. Tailor-made short courses are provided for industry and the public services and research, testing, consultancy and conference facilities are available; please contact the Commercial and International unit.

Rotherham College of Arts and Technology
(1988) 'Open Workshop' courses offering a choice between attending the workshop at a time and pace to suit the learner, or by Flexistudy, with occasional contact with a tutor. Courses available include: Improve Your

English, Improve Your Maths, Skills for Returning to Study, Preparatory Course for the Police Entry Test, Preparatory Course for the Mature Nurse Entry test, Job Application and Interview Skills, Setting up Your Own Business, English as a Second Language, Teach Yourself Word Processing and Typing – together with a wide range of conventional GCSE and A-level courses. This workshop is open Monday-Thursday 10 a.m. – 7 p.m. and Fridays 10 a.m. – 4 p.m.

Rotherham: Rockingham College
Co-operating in Open College of South Yorkshire to provide open learning packages for adults who require no previous entry qualifications. Students should be 24-plus to take advantage of this provision. Also Flexistudy courses for GCSE and A-levels, for professional qualifications in such areas as Marketing, and leisure subjects such as Gardening, Dressmaking and Beauty Care. Also science and technology open learning packages originally developed with funding from the Open Tech project.

Runshaw Tertiary College
Centre for Open College of the North West (see Accrington and Rossendale College).

Sheffield: Loxley Tertiary College
Open Learning Workshops for learning skills: Communication, Numeracy, Keyboarding and Information Technology. Flexistudy – wide range of NEC Telecommunications packages. The Open College: 'The Effective Learner'. GCSE packages available for English Language, English Literature, Sociology, History (Social and Economic and World Powers), Maths, Human Biology. GCE A-levels – English Literature, Sociology, History, Art. All the above will be expanded upon during 1989/90.

Sheffield: Stradbroke College
'Who would have thought that I could have obtained employment so easily at 57 years of age?' College states: 'Thanks to our flexible retraining programme in Secretarial Skills, this was possible and the student had the confidence to apply for and obtain a job as a secretary. We are able to offer a wide range of subjects on a flexible basis – Languages, GCSEs and Secretarial Skills. There are no formal entry requirements. The flexible nature of attendnce should suit housewives, shiftworkers – in fact anyone who cannot, or does not want to attend ordinary classes. The training is available on a "pick and mix" basis to allow individuals to select from a menu of options. The college also has an Information Technology workshop with excellent facilities where students can attend on a flexible basis and familiarise themselves (at their own pace) with word processing packages, spreadsheets, databases etc.

Shipley College
Open Learning Workshops: Keyboard and Typing; Numeracy and help with Basic Maths; Maths; Business Training Packages (include Word Processing, Getting Finance, Taxation, Designing a Promotion Campaign, Understanding Stock Control etc.); Study Skills; Information Technology.

Skelmersdale College
Centre for Open College of the North West (see Accrington and Rossendale College).

Southport College of Art and Technology
Centre for Open College of the North West (see Accrington and Rossendale College for details). Open Learning Guest House Owners course, with audio-cassette guidance, telephone help line and tutorial back-up (on student's premises if necessary). Customised learning packages to suit individual students' needs, covering every subject at every level, enabling people to learn at their own speed, in their own home (or at a place of work) with tutorial support as needed. Also support centre for The Open College.

Wakefield: Bretton Hall College of Higher Education
Distance-learning packs can be provided for students wishing to take the Mature Matriculation examination

Warrington: North Cheshire College
Part of the Manchester Open College Federation; provides Access courses (see 'Pre-Entry, Sample and Access Courses').

Whalley Adult Centre
Centre for Open College of the North West (see Accrington and Rossendale College).

Widnes: Halton College of Further Education
A wide variety of Open Learning and Flexible Learning packages available, including Information Technology, Word Processing, Selling a Service and Telephone Techniques. Drop-In Skils centre for training by appointment

Wigan College of Technology
Centre for Open College of the North West (details from Accrington and Rossendale College).

Wigan: TRACE (Training Research Advisory Consultancy) Enterprises Ltd
(1988) A Wigan College of Technology Company. Distance-learning Return to Study course, home-based study packages plus postal andtelephone tutorial contact, plus five group meetings on Saturdays. Based on six-month

completion, but you may take longer ifyou wish. NB: TRACE produces specialised distance-learning materials, e.g. updating courses for Radiographers. If you are a manager or are professionally qualified and want to update, their brochure could produce some useful ideas for you.

Wales and Western England

Barnstaple: North Devon College
Open Learning packages developed with funding from the Open Tech project. College is also associated with The Open College – details from college.

Bath: Norton Radstock College
Flexistudy courses including: How to Study Effectively, Wordpower, Numbers at Work, Fleximaths. Open University Community Education courses: The First Years of Life, The Pre-School Child, Parents and Teachers, Work Choices, Action Planning for the Unemployed. Flexible Access by arrangement, to certain specialist rooms for self-directed study; these include the Pottery, Darkroom, Computer Room and Workshop/Woodwork Room. A growing range of courses including Open University Group and Study packs, courses from The Open College and others. Subjects include 'The Carers' (The Open College); Information Technology Workshop; Small Business courses; Word Processing and others.

Bristol: Filton Technical College
Flexastudy: approximately 70% of your time at college is spent in guided private study, with regular individual tutorials from qualified staff who supply schemes of work and learning resources, and assess each student's work. Students can choose to attend morning, afternoon or evening sessions. The Flexastudy sessions are offered two days a week from 9 a.m. to 9.15 p.m. Choices include: BTEC Continuing Education Units in Computer Studies, Working with People, Information Technology for Managers, Improve your Financial Decision Making, Making Sense of Economics, Making Sense of Marketing, Making Sense of Exporting. Also Institute of Industrial Managers' Certificate and Diploma, NEBSS Introductory course in Supervisory Studies, Institute of Management Services Certificate and Diploma, Institute of Transport Administration Graduateship and Corporate Membership, Institute of Administrative Management Certificate, Association of Accounting Technicians Intermediate and Final, Finance Houses Association Part I, Institute of Chartered Secretaries and Administrators, Diploma in Marketing Foundation, Course in Overseas Trade,

Computer Programming (BASIC, COBOL, PASCAL, etc.). Mathematics at GCSE and A-level by Open Learning. Also 'Freeway' courses in Sociology and Social and Economic History, using study materials of the National Extension College: you decide how, when and where you'll study.

Flexastudy Courses: viewpoint
'There are lots of quite reputable professional institutes, each of whom, in our catchment area, would only come up with five or six students in any given academic year. We're faced with meeting the LEA minimum recruitment number of 12 students before we can offer a course. By grouping all these minority professional institute students together in the one Flexastudy facility, we've overcome our numbers problem. On a typical evening in the past year we would have anything up to 40 or 45 students taking anything up to six or seven different professional institute schemes, supported by three full-time members of staff, who would be circulating round the room giving tutorials. So far, all our learning materials have been produced by our (intensely overworked) staff, but we are planning to buy in correspondence materials for the scheme in our area in the future.'

(Spokesperson, Filton Technical College, Bristol)

Bristol Polytechnic
Distance Learning is available in some subject areas, such as Town Planning and Construction.

Chippenham Technical College
(1988) Flexistudy courses for GCSE, various subjects. Computing in BASIC, Archaeology A-level, Hairdressing, Office Skills.

Exeter College
Open Learning: a wide range of packages is offered with tutorial support. Subjects covered include Return to Learn, Study Skills, Numeracy, GCSEs, A-levels, Business and Management, Office Skills, Computing, Electronics and Microelectronics.

Haverfordwest and Neyland: Pembrokeshire College
Pembrokeshire College offers distance learning with coursebooks and audio or video cassettes. Telephone, face-to-face tutorials and seminars are arranged. A wide range of study programmes is available, tailor-made to suit the individual's specific requirements. Areas covered include Agriculture, Beauty Therapy, Business and Finance, Catering, Computing, Construction, Engineering, Hairdressing, Health Studies, Office Skills and Tourism.

Llanelli: Carmarthenshire College of Technology and Art
(1988) Distance learning provision for NEBSS Supervisory Studies award.

Newtown: Montgomery College of Further Education
In Distance Learning, the Association of Accounting Technicians' course is particularly successful and A-levels are available.

Plymouth College of Further Education
The Plymouth Open Learning Systems Unit, a Department within the college, produces Microelectronics and Electronics Distance Learning packages, each of which provides a BTEC Certificate of Achievement at the new National level. These units are part of a full Distance Learning National Certificate which is available in Engineering (Electrical/Electronic). Telephone tutorial support is available for those who register on the college courses; learners may join at any time of year. NEBSM Super Series Open Learning Units and Modules. Institute of Personnel Management (IPM) Certificate in Personnel Practice. Workshops/Open Learning. Supervisory and Management tailor-made courses and other specialist training programmes constructed to meet your specific training needs. Totally flexible in subjects covered; as long or as short as you require, delivered in whatever way or location is best. The college is a Gateway centre for The Open College and is available to offer all The Open College materials with tutorial support as required.

Pontypool College
Certain subjects can be taught using Open Learning methods, which involve a combination of study packs and personal tutorials at the college. Please ask for details.

Pontypridd: the Polytechnic of Wales
(1988) Participates in the Morgannwg Open Learning Project for Mid, South and West Glamorgan. Has produced open-learning materials in Computer-Aided Manufacturing Systems V, for BTEC Units and is producing them in Production Planning and Control IV and Computer-Aided Engineering IV, for BTEC Units.

Salisbury College of Technology
(1988) Open Learning. Distance-learning packages for GCSE Biology/Environmental Studies, English, English Literature, Human Biology, Local History, Psychology, Sociology and GCE A-level Biology/Botany/Environmental Studies, English, Human Biology, Zoology. Also distance-learning for BTEC Continuing Education Units.

Street: Strode College
Open Learning at Pre-GCSE, GCSE and A-level in wide range of subject areas. Also Business and Secretarial, Transport Studies, Garage and Transport Management and Caring. Open Learning workshops available in Mathematics, English and Motor Vehicle Engineering.

Taunton: Somerset College of Arts and Technology
Open Learning with wide range of subjects. Details from the college's Open Learning Co-ordinator.

Weymouth College
(1988) Open Learning Unit providing self-study packs and tutorial support over a wide range of subjects, and with some courses leading to qualifications such as GCSE, A-levels, City and Guilds and BTEC awards. The unit has an Open Access Computer Room and Preview Room for viewing course materials, as well as providing audio-visual and photocopying facilities. The Unit has databases which give access to records of courses and open learning materials which may not yet be available through the Unit. In addition, the Open Learning Unit has been selected as Dorset's main Open Access Centre for The Open College. Packages currently available include Autocare, Basic Calculation, Circuit Training, Computers in Business, Introduction to Selling, Is Self-Employment Right for You?, Library and Information Skills, Looking After Children, Pub Business, Report Writing, Understanding Information Technology, Women – the Way Ahead.

Scotland and Northern Ireland

Clydebank College
Open Learning facilities available – details from college.

Dumfries and Galloway College of Technology
Distance-learning courses with monthly meetings with the course tutor, or telephone tutorials where this is impractical. SCE O-grade Accounts, Arithmetic, Economics, English, History, Mathematics, Sociology. H-grade English. GCE A-level Sociology. Teeline Shorthand. 'Learning by Appointment' system: attendance to use college equipment at negotiated times with monthly tutorials. Computing – 30-hour BASIC, Advanced Structural BASIC. Modern Languages: French, German, Modern Greek, Italian, Portuguese, Russian, Spanish, English as a Foreign Language. Pitman's Shorthand – Beginner, Refresher Course, Speed Building. Typing – Beginner, Speed Development, Audio. Word Processing, Keyboarding. Open Learning packages developed as the result of funding from Open Tech project in: Analogue Electronics – Devices; Analogue Electronics – Waveform Generators; Basic Electrical Skills; Computer Numerical Control – Part-Programming, Computer Numerical Control – Machine Tool Applications; Digital Electronics – Basic Digital Electronics, Digital Electronics – Decoders and Combinatorial Logic, Digital Electronics – Digital Devices. Electronics – Introduction, Fault-Finding. Fault-Finding methods: Process Control, Hydraulics; Microprocesser Applications in Business and Commerce. Introduction to Electronics. Pneumatics; Servicing Video Recorders.

Edinburgh: Napier Polytechnic of Edinburgh
Open Learning courses using study materials in text, audio-visual media and computer software for self-study facilities. Wide range of subjects starting from the pre-entry level.

Edinburgh: Queen Margaret College
(1988) Main delivery centre in Scotland for the distribution of SCOTVEC Open Learning course Start Your Own Business. Tutorial backup here and at Clydebank Technical College and Dumfries and Galloway College of Further Education.

Edinburgh: Telford College of Further Education

I am grateful for this information from a reader working as library orderly in a West Country prison, who took the trouble to send me his copy of the Telford College 'Open Learning Opportunities' brochure when he found there was no entry for that college in *The Mature Student's Handbook*. He further advised me that the cost of the Telford College open learning course leading to City and Guilds 737, Library and Information Assistant's certificate was £150 for UK students. The prospectus lists a most extensive range of study subjects, most of which lead to a specific qualification, e.g. SCE O-grade or City and Guilds or SCOTVEC or HCIMA. Study areas are: Business Management/Secretarial Studies: Building/Construction: Catering; Communication Skills: Computing: Engineering; Hairdressing; Languages,Library and Information Studies; Life Sciences/Health Studies; Numeracy, Mathematics and Statistics; Physical Sciences/Electronics; Social Sciences. For general information, contact the Course Information Officer, tel: 031-332 2491 ext 290. (Answerphone service available on 031-332 0127 outside college hours.)

Glasgow: Strathclyde Business School, University of Strathcylde

Open Learning MBA postgraduate course.

Open Learning MBA: viewpoints

'I had to make a choice – did I want to take the full-time MBA course, which would have meant taking a year out of work, or was I prepared to fit open learning in with my job? With the way things are developing in my company, giving up work for a year would have been inappropriate. To cover the reading, tutor-marked and other assignments that I have to do on the open learning MBA takes up to about 10–15 hours a week, but if you are experiencing any difficulties with any part of the course at all, you can phone up the tutor assigned for each course and you will receive guidance and advice. You are left to a great extent to rely on your own devices, but you can meet people whose experience is of consummate value to you when you need access to tutors.'

(Student, Open Learning MBA, Strathclyde Business School)

'Open learning solves three problems. It keeps people in their jobs, so that they can keep up to date with what's happening in their company. Then they can give their company instant feedback on ideas that are starting to emerge from the course and inject suggestions for new approaches to company problems that may crop up as they study. And open learning gives people flexibility. If they are promoted into demanding new jobs, they can stop their studies for a while, and plug back into the system later on, picking up where they left off.'

(Spokesperson, Open Learning MBA, Strathclyde Business School)

Glasgow: University of Glasgow
Department of Scottish Literature. MPhil programme in Scottish Literature taught over three years by correspondence with one day and week long schools. 'Open to suitably qualified graduates, the course provides a comprehensive study of 600 years of literature in English and Scots, and is aimed at schoolteachers and all those with interest in the subject.'

Inverness College of Further and Higher Education
(1988) Open Learning with telephone tutorials in SCOTVEC National Certificate modules: Communications, Learning and Study Skills; Mathematics Grade 2; Cost Control in Catering; Introduction to Economic Analysis; Organisation of Industry; Starting and Running a Small Business; Financial Record Keeping; Health and Safety in the Work Environment; People and Politics; Local Authorities; Central Government; Fundamentals of Technology: Mechanical; Fundamentals of Technology: Electrical; Basic Telecommunications; Communication 1/2; Communication 2/3; Introduction to Computers; Computer Software; Marketing; SCOTVEC Higher National Certificate in Business Studies; City and Guilds 232 Electrical and Electronic Craft Studies; 236C Electrical Installation; BTEC/SCOTVEC subjects and modules for technical training; City and Guilds 760/2 Advanced Hairdressing.

Motherwell College
The college has an Open Learning Unit providing a wide range of courses leading to SCE or SCOTVEC National Certificate modules. Students with disabilities can be accepted on to most courses and are supported in their studies by the considerable resources of the Special Needs Department.

Newcastle College of Further Education
Open College. Flexistudy packs etc.

Newtownabbey College of Further Education
Open-learning packages are available for many of the subjects and courses listed for this college in the 'Retraining and New Skills Courses' section of *The Mature Student's Handbook*. Ask for details from the college.

Newry: the Continuing Education Programme (Southern Education and Library Board)
We are the contact for Open Learning. We offer careers and educational counselling for adults.

Perth College of Further Education
Courses/packages provide flexible learning opportunities in the following categories: SCE and GCE subjects and Basic Skills, including Study Skills and Communications. SCOTVEC modular courses in Computing, Special

Needs Care course, City and Guilds qualifications in Construction Crafts (600 series), Motor Vehicle Craft Studies (381) and 15th Edition IEE wiring regulations. SCOTVEC Diploma in Business Development. City and Guilds qualifications in Report Writing; specialist qualifications related to Tourism, Private Hotel Management and Outside Catering. The Centre of Open Learning is also Tayside Region's Gateway centre for all courses offered by The Open College and in combination with other Open Learning provision, e.g. Hotel & Catering Training Board, Road Transport Industry Training Board, Seafish Industry Authority, National Examination Board for Supervisory Studies etc. the centre is able to provide a comprehensive range of flexible, individualised learning.

DEGREE
AND
ADVANCED COURSES

Higher education and further
qualifications: full-time and
part-time opportunities

Introduction

'Graduate status' is valuable. There are all kinds of reasons why adults embark on degree courses late in life, but one of the most popular is that it widens the range of careers anyone can be considered for. In some cases, there are special 'graduate training schemes'. In others, graduates are entitled to a shortened form of training. And even if you stay in your own career field after taking a degree (as many Open University graduates choose to do), the achievement of a degree can substantially improve your career prospects.

There are also careers for which 'graduate status' is the bottom line. The minimum qualification for entry to the professional course of training is a degree. Librarianship is a good example. But it also gets more difficult every year to obtain training in accountancy if you are a non-graduate. (In chartered accountancy, 90% of articled clerks are graduates.) A first- or second-class honours degree is necessary if you want to read for the Bar, and most solicitors considering mature applicants are likely to favour graduates over non-graduates. Degrees can win you concessions in professional training entry requirements in a range of occupations from journalism to social work.

LATE STARTERS WELCOME

Mature students often need convincing that they're really welcome at universities, polytechnics and colleges of higher education. As one student puts it, in the *Birmingham Polytechnic* student viewpoint on page 302, '...at the start, when I saw the younger students and they were discussing topics I knew nothing about, I felt very unsure of myself'.

That same student goes on to say... 'After a period of time, I realised that as far as the course was concerned, the young students were basically at the same level as I was. They were no better than me, and I was no better than them. It gave me security...'

In fact, mature students are often at an advantage in higher education. Staying with Birmingham Polytechnic, their official spokesperson says 'The 18 and 19-year-olds can be intimidated by the self-confidence and experience and knowledge of the world that the mature student has. There is a dedication and motivation among mature students that I, as a teacher, find positively exhilarating and very, very rewarding.'

RECORDS OF SUCCESS

What is undeniable is that mature students have built up a reputation of success in higher education. For example, at the University of Warwick, where nearly one in eight students is a mature student, the prospectus states: 'It is noticeable that mature students generally obtain better degree results than younger students, even though in the majority of cases, the mature students did not have qualifications normally acceptable for entrance when they applied for the course.'

This experience is mirrored at polytechnics. The Council for National Academic Awards (which approves degrees offered in polytechnics and other institutes of higher education outside the universities) carried out a research project that showed that students who went into higher education *without* A-levels tended to do better than those *with* A-levels.

CONCESSIONS FOR MATURE STUDENTS

This is all good news, but the average 'late starter' who may well have left school without A-levels or even O-levels often feels it's hardly practicable to start on a course of study that may or may not lead to them starting a degree course in three or four years' time. The idea of starting all over again to get the entry requirements for a degree is what puts many people off – which is why special 'Access courses' for mature students have been so enthusiastically received. (For examples, see the 'Pre-Entry, Sample and Access Courses' section of this directory.)

As well as Access courses, many universities, polytechnics and colleges of higher education offer a range of concessions in entry requirements to people applying later in life. The minimum age for mature student concessions, according to colleges that answered my enquiry, ranges from 19 (at the University of Keele) to 25 (at Glasgow College of Technology). As a rough guideline, a majority of higher education institutions set 21 as their minimum age for mature students.

Concessions vary considerably from place to place. You may be offered a place on the basis of your performance at an interview, your work experience and/or an essay or two, written on subjects suggested by the selectors. You may offer success in an Access course or an Open University Foundation course instead of A-levels. Often higher education establishments reduce their A-level requirements – from three or two passes to just one – in the case of a promising mature student.

Then there's the *Associate Student* scheme. This is primarily for people who may want to study just one subject or part of a subject in a degree course – often because it will help them in their work. On page 293, you'll see how one student is released by his employers to take a unit of Advanced Maths at Hatfield Polytechnic because it helps him with the computer he has to use at work.

However, quite a few people who begin as *Associate Students*, just visiting college for one study session a week and doing their course work at home, later decide they'd like to aim at a degree. Usually this is possible; often the *Associate Student* achievement satisfies entry requirements and success in a unit exam may count towards their final degree.

VALUE OF WORK EXPERIENCE

APEL is the latest bridge into higher education for mature students. The letters stand for 'Assessment of Prior Experiential Learning', which in turn means that you may be accepted for a degree course at a polytechnic or college, without any formal qualifications but on the basis of your work experience and training.

A study was carried out by the Learning from Experience Trust and financed by the Council for National Academic Awards. It covered 147 students aged between 22 and 56. Among those interviewed was a 48-year-old who had no formal educational qualifications but was accepted on the basis of her work experience, from clerk to information consultant, for a BA in Information and Library Studies. Another 33-year-old had only O-levels, but was accepted to take a BEng (Hons) degree course because of his experience and technical certificates in motor engineering.

APEL promises to open more routes into more courses for people whose work experience and increasing responsibilities may have left them little time to get formal qualifications. You should always ask Admissions Tutors at colleges what factors they take into account when considering applications from mature students; new entry routes are opening up all the time.

CREDIT ACCUMULATION

'CATS' is another acronym to look out for when you are looking through prospectuses of degree courses (and do send for them; this book can only give shortened versions of individual colleges' arrangements for mature students). It stands for 'Credit Accumulation and Transfer' and it means students can be credited with their successes in individual units of a pre-degree or degree course and that these credits will be recognised by other higher education establishments taking part in the CATS scheme (generally all those which offer CNAA-validated courses and other colleges which have applied to take part in the scheme).

The mention of 'transfer' in the CATS title means that if you have to give up a course part of the way through – perhaps because you've moved your job to a different part of the country - you can transfer your accumulated credits to a college offering a similar course in the new location, and carry on studying.

CREDIT ACCUMULATION – DEVELOPMENTS

An agreement in March 1989 between the CNAA and the English National Board for Nursing, Midwifery and Health Visiting will enable post 1985 courses leading to registration as a first-level nurse, together with many well-established post-registration qualifications to count for academic credit towards a degree.

The example they give is that someone with the Health Visitor's Certificate has earned 110 out of the 120 points needed for completion of the first year of a degree, plus 30 points towards the 120 needed for the second year of a degree. (The address for more details of this scheme is: The ENB Careers Service, Chantry House, 798 Chesterfield Road, Sheffield S8 0SF.)

'ERASMUS' deserves a mention, too. This acronym stands for the European Community Action Scheme for the Mobility of University Students. The CNAA's 'CATS' scheme has been selected by ERASMUS to take part in an experimental pilot project that will enable students at certain colleges to receive credit for the study they've completed in one country, and then to transfer to a higher education establishment in another country within the EEC. Only a small number of UK polytechnics and one university have been chosen for the initial project, but if it works, it could mean that eventually, students can combine courses at two or even more higher education establishments here or on the Continent to build up credits towards a degree.

APPLICATIONS AND ENTRY

Skimming through the past pages of information, you'll have noticed that universities, polytechnics and colleges of higher education are great ones for acronyms. This too can put off people who have been away from education for some time and indeed, may have been taught in the workplace that the simplest, most widely understood description is the best.

All the same, life's too short to have to keep on referring to the 'Universities Central Council on Admissions' and the 'Polytechnics Central Admissions System' – whose forms you usually have to complete if you want to apply for a full-time or sandwich course degree place.

They're shortened to UCCA and PCAS and you will find that prospectuses always tell you where to write for your UCCA or PCAS form and instructions on how to apply.

While we're on the subject, anyone applying for a degree place that will qualify them to teach (a BEd) will find they have to apply through something called CRCH – the Central Register and Clearing House. Again, prospectuses give details. And if you're after an art and design course, your acronym is ADAR – the Art and Design Admissions Registry, which sifts these applications.

STEP BY STEP GUIDANCE

Sounds a bit heavy? Let me recommend Chapter 3 'Your Applications' in Brian Heap's book *Degree Course Offers* (Careers Consultants) – available in most public libraries – for the simple and methodical way in which he explains how to tackle these organisations. I won't attempt to condense into a few paragraphs what takes him 18 closely-packed pages, but it's all there, and it's all valuable. Any would-be mature student who finds himself or herself keen but puzzled by the complexities of applying for a course that sounds ideal will find that Mr. Heap will take them step-by-step though the whole process.

PART-TIME DEGREES

You can make a direct application to the university, polytechnic or college of your choice if you want to take a part-time degree course. I have made a point of asking higher education establishments about the courses they offer on a part-time basis because so many people want to keep on their jobs while they are studying to better themselves or change careers. The demand for part-time study facilities has increased very much in recent years, and it's interesting to see how some colleges are making a special effort to cater for the people who want to get letters after their names without giving up their jobs in the process.

Don't overlook the wide range of courses offered by the Open University when you are considering part-time study. OU degrees are highly valued, not least because most employers recognise what an effort it is to study part time, while working, let alone motivating yourself when you study at home.

MAKING YOU WELCOME

Throughout the courses section that follows, I've listed the entry concessions offered to mature students by each higher education establishment that responded to my enquiries. Not all of them did – and since they all received two requests for information in 1988 and a further request in 1989, it does suggest that any college without an entry probably has no special policy with regard to mature students.

They are more than made up for by the enthusiasm of the majority who *do* give concessions, *do* put on part-time courses (some even during the evenings for people at work all day) and *do* use phrases like 'mature students welcomed' or 'mature students encouraged to apply'. The attitude of the University of Bradford should encourage anyone, and it's nice to see the University of Cambridge pointing out which are the likely colleges for late starters.

HIGHER EDUCATION – THE BENEFITS

Welcomes apart, do you sincerely want to enter higher education? It does need thinking about because of the time it takes – at least three years, sometimes longer, if you are on a full-time honours or sandwich degree course, and maybe between five and eight years if you study part-time for a degree. It will mean loss of earnings, if you are a full-time student, or loss of freedom, in evenings and weekends devoted to study, if you take up a part-time place. Not surprisingly, degree course selectors often say they place 'motivation' high on their list of requirements when they are considering whether to give a place to an older student.

In return for all that effort, rewards can be substantial. According to the latest Open University study, which covered 5000 OU graduates, 57% claimed that their job performance or career prospects improved as a result of their studies. 80% said the experience was good for them as individuals. Only 7% warned that there were some bad effects on family life.

EMPLOYMENT PROSPECTS

About one third of all graduate traineeships are open to graduates in any subject (or 'of any discipline' – the phrase often used in prospectuses). Unless you are substantially older than the usual graduate trainee (say in your late 40s or 50s rather than your 30s or 20s) you could have an advantage over an untried graduate, bearing in mind that you can probably offer work experience and a work reference as well as a degree. You're offering prospective employers two valuable demonstrations of ability – you can hold down a job and you've reached an academic target, demonstrating intellectual strength and staying power.

Apart from those jobs that require the status of graduate for you to be considered, there are others you can train for on a postgraduate course. You get concessions in the length of training or in the exams you have to take. For example, the courses section identifies shortened courses for graduates who want to qualify as registered nurses. There are 'fast stream' management training opportunities for graduates in the police, in banks, in building societies, in retailing. Then there are graduate 'conversion' courses for which you can be considered once you have demonstrated intellectual potential by getting a degree. You'll find information technology and hotel and catering management courses for graduates mentioned in the course lists.

Finally, a degree can help you in the promotion stakes. Given two candidates of equal merit, one who has a degree and one who does not, the person with the degree is likely to get the job because he/she has proved to have the staying power to withstand the undergraduate course and the temperament to succeeed in competitive exams and assessments. This stamina is demonstrated even more by those who take part-time or distance learning degrees. The OU survey mentioned earlier showed that 44% of its graduates had been promoted as a result of their studies, whilst another 22% had changed their jobs. About 17% had moved on from the 'shop floor' to achieve managerial status.

PERSONAL FACTORS

At the end of the day, though, it's not enough just to take a degree course for job reasons. You may choose a very 'useful' subject, but if it bores you, you are unlikely to do well.

The best reason for going after a degree or advanced level qualification is that you really do want to spend your time studying the subject or subjects concerned. You can't think of anything more enjoyable than being freed of the burden of going to a job, or looking after a house, and allowed to learn all about Music, or Modern History, or Biotechnology – or whatever your own pet subject might be. When you leaf through prospectuses with pictures of groups of people eagerly discussing new ideas, or using the latest technical equipment or choosing from a library full of books, you wish you were one of them. You wouldn't mind living on rice and lentils, or dressing out of the Oxfam shop in return for three years of freedom to learn.

GRANTS FOR (NEARLY) ALL

People who have not previously had a grant for education and are self-supporting are entitled to one when they are accepted for a full-time degree or similar course. It's not a lot, but it covers your fees and a spartan lifestyle. You get extra if you are over 26 when your course starts and have earned, or received in taxable unemployment or supplementary benefits, at least £12,000 during the three years before the start of the first academic year of your course (see 'Costs and Grants' section).

It's less easy to get a grant for a postgraduate course, though if you are a graduate wanting to make a career change, this can be one of the most convenient bridges into a new career that you can find. Some courses of the 'conversion' kind may attract support from the Training Agency. Others attract grants from research councils, but you may have to look for a part-time version of your ideal full-time course so that you can 'work your way through college' as American students do.

There's also the possibility of a Career Development Loan for a course lasting not more than a year in length. Under this government scheme, you don't have to start paying your loan back until three months after you have finished your course (see 'Costs and Grants' section again).

As in the earlier sections, students who have gone into higher education when making a fresh start – and sometimes those who teach them – have contributed their views to the courses section. For future editions of *The Mature Student's Handbook* I would be delighted to hear from others who have experience of mature-age study at university, polytechnic or college.

Useful free booklets are *Universities Welcome Mature Students* from UCCA, PO Box 29, Cheltenham, Glos. GL50 1HY and *Open Doors to Higher Education – Opportunities for Everyone Over 21* from the Commiteee of Directors of Polytechnics, Kirkman House, 12/14 Whitfield Street, London, W1P 6AX.

Though initially written for prospective mature students going to Manchester Polytechnic, their free Handbook is well worth reading – write to Manchester Polytechnic, The Registry, All Saints, Manchester M15 6BH.

University, polytechnic and college prospectuses are free and give you masses of information about individual courses. (See addresses at the end of the book). It is worth mentioning whether you are interested in full-time courses or part-time courses as some institutions, notably polytechnics, often produce two separate prospectuses, one listing full-time and sandwich courses and the other listing part-time courses.

London and Middlesex

Birkbeck College: University of London
The prospectus states: Birkbeck is primarily a College for working people; we specialise in providing degree level and research facilities for students who are, in the words of the College Charter, 'engaged in earning their livelihood during the day time and are, therefore, only able to study on a part-time evening basis. If you are not working because you have to look after your children or an elderly or infirm relative during the day time, or if you are retired, please make this clear on your application form'. Mature student concessions are possible at age 23 via interview plus a record of successful study at mature age (e.g. an A-level, extra-mural diploma or OU credit). Sometimes students are offered a place for a year on a probationary basis. Most popular courses among mature students (NB: these are all Part-Time degrees) are: BA Classics, English, French, German, Hispanic Studies, History, History of Art, Philosophy, and BSc Biology, Chemistry, Financial Economics, Geography, Geology, Mathematics (including Statistics and Computing), Physics and Psychology. Combined Subjects degrees of interest to mature students include: BA Humanities, Politics/Philosophy/History, Philosophy/Psychology; and BSc Cognitive Science, Environmental Science, and other science combinations. For details ring 01-631 6561.

Central London: Polytechnic of Central London
The prospectus says: 'Normally, but not necessarily, mature students seeking special consideration should be over 21'. The polytechnic's letter adds: 'The Business Studies degree course will consider students over the age of 21 years. Most degree courses .... will consider students as mature students as long as they are 25 years or over. Concessions usually take the form of an informal interview with the course leader.' *Part-Time Degrees*: BA/BA (Hons) Social Science; BA/BA (Hons) Business Studies, in association with the City of London Polytechnic and Polytechnic of the South Bank. LLB/LLB (Hons); BA/BA (Hons) Arabic, Chinese, Russian Studies, BSc/BSc (Hons) Chiropody, in conjunction with the London Foot Hospital and Chelsea School of Chiropody. BSc Computing; BA Photography. *Postgraduate Vocational Courses* include: Diploma in Law, full time – conversion course for non-law graduates who wish to read for the Bar. Foundation course in

Accountancy, full time – any graduate. Diploma in Conference Interpretation, two terms, full time – for candidates with university degree or equivalent and thorough knowledge of their working language. Diploma in Technical and Specialised Translation, full time – for candidates with degree or equivalent in any two of the five major languages: French, German, Italian, Russian, Spanish. Postgraduate Diploma in Office Technology and Business Administration, full time – for any graduate.

City University
(1988) Mature student concessions for those aged 23-plus. Each student is treated individually. The Continuing Education department offers a one-year Open Studies course, part time, day or evening, for adults wishing to return to HE. 'The Department of Social Sciences and Humanities finds a high number of mature students attracted to Sociology and Philosophy degrees and a fair number to Psychology.' *Postgraduate Vocational Courses*: wide range but note particularly Diploma in Industrial and Administrative Sciences, part time, for those with a degree or equivalent in any technical subject, wishing to train in management. MA/Diploma in Arts Administration, MA in Museums and Gallery Administration, MA in Arts Management in Education, for those with experience in the relevant fields seeking further qualification; MA in Librarianship and Arts Administration, for Senior Librarians; all of these may be studied full time or part time. Diploma in Music Information Technology, full time or part time, for graduates in music/the arts, business studies, computing or engineering, hoping to work in the media, and others with relevant experience. MBA in Finance, Industrial Relations and Personnel Management, Export Management, full time or evenings. MSc in Shipping Trade and Finance, full time or evenings. Diploma in Newspaper Journalism, Periodical Journalism, Radio Journalism, International Journalism, full time, any degree acceptable, plus commitment to career in journalism. Diploma in Law, full time, any degree acceptable, for those who wish to become barristers but do not have a qualifying Law degree. Diploma in Clinical Communication studies, full time (acceptable for membership of College of Speech Therapists) any degree considered, but graduates in Psychology, Linguistics or other relevant subjects may gain exemption.

East London Polytechnic
The prospectus does not specify age for mature student concession, but the Polytechnic encourages applications from older people, with or without the normal entry requirements for a course of higher education. In fact more than three-quarters of the full time and sandwich students are over 21 and more than one third are over 25. The School for Independent Study admits students aged over 21 without formal entry requirements and in addition, students may be admitted who are aged between 18 and 21 and do not have the usual entry requirements. *Part-Time Degrees:* BA/BSc (Hons) by Independent Study, BSc (Hons) Life Sciences, BA/BA (Hons) Business Studies,

BEng/BEng (Hons) Civil Engineering (day release), BSc Land Administration, LLB (Hons), BSc/BS (Hons) Mathematics, BSc (Hons) Applied Biology, BA (Hons) Health Studies (for registered nurses and other health professionals, day and evening release), BSc Archaeological Sciences, BSc/BSc (Hons) Psychology. *Postgraduate Vocational Courses:* these include: Diploma in Careers Guidance, full time – any degree acceptable; Diploma in Management (self-managed), open to self-employed as well as employed; MBA part time. Many courses on day-release basis for those already employed in professional/management areas.

Goldsmiths' College: University of London
The College welcomes applications from mature students to all its degree courses. Those over 21 are exempted from the general entrance requirements and any course requirements if they have or will have gained alternative qualifications which demonstrate that, in the College's opinion, they have achieved sufficient competence to justify admission. This could be demonstrated by, for example, a GCE A-level pass gained after leaving school, an Open University Credit or an Access course acceptable to the University. There are many other categories; see the Undergraduate Prospectus for further information. *Part-Time Degrees:* Anthropology, Anthropology and Psychology, Anthropology and Sociology, Craft Studies (Ceramics and Textiles), Design Studies, English, English and French Studies, English and History, English and German Studies, Historical Studies, French Studies, French and German Studies, German Studies, Mathematical Studies, Music, Psychology and Sociology. Mature students are welcome to apply for the following full-time degree courses: Anthropology and Communication Studies, Art and Art History, Communications, Communications and Sociology, English and Theatre Arts, Education (Primary with Subject Study), Education (Secondary with Design and Technology), Fine Art, History and Sociology, Mathematical Studies and Psychology, Social Science and Administration, Textiles. A wide range of *Postgraduate and Post-Experience* courses is available, including Art Therapy, Computer Science, Educational Guidance for Adults, Initial Teacher Training, Social Work. For full details of these and other advanced courses, write for the Postgraduate Prospectus.

London College of Printing
Mature candidates without conventional qualifications considered for BA (Hons) Photography and BA (Hons) Film and Video. *Postgraduate Vocational Courses:* Diploma in Design and Media Technology, full time – for graduates in Graphic Design or equivalent. Periodical Journalism course for graduates, full time - any degree, or those over 21 with equivalent qualifications considered. Diploma in Radio Journalism, full time – any degree or equivalent qualification. Diploma in Printing and Publishing, full time – any degree.

London School of Economics and Political Science, University of London
Mature student concessions possible for those aged 22: the normal number
of GCE passes is not always required. The prospectus states: 'To have a
larger than normal proportion of older students in its population is one of
the traditions of the School, and it is glad to consider applications from
candidates who have had several years' work experience, or, for example,
from married women who wish, after an interval of some years, to return to
full-time study.'

Middlesex Polytechnic
Mature student concessions normally start at 21. For entry to the modular
degree scheme, mature students aged 21 or over without formal qualifications, who can demonstrate capability and motivation to succeed on the
courses within the scheme, are welcome to apply. For entry to BEd course
'consideration is given to candidates over 21 who lack the formal entry
requirements. Such applicants must either undertake a written examination
and tests or provide evidence of a sustained interest and study in an
appropriate subject or activity. They must also satisfy the requirements for
literacy and numeracy (O-level English and Maths or equivalent), or, *for
those over 25*, successfully complete polytechnic tests in these areas prior to
entry.' Concessions for mature students on other degree courses are broadly
similar to above, though more specific requirements are likely to be made for
subjects such as Engineering. *Part-Time Degrees* BA (Hons) Textiles/Fashion,
BA (Hons) Three-Dimensional Design, BEng (Hons) Electronic Engineering, Design and Production (for students with HND/HNC or equivalent),
BA/BA (Hons) Humanities, BA (Hons) Literature and Philosophy, BA
(Hons) Historical Studies, BA (Hons) History of Art, Design and Film, BA
(Hons) Contemporary Cultural Studies, BA (Hons) Social Science, BSc/BSc
(Hons) Science, Technology and Society, BA (Hons) Studies in Contempo-
rary Writing, BA (Hons) English Literary Studies. The Modular Degree
Scheme offers part-time study in Art History, Communication Studies,
Dance, Drama, Economics, Education, English, Environment and Society,
French, Human Geography, History, History of Ideas, Information Tech-
nology, Law and Society, Music, Natural Science, Physical Geography,
Philosophy, Politics, Psychology, Quantitative Studies, Religious Studies,
Social Policy, Spanish, Trade Union Studies, Third World Studies, Urban
Studies, Visual Arts and Women's Studies. *Postgraduate Vocational Courses*:
MA in Video, full time. Diploma in Personnel Management, full time or part
time. Diploma in Marketing, part time. Institute of Chartered Secretaries
and Administrators, part time. Diploma of the Market Research Society,
part time. Conversion course: Diploma in Craft, Design and Technology
Education, full time, for qualified teachers wishing to move to secondary
education. Postgraduate Diploma in Microelectronics Technology, part
time, for graduates in electronic engineering or physics; exceptionally,

graduates in mathematics, computing or chemistry considered. Postgraduate Diploma in Air/Water Pollution Control, part time, for graduates in science or engineering others considered. Postgraduate Diploma in Geotechnics, part time, for graduates in civil engineering, geology, mining engineering or related subjects; other candidates considered if employer-sponsored. Postgraduate Diploma in Water Supply and Public Health Engineering, full time, for professional engineers and scientists employed in or affiliated to the water industry. Diploma in Highway and Traffic Engineering, part time, for graduates and others with HE qualifications in civil or municipal engineering or town planning; others considered. Postgraduate Diploma in Computer Graphics, part time, to retrain graduates in engineering, mathematics or computing. Postgraduate Diploma in Social Work, full time.

North London Polytechnic
Mature student concessions for those aged 21 and over. Those without the standard entry requirement who can offer alternative qualifications or relevant experience my also be considered, and will need to demonstrate (i) evidence of commitment and (ii) evidence of likelihood to benefit. They may do this in written applications or in personal interview. Tutors may require a brief examination of literacy/numeracy. The polytechnic says: 'Older students are very welcome at PNL' and emphasises commitment to mature students, second-career trainers and 'second chances'. *Part-Time Degrees:* New modular degree schemes in Humanities, Science and Social Science allow a flexible approach to part-time day and evening study, with a wide range of subjects. BA/BA (Hons) Combined Studies – specifically for students over 21, special consideration for non-standard qualifications; BSc Architecture; BSc/BSc (Hons) Chemistry; BEd (Hons) – in-service for qualified teachers. *Associate Student Scheme:* Over 50 units available at preliminary, intermediate and final levels, day and/or evenings, can lead to a degree. No specific experience needed for preliminary units. Advisory service to help you choose your level of entry. *Postgraduate Vocational Courses:* Diploma in Computing, full time or part time (conversion course for graduates *without* existing qualifications in computing). Diploma/MA in Health Facility Planning, full time or part time, for graduates with planning experience, architects, doctors, nurses, engineers, administrators. Diploma in Labour Studies, full time or part time, for those seeking graduate membership of the Institute of Personnel Management. Diploma/MA in Information Studies, full time or part time – any degree, preferably but not essentially with library experience (PNL can arrange this). Diploma in Management Studies (Recreation), part time – for graduates or those with HND/professional qualifications.

Entry to BEd degree courses at PNL: viewpoint
'You may like to know that at the Polytechnic of North London, A-levels are not necessarily essential, and we also give a lot of help to students who don't

have Maths O-level/GCSE at the time of applying. This year 90% of our teaching studies students were over 21 and 90% were women.'

'A student may be conditionally accepted without that O-level/GCSE providing she/he is working towards it and has passed it by the time of starting the course. PNL runs two special revision workshops over the summer (one-week long and only £5 for students with fee concessions, £25 for waged) to help people brush up on their maths. They get special coaching and advice from tutors, before the BEd courses. Six out of the seven students who took O-level Maths in this way passed,last summer.'

'This is all the result of our policy of welcoming students to PNL at whatever stage in their life they choose to study. Over 50% of our students are mature (and 52% of our 1987 graduates were women – the highest ratio for any polytechnic). My post exists precisely to help people like your readers. At PNL we all share the hope that they will manage to get as close to achieving their career dreams as they can.'

(Mature Student Liaison Officer, Polytechnic of North London)

Queen Mary College: University of London
(1988) Welcomes applications from mature students, and over 10% of undergraduates are in this category. Many enter with the usual qualifications, but some are admitted on the basis of other evidence of their ability to study; for example, candidates who have been studying with the Open University and have at least two full credits (gained by course work and examination) with at least one above Foundation level. Access courses are also taken into account. Applicants, who should be aged 21 or over at the proposed date of entry, can obtain advice about the acceptability of their qualifications. *Postgraduate Vocational Courses*: MSc/Diploma in Information Technology, full time, for graduates with little computing or electronic experience. MSc Chemical Research, full time, graduates with relevant degrees wishing to develop research expertise. MSc Biochemistry and Chemistry Applied to Medicine, full time (in association with London University Medical College), for Chemistry and Biochemistry graduates who wish to develop interests in clinical applications of science, and Medical or Dental graduates wishing to develop aspects of basic sciences related to other subjects. MSc/Diploma in Astrophysics, full time or evenings. Diplomas in Intellectual Property Law, International Commercial Arbitration Law, Media Law, full time, for graduates in any discipline whose undergraduate course or previous training/experience is such as to qualify them for admission. (Non-graduates may be admitted in appropriate cases.) MSc in Law and Science: Intellectual Property, full time, for graduates in Mathematics, Engineering and the Natural, Medical and Computer Sciences.

St Mary's College, Strawberry Hill
Mature student concessions possible for those aged 21 and over. They must offer qualifications of equivalent value to the normal entry requirements and

demonstrate capacity and academic attainment to enable them to manage the course they have chosen. *Postgraduate Vocational Courses:* Postgraduate Certificate in Education, full time – any graduate. Diploma in the Teaching of English as a Second Language, full time or part time – for those with qualified teacher status; teachers without a teaching qualification considered. Diploma in Drama and Theatre Arts, evenings and two weekends – for secondary school teachers of theatre arts courses, those involved in community work and those involved in amateur theatre. Diploma in Heritage Interpretation, full time – any degree entry.

South Bank Polytechnic
Mature student concessions possible for those aged over 21. Selection by many methods. 'Course directors need to be satisfied that the applicant will benefit from the course and is likely to pass. All courses have a number of mature/exceptional entry students.'

Thames Polytechnic
Polytechnic states: 'A wide variety of degree and advanced courses are offered on several sites. *Most courses offered in full-time and part-time modes.* Applications are welcomed from candidates of 21 years and over without the formal entry requirements if they can demonstrate that they have the work experience, interests, abilities and skills to enable them to complete the course successfully.' *Degrees* (NB: Polytechnic does not identify which of these are available part time.) BA/BA (Hons) Accountancy and Finance, Architecture, Landscape Architecture, Business Studies, International Marketing, Humanities, Economics, Sociology, Theological Studies, Management and Design for Building. BEng/BEng (Hons) Civil Engineering, Electrical and Electronic Engineering, Mechanical Engineering. BSc/BSc (Hons) Building Surveying, Quantity Surveying, Estate Management, Applied Biology, Applied Chemistry, Applied Geochemistry, Applied Science, Materials Science, Environmental Biology, Earth Science, Biochemistry, Metallurgy and Materials, Science in the Environment, Environmental Health, Computing Science, Computer and Communication Systems, Mathematics, Statistics and Computing. BEd/BEd (Hons) Primary, Secondary. *Postgraduate Vocational Courses* MA/PgDip Architecture, Landscape Architecture, Business Administration, Building Rehabilitation Studies, Historical Studies, Modern European Thought, Management Studies (Health Service), Environmental Health, Biotechnology, Chemical Analysis, Molecular Science of Materials, Electronical Materials and Devices, Scientific and Engineering Software Technology, Bulk Solids Handling Technology, Synthesis and Synthetic Methods, Statistics, Youth and Community Work, Postgraduate Certificate inEducation (Primary, Secondary). In-service courses for teachers – Primary, Secondary, Further Education.

Thomas Guy and Lewisham School of Nursing
Postgraduate Vocational Course: Shortened course of training (116 weeks, full time) leading to Registered General Nurse qualification for graduates with a degree in subjects related to nursing and good grades in science subjects at GCE level. Subjects include Biology, Chemistry, Microbiology, Physics, Psychology, Physiology and Sociology. A copy of the degree syllabus should be forwarded in order to assess eligibility.

University College: University of London
(1988) Mature candidates 21 and over are given individual consideration. They must satisfy course requirements but in some circumstances may be exempted from the general entrance requirement.

Uxbridge: Brunel University
(1988) Mature student concessions apply at 23. Students selected by interview. The university states: 'Most courses welcome mature students. Particularly popular courses for mature students include Sociology, Psychology and Government. The Mental Nursing option in some Social Science courses also attracts mature entrants.'

West London Institute of Higher Education
Special entry procedures for candidates who are not less than 21 on 31st December in the year of entry. Normally, evidence of academic ability at the appropriate level is required, as well as the motivation and potential for study. *Part-Time Degrees:* BA/BA (Hons) Humanities, choosing two subjects from American Studies, English, Geography, History, Religious Studies. *Postgraduate Vocational Courses:* Postgraduate Certificate in Education, full time. Bilingual Secretarial, full time – for those with relevant degree and A-level in French or Italian. Personal Assistant, full time – any degree acceptable. Accountancy Conversion course, part time.

Southern and Eastern England

Bedford College of Higher Education
(1988) Mature students over the age of 21 may apply for courses even though they do not possess specified academic qualifications. Special consideration is given to each individual case. *Part Time Degrees*: BA (Hons) Combined Studies, open to students aged 21 and over, selected on the basis of individual merit rather than formal qualifications alone. Students with certain relevant qualifications, such as Open University credits, may claim exemption from part of the course. Group I options are: Ecological Studies, English, French, History, Human Geography, Outdoor Recreation Studies, Sociology. Group II options are Computer Studies, Drama, Ecological Studies, Romanticism and Realism. You must take two from Group 1 and one from Group II. *Postgraduate Vocational Courses*: Postgraduate certificate in Education (Primary) or PE/Dance (Secondary) full time.

Bognor Regis: West Sussex Institute of Higher Education
Entry concessions possible for students over 21. Mature entry test procedure is essay followed by interview. All degree courses attract late starters.

Brighton Polytechnic
(1988) Entry concessions possible for students over 21. Each candidate's application considered on individual merits – education, job experience, personal background etc. BA Social Administration and BA Humanities are among the most popular courses. *Part-Time Degrees*: BA (Hons) Humanities, DipHE/BA (Hons) Business Studies, BSc Nursing Studies – practising Registered nurses. BEd (Hons) – for serving teachers. *Postgraduate Vocational Courses*: Postgraduate Certificate in Education, full time. MSc/Diploma Information Systems, full time, any first- or second-class honours degree acceptable, but employment experience is an advantage. MSc/Diploma Microprocessor Technology and Applications, full time, any degree in engineering or science acceptable, but usually not *recent* degrees in electronic engineering. MA/Postgraduate Diploma in Printmaking, part time, for graduates in Art and Design. MA Social Policy, for experienced practitioners with relevant first degree and, exceptionally, applicants with relevant experience without relevant degree qualification, on demonstration of ability to achieve postgraduate level. Mode not specified – please ask

college. MA/Postgraduate Diploma in Regional History, for applicants with established interest in History and/or related first degree. Mode not specified – please ask college.

Brighton: University of Sussex
Entry concessions for mature and/or unqualified candidates. 'The University will consider mature unqualified candidates for all courses in the Arts and Social Studies area, but candidates without the required Science qualifications will have to demonstrate their abilities in this field if they are applying for a course in the Science area. However, the University does offer a four-year course in Physics or Engineering for candidates without qualifications in science. Special Entry Scheme for Mature and/or Unqualified candidates: all selected will be required to complete a supplementary application form and either write an essay of not more than 2000 words based on one of two books nominated by the University, related to their proposed course of study, or they may, on request submit a recent piece of written work. They are also interviewed. A mathematics test may be given to candidates applying to courses with a specific requirement for O-level Mathematics.

Cambridge: Cambridgeshire College of Arts and Technology
This college is merging with Essex Institute of Higher Education and no information on courses is available during this process.

Cambridge: University of Cambridge
Intercollegiate Applications Office states: 'If you have not previously completed a course at a University or a similar institute of higher education, and will be 21 years of age or over, by October 1 of the year in which you hope to come to Cambridge, you may apply as a mature student. Most Colleges admit some mature students, but the greatest numbers are admitted by Lucy Cavendish (only for women), St. Edmund's, and Wolfson and are over 25. You will have to follow the same three year course as other undergraduates. You will normally be expected to produce evidence of high academic potential and recent study. In some cases you may be asked to take A-levels and possibly STEP (NB: the initials stand for Sixth Term Examination Papers, as offered to school-leavers) (as the College agreement only to use STEP alongside A-levels does not apply to mature candidates), or a written exercise may be set by the College. The normal matriculation requirements may be relaxed. Because every mature candidate is a special case, and personal qualities, motivation and experience will be considered in the selection process, it is best to approach one or more Colleges before you make your formal application, sending a short curriculum vitae and outlining your future plans. As a Mature applicant, you should submit an UCCA form by October 15 1989 and a special (yellow) form, obtainable from any College or from the Cambridge Intercollegiate Applications Office,

which must be returned by October 31 1989 (although some Colleges may consider applications received later). You are strongly advised not to make an Open Application. Interviews will normally be held in November or December and decisions will, as far as possible, be notified at the same time as those for normal undergraduate applications.' Also *Affiliated Students*: a graduate with an approved degree of another University may apply for admission to work for a Cambridge BA as an Affiliated Student. As such you would be exempt from the normal matriculation requirements and can take the degree in two years instead of the usual three – normally after passing Part II of the Tripos. About 100 Affiliated Students are admitted every year. Because of the quota system in some subjects, not all Colleges can consider applications for Architecture, and in the case of Medicine and Veterinary Medicine, Affiliated applications are only considered by Lucy Cavendish and Wolfson. In every subject high academic standards are required. You should write for an application form to the Admissions Tutor of *one* college and return it by October 31, together with a fee of £10. You do not need to apply via UCCA if you are applying to Cambridge as an Affiliated Student.'

Canterbury: Christ Church College
(1988) Entry concessions possible for students aged 23 on 1st October in the year of admission. Candidates may be accepted with one A-level or equivalent (e.g. an Access course) rather than the usual two A-levels for entry. Degrees which attract late starters are Art, Education, English, Geography, History, Maths, Movement Studies, Music, Radio/Film/TV Studies, Religious Studies, Science and Occupational Therapy (the Occupational Therapy Honours degree is the first in England). *Postgraduate Vocational Courses*: Postgraduate Certificate in Education, full time. Diploma in Teaching English as a Foreign Language, full time.

Canterbury: University of Kent
Entry concessions sympathetically considered for those aged 23 and over (also minimum age limit for entry to part-time degrees). Candidates without standard A-level qualifications asked to produce evidence of mature age study – written work or alternative qualifications, such as Access or BTEC awards. *Part-Time Degrees:* BA (Hons) French, BA (Hons) Humanities (English), BA (Hons) Social Sciences, BA (Hons) Specialised Social Sciences - e.g. Economics, Politics and Government, Industrial Relations, Social Statistics etc. Students specialise in a subject selected from the range of options within the full-time Social Science course (15 options). Also part-time Diplomas, including Ecology, Women's Studies, Theology, Local History, English Literature, Archaeology, German, Italian, Social Sciences, Law. *Postgraduate Vocational Courses:* TA-sponsored Diploma in Computing, full time – for graduates in subjects other than computing.

Higher Education in Later Life: viewpoint
'When people reach their later 20s, 30s, 40s, many of them feel they have somehow missed out on educational opportunities that are still there, and this is a very important part of their motivation. There are also many adults who feel that if only they had that magic piece of paper, their potential would be much better used, either by their present employer, or another employer. Some are nervous when they first come to university, but the chances are that, because they've been around, perhaps travelled abroad and had some experience of life, they begin to see the relevance of what the teachers are trying to put across and then everything starts to slot into place. Your mind is that much more receptive if you've had some experience.'

(Spokesperson, University of Kent at Canterbury)

Colchester Institute
The Institute has a positive policy towards mature students. 'In general, admission of mature students with unconventional qualifications is at the discretion of individual course tutors, but most tutors are sympathetic. The overriding considerations are: Will the student be successful on the course? Will they benefit by being on the course? Would they deprive another student of a place who would be more likely to be successful or benefit more?' Late starters particularly attracted by the BA Music and Graduate Diploma in Music. The college says 'We encourage adult students to apply for courses and course tutors will waive formal entry requirements where a mature student will show that they can benefit from the course. We are increasingly finding that the inclusion of adult students in full-time classes previously largely composed of school leavers creates a more stable learning atmosphere for the youngsters.'

Colchester: University of Essex
Entry requirements more flexible for students over 21. Selectors look for evidence of ability to undertake degree-level work, adequate preparation in terms of study skills and, where first-year courses presuppose it, detailed subject knowledge (principally for Science, Mathematics and Engineering). Open University Foundation courses, Return to Study, Access and similar courses are considered in lieu of A-levels or AS-levels. Applicants for Comparative Studies, Social Sciences and Law degree couses may be asked to take an entrance examination.

Croydon College
(1988) *Postgraduate Vocational Courses*: Diploma for Personal Assistants, full time, any degree. Certificate of Qualification in Social Work, full time, appropriate degree plus one year of social work experience.

Egham: Royal Holloway and Bedford New College, University of London
Mature student concessions apply at 23. Each case is considered on its merits, but mature student applications are welcomed. In some Arts departments, more than 20% of the intake is made up of mature students.

Guildford: University of Surrey

A wide range of entry qualifications is acceptable as an alternative to A-levels for applicants aged 21 and over. These include Open University credits, CNAA certificate courses and other courses specially designed to assist mature students to re-start academic study. Surrey University has links with a number of Access programmes and currently offers a one-year linked Access course in Science and Engineering with Guildford College of Technology.

Hatfield Polytechnic

Entry concessions possible for students over 21: entry by interview and/or essay. *Associate Student* scheme may also lead into degree course. *Part-Time Degrees* BSc/BSc (Hons) Mathematics, BSc/BSc (Hons) Applied Biology, BSc/BSc (Hons) Applied Chemistry, BSc/BSc (Hons) Computer Science, BA/BA (Hons) English, BEd, BA/BA (Hons) Contemporary Studies, BA/BA (Hons) Humanities. *Postgraduate Vocational Courses* include Diploma in Careers Education and Guidance, full time – any degree acceptable.

Associate Student Route: viewpoints

'After I'd taken a New Opportunities for Women course, I decided to carry on and become an Associate Student. I was committed to attend college just one morning a week, and chose the course "Introduction to Sociology". I followed on with two more courses as an Associate, and at that point, I thought I would join the degree course as a proper student. It is a part-time degree, and because I have done course units as an Associate, I was exempted from those and could join the appropriate year.'

'My company gives time off during the working week for staff to take individual Associate Student courses. I'm taking Advanced Maths, which fits in with the sort of work I do. This is a subject that is used in my job that I haven't really covered before, where you tend to use computer programs. The course lets you look inside the black box of the computer, which enables you to understand better what's going on and make better decisions.'

'Having taken the Polyprep course, I couldn't wait to get to the Polytechnic to start on the degree course. It takes four years part time, but I'm at the end of my sixth year, as I've failed twice to do exams, which you must pass to go forward to the next year. Nevertheless, I have now arrived at the final year. I've passed 11 subjects (22 modules) and now need just two more to get my degree. Yes, it's very tough, but stimulating beyond words.'

(Part-time students, Hatfield Polytechnic)

'Associate Student courses are not special courses; they are constituent parts of all the degrees we run. We originally put forward a policy statement to our Academic Board saying that we were willing to open up all our degrees to mature students – undergraduate or postgraduate courses. The only proviso would be that the students must be counselled beforehand. Obviously if someone comes along and wants to take a third-year course in Pharmacology and they'd never done any, we'd be crazy to accept that student. Students come in for their counselling sessions and can then take from one to three units, either from the same degree, or from different degrees if that helps them, and they share lectures and seminars with normal enrolled degree students. They have to do their course work but they don't have to take the examinations unless they want to do so.'

(Spokesperson, Hatfield Polytechnic)

High Wycombe: Buckinghamshire College of Higher Education

Entry concessions possible on BSc Furniture Production, sandwich, BSc Timber Technology and BSc Sociology. Candidates over the age of 21 with relevant industrial experience may be admitted without usual academic qualifications. *Postgraduate Vocational Courses:* Diploma in Timber Studies, full time – conversion course for graduates from other disciplines. Senior Secretarial course, full time – any degree acceptable. Bilingual Secretarial course, full time – degree in one foreign language. Diploma in European Marketing Management, full time, degree plus oral ability in French, German, Spanish or Italian plus three years' work experience. Diploma in Export Marketing, full time – any degree acceptable.

Kingston Polytechnic

Entry concessions possible for students over 21. Wide range of Access courses available from local FE colleges to allow entry to BEd, BA and BSc degrees at the polytechnic (details from Admissions Office). The usual method of deciding on concessions is for students to be interviewed: then a decision as to any entry waiver will be made. There are specific problems with waiver of entry requirements where the course also leads to exemption from a professional body examination. *Part-Time Degrees*: BA/BA (Hons) Combined Studies (two fields, chosen from Economics, Geography, History, History of Art, Architecture and Design, Financial Services, History of Ideas, Labour Studies, Literature, Mathematics, Music, Public Sector Policy Studies, Politics and Sociology). No formal entry requirements – course is specifically for mature students 21 and over. Also BEd for serving teachers, part time, within the Diploma in Professional Studies in Education modular course. BEng/BEng (Hons) part time, for HNC entrants; BA/BA (Hons) and BSc/BSc (Hons) Geography, part time. *Postgraduate Vocational Courses*: include Engineering, full time; Diploma in Marketing, full time, any degree acceptable. Postgraduate Certificate in Education, full time. MSc Information Technology, any degree acceptable, preferably including computing experience. MSc Artificial Intelligence, with Training Agency support. HNC and Graduateship of Royal Society of Chemistry, part time. Contact Admissions Office for advice and information.

Luton College of Higher Education
(1988) Entry concessions possible for students aged over 21. *Part-Time Degrees*: BSc (Hons) Biology or Geography and Geology. *Postgraduate Vocational Courses*: Diploma for Personal Assistants,full time, any degree acceptable.

Milton Keynes: The Open University
All courses are by distance-learning methods. Not only are there no qualifications required for entry to an OU *undergraduate degree course* – there is no selection as such. Applications are dealt with in order of receipt, i.e. on a 'first come, first served' principle. You, the student, decide if you are able to study for a degree. You also decide how many years it will take. If you need to take a year off because of a change of job or house, or home circumstances, you are free to do so, and resume study when you are ready. Courses are based on the credit system. You build up your record of successful work through full or half credits. If you've successfully completed previous higher-level study, you may gain exemption from up to three credits. An ordinary degree requires six credits; an honours degree eight credits. You have a choice of more than 130 courses from which to build up your credits. They span the Arts, Social Sciences, Mathematics, Science, Technology and Educational Studies. All students have to take a Foundation Course, which assumes no previous knowledge of the subject and provides a broad introduction to a range of subjects and to study skills. After that they can choose courses at any level. Tuition uses correspondence texts, television and radio broadcasts, home experiment kits, tutorial help through 250 study centres spread throughout the UK (telephone tutorials may sometimes be possible), and summer schools. For people not ready to commit themselves to a full degree course, there is an *Associate Student* programme; you can choose to study part of an undergraduate course, and if you later want to apply for a degree course place, the work you've done can be assessed and counted towards your Open University degree. The University also offers *Higher Degrees* and *Continuing Education* provisions, including the Open Business School with courses that include an Open University MBA programme. NB: The application period for undergraduate study is from January to the end of September for studies beginning the following year.

Questions people ask about the Open University
'Can I qualify as a doctor through the Open University?'
   'No, there are no OU first degrees in medicine (nor are there first degrees in dentistry or veterinary science). For these you must attend a conventional university.'
   'Can I study with the Open University if I go abroad?'
   'Yes, if you are a member of the British armed forces serving in West Germany or Cyprus or a dependent of such a person (limited range of

courses). Yes, if you are a resident of Brussels or Luxembourg. Yes, if you are a merchant seaman: your course material can be forwarded by the College of the Sea. If you begin your degree studies in the UK, but subsequently have to move abroad, you can usually continue your studies if you have a forwarding address in the UK, i.e. someone who'll act as your intermediary and send course materials to you.'

'Can I get a grant to take an Open University degree?'

'Some local authorities or employers will help with the cost of fees or attending summer school. The OU itself has a scheme to help people who are unemployed or on a low income with the cost of fees. Many employers help their staff with OU fees and/or paid time off for summer school.'

'Do I have to be a mature student?'

'Depends what you mean by "mature". The minimum age limit for entry is 18. There is no upper age limit.'

The Open University, viewpoint
'Many of the Open University's 95,000 and more graduates have gone on to establish themselves in new careers, take further professional qualifications or achieve substantial job advancement, sometimes after starting to study for interest alone. 52% of the graduates questioned in a sample survey (in 1986) said they had gained some "occupational benefit" from their degree. (More than 4,500 responded, 72% of the sample.)

'In general terms, almost 50% of the respondents said they had gained "great benefit" from their OU degree. More than 80% said they had "become more self confident" and more than 70% had "acquired a new way of looking at things, a different perspective on life", or developed new ideas or gained knowledge that they wanted to put to practical use.'

(Spokesperson, The Open University)

Norwich City College
Students over 21 are given special consideration. For the BA Hospitality Management course, students over 21 may be admitted without formal qualifications if in the view of the college, they have the necessary motivation, potential and knowledge to succeed. (See also 'Retraining and New Skills Courses'.)

Norwich: University of East Anglia
(1988) Entry concessions possible for students over 23. They must submit evidence of ability to pursue the course, for instance, professional qualifications obtained by examination or examinations deemed equivalent to A-levels. (Individual schools may have different/additional requirements.) The university says: 'The Schools of English and American Studies, Economic and Social Studies, Development Studies and Environmental Sciences all run courses attractive to mature students, particularly History and Philosophy. Law generally has a few mature students, while the School

of Information Systems attracts mature applicants who have a flair for computing but need to obtain formal qualifications.' *Part-Time Degrees*: American Studies, Development Studies, History of Art, Philosophy, Sociology, also part-time BEd for serving teachers. Wide range of part-time postgraduate degrees. *Postgraduate Vocational Courses*: Apply to the university, but note that a programme of Museum courses is offered in the Sainsbury Centre for Visual Arts and the Audio-Visual Centre has occasional openings for graduates wishing to train for work in television.

Portsmouth Polytechnic
The Polytechnic is particularly keen to encourage applications from students aged 21-plus. Experience and motivation to succeed are very important factors in academic study and applicants who do not hold the minimum qualifications for entry are therefore encouraged to contact the admissions tutor in the appropriate department, who will be pleased to offer advice about the wide-ranging possibilities available. Each application will be considered by the Polytechnic on its merits. Applicants may also contact the Polytechnic's counsellors or career advisers if they feel unsure about returning to study and need advice.

Reading: University of Reading
Entry concessions possible for students over 21 on Arts and Social Sciences and Education courses, over 23 on other courses. Applications are welcomed from students on Access courses. Late starters are generally valued on all full-time degree courses. *Postgraduate Vocational Courses:* Wide range of Master's degrees; also: Postgraduate Certificate in Education, full time, Certificate in Vocational Guidance, full time – candidates with any degree considered. Interesting range of Diploma and Master's courses for graduates from, or with experience of, developing countries.

St Albans: Hertfordshire College of Art and Design
Entry concessions possible for students over 21 – alternatives to A-levels, for example. Candidates may be required to demonstrate their academic ability with a short piece of writing organised as part of an interview. *Part-Time Degrees:* Fine Art. *Postgraduate Vocational Courses:* Diploma in Dramatherapy, full time or part time – for those with an appropriate degree or professional qualification in occupational therapy, psychiatric nursing, social work or drama teaching, plus relevant work experience and developed interest and practice in drama. Diploma in Art Therapy, full time or part time. Candidates must be over 21, with a degree in Art and Design (other disciplines involving Art considered), plus professional qualification in occupational therapy, psychiatric nursing, psychiatry, psychotherapy, social work, teaching or clinical psychology, plus portfolio of work plus relevant work experience.

Southampton: Institute of Higher Education
(1988) In association with the La Sainte Union College of Higher Education, the Institute offers a *Part-Time Degree* in Modern Languages and European Studies, including a programme for DipHE. The course incorporates a Foundation Year, from which applicants with the normal entry requirements may be wholly or partially exempted. Mature students who do not possess the usual five GCE passes with two at A-level, including a modern language other than English, may apply for exceptional entry to the course. A preparatory course of one year is advised for students without previous knowledge of a modern language or who have reached less than O-level standard. The degree is organised in three-hour modules over morning, afternoon and evening study periods, so it should be possible to devise a study programme, with the help of tutors, to fit in with other commitments at work and at home.

Southampton: University of Southampton
Entry concessions possible for students over 21. Normal entry requirements waived but evidence of 'recent serious study' is required. One or two A-level passes, successful completion of an Open University Foundation course or of an appropriate Access course could be accepted. Departments which admit significant numbers of mature students include English, Sociology and Social Policy, Social Work Studies, Psychology.

Surbiton: Hillcroft College
Residential college for women. Provides full-time and part-time CNAA Modular Certificate courses open to unqualified students seeking to reassess their capabilities and plan for a future career or higher education. Those who complete the two-year option may be able to enter directly into the second year of a degree course. Those who choose the social work option within the Certificate improve their prospects of a place on the Certificate of Qualification in Social Work (CQSW). There are also part-time Returning to Learning courses, afternoon and evening classes and one-week residential courses at Easter and in the summer holiday period. Candidates should be at least 21 and there is no upper age limit. Mandatory grants are available for students on full-time courses.

Watford College
Entry concessions for mature students possible at any age, says college. Students may be selected on the basis of industrial experience plus interview. BSc (Hons) Printing and Packaging Technology and HND in Printing are attractive to late starters. *Postgraduate Vocational Courses:* Postgraduate Diploma in Publishing, full time – any degree acceptable.

Wimbledon School of Art
Entry concessions possible for students over 21. All are interviewed at first choice stage, some may be accepted with reduced GCE requirements.

Significant mature entry to Art Foundation course. *Postgraduate Vocational Courses:* CNAA Diploma in Printmaking for graduates in Art and Design or equivalent; other degree subjects and non-graduates are also considered. CNAA Diploma in Higher Education/BA (Hons) Theatre Design, full time, options Costume Design as well as Costume Making. College emphasises that this is an *advanced* course. Selection is by interview. Candidates must submit examples of their work, which must include evidence of ability in the area of specialism.

Winchester: King Alfred's College
Entry concessions possible for students over 21. Candidates may be accepted with only one A-level, or via Access course, Return to Study, essay, Open University credit, certain professional qualifications etc. *Part-Time Degrees:* BA (Hons) History with English.

Central England

Birmingham: Newman and Westhill Colleges
Entry to BEd possible for mature students via special university examinations and/or Access courses. *Postgraduate Vocational Courses:* Postgraduate Certificate in Primary Education, full time.

Birmingham Polytechnic
Entry concessions for mature students, 21 and over. Various routes: Special Admissions Procedure – interview and/or submission of piece of written work; Access course via college of further education; *Associate Student* entry (see below). Direct entry to second year of some courses for candidates already holding advanced qualifications: e.g. someone with HND may be admitted directly to second year of a degree. Mature students welcome on all courses. *Part-Time Degrees:* BA (Hons) Architecture, BA/BA (Hons) Business Studies, BA/BA (Hons) Economics, BEng Electronic Engineering, BSc Nursing (qualified nurses with advanced qualifications), BSc Quantity Surveying. *Associate Student* scheme: incorporates Visiting and Listening Students Programme. You can choose any of over 200 units of study, in areas such as Business Studies, Law, Social Science, Health Science, Art and Design, Primary Education, Built Environment, Computing and Information Studies and Engineering and Science. Associate students attend daytime or evenings, usually for about two hours a week for each unit studied. *Postgraduate Vocational Courses* include: Postgraduate Certificate in Education, full time; Diploma in Industrial Design, full time or part time – for graduates in Art and Design, or, exceptionally, Engineering, Architecture, Management or Education; Diploma in the Management of Modern Technology, part time for graduates in Engineering, Technology, Science or Business Studies, or with relevant experience; Diploma in Librarianship and Information Studies, full time or part time – any graduate with at least nine months' library or information experience. For Science graduates, TA-sponsored full-time conversion courses at postgraduate level in Software Engineering. Microelectronics and Computer Technology and Electronics Manufacture are also available.

Part-Time at the Polytechnic: viewpoints

'I was at a disadvantage at school from the start because I only came to Britain from the West Indies when I was ten. I left school at l5 feeling I'd done very little. It was much later in life, after my divorce, when I had children to look after, that I thought of trying to do something that would give me a better position in life and make a future for them. I've started on a Listening Student course, and at the start, when I saw the younger students and they were discussing topics I knew nothing about, I felt very unsure of myself. After a period of time, I realised that as far as the course was concerned, the young students were basically at the same level as I was. They were no better than me and I was no better than them. It gave me security and I felt I was really laying a foundation for the future.'

'I wanted to do something on a Friday morning when I had time to spare, so I just looked in at the Poly to see what was on on a Friday. It turned out to be Comparative Government. It was such a long time since I'd studied (I had taken an HND before) that I just sat and shook for the first quarter of an hour. I couldn't write at all. But I managed to pass Comparative Government in the end, partly because it was continuous assessment and the marks I'd got for my essays were taken into account. Then they asked me if I would like to take the part-time degree in Government. I had two exemptions because of my HND, so I did two years as a part-time student and then the Polytechnic advisers suggested I went full-time – they found that because I'd only had two years of grant for my HND, I could get another year of grant to finish my degree. I'm now enrolled as a postgraduate student doing research into politics abroad.'

(Students, Birmingham Polytechnic)

'It's my experience, having worked with adults now for going on 15 years, that very often their intellectual horizons broaden, and as they broaden, so does their belief in themselves and what they can do. They start by thinking the young 18 and 19-year-olds who've come in with A-levels are so much better and brighter, when in practice what we find is somewhat the reverse. The 18 and 19-year-olds can be intimidated by the self-confidence and the experience and knowledge of the world that the mature student has. There is a dedication and motivation among mature students that I as a teacher find positively exhilarating and very, very rewarding.'

(Spokesperson, Birmingham Polytechnic)

Birmingham: University of Aston
(1988) Entry concessions possible for mature students aged 23 or over on entry who have pursued study to a suitable level, even though they may not meet the formal entry requirements.

Coventry Polytechnic
Entry concessions possible for students over 21. 'Often they will simply be interviewed to satisfy course admissions tutors they have the commitment/

capacity to cope with the course. They may have to demonstrate aptitude in certain subjects for certain courses e.g. Mathematics and English, but this could be decided on an individual basis with the tutor and potential student. This polytechnic sent a long list of full-time degree courses for which mature entrants are considered – please check their free prospectus for details. *Associate Student* scheme – may also lead into degree courses. *Part-Time Degrees:* BSc Remedial Health Sciences (for professionally qualified occupational therapists, physiotherapists etc.) DipHE/BA/BA (Hons) Social Studies. DipHE/BA/BA (Hons) Modern Studies. BA/BA (Hons) Applied Economics. *Postgraduate Vocational Courses:* Diploma/MA in Electronic Graphics (for graduates in Art and Design subjects). Diploma/MA in Regional Planning (for graduates of Planning or Social Science). Diploma/MA in Modern Historical and Political Studies. Diploma/MSc in Advanced Manufacturing Technology. Diploma/MSc in Computer Aided Engineering. Diploma/MSc in Robotics – Systems and Application. Diploma/MSc in Control Engineering. Diploma/MSc in Engineering Manufacture. Diploma/MSc in Mathematical Modelling and Computer Simulation. Diploma/MSC in Information Technology for Management. Diploma in Management Studies. Diploma in Policy Studies.

Derbyshire College of Higher Education
Entry concessions possible for mature students with experience or aptitude for the chosen course. Students may like to note: BA (Hons) Photographic Studies – those lacking normal entry qualifications may be admitted if they show particular aptitude for photographic studies. BA (Hons) Earth and Life Studies; BSc Power Engineering and BSc Applied Chemistry, part time, where special provision is made for mature students; and BEd (Hons) for which mature candidates over 23 who lack the usual qualifications but who have recently studied at an appropriate academic level and show special promise may be allowed to sit a Special Entrance Examination set by the University of Nottingham. All BEd candidates must have a GCE O-level or equivalent in both English Language and Mathematics. For the Bachelor of Combined Studies (Hons) candidates may sit the Special Entrance Examination or enrol for the college's Pathway course, part time, which offers direct entry. *Postgraduate Vocational Courses*: Postgraduate Certificate in Education, full-time. MBA, three-year part-time course; MSc in Advanced Manufacturing Management, two-year part-time course.

Keele: University of Keele
(1988) Entry concessions possible for mature students aged 19 or over on 1st October of the year in which they wish to be admitted, who have been away from full-time education for three years, and have in the recent past, attended a systematic course of study (Adult Education classes, Further Education course, Open University, Access course etc.). NB: though candidates for three-year degrees must satisfy *course requirements*, i.e. have

passes in any A-level exams or OU/Access credits specified for a particular degree, there are *no course requirements* for any four-year degree course. These begin with a multidisciplinary Foundation Year. About 10% of the undergraduates at Keele are mature students.

Leicester: University of Leicester

For detailed information, write for the booklet *Over 21? Opportunities for Mature Students at Leicester University*. A range of UK vocational qualifications are accepted as equivalent to A-level for meeting the general entrance requirements of the University, e.g. HND, HNC, OND or ONC, with an average mark of at least 60% in three subjects at the final examination; BTEC National Certificate or Diploma with merit passes in at least three Level III units. Other vocational qualifications may be acceptable. In the East Midlands, two Access course schemes are recognised by Leicester University so that all who achieve a Merit pass on the course meet the University's general entrance requirement. *This does not guarantee admission and candidates must apply on the UCCA form in the usual way and meet any specific course entrance requirements that may be imposed.* The local courses recognised by the University are the Charles Keene College Access Programme in Leicester, and the Northamptonshire Access Courses available at the Adult Education Centre, Northampton, Northampton College of Further Education, Tresham College of Further Education, Corby and Wellingborough College of Further Education. Of other access courses, the University says: 'Generally those which are validated by a university or polytechnic will be recognised by Leicester University; the Admissions Office can provide advice about those which are recognised. Another alternative is to take one of the University's own adult education Certificate courses which can provide automatic transfer to the University's degree courses. In some cases, e.g. Social Sciences and Modern Social History, specified level of achievement can gain you exemption from part of some full-time degree courses. Mature students who have obtained a Credit pass on an Open University Foundation Course meet the general entrance requirements of the University. *Part-Time Degrees*: BA Combined Arts, BA Modern Language Studies, BSc Combined Science, BA/BSc Social Sciences (options: Economic and Social History, Economics, Geography, Politics, Sociology, Applied Sociology, Economics and Economic History, Politics and Economic History, Economics, Sociology, Applied Sociology). NB: It is hoped to provide opportunities for mature students to take *evening* degrees from October 1989. Options are BA Humanities and BSc Human and Natural Sciences. For more details, see the free booklet mentioned above.

Loughborough: Co-operative College

See 'Pre Entry, Sample and Access Courses' which is the section in which the college authorities requested that details of their courses should appear.

Loughborough University of Technology
Considers sympathetically applications from mature students aged 21 and over, outside its normal matriculation requirements. Admission may be granted on the basis of individually approved qualifications, such as Access courses, or interview and special assignments. *Part-Time Degrees:* BA (Hons) English, BA (Hons) Library Studies. *Postgraduate Vocational Courses:* TA-sponsored Information Technology, full time or part time – conversion course for graduates of any discipline. TA-sponsored Theory and Applications of Computation, full time – conversion course for graduates in disciplines other than Computer Science. TA-sponsored Computer Integrated Manufacture – full time, aimed at Mathematics graduates and others who are mathematically inclined. Postgraduate Diploma/MA/MSc in Library and Information Studies/ Information Studies/Archives/Publishing/ School Librarianship, full time – for graduates of any discipline, normally with a year's experience of work in a library, documentation centre, records office or the book trade. MSc Recreation Management, full time – open to graduates from industry, recreation, tourism, local government, town and country planning, professional sport, community development and education, preference for those with work experience, but others considered. MSc Polymer Technology, full time or part time – for graduates in Science, Engineering or an appropriate Technology-based discipline. MSc Airport Planning and Management, full time or part time – for graduates in Transport, Human Geography, Economics, Business and Management Studies, Civil Engineering or Planning, or other graduates with work experience in airports or other organisations concerned with aviation. MA/MSc Negotiated Studies, full time or part time – appropriate for mature students who have clear ideas about their needs and who are prepared to devote considerable effort to developing a personal syllabus of study. Any first degree is acceptable and mode of attendance is determined by the negotiated syllabus.

Northampton: Nene College
Entry concessions for mature students. Note specially BA/BSc (Hons) Combined Studies (choice of 29 subjects). One half of all enrolments are mature students; those without the normal academic requirements, but with equivalent professional qualifications, or OU Credit, or one A-level, or successful completion of an Access course are invited to apply. *Part-Time Degrees:* BA/BSc (Hons) Combined Studies (choice of 29 subjects, as for full-time course). BSc (Hons) Chemical Science, for holders of BTEC HNC Science (Chemistry) or equivalent. BSc (Hons) Health Science Studies – for members of one of the recognised Professions Supplementary to Medicine, or for Registered Nurses, with at least two years' post-qualification experience. BEd (Hons) for qualified teachers. *Postgraduate Vocational Qualifications:* Postgraduate Certificate in Education, full time.

Nottingham: Trent Polytechnic

The Polytechnic welcomes applications from mature candidates for all of its degree courses; entry requirements may be waived and suitable experience will be taken into consideration. *Associate Student* scheme also available; contact the Centre for Access and Continuing Education, 0602 418418 ext 2333/2158. Degree courses are in: Accounting and Finance; Applied Biology; Applied Chemistry; Applied Social Studies with CQSW; Building (plus Residential Development option); Business Studies, Civil Engineering; Clothing Studies with Textiles; Combined Studies in Sciences; Communication Studies; Computer Aided Engineering MEng/BEng; Computing Systems; Creative Arts; Economics; Electrical and Electronic Engineering; Engineering Surveying; European Business; Fashion Design; Fine Art; Furniture Design; Humanities; Industrial Studies; Information Graphics; Integrated Engineering; Interior Design; Knitwear Design; Law (full-time or sandwich); Manufacturing Enineering; Manufacturing Systems Engineering with Management MEng; Mathematical Methods for Information Technology; Mechanical Engineering; Modern European Studies; Photography; Primary Education: Public Administration; Quantity Surveing; Secondary Education (Craft Design and Technology); Secondary Education (Mathematics and Sciences); Secondary Education (Shortened); Mathematics or Science or Design and Technology); Social Sciences; Sport (Administration and Science); Tetile Design; Theatre Design; Urban Estate Surveying. Mature students interested in studying on a *part-time* basis for the wide range of degrees, HNDs and professional qualifications offered should contact the Polytechnic for the Part-Time prospectus. Full-Time prospectus is also available from 0602 418418, ext 2062 (Academic Registry).

Oxford: Plater College

This is the Catholic Workers' College. For students aged over 21 (no upper age limit), offering the chance to study for one or two years at university standard. All courses lead to qualifications of the University of Oxford or the College and involve a study of Catholic social teaching. No formal educational qualifications are neeed. 'Average intelligence and love of God and neighbour are qualifications enough. Students come from all walks of life – manual and office workers, skilled and unskilled, married and single, laity and religious – and from all parts of the world, although most come from the United Kingdom.' Adult Education Bursaries are available for more students to cover fees and maintenance. The college has asked that all their courses should be listed: Two-year courses: Oxford University Special Diploma in Social Studies; Oxford University Special Diploma in Social Administration; Plater College Diploma in Theology and Social Studies; Plater College Certificate in Youth and Community Studies. One-year courses: Plater College Certificate in Social Ethics; Plater College Certificate in Social Studies for Pastoral Ministry.

Oxford Polytechnic
Entry concessions possible for mature students aged 21 and over. Note specially modular degree course available on *full-time, part-time* or *mixed-mode* basis; you can vary the amount of time you spend studying. A 'module' is a study unit; there are 800 different modules available. Each module represents between one-quarter and one-third of a term's work for most full-time students. A DipHE can be achieved by studying 20 modules, a degree by studying 28 and an honours degree by studying 30 modules. Most students on modular courses combine the study of two 'Fields' – a field is a single area of study like Psychology or Law, Food Science, Catering, Publishing, Musical Studies, Microelectronic Systems and so on. Full list from polytechnic. Also available: non-modular degrees, including BA (Hons) Business Studies, for which mature students are encouraged to apply, even though they may not hold the minimum entry qualifications. *Postgraduate Vocational Courses:* include Postgraduate Certificate in Education, full time; Diploma in Urban Planning, full time or part time – for graduates from social science or design disciplines.

Oxford: Ruskin College
A college providing further education for working men and women, which from its foundation has had close links with the trade union movement (many scholarships are offered by individual trade unions and by the Trades Union Congress Educational Trust). The minimum age of entry is 20, the average age of students is normally about 30 and formal entrance qualifications are not required for admissions (preference is given to those who have had little or no full-time education beyond the statutory school-leaving age, though evidence of efforts towards self-education, e.g. serious reading, adult education classes, trade union schools etc. is an advantage). Students are selected partly on the basis of their record in voluntary work and service to the community, especially through the trade union movement and associated bodies. Adult Education Bursaries are usually available for fees and maintenance. Course choices include: Labour Studies, Literature, Devlopment Studies, History, Social Studies, Applied Social Studies. A four-week residential course in Advanced Trade Union Studies is also available and can be followed by a one-year distance learning programme. Computer Access and Language Study facilities are available:

Study at an Adult Residential College: viewpoints
'I left school at 16 with three O-levels and went to work in the Health Service where I stayed for about 13 years, ending up with a job as a technician in a cardiac unit. I was active in a Union branch and became branch secretary, finding that I was a good organiser. I began to realise, though, that there were great gaps in my education and I needed the discipline of being somewhere to study. Just reading by yourself and studying by yourself, you feel there's always something else to take you away from what you're doing.

I thought Ruskin College was the kind of place I could function in because I would be studying with people who were older, like myself. I felt I would meet people from a similar background and therefore, we'd all be starting from the same point. The hardest part of the selection was having to write an essay – the first one I'd done since "compositions" at school. The interview wasn't too bad; it was arranged through my union and the college tutor and wasn't too daunting. I've chosen to take Labour Studies – things like labour history, the sociology of work, economics and industrial relations.'

(Student, Ruskin College, Oxford)

'Our selection is based broadly on the applicant's record of activity at work and service to the community, with an emphasis – given our particular background and tradition – to work undertaken in the trade union movement and similar bodies. Courses are designed for adults. Many of the students have forgotten, if they ever mastered, the techniques of structuring arguments and of written expression. That, from our standpoint, is what an educational process means. It's not to buttress prejudices. It's not simply to solidify beliefs that students may have had before they came to Ruskin. It's to give them a whole range of views and thinking that otherwise they may not have confronted. At the end of the course, some are content to go back to their original jobs (though they may seek more responsibility), but many also go on to university or to careers like social work.'

(Spokesperson, Ruskin College, Oxford)

Oxford – University of Oxford
All colleges are happy to consider applications from mature students. Application and selection procedures for mature students are formally the same as for school-leaver students – but the Admissions Office is happy to advise on your application or to put you in touch with a college tutor in the subject of your choice. (Tel: 0865 270210) In addition, in 1989, Manchester College (an independent institution) will begin a scheme to admit 6 mature students per year for a trial period of 3 years to read for Oxford University degrees in arts and social studies subjects. (Tel: Manchester College, 0865 241514)

Stoke-on-Trent: Staffordshire Polytechnic
(1988) Entry concessions for students over 21 on entry. 'Almost 15% of our students are over 21 on enrolment and nearly 5% are over 25 (all types of course).' Thirty per cent of students at the polytechnic attend in various part-time modes. There is a Mature Students' Association. *Associate Student* scheme; wide range of units available part time, day and evening, may lead to degree entry. BA (Hons) Design – 'Exceptionally, students without the minimum academic qualifications but with evidence of outstanding talent will be admitted.' BA (Hons) History of Design and the Visual Arts – 'We welcome applications from mature students (21 and over) who may in

certain cases be admitted to the course without the standard qualifications.' BA (Hons) Economics – 'Mature students (over 21) with minimal formal qualifications who satisfy us that they can cope with the course will be admitted.' BA (Hons) Geography – 'We are pleased to welcome applications from mature students, for whom special conditions apply.' BA (Hons) Literature and History – 'We have a positive attitude towards mature students, who may be admitted to the course without standard qualifications in certain circumstances.' BA (Hons) International Studies – 'In exceptional cases, mature students with minimal formal qualifications will be admitted.' LLB (Hons) – 'If you are a mature student, you can be considered on the basis of work or other experience if, in our opinion, you would benefit from the course.' BA (Hons) Modern Studies – 'We have an active policy of encouraging mature students who may have missed a conventional sixth-form education to apply.' BA (Hons) Sociology – 'We are pleased to receive applications from mature students for whom special conditions apply.' BSc/BSc (Hons) Computing – 'Mature students lacking formal qualifications are considered on an individual basis.' *Part-Time Degrees* BA Business Studies, BA (Hons) Economics, BA (Hons) International Studies, BA (Hons) Sociology, LLB (Hons). LLB plus Hons conversion course. *Postgraduate Vocational Courses:* MSc Computing Science, full time, for graduates in any discipline. Postgraduate Diploma in Marketing Management, full time, for graduates in any discipline. Postgraduate Diploma in Management Studies, full time, for graduates in any discipline. Postgraduate Diploma in International Marketing, full time, for language graduates and others with equivalent qualifications. Certificate in Microelectronics Applications for Scientists, part time, for teachers, engineers and industrialists.

Walsall: West Midlands College of Higher Education
(1988) Entry concessions possible for mature students over 21 on 31st December in the year their course commences. For candidates over 25, internal tests in English and Mathematics may be provided, to meet the needs of initial teacher training, through BEd (Hons). *Postgraduate Vocational Courses* Postgraduate Certificate in Education, full time.

Warwick: University of Warwick
(1988) Entry concessions possible for mature students 21 and over at the proposed date of entry who have been unable to complete a normal secondary education. Selectors look for evidence of the candidate's general motivation and indication of appropriate academic ability, e.g. participation in Open Access/Evening courses. Candidates are interviewed and may be required to submit written work. *Part-Time Degrees*: Historical Studies, Literary and Cultural Studies, Social Studies, Classical Civilisation, European Studies, French Studies, French and European Literature, European Studies, French Studies, French and European Literature, History. 'Approximately one in every eight undergraduates arriving at the University is a

mature student. A steady rise in the number of older students has led to the formation of a Mature Students' Society at the University ... It is noticeable that mature students generally obtain better degree results than younger students, even though in the majority of cases, the mature students did not have qualifications normally acceptable for entrance when they applied for the course.'

Wolverhampton Polytechnic

(1988) Entry concessions possible for mature students – those 21 and over by 31 December in the year their course commences. Work experience is taken into account and GCE requirements can be reduced. Students are normally counselled. All degree courses encourage applications from mature students. 'Great stress is placed on the value of past practical experience in admissions procedure. Mature candidates can discuss their specific requirements and personal circumstances directly with course admissions tutors, or, in the first instance, with experienced counsellors in the Polytechnic's Advice Centre. (A professionally staffed playgroup is provided for students with children under five.) The polytechnic currently recognises Access courses, run at the following centres: Bilston Community College, Dudley College of Technology, Garrets Green College, Walsall College of Technology, Wulfrun College of Further Education, and if 1988 plans have been fruitful, further Access courses will be available at Sandwell College of Further Education and Kidderminster College of Further Education. This polytechnic also operates an *Associate Student* scheme and plans to publish an Associate Students' Handbook – write for details.

Worcester College of Higher Education

The College welcomes enquiries and applications from mature students (over 21) with no formal qualifications. Each applicant is offered an advisory inteview, and in the majority of cases we are able to accommodate their requirements, either by recommending attendance on one of the many Access courses running at local Colleges of Further Education, or by direct entry on to the Diploma of Higher Education. Those interested in teacher training must have an O-level or GCSE pass in Maths and English Language. Students who wish to continue in full- or part-time work may study under the *Associate Student* scheme and accumulate credits over a period of time towards a Certificate, Diploma and Degree. For full details please contact the Registry (tel: 0905 748080). No *Part-Time Degrees* but Diploma in Higher Education is available full time or part time and students may choose any three options available for the BA/BSc (Hons) in Combined Studies and transfer after two years either on to the BA/BSc(Hons) or to another institution by individual negotiation. Mature students welcomed on the BEd (Primary or Secondary) full time and BA/BSc (Hons) full-time Combined Studies degree (19 courses). *Postgraduate Vocational Courses:* Postgraduate Certificate in Education (Primary or Secondary).

Northern England

Blackburn College
Part-Time Degrees: Mature students with various entry qualifications can study for Levels One, Two and Three of the LINCS Combined Studies degree. (LINCS = Lancashire Integrated Colleges Scheme; where necessary, students can study and obtain credits, building up into a degree, at more than one college, i.e. if you have to move home and away from the college in Lancashire where you have been studying, you can pick up your course in the new area, at the same level). Subjects offered in the LINCS Combined Studies degree are Linguistics, History, Organisation Studies, Psychology, Economics, Maths, Computing, Law, Politics, English.

Bolton Institute of Higher Education
Entry concessions possible for students aged 21 or over (e.g. reduced GCE requirements after interview). Mature students are particularly attracted to the BA (Hons) Humanities and Combined Studies and BSc (Hons) Psychology degrees, all three available either full time or part time. *Associate Student* scheme for entry to the BA (Hons) Humanities, part time. *Part-Time Degrees:* In addition to those mentioned: BA Business Studies, BEd (Hons) – for qualified teachers. *Postgraduate Vocational Courses* include Postgraduate Certificate in Education.

Bradford and Ilkley Community College
(1988) Entry concessions possible for students over 21. BA Art and Design – exceptional entry can be given if an applicant shows marked creative promise but does not possess the formal entry qualifications. DipHE/BA(Hons) Community Studies, over-21s admitted if their qualifications may be considered relevant; evidence of work with children and/or ability to speak a second community language would be an advantage. DIpHE/BEd (Hons) Home Economics for Secondary Education, possible concessions. *Part-Time Degrees*: BEd (Hons) for qualified teachers. BEd (Hons) Organisation Studies. *Postgraduate Vocational Courses* include Postgraduate Certificate in Education (Primary), Postgraduate Certificate in Education (Secondary), Home Economics, Professional Diploma in Education (Special Education), part time.

Bradford – University of Bradford

'Bradford has always encouraged applications from those who were unable to complete their secondary education, or who have delayed their entry into higher education, or who wish to return to academic life to either develop their careers or make a fresh start.' Applicants aged 21 and over do not necessarily have to meet the standard entrance requirement but do need to demonstrate that they will derive benefit from their studies and also that they have the potential to succeed on their chosen course. The University accepts a wide range of alternative qualifications to the traditional GCE A-levels in satisfaction of the General entrance requirement including, for example, one Open University credit at Foundation Level, or a pass in certain Return to Study or Access courses approved by the University. *Note* This policy applies to *all* undergraduate degree courses. Holders of a BTEC HND or HNC are eligible for direct entry to the second year of undergraduate courses within the Board of Studies in Engineering, subject to the conditions set by the Department. Applicants with suitably advanced qualifications in social science subjects (such as a DipHE) may be exempted from two years of the part-time BA (Hons)/Diploma course in Social Studies. *Part-Time Degrees:* BA (Hons)/Diploma Social Studies. *Postgraduate Vocational Courses:* These include a part-time MBA. Like the full-time MBA, this is designed for good honours graduates who ideally have had at least three years' experience. Diploma in Computing, full time – a conversion course for people qualified in a field other than computing who seek a formal qualification in computing to obtain jobs. Diploma/MSc in Computing, full time and part time. Candidates for the MSc course must satisfy the University entrance requirements and will normally be expected to be graduates (or hold equivalent qualifications) and to have proven experience of computer programming. Candidates who are graduates or hold equivalent qualifications but are not qualified for admission to the MSc course may be admitted to the postgraduate Diploma. New postgraduate courses being introduced from October 1989 include a Diploma/MSc Nursing Studies, part time, lasting five terms for the Diploma or two years for the full MSc. The course, providing nurses with an opportunity to obtain a higher level of qualification, includes not only scientific subjects but also aspects of management, psychology, sociology and other relevant topics. Also the MSc Biomedical Sciences is a new full-time 12-month course aiming to train highly qualified professional laboratory staff for hospitals and industry. Laboratory skills and management practice will be developed and an insight into the various specialisms given.

Chester College of Higher Education: an Affiliated College of the University of Liverpool

The College welcomes mature students (over 21) to its Liverpool University BA, BSc and BEd courses. One in five students enters at the age of 21 or over. Entry concessions for students over 21 who have not already matriculated are negotiated at interview. The JMB Mature Matriculation scheme is the basis of admission: this involves a 2-hour examination to test comprehension and the ability to construct an essay. Departmental requirements vary according to the subjects chosen for study in the BA (Hons) and BSc (Hons) Combined Subjects degree. All departments accept Access courses in relevant subjects; one A-level entry is also acceptable. BA (Hons) in Health and Community Studies has proved particularly popular with mature entrants. For BEd (Hons) an O-level or GCSE pass in Mathematics and English is a national requirement.

Doncaster: Humberside College – see under Hull

Durham: New College Durham
Entry concessions possible for students aged over 21. BA (Hons) Travel and Tourism, in association with Newcastle Polytechnic. *Part-Time Degrees:* BEd (Hons) for qualified teachers; BA (Hons) Criminal Justice Studies (in association with Newcastle Polytechnic).

Gateshead Technical College
Postgraduate Vocational Course: MA Conservation of Fine Art, full time – any graduate considered.

Grimsby: Humberside College – see under Hull

Huddersfield Polytechnic
(1988) The college wishes to encourage applications from mature entrants. No set level of qualification (or lack of qualification) for mature students – each course considered individually. Mature students are defined as 21 or over at the time of admission. The following degree entries indicate that mature candidates are expected to apply: BSc (Hons) Behavioural Sciences – 'Mature students may be exempted (from usual requirements) and are encouraged to apply.' BA/BA (Hons) Computing in Business – 'Mature students who do not meet the entry requirements may be admitted if they can show evidence acceptable to the polytechnic of their suitability for the course.' BA/BA (Hons) Humanities – as previous degree. BSc (Hons) Human Ecology – 'Applications are welcomed from mature students.' BSc (Hons) Transport and Distribution – 'special arrangements can be made for mature students, from whom applications are encouraged.' *Part-Time Degrees*: BA/BA (Hons) Social Welfare Administration, for holders of the Certificate of Qualification in Social Work (CQSW), others considered; BEd (Hons) for serving teachers in further education establishments. BEd (Hons) for serving teachers in schools and further education; BA/BA (Hons) Humanities; BA (Hons) Business Studies; BSc (Hons) Textile Technology. *Postgraduate Vocational Courses* include Postgraduate Certificate in Education (Further Education), full time.

Humberside College of Higher Education
(1988) Campuses also in Doncaster, Grimsby and Scunthorpe. Entry concessions possible for mature students – see individual courses. BA (Hons) Architecture – mature students especially welcome; BA (Hons) Fine Art – applicants with less than the minimum requirements admitted when there is clear evidence of exceptional merit; BA (Hons) Graphic Design – some entry requirements waived for mature students; BSc (Hons) Fishery Studies – candidates with maritime, fishing or other industrial qualifications, plus evidence of suitable industrial experience and academic potential admitted without usual academic qualifications; BSc/BSc (Hons) Industrial Food Technology – over-21s may be granted concessions in entry requirements if they satisfy college they have the necessary motivation, potential and knowledge to succeed; BA (Hons) Social Science – over-21s without usual qualifications considered; DipHE, full time Hull, part time Grimsby – over-21s without usual qualifications considered, can lead to entry to third year of BA (Hons) Business Studies; BA (Hons) Combined Studies; BA (Hons) Social Science; full time. *Part-Time Degrees*: see college statement at the end of this entry. Certificate/DipHE/BA/BA (Hons) and Certificate/DipHE/BSc/BSC (Hons) as appropriate, in Applied Biology; Business Studies (also at Grimsby); Combined Sciences; Combined Studies (also at Grimsby and Scunthorpe); Humanities (also at Scunthorpe); Office Systems Management; Social Studies (also at Scunthorpe); Visual Studies. BEd (for qualified teachers) also at Doncaster and Scunthorpe. BSc Engineering. *Postgraduate Vocational Courses* include: Postgraduate Diploma in Food Technology, full time, any graduate considered; Postgraduate Diploma in Fishery Harbour Operations and Management, full time, any graduate considered; Postgraduate Diploma in Port Operations and Management, full time, any graduate considered; Postgraduate Certificate in Education, full time, any graduate considered; Postgraduate Diploma in Refrigeration and Air Conditioning, full time, any graduate in engineering discipline. The college says: 'Evening-only attendance with occasional Saturday Day Schools. Mixed-mode attendance available in some areas. No specific entry requirements for over-21s. Courses to Honours Degree level, with intermediate qualifications available in Applied Biology, Applied Social Science, Business Information Systems, Business Studies, Documentary Studies, Humanities, Office Systems Management, Visual Studies or Combined Studies. All are run in Hull, with selected courses at Grimsby.'

Lancaster: St. Martin's College
Entry concessions for mature students on BEd (Primary Teaching) and BA (Hons) Humanities courses. Alternatives to A-levels include OU Foundation Credit or Open College awards. Access course students are considered. Mature students should normally be under 50 years of age. BA Youth Studies (recognised CETCYW qualification). Experience of working with young people is most important. A wide range of formal qualifications can

be accepted – ask College. *Postgraduate Vocational Courses:* Postgraduate Certificate in Education (Primary and Secondary), full time. Postgraduate Diploma in Youth Work – degree-equivalent training accepted. Department of Education and Science Special Initiatives: 2-year courses for Maths and Physics Teaching. Degree-equivalent courses and/or industrial experience acceptable. Please contact the Registrar for details – tel: 0524 - 63446.

Lancaster: University of Lancaster
Entry concessions for students aged 21 and over. Very welcoming; has special free *Guide for Mature Students* – ask for a copy. For entry to degree courses, there are numerous alternatives to A-levels: BTEC and similar awards at specified levels and a wide range of professional qualifications – for example, Registered General Nurse, Registered Mental Nurse, Institute of Chartered Secretaries and Administrators, Institute of Linguists Grade II, police promotion examinations with further study experience etc., and Open University. Lancaster University, jointly with Lancashire Polytechnic, validates a wide range of courses of the Open College Federation of the North West as alternatives to A-levels for adults. These are offered at colleges of further and adult education in Nelson & Colne, Accrington, Blackburn, Burnley, Preston, Blackpool, Leyland, Wigan, Kirby, Southport, Oldham, Morecambe and Lancaster. Degrees attracting mature students: potentially all courses, but, in practice, the social sciences – Psychology, Social Work etc. *Postgraduate Vocational Courses* include Postgraduate Diploma in Social Work; Postgraduate Diploma in Business Administration – any degree acceptable.

Leeds Polytechnic
(1988) Welcomes applications from mature students aged 21-plus without normal entry qualifications, who are considered on merit. BSc/BSc (Hons) Environmental Health – entry for mature students without normal entry requirements is possible. BA (Hons) Architecture – mature students without qualifications are assessed on portfolio and at interview; BA (Hons) Landscape Architecture – regulations as preceding degree; BA (Hons) Fine Art, Graphic Design or Three-Dimensional Design (Furniture, Industrial Design or Interior Design) – exceptionally gifted students without normal qualifications may be admitted; BA (Hons) Food and Accommodation Management – mature students may be admitted; BSc (Hons) Information Science – 'The School actively encourages mature students without formal qualifications to apply.' *Part-Time Courses*: BA/BA (Hons) Management and Administration; BEd/BEd (Hons) for qualified teachers; BSc (Hons) Nursing Studies; LLB/LLB (Hons) Law; BA/BA (Hons) Librarianship; BSc Production Engineering; BA (Hons) Social Policy and Administration. *Postgraduate Vocational Courses*: Graduate Conversion course in Accounting, full time, any graduate considered; Postgraduate Diploma in Personnel Management, full time, any graduate considered; Postgraduate Certificate in Education,

full time, any graduate considered; Postgraduate Diploma in Dietetics, full time – any graduate in science who has read human physiology and biochemistry to an approved standard. HCIMA graduate Conversion course, full time, any graduate. Polytechnic Diploma in Hotel, Catering and Institutional Management, full time, any graduate. Postgraduate Diploma in Health Education, full time, any graduate. Postgraduate Diploma in Information Administration for Linguists, full time, graduates in French, German, Italian or Spanish. Postgraduate Diploma in Information Administration, full time, any graduate. Law – Common Professional Examination, full time, any graduate. Postgraduate Diploma in European Community Law and Integration, full time, graduates in Law, Economics, Business Studies, Political Science, Modern Languages. Postgraduate Diploma in Librarianship and Information Work, full time, any graduate with a year's approved library/similar acceptable experience. Postgraduate CQSW Social Work, full time, graduates in social sciences/other approved degree, plus relevant experience. Business Automation Analysis/Electrical Engineering Conversion course for arts graduates. Part-Time prospectus available.

Leeds: Trinity and All Saints College
(1988) Entry concessions possible for students aged 21-plus. JMB Mature Matriculation process used (see description under Liverpool University). All BA/BEd degrees attract mature students, but the Home Economics BEd is particularly popular. Honours degrees of the University of Leeds awarded in BA/BSc Planning and Administration; BA/BSc Public Media; BEd (Primary or Secondary). *Part-Time Degrees*: In-service BEd (Primary or Secondary) for qualified teachers.

Home Economics BEd: viewpoint
'A government grant has enabled the college to equip spacious and attractive new premises for Secondary Education,and this means more opportunities for the growing number of mature students who wish to train for a career in teaching. For such would-be students, the combination of Home Economics with Secondary Education is particularly attractive.'

'We recognise that many mature students will not have the same qualifications as students coming straight from school, but mature students do bring to their studies other skills. Alternative means of entry to the course are available, and qualifications such as BTEC may be acceptable for entry, so it is worth writing to us to find out.'

'The Home Economics component includes units on health education, textiles, social studies, consumer studies, design in the home, nutrition and food science and technology.'

'The Education component develops the knowledge and skills needed to become a secondary school teacher and includes regular and frequent contacts with pupils in schools. The course enourages mature students to bring their own experience to their studies and eventually into the classroom.'

'Job prospects are very good. Indeed since 1985, everyone graduating with a BEd in Home Economics has obtained employment and many of the former students have found that progress can be rapid.'

(Spokesperson, Trinity and All Saints College, Leeds)

Lincoln, Gainsborough, Louth: North Lincolnshire College
The first year of the Leicester Polytechnic Combined Studies degree can be taken as modules from Computing, Marketing, Mathematics and Accountancy.

Liverpool: Institute of Higher Education
'The Institute wishes to promote enquiries and applications from mature students.' An explanatory booklet has been produced by the Joint Matriculation board, Manchester: *A University Degree: A Second Chance at 21-plus* (see under Liverpool University for admissions procedure) and can be obtained from this Institute as well as any of the participating universities (see address list).

Liverpool: University of Liverpool
Students over 21 who are not matriculated in the usual way may opt for the Mature Entry Scheme of the Joint Matriculation Board. Candidates using this procedure may be interviewed following their application to the university and given conditional offers of places, subject to their passing a 'package' of tests to be set by the university. These may include: a mature matriculation interview, a general test of comprehension and essay-writing, a test or tests set by the department they wish to enter. All undergraduate courses consider mature students, but departmental tests vary with the character of the subject and the level of demand from students. NB: This JMB Mature Entry scheme also applies to the universities of Birmingham, Leeds, Manchester and Sheffield and to colleges affiliated to the five constituent universities.

Manchester Polytechnic
(1988) An excellent *Mature Students Handbook* is available free from The Registry, Manchester Polytechnic, All Saints, Manchester Ml5 6BH. Entry concessions possible for students aged 21 and over. In general, admissions tutors must be satisfied you can cope with the course, and normally you should have done some preparatory study (Access course, Open College, Gateway, Threshold, Polymaths – see 'Pre-Entry, Sample and Access Courses'). BA (Hons) applied Community Studies, applications welcomed from mature students; BEd (Hons), mature students invited to apply and may be considered under exceptional entry arrangements; BSc/BSc (Hons) Environmental Management, mature students lacking normal requirements should contact the department for discussion; BSc Speech Pathology and Therapy, applications from mature candidates always welcome; BA/BA

(Hons) English Studies or Historical Studies, special consideration given to unqualified mature students; BA/BA (Hons) Humanities/Social Studies, special consideration given to unqualified mature students; BA/BA (Hons) Economics, entry requirements may be waived for over-21s who show evidence of continued study since leaving school. *Part-Time Degrees*: BA (Hons)/BSc (Hons) Business Studies; BA/BA (Hons)Humanities/Social Studies; BA (Hons) Public Administration; BA (Hons) Social Science; BEng/BEng (Hons); Electrical and Electronic Engineering/Mechanical Engineering/ Engineering; BSc/BSc (Hons) Applied Biological Sciences; BSc (Hons) Combined Studies (Science and Technology subjects); BSc (Hons) Polymer Science and Technology; BSc (Hons) Psychology; LLB (Hons). *Postgraduate Vocational Courses* include Postgraduate Diploma in Personnel Management, any graduate; Accountancy Foundation course, full time, any graduate; Law – Common Professional Examination course, full time, any non-Law graduate; Postgraduate Diploma in Hotel and Catering Administration, full time, any graduate; Polytechnic Diploma in Tourism, full time, any graduate; Polytechnic Diploma in Clothing Technology, full time, any graduate; Postgraduate Diploma in Librarianship, full time, any graduate with at least six months' experience in librarianship/other approved experience; Postgraduate Certificate in Education, full time.

Mature Student routes in Science and Technology: viewpoints
'I started out in a job in industry where I had to do Chemistry and that involved taking the TEC (now BTEC) part-time college course. Then I was made redundant, so I went through the telephone directory and just phoned people up till somebody gave me an interview for another job. I asked them to send me to college and they said yes, I could do the Higher National Certificate in Chemistry. Then, round about Christmas, the firm started going under and I asked Manchester Polytechnic if I could transfer from the HNC to the degree course. They said to stay on at work if I could and keep doing the HNC because if I did, I'd get the necessary industrial experience for the sandwich degree, and I could do it in two years – which is what I did.'

'People don't expect middle-aged Mums like me to want day release but when I got a job in a hospital laboratory, I applied to come to the polytechnic. It was only after a lot of persuasion that I managed to get on this medical laboratory technology course (I think they'd originally wanted somebody who'd just be an extra pair of hands at the hospital.) Now that I've got the chance, I can't afford to fall behind with the course. That means working my diary out very carefully, because at times I'm 'on call' at work, and there are things like visiting my children's school on various occasions, which have all got to be fitted in. Unlike young students, I don't feel I can take time off work to catch up if I get behind with homework, so I have to be organised.'

(Students, Faculty of Science and Engineering, Manchester Polytechnic)

'In virtually all our CNAA degree courses, we have a clause which allows the admission of students without the standard entry qualifications as prescribed in the prospectus. This may range, for example, from leaving school with very modest attainments but having a period of relatively mature experience in industry, which we deem experiential learning as it's called, or again, there may be a gap in the education record which we feel has been made up in other ways.'

(Spokesperson, Faculty of Science and Engineering, Manchester Polytechnic)

Manchester: UMIST (University of Manchester Institute of Science and Technology)

Entry concessions possible for students aged 21 and over. Mature Matriculation entry: could be by interview or directd reading programme and written examination. Students also accepted via Access courses and HITECC courses.

Manchester: University of Manchester

Entry concessions possible for students aged over 21. Selection by interview, possibly involving the submission of an essay or essays, or taking an examination. Preparatory courses available (see 'Pre Entry, Sample and Access Courses'). *Part-Time Degrees:* Comparative Religion, Economic and Social Studies, Education, Environmental Studies, History, History of Art, Literary Studies, Nursing Education, Nursing Studies, Theology and Religious Studies. Also conversion courses, both at graduate and undergraduate level. For details, contact the Office of Continuing Education and Training at the University.

Middlesbrough: Teesside Polytechnic

Mature students (over 21) are exempted from minimum qualifications if, in the opinion of the course officers, they would be capable of completing the course without formal qualifications. Entry to BA Humanities, full time and part time, and BSc Social Studies, full time, via Access/Gateway courses. *Part-Time Degrees:* Humanities, with a wide range of courses in the areas of Literature, History, Politics, French and Sociology, which may be studied either as single subjects or in combination.

Newcastle-upon-Tyne Polytechnic

(1988) Mature students may be admitted without the usual minimum qualifications at the Polytechnic's discretion. NB: a Higher Education Foundation course is offered at Newcastle-upon-Tyne College of Arts and Technology, Gateshead Technical College, Derwentside Technical College, Peterlee College and North Tyneside College of Further Education on a part-time basis for candidates over 20. The Polytechnic also runs an *Associate Student* scheme for over-21s to take units from degree/diploma/certificate courses, part time. (See also 'Pre-Entry, Sample and Access Courses'.) BA

320 Degree and Advanced Courses

(Hons) Design for Industry, mature candidates with relevant experience considered; BA (Hons) Media Production, over-21s and those of marked creative promise without minimum qualifications considered; BA (Hons) Travel and Tourism, mature applicants welcomed and fully considered; BA (Hons) Business Studies, over-21s considered without minimum entry requirements, aptitude tests may be given. BSc (Hons) Mathematics, mature students and those with non-standard qualifications considered. BSc/BSc (Hons) Computing for Industry, over-21s considered without minimum entry requirements; BA Secretarial Studies, over-21s considered without minimum entry requirements; BSc (Hons) Sociology, mature students without formal entry qualifications welcomed. BSc (Hons) Applied Consumer Sciences, over-21s considered without minimum entry requirements; BEng/BEng (Hons), mature applicants welcome, including those with non-standard qualifications. BA/BA (Hons) English and History, mature candidates are specially and sympathetically considered. BA (Hons) Geography, mature candidates without formal qualifications welcomed; BA (Hons) Information and Library Studies, mature students are always welcome. BA (Hons) Economics, over-21s encouraged to apply even without minimum entry qualifications; BA (Hons) Government and Public Policy, older candidates who do not possess the formal qualifications outlined will be welcomed; LLB (Hons), mature students may submit applications for consideration *Part-Time Degrees*: BA/BA (Hons) Business Studies; BA Applied Computing; BSc (Hons) Health Studies (for Registered nurses, paramedical professionals, NHS administrators etc.); BSc Applied Chemistry; BEng EngineeringTechnology, BSc/BSc (Hons) Physical Electronics; BEd/BEd (Hons) for qualified teachers; BA/BA(Hons) English and History; LLB/LLB (Hons) Law. Projected BA (Hons) Criminal Justice Studies. *Postgraduate Vocational Courses* include: Postgraduate Certificate in Education, full time; Postgraduate Diploma in Library and Information Studies, full time, for any graduate; Postgraduate Diploma in Optoelectronics, full time, for graduates in physics, electronic engineering or similar; Postgraduate Diploma in Computer-Assisted Manufacture, full time, for graduates in engineering, science or similar; Postgraduate Diploma in Offshore Materials and Corrosion Engineering, full time, for graduates in Applied Science (Physical or Chemical) or Engineering or similar; Postgraduate Diploma in Secretarial/Bilingual Secretarial Administration, full time, any graduate for the former, graduates in French, German or Spanish for the latter; Postgraduate Diploma in Business Information Technology, full time. NB: Part-Time Prospectus available.

Ormskirk: Edge Hill College of Higher Education
(1988) Entry concessions possible for mature students aged 21 and over; applicants are considered by the Special Admissions Committee of Lancaster University but would normally be expected to have undertaken recent academic study at an appropriate level and might be asked to undertake an

assignment related to their chosen course. 'Each year, some 100 older students of widely varying ages enter the College's undergraduate courses; indeed a few of them have reached the pinnacle of success by achieving a first-class honours degree, and most of them achieve degrees of a good honours standard.' *Part-Time Degrees*: DipHE/BA (Hons) Applied Social Science, English, Geography, History, Urban Policy and Race Relations. DipHE/BSc/BSc (Hons) Geography. Courses are credit-based with a wide choice of options. Part-time students may move on to a full-time course by arrangement.

Preston College
LINCS – 1st year combined studies BA/BSc in partnership with Lancashire Polytechnic.

Preston: Lancashire Polytechnic
Entry concessions widespread for students aged 21 or over. May be admitted by virtue of prior experience, ability to cope with and benefit from the course, advanced standing from previous learning plus disadvantage criteria. Credit Transfer possible, particularly to 25-subject Combined Studies Programme. Open College entry via local colleges. Access courses and Foundation courses (see 'Pre Entry, Sample and Access Courses'). Mature students particularly attracted to Social Sciences, Humanities, Business Studies, Science, Technology, Law and Languages courses (Combined Studies modular scheme). *Associate Student* scheme, part time, choice of study units from hundreds in most subject areas within the polytechnic. *Part-Time Degrees*: BA (Hons) Business Studies; BA (Hons) Fine Art; LLB (Hons) Law; BSc Quantity Surveying; BSc Building Management; BEng(Hons) Building Services Engineering; BA (Hons) Applied Social Studies; BA (Hons) Nursing; BSc (Hons) Chemistry; BEd (Hons)/BSc (Hons)/ BA (Hons)/BA/DipHE/Polytechnic Advanced Certificate Combined Studies credit accumulation programme: 25 subject choices. Some first-year subjects from Combined Studies programme available in local further education colleges (enquire at Polytechnic). *Postgraduate Vocational Courses:* – various, including: research by thesis, Social Work Diploma, Journalism, MSc in Biotechnology, MBA, Bilingual Executive Assistants' course. Prospectus not supplied, so enquire at the polytechnic.

Salford College of Technology
Part-Time Degrees: BSc Environmental Health (in association with Manchester Polytechnic).

Salford: University of Salford
Entry concessions possible for students aged 21 or over at the start of the degree programme. Wide variety of concessions: reduced GCE requirements for candidates who demonstrate ability and potential. Interview plus

written work plus other exam qualifications plus work experience may be considered. Access course candidates accepted, particularly from courses available in the region. Mature students are particularly welcome on courses in Business and Management, Information Technology, Sociology and Social Sciences, but will also be considered for courses in Science and Engineering subjects. *Part-Time Degrees:* BA Politics and Contemporary History, BSc Sociology, BSc Applied Physics with Electronics.

Sheffield City Polytechnic

This Polytechnic chose to provide a statement: 'All Sheffield City Polytechnic's mainstream degree and higher diploma courses welcome applications from mature students who do not necessarily need to have the standard GCE/GCSE entry requirements expected of school leavers. There are nearly 100 full-time courses, matched by a similar number of part-time courses to choose from. Recently the Polytechnic has introduced a new Credit Accumulation and Transfer Scheme (CATS) which is ideal for mature students and has a number of special features. For instance CATS enables students to study units from any of the Polytechnic's mainstream courses, gain credit for each unit completed successfully and "save" up the credits towards qualifications ranging from an advanced certificate to a degree course. Using CATS, students could also, if they wish, study either full time or part time, negotiate their own programmes of study, study mainstream degree courses at a slower pace and may gain credit from previous work experience which will count towards their eventual qualification.' (*NB: see references to CATS and ERASMUS in Introduction to this section.*) General Prospectus available; see address list for Northern region at the end of the book.

Sheffield: Loxley Tertiary College

University of Sheffield Certificate course in Computer Control of Manufacturing Systems, part time. University of Sheffield Certificate course in Non-Destructive Testing of Materials, part time. University of Sheffield Certificate course in English Studies, part time. These courses are linked to the CNAA Credit Accumulation and Transfer (CATS) scheme; admission by interview.

Sunderland Polytechnic

Mature students are welcome to apply for all degree courses. For the following list of courses, candidates aged over 21 without formal entry requirements are considered, especially those with relevant experience: BA (Hons) Fine Art; BA (Hons) 3D Design; BSc (Hons) Information Technology; BSc (Hons) Technology Management; BSc (Hons) Manufacturing Management; BSc (Hons) Product Innovation Management; BSc (Hons) Environmental Technology; BSc (Hons) Mechanical Engineering (with European Studies option); BEng (Hons) Digital Engineering; BEng (Hons) Civil

Engineering; BA (Hons) Business Studies (with European Languages and Accountancy options); BA (Hons) English Studies; BA (Hons) Combined Arts; BA (Hons) Economics; BA (Hons) Social Sciences; BA (Hons) Communication Studies; BA (Hons) Business Computing (with Languages option); BSc (Hons) Maths, Computing and Communications. BEd (Hons) Early/Middle Years; BEd (Hons) Technology; BEd (Hons) Education and Business Studies; intercalated Teachers Certificate within Joint Scheme and BEng degree; 2-year BEd in Maths, Physics, Technology, Business Studies. *Please note*: Mature candidates for any BEd course must be aged 25 years or over and hold O-level/GCSE in Maths and English Language. Candidates applying for entry to the 2-year BEd courses must also hold an HNC/D in a relevant subject. There are other-full time degree courses for which mature students can apply but no specific concession has been quoted for them: check the Undergraduate prospectus for details. *Part-Time Degrees:* (normal entry requirements) BEng; BSc (Hons) Chiropody. Mature applicants without formal entry requirements considered: BSc (Hons) Material Science; BSc Science Subjects; BA (Hons) Combined Arts; BA (Hons) Management Studies; BA (Hons) Information Technology; BA (Hons) Art and Design. Also: Higher Diploma in Psychology, Diploma in Humanities. Wide range of postgraduate courses available.

Mature students, viewpoint
'Sunderland Polytechnic welcomes applications from "late starters" as it is generally accepted that their very maturity and its attendant qualities are an enhancement to study. As an institution which has chosen to adopt an Equal Opportunities Policy, this Polytechnic is keen to encourage and support those returning to study. In particular, we are hoping to provide creche facilities for those students with pre-school children in the academic year 1989–90.'

Wakefield: Bretton Hall College of Higher Education
Entry concessions for students aged over 21, via JMB Mature Matriculation scheme (see under Liverpool University for details). 'It should be stressed that the college welcomes adults as mature students on degree courses ... the Mature Student Qualifying Examination as mentioned above is based on an intelligent awareness of the contemporary world and a capacity to present ideas and opinions in clear written English. To help adults succeed in this examination, preparation courses are provided by the college.' The college has degrees in all the major Arts: BA (Hons) Art and Design (Fine Arts and Fashion and Textile Design); BA (Hons) Dance; BA (Hons) Drama; BA (Hons) English; BA (Hons) Music. There is a long tradition of teacher training, the college offering BEd (Hons) Early Years (3–8 year olds), BEd(Hons) Primary/Middle (5–8 year olds and 8–13 year olds) with specialisms in Art, English, Environmental Studies, Maths and Computing or Music. *Postgraduate Vocational Courses:* Post Graduate Certificate in Education (Primary and Secondary).

Warrington: North Cheshire College
A BA (Hons) degree in Media Studies or Leisure and Recreation, both combined with Management Studies is available. Thirty places are available for mature students; Access courses provide individually tailored programmes to entry standard (see 'Pre-Entry, Sample and Access Courses').

York: College of Ripon and York St John
Mature student concessions unspecified, but there is part-time provision. *Part-Time Degrees:* DipHE/BA/BSc, wide range of options. *Postgraduate Vocational Courses:* Postgraduate Certificate in Education, full time – any graduate.

Wales and Western England

Aberystwyth: University College
Exemption from minimum entry requirements for students aged over 21. Selection by interview, possibly including the submission of work done at home/on any pre-university course. Preparatory courses available in Science subjects (see 'Pre-Entry, Sample and Access Courses'). BSc Ordinary degree available with Maths or Physics options as appropriate, designed with older students in mind. Mature students, candidates with non-traditional Access qualifications or relevant experience considered by all departments for entry. *Postgraduate Vocational Courses:* Computer conversion course for non-computing graduates; Biological Electron Microscopy course for intending BEM users; Environmental Impact Assessment Diploma; Diploma in Archive Administration. Post-experience courses in Education available, full time, part time and unit-based; Fine Art vocational Diploma; Diplomas in aspects of Law, Accounting and Economics available for non-specialist graduates in these fields; Vocational Agricultural courses available; MBA; Micropaelaeantology course for intending Geologists. Non-graduates over 30 with relevant work experience considered for any appropriate postgraduate course. Courses available part time and full time.

Bath: College of Higher Education
All courses – individual and sympathetic consideration given to mature candidates over 21 years of age. Successful completion of the Access courses offered by City of Bath College of Further Education, Weston-Super-Mare College of Further Education and, subject to approval by the CNAA, Trowbridge Technical College, qualifies candidates for admission to the following: BEd (Hons) full time; BSc (Hons) Home Economics, full time; BA (Hons) Music, full time; BA (Hons) Combined Studies, full time; DipHE, full time. Mature candidates are also admitted to the following Art and Design courses on the strength of their portfolio submission: BA (Hons)Fine Art (Painting or Sculpture), full time; BA (Hons) Graphic Design, full time; BA (Hons) Three Dimensional Design (Ceramics), full time. *Postgraduate Vocational Courses:* Postgraduate Certificate in Education for Primary Teaching (candidates with degrees in subject areas relevant to the primary school curriculum), full time. Postgraduate Certificate in Education for Secondary

Age Range: options are Home Economics, Music, Rural and Environmental Science, full time – special entry requirements.

Bath: University of Bath
Some concessions for mature students; applicants should write to the relevant Admissions Tutor (see prospectus).

Bristol Polytechnic
Successful completion of Access courses at local technical colleges leads to places at Bristol Polytechnic on degree/diploma courses in: Teacher Education; Social Work; Community and Youth Work; Law; Business Studies; Mathematics, Statistics and Computing; Systems Analysis; Systems Design; Science (Applied Biology); Housing; Town and Country Planning; Valuation and Estate Management; Building; Social Science; Humanities; Modern Languages. 'The Polytechnic also welcomes enquiries from mature people without the standard entry qualifications, or who wish to update, or add to existing qualifications, or to change the direction of their careers/lives.'

Cardiff: South Glamorgan Institute of Higher Education
(1988) Entry concessions possible for students aged 21 or over on CNAA courses or aged 23 or over on University of Wales degree courses. These may include reduced GCE requirements, admission by interview and submission of case to University of Wales for approval. The Institute lists the following degrees as attracting mature students: BA (Hons) Fine Art; BA (Hons) Ceramics; BA (Hons) Industrial Design; BA (Hons) Interior Design; BA (Hons) Art Education Studies; BEd (Hons); BA (Hons) Human Movement Studies; BSc (Hons) Dietetics; BSc (Hons) Speech Therapy; BSc (Hons) Applied Life Sciences; BA Tourism. *Postgraduate Vocational Courses* include: MA Fine Art; MA Ceramics; Postgraduate Certificate in Education (various options), full time; Graduate Entry to Journalism, full time (mainly for those sponsored by the newspaper industry; some places available for non-sponsored students). Bilingual and non-linguistic Secretarial courses.

Cardiff: South Glamorgan School of Nursing
Postgraduate Vocational Course: A 116-week course (exclusive of holidays) leading to the qualification of Registered General Nurse is available for graduates bi-annually.

Cardiff: University of Wales College of Cardiff
This new college was formed by the merger of University College, Cardiff and University of Wales Institute of Science and Technology. Mature students (aged 21 or over) with good general educational background are not necessarily subject to the standard undergraduate entry requirements. Mature applicants are usually interviewed. Undergraduate degrees in the Faculty of Humanities and Social Studies attract significant numbers of

mature age students. *Part-Time Courses/Degrees* BD, Diploma in Theology. Many full-time and part-time postgraduate taught courses which may be defined as vocational. See Undergraduate and Postgraduate prospectuses for details, including postgraduate entry requirements.

Cheltenham: College of St Paul and St Mary
(1988) Entry concessions for students aged 21 and over on 31 December of the year of entry. They still need O-level English and Mathematics, but those over 25 may be able to take an alternative test for Mathematics. Special Access course mainly for members of ethnic minorities (see 'Pre-Entry, Sample and Access Courses'), leading to the BEd (Hons) degree. Mature students are also attracted to part-time degrees and to the BA (Hons) Combined Studies and BSc (Hons) Geography/Geology courses. *Part-Time Degrees*: BA (Hons) Combined Studies – options English and History, English and Geography, English and Religious Studies, Geography and History, History and Religious Studies; BSc (Hons) Geograpy and Geology; BEd (Hons) of Bristol University for serving teachers. *Postgraduate Vocational Courses* include Postgraduate Certificate in Education, full time, any graduate. Conversion course, full time, for secondary teachers wishing to teach in primary schools.

Dartington College of Arts
We welcome applications from mature students. Our CNAA degrees (Music, Art and Social Context and Theatre) all have flexible entry requirements for applicants over 21 who may not have the standard academic qualifications. 'I was greatly encouraged by the number of other mature students on the courses' (Student on BA (Hons) Music degree). Also courses specifically aimed at people returning to higher education (see 'Pre-Entry, Sample and Access Courses').

Exeter University
Entry concessions possible for students aged 21 and over. Concessions depend on recommendation by department, based on interview, and taking account of academic background and experience. The prospectus states: 'applications are welcomed from those who for a variety of reasons may not have had the opportunity of embarking upon University education when they left school but are now interested in doing so.' Mature applicants are welcomed for all degree courses, but they find Social Studies to be among the most attractive. *Postgraduate Vocational Courses* include two new two-year degrees for students who *either* have already completed two years of a degree course in Physics, Mathematics or Engineering or are HND holders with relevant professional experience, *or* mature students with degrees or professional qualifications including one year's relevant main subject study, with at least four years' professional experience.

Lampeter: St David's University College

(1988) Entry concessions for students over 21 at the time of admission – the need for formal GCE qualifications may be waived. Mature applicants are normally called for interview and occasionally asked to submit written work. Wide range of BA (Hons) degree choices and BD of the University of Wales.

Plymouth: Polytechnic South West

Amalgamation of Plymouth Polytechnic with Exeter College of Art and Design, Seale Hayne College (Newton Abbot) and Rolle College (Exmouth). (1988) Applications welcomed from mature students for all courses, no minimum age limit specified, 'a place will be offered if we feel someone will benefit from and complete satisfactorily the particular course.' *Part-Time Degrees*: DipHE/BSc/BSc (Hons) Combined Honours – Science, Social Science, Science and Social Science; BSc Applicable Mathematics. *Postgraduate Vocational Courses* include MSc Intelligent Systems, full time or block, any honours degree acceptable provided candidates have a strong interest in artificial intelligence and some knowledge of computers; Doctor of Clinical Psychology, full time or part time, good honours degree in Psychology needed; Postgraduate Diploma/MSc Applied Fish Biology, full time or part time, for honours graduates in biology or a joint honours/modular degree with biology forming the major part (includes option in Fish Farming).

Pontypridd: Polytechnic of Wales

(1988) Entry concessions possible for mature students (age unspecified) if the polytechnic is satisfied they will benefit from the course and have the necessary motivation, potential and knowledge to complete it satisfactorily. *Part-Time Degrees*: BEng/BEng (Hons) Civil Engineering; BSc/BSc (Hons) Chemistry; BSc/BSc (Hons) Computer Studies; BA/BA (Hons) Humanities; LLB/LLB (Hons); BA (Hons) Police Studies – majority of students will be serving police officers. *Postgraduate Vocational Courses* include: Common Professional Examination in Law, full time, for graduates with non-Law degrees; Polytechnic diploma in Craft, Design and Technology, part time, for practising teachers; Postgraduate Diploma in Computer Science, part time, for any graduate; MSc Education Management, part time.

Poole: Dorset Institute of Higher Education

(1988) Most full-time courses are open to those mature students without formal qualifications who can present evidence that convinces admissions staff that they have the capacity and ability to succeed and benefit from the course. Choices include: BA (Hons) Business Studies; BA (Hons) Combined Studies; BSc (Hons) Engineering Business Development; BA (Hons) Financial Services; BSc (Hons) Food and Catering Management; BA (Hons) Hospitality Management; BSc (Hons) Information Systems Management; BA (Hons) Media Production; BA (Hons) Tourism Studies. *Part-Time Degrees* BEng Computer-Aided Engineering; BA/BA (Hons) Business Studies.

Swansea: University College of Swansea
Entry concessions possible for students aged 21 or over. They are required to attend for interview with the chosen department and the department's recommendation is considered by a special committee. The College looks for a genuine commitment and the ability to pursue a course of study; this can be demonstrated in a variety of ways, e.g. by pursuing an Open University course, success in GCE, or attendance at the College's own Adult Education Department.

Weymouth College
Postgraduate Vocational Courses: Diploma in the Conservation of Stonework, full time, for graduates in any subject.

Scotland and Northern Ireland

Aberdeen: Robert Gordon's Institute of Technology
Applications are welcomed from mature students and candidates may be admitted without the normal minimum qualifications at the Institute's discretion. Each application is treated on an individual basis and entry to the later stages of a course may be possible, depending upon experience. A wide range of courses is available for which mature candidates may be admitted without minimum qualifications: (1) *Interlinked HND and Degree Courses* which allow entrance to an HND and subsequent transfer to the degree course with no time penalty – Electronic and Electrical Engineering; Mechanical Engineering; Applied Chemistry; Applied Physics; Hotel, Catering and Institutional Administration. Also degree/honours degree courses – BSc Electronic and Electrical Engineering; BEng/BEng (Hons) Electronic and Electrical Engineering; BEng/BEng (Hons) Information Engineering; BSc Mechanical Engineering; BEng/BEng (Hons) Engineering Technology; BSc/BSc (Hons) Computer Science; BSc/BSc (Hons) Mathematical Sciences with Computing; BSc/BSc (Hons) Applied Science; BSc Food, Textiles and Consumer Studies; BSc/BSc (Hons) Nutrition and Dietetics; BSc/BSc (Hons) Human Nutrition; BA Hotel, Catering and Institutional Management; BA Applied Social Studies; BA/BA (Hons) Business Studies; BA Commerce; BA/BA (Hons) Librarianship and Information Studies; BA/BA (Hons) Public Administration; BA/BA (Hons) Fine Art; BA/BA (Hons) Design and Craft; BSc (Hons) Architecture; BSc Quantity Surveying. *Diploma courses* Computing; Health Visiting, Occupational Health Nursing. *Postgraduate Vocational Courses:* Offshore Engineering; Offshore Materials and Corrosion Engineering; Computer Applications in Engineering; Computer Aided Monitoring and Control; Computer Aided Project Management; Computer Aided Drawing and Design; Computer Aided Manufacture; Systems Modelling and Simulation.

Belfast: Stranmillis College
Mature students accepted for BEd courses on offer; appropriately qualified mature students who wish to take Craft, Design and Technology as the main academic subject may be permitted to enter the second year of the degree course. *Postgraduate Vocational Courses:* include Postgraduate Certificate in

Education, full time – any graduate considered. Postgraduate Certificate in Education in Technology – for graduates in appropriate discipline. Graduate Certificate in Education (Honours Psychology option) full time – for intending educational psychologists who wish to proceed to the MSc in Development and Educational Psychology of Queen's University.

Coleraine: University of Ulster

University states: 'Persons of at least 21 years of age at the date of entry to a course who have useful experience to bring to University studies but who do not satisfy the entry requirements may apply for admission to an undergraduate course. The University has a sympathetic attitude towards such applications, the major concern being that mature students have a realistic chance of completing their course. Applicants may be asked to take a test or to take part in some other selection procedure to assess whether they are likely to be able to cope with the work expected of a University student.' The University organises information evenings, particularly for those interested in part-time degrees and access courses (see 'Pre-Entry, Sample and Access Courses'), as well as holding open days and arranging for talks to groups of mature students. No information about part-time degree subjects was supplied; please check prospectus.

Dundee: Duncan of Jordanstone College

Entry concessions possible for students aged 23 and over. Up to 10% of admissions may be without any formal qualifications for the first year course in Art and Design; however, applicants must present outstanding portfolios of art and/or design work, appear for interview and convince the committee of an ability to complete the course satisfactorily, including written assignments. BA (Hons) Fine Art attracts most mature students. *Postgraduate Vocational Course:* It is hoped that a MA course in Catering Managment will start in September 1989. Validation by the University of Dundee is still awaited.

Dundee: University of Dundee

Entry concessions possible for students aged 21 or over at the time of entry to the university. The minimum level of attainment expected will be the equivalent of two A-levels or three SCE Highers, or an approved national certificate or diploma. In some faculties, candidates can qualify with Open University credits or by attending the University's Return to Study course. *Part-Time Degrees:* The MA degree in the Faculty of Arts and Social Sciences is available by part-time study and some BSc courses may also be available on this basis; details are available on request from the Admissions Office.

Edinburgh: College of Art

Entry concessions possible for students aged 23 or over. The college's assessment of the standard and promise indicated by the portfolio of work is of great importance in arriving at the final selection of candidates. *Postgraduate Vocational Courses:* MArch, full time or part time; MSc Architectural Conservation, full time or part time; MSc Urban Design, full time or part time; Postgraduate Diploma in Art and Design, Painting, Printmaking of Sculpture, full time; Postgraduate Diploma in Town and Country Planning, full time or part time – recognised by the Royal Town Planning Institute; Postgraduate Diploma in Housing, full time, recognised by the Institute of Housing; Postgraduate Diploma in Architecture, full time; Postgraduate Diploma in Urban Design, full time – recognised by the Royal Institute of British Architects; Postgraduate Diploma in Architectural Conservation, full time.

Edinburgh: Heriot-Watt University
(1988) Entry concessions possible for students aged 21 or over. *Part-Time Degrees*: BA Business Studies; BSc General. *Postgraduate Vocational Courses* include: Diploma in Accounting, full-time conversion course for graduates wishing to enter a professional accounting studentship; MSc/Diploma conversion course in Digital Techniques for Information Technology, full time, for graduates in mathematically based subjects; Diploma in Optoelectronics, full-time conversion course for science graduates.

Edinburgh: Napier Polytechnic of Edinburgh
The polytechnic states: 'Minimum entry requirements for all full- and part-time degrees or HND courses are normally two SCE Higher Exam passes or two GCE A-level passes, but mature applicants (over 21) who lack these qualifications but who have relevant work experience are welcome to apply. These requirements do not apply to the Open Learning Centre. (See 'Open and Distance Learning Courses'.) This polytechnic supplied information in a form that does not lend itself very readily to the style of *The Mature Student's Handbook* and readers may like to refer to the actual prospectus. However, a special mention should be made of *Part-Time Degrees* in Applied Economics, Business Studies, Life Sciences, and of the fact that 'multi-mode' attendance is allowed for Quantity Surveying. *Postgraduate Vocational Qualifications:* again, the material supplied by the polytechnic does not lend itself very readily to assessment in the terms of this book, but the subjects of Accounting, Business Administration, Careers Guidance, Computer-Aided Engineering, European Marketing and Languages, Information Technology, Personnel Management, Secretarial Studies, Software Technology and Systems Analysis and Design would seem promising for any graduate seeking a vocational course. There is also mention of a Postgraduate Diploma in Software Technology lasting 33 weeks 'designed to retrain people with programming skills. A degree is usually required, but exemption may be given to applicants with recent, relevant skill of a similar standard.'

Edinburgh: Queen Margaret College
(1988) Entry concessions possible for students over 21 who are warmly welcomed. Send for booklet *A Second Chance to Learn*. Note especially: BSc Dietetics (preliminary study of Chemistry advised); BA Nursing Studies – the college says 'we find that older and more experienced students also tend to be determined and adaptable, and our mature stuents have had a strong record of success on the course'; BSc Occupational Therapy, now 30% of entrants are over 21 but the course is a strenuous one, and those over the age of 40 have sometimes found it excessively so; BSc Physiotherapy; BSc Speech Pathology and Therapy; BA Communication Studies – in recent years, the majority of entrants have been away from school for some time, with a significant proportion being in their late 20s and 30s.' BSc Food Studies; BA Applied Consumer Studies, with Retailing and Home Economics options. *Postgraduate Vocational Courses*: HCIMA conversion course in hotel, catering and institutional management for those with non-catering degrees; new graduates and graduates wishing to retrain equally welcome.

Catering and Hotel Management Conversion Course
'I had been working in libraries for seven or eight years, but I felt a bit stifled. I wanted to choose a course where I might be able to forge ahead and one day run my own establishment. We had a spell in the first term in the kitchens on the production side, organising meals and banquets and that I hadn't encountered before; it was enormously interesting and good experience, even though what we are learning to do is not being trained as chefs but see the pressures on the chef. A great change from librarianship? Well, yes, but certain things are in common; dealing with people, getting on with them,sociability of approach and so on. I hope I may begin as an assistant trainee manager. That's a sort of manager's dogsbody – a jack of all trades who can take over in any supervisory or management function if someone's off duty.'

(Student, HCIMA Conversion course, Queen Margaret College)

Edinburgh: The University of Edinburgh
Entry concessions possible for students aged over 21 by 1 October in the year in which they begin their degree course. The normal minimum level of attainment will be recent passes at the Higher Grade in three subjects or GCE A-levels in two subjects. Alternatives are two full credits at OU Foundation level or adult residential college diplomas. There is also an Exceptional Admissions Procedure for students without the normal type of examination pass but with some evidence of appropriate achievement in a related professional field, or other evidence of intellectual promise. Candidates complete a special application form and, if considered for the Procedure, spend a day at the University where they tackle a test in reasoning skills, write two essays (one on a general topic, one on a topic relating to the individual's area of interest) and undergo an interview. *Part-*

Time Degrees: Faculty or Arts, MA (General); Faculty of Divinity, BD, BD (Hons): BA Religious Studies and MA Religious Studies; Faculty of Music, BMus/BMus (Hons); Faculty of Social Sciences, BSc (Social Sciences).

Glasgow Business School of the University of Glasgow
The Glasgow Business School offers a full-time International Master of Business Administration degree, a part-time Executive Master of Business Administration degree, a Corporate Management Development Programme and an MSc in Information Technology. The School's Centre for Entrepreneurial Development has a complete portfolio of full-time and part-time programmes for people wishing to start, expand or rescue small and new businesses.

Glasgow: The Queen's College
Mature students accepted for the BSc Physiotherapy. (See 'Retraining and New Skills Courses'.)

Glasgow: The University of Strathclyde
Entry concessions for students aged 21 and over. Competitive entry standard or General Entrance requirement may be relaxed (less likely in Science and Engineering). The Faculty of Arts andSocial Studies and the Strathclyde Business School run tests for admission for their BA degree courses. The test consists of an unseen essay on a general topic, aptitude tests and interview. There are also preliminary courses (see 'Pre-Entry, Sample and Access Courses'). *Part-Time Degrees:* BA Certificate/Pass degree programme in Economics, English Studies, French, Geography, German, History, Italian, Politics, Psychology, Russian, Sociology, Spanish, Women's Studies; you must take at least two subjects plus other selected classes or three full subjects to obtain a BA Pass degree. *Postgraduate Vocational Courses* include: Legal Practice, Accounting and Finance, Librarianship, Personnel Management etc. (See also 'Open and Distance Learning Courses' for details of MBA.) The Strathclyde Business School also offers an Effective Management Programme in seven modules, which may be taken individually, together with an Effective Supervision Programme lasting 3 days and offered at regular intervals throughout the year.

Paisley College of Technology
The College welcomes applications from mature students (normally 23 years and over) and special consideration will be given to applicants who, lacking conventional entrance qualifications, have over the years shown an interest in their educational advancement and an aptitude for academic study. Prospective mature students might also like to note that Paisley is a participating member of the Scottish Wider Access Programme (SWAP). The scheme involves one year full-time study of National Certificate modules with guaranteed entry to higher education for successful candidates. Information of the full range of subjects available can be obtained

from the Gateway Guidance Unit (041-422 1070) or the SWAP offices (041-553 2471). *Postgraduate Vocational Courses:* Postgraduate Diploma in Information Technology, full-time conversion course – any graduate considered (with introductory courses for those whose degrees did not include courses in Maths, Physics and Programming). Postgraduate Diploma in Computer-Aided Engineering, full time or part time through Module Credit accumulation – for Engineering and Science graduates or those with equivalent experience in a relevant industry.

St Andrews: University of St Andrews
(1988) Entry concessions possible for students aged 21 and over by October of year of entry. The general entrance requirement may be waived but current evidence of ability to perform well in public examinations is required.

GENERAL INFORMATION

Costs and grants, sources of information and useful addresses

Costs and Grants

Colleges and other providers of training are often loath to quote the fees charged for the courses they offer. Almost certainly this is because fees go out of date so quickly. Prospectuses have to be available early (often a year before a course will start) to give candidates a chance to apply for courses which may start in October 1989 but for which applications should be made by December 1988. Yet fees may not be definitely decided upon until May 1989 for the October 1989 start courses. It's not surprising that most colleges put a note in their prospectuses to the effect that 'Enquiries about fees should be directed to the Registrar.'

Yet for most people, the cost of any course is a major factor in deciding whether to enquire further about their eligibility. An adviser at Paddington College told me that they always encourage applicants for their Access courses to look at the whole cost of studying before they start. 'You could say that the average fee for a year's Access course is £500' she said. 'But students should add to that the cost of travelling from home to college and back for 36 weeks, the cost of a midday meal – say £1.50 in the canteen – for five days a week, the cost of pens and stationery. These extra factors are important for all students, not just Access course students, but we make a particular effort to explain costs for mature students who may be making considerable sacrifices to return to study.'

It is with this in mind that I have compiled a list of examples of typical fees charged by colleges for different kinds of courses. Obviously, there can be variations from college to college, as there are from one year to the next. The fees I am quoting are those published in prospectuses or given to me by phone in April 1989. By May 1989 they may have changed. By May 1990, I'd be surprised if there wasn't a small increase. The cost of most products goes up annually so why not education?

Even so, I think most people would prefer to have an approximate fee to consider than be given no information at all. It helps to know if something will cost you £20, or £200, or £2000 – and to get some idea of whether there's a chance of a grant in your case.

Rates of grant and benefit alter every year too (in November for benefit or Spetember for grants). The figures I quote are from official literature available in April 1989. You can get the latest leaflets on grants from the

Department of Education and Science, Elizabeth House, York Road, London SE1 7PH, and your local Department of Social Security office (formerly DHSS office) has leaflets on benefits. Your Jobcentre will have details of training allowances payable for full-time courses of Employment Training. Colleges themselves can tell you what might be offered for a course sponsored by theEuropean Social Fund (ESF in the course lists); sometimes a maintenance allowance is payable to students.

ALWAYS ASK

In matters of finance, you lose nothing by asking. The worst thing that can happen is that people will say, regretfully, 'No, sorry, nothing is available that suits your situation.'

The best is that they might discover that by slightly altering the hours of your attendance at college, you can move yourself into the category covered by the 2l-hour rule (explained in the second half of this section, headed 'Grants and Concessions'); or that because you were born in Little Wychwood, you're eligible for a special award only open to residents of that town who are over 30 and retraining. This kind of offer can sometimes be found tucked away at the back of prospectuses, particularly for higher education (universities, polytechnics, colleges of higher education). Check the index in each prospectus for 'awards', 'scholarships', 'bursaries'.

Unemployed people are often entitled to drastically reduced fees; again always check with the college.

Meanwhile, here are some sample costs. Please remember that they are likely to increase a little each year, so you are unlikely to find yourself paying the same at the end of a 3-year course as you did at the beginning!

ACCESS AND SIMILAR PRE-DEGREE COURSES

Some local authorities will consider giving discretionary grants to cover the cost of full-time Access courses, and for some people there may also be the chance of a maintenance allowance. However, if you are required to pay fees, Paddington College quotes 'approximately £500 a year' for the cost of an Access course from its extensive range (see 'Pre-Entry, Sample and Access Courses' in the London section).

The 'Cross ILEA Access Courses Guide' (see 'Pre-Entry, Sample and Access Courses') points out that students on part-time Access courses who are not eligible for grants may be eligible for substantially reduced fees in certain circumstances. They could be eligible if they are in receipt of unemployment benefit, DSS benefits (e.g. income support and family credit) or National Insurance state retirement pension.

Very moderate fees may be payable in the case of some Nursing Access courses. Doncaster Health Authority charges only £36 for a 12-week part-time Nursing Access course that prepares entrants to take the UKCC entry test – the fee for this is £5.

ADULT RESIDENTIAL COLLEGES
Bursaries are normally available to cover tuition and maintenance. Which-ever of the adult residential colleges you want to attend, you should make enquiries about bursaries by writing to the Awards Officer, Adult Education Bursaries, c/o Ruskin College, Oxford, OXl 2HE.

ASSOCIATE STUDENT COURSES
Costs are likely to vary a lot, partly because some courses involve the use of equipment which may be costly to buy or borrow, and partly according to the amount of work which might make up a unit of study. But a very helpful outline came from Birmingham Polytechnic, whose 'Listening and Visiting Student' programme is described on page 53 of the 'Pre-Entry, Sample and Access Courses' section. A Listening Student, who sits in on lectures but doesn't do coursework or take any exams, can expect to pay about £13 a year to attend for one hour a week. A Visiting Student, who not only listens but does coursework and has it marked, and may take an exam, if appropriate, pays £70 a year to attend for up to 4 hours a week, £145 a year to attend for between 4 and 8 hours a week, or £225 if attending for 8 hours a week or more. These are approximate fees, accurate in April 1989 but as with all costs, they could increase as time goes on.

GCSE AND GCE A-LEVEL COURSES
Sutton College of Liberal Arts quoted £48 for a 30-week course on an evening class basis (once a week) leading to the GCSE exam of the London and East Anglian Group. The same college quoted £96 for a 60-week course (once a week for two years) for an English Literature A-level course leading to the exam of the University of London.

WIDER OPPORTUNITIES
These are usually Training Agency (TA) sponsored courses and free to unemployed people and those returning to work after a break.

BTEC NATIONAL DIPLOMA
Sometimes local authorities will give a small discretionary grant to a mature student, to help with fees. Merton College quoted £439 a year for the full-time two-year course leading to the BTEC National Diploma in Health Studies, which can lead on to courses in nursing, radiography, physio-therapy, chiropody etc. You must also pay a registration fee to BTEC which at the time of writing is £42.

BTEC HIGHER NATIONAL DIPLOMA
Courses usually attract mandatory grants, just like degree courses. But if you have already had a grant for a degree, or HND or similar designated course, you may have to pay your own way. The South Bank Polytechnic quotes £566 a year for the two-year full-time HND. If you want to study part-

time and go for the Higher National Certificate, the cost would be £114 a year if you attended one day a week. Each evening a week up to two hours would cost £38 a year, and each evening longer than two hours would cost £57 a year. You must also pay a registration fee to BTEC which at the time of writing is £48.

PROFESSIONAL COURSES
As an example of a full-time course, the National Nursery Examination Board two-year full-time course at the North London College costs £410 a year. Evening and day-release part-time courses for the examinations of other professional bodies compare with fees charged for BTEC part-time courses.

OPEN COLLEGE UNITS
These are the college-based study units run by Open College Networks, which you'll find explained in the 'Open and Distance Learning Courses' section. Please note that you attend college (these are not distance-learning courses), but you do not need any qualifications to start on the beginners' units, and you can build up units to reach degree-entry standard. In 1988/9 the fee for a single unit (two and a half hours a week at college) was £38 a year. Fees may be waived for those registered unemployed or people on retirement pensions. The address list for the Northern Region includes that of the Mailbox for the National Open College Network, from which you can get the address of your nearest college offering this type of study course.

THE OPEN COLLEGE
This is the national organisation providing study packages you can use at home (or at work, perhaps, if your employer's paying!). Examples of costs: 'Looking After Children' – leads to the Certificate in Human Development, Child Care and Family life from the National Association for Maternal and Child Welfare. £44 including 7 workbooks and textbook. 'It's a Deal – an Introduction to Effective Selling' £49.95 including video tape, audio tape and three workbooks.

THE OPEN UNIVERSITY
A Foundation course leading to an OU credit can cost up to £186 plus £122 for attendance at summer school. (NB: some local education authorities may help with a grant towards the cost of the summer school). Degrees are credit-based (see OU information on pages 295-296) and a complete BA degree (for someone who was not entitled to any exemptions but obtained the six full credits and attended the minimum of two summer schools necessary) would cost £1360. Among OU specialist courses, 'The Effective Manager' from the Open Business School costs £630 and can lead on to study for the MBA.

DEGREES – EXTERNAL
The Secretary for External Students, University of London, estimated that a complete course taken over five years at 1990 rates, registration and

examination for the LLB degree would cost £910 (home) and £1115 (overseas students) and for a BA in Philosophy would cost £610 (home) and £765 (overseas students). To this must be added the cost of books and materials and of any tuition arranged.

DEGREES – PART TIME
It is unusual to be offered any help from the local education authority with fees on a part-time degree course, as it is assumed you will be working and earning while you study. As an example of costs, the University of Bradford quoted £210 a year for its part-time BA (Hons) Social Studies course.

DEGREES – FULL TIME
These usually attract mandatory grants, though if you've already had a grant for an HND, degree or equivalent course, you will probably have to finance your second degree course. West London Institute of Higher Education quotes £578 a year as the 1988-89 fee charged for its three- and four-year degree courses, plus CNAA Registration fee of £55. Again, if you are not in receipt of any grant, remember to allow for your living expenses. If you will be living at home, you might estimate not less than the standard rate of LEA grant (see 'Grants and Concessions' on page 346). However, students coming from overseas who will have to live in university residences or find lodgings are usually told to allow not less than £4000 for each year's living costs.

POSTGRADUATE DEGREES AND DIPLOMAS
Grants are hard to get, but ask the university or polytechnic where you want to study if there is an official grant-awarding body to which you should apply. Ask, too, if there are any bursaries or company sponsorships available. Fees vary widely, but the South Bank Polytechnic quotes £1730 for a full-time postgraduate course. For a part-time MBA postgraduate course, the University of Bradford quotes £967 for the first year, £720 for the second year and £607 for the third year. These figures are accurate for April 1989.

SMALL BUSINESS COURSES
Many of these are free under the Enterprise Training provision in the government's Employment Training scheme. Otherwise costs for short courses can be very modest – typically, Sutton College of Liberal Arts charges £16 for a 10-week evening course called 'Mind Your Own Business' on setting up and managing your own small business. A 10-week evening course on 'Desk Top Publishing' costs £22 at the same college.

RESIDENTIAL BUSINESS COURSES
These are often aimed at and paid for by employers on behalf of their employees. However, colleges do accept independent students who pay their own fees. Typically, St. Helen's College quoted £250 for a three-day

residential course in 'Effective Salesmanship' plus residence fee of £36 per night. A three-day residential course in 'Retail Food Management' cost £120, plus residence fee of £36 per night.

GRANTS AND CONCESSIONS

Many of the courses in this book are free to unemployed people or anyone receiving Department of Social Security benefits. To give you examples, courses that are headed 'Restart' or 'Replan' are likely to be free and so is anything headed with the description 'TA-sponsored'. TA stands for the Training Agency which involves colleges in providing training so that the 'workers without jobs' will be capable of doing the 'jobs without workers'.

Courses with the title 'Wider Opportunities' or 'New Opportunities' may also be free, but don't count on it. Ask the organisers, because both the Training Agency and individual colleges use these titles for courses provided by people who want information about new directions they can take.

Some courses available under the 21-hour rule are provided at very low costs to unemployed people.

WHAT IS THE 21-HOUR RULE?
The 21-hour rule is a concession to help unemployed people who have left full-time education but wish to take up study/attend training courses while continuing to receive benefit. The courses do not have to be job-related; if you want to take a part-time degree in English Literature or learn to play the guitar, and you can find a course of suitable hours, you are still eligible. Many colleges, as you will see when you look through the course lists, put on special job-related courses, often leading to City and Guilds awards or other highly-regarded qualifications, in such a way that they fit conveniently into the 2l-hour rule regulations.

There are rules, though. Claimants of all ages must:
(a) Be prepared to give up the course or training immediately a suitable job comes up.
(b) Be receiving Income Support, Unemployment Benefit or Sickness Benefit.
(c) Have been signing on as available for work or being incapable of work for three months, or have been on a YTS scheme.
(d) During the 6 months before starting their course, have been getting Income Support, Unemployment Benefit or Sickness Benefit for 3 months in total, between periods of temporary or seasonal employment.

There are a number of additional regulations/concessions: for instance, single parents with a dependent child living with them, or severely disabled people who are regarded as unlikely to get employment within the next 12 months do not have to be available for employment in order to get benefits while studying under the 21-hour-rule. For exact details contact your local DSS office or ask the College Counselling Service.

THE 21-HOUR RULE – THINKING IT THROUGH

Most colleges offer a range of ways of studying particular subjects – part-time day, part-time evening, distance learning and so on – so that you can satisfy the DSS that you will genuinely be 'available for work' if a job is offered. Make sure you can show the DSS that you have found a way to continue any studying or training programme you start under the 21-hour rule should you be offered a job.

In some areas, particularly those noted for high unemployment, special 21-hour programmes have been set up with provision for people to build on to any qualification they get over a number of years. This helps people who take seasonal work when it's offered, for they can still go back to studying when their job ends and they are unemployed again.

LEA GRANTS

The LEA is your Local Education Authority, and that means the one governing the place where you were educated, not the place where you happen to be living now. They provide grants that are *mandatory* and other grants that are *discretionary*.

To be considered for a *mandatory* grant, you have to be accepted on a 'designated course' (more about that presently), and not previously have had a grant.

To be considered for a *discretionary* grant you have to meet your own LEA's specific requirements.

'Discretionary', as you can see, means what it says. The grant is at the discretion of the local education authority, and whether you get it depends on how much money they have to spend, how many people are applying for it and how much they think you deserve financial help compared with everyone else applying, so it's a bit like being on a housing waiting list. Your suitability for the course you have chosen and your prospects of work at the end of it are also likely to be taken into account.

Don't let the uncertainty of discretionary awards discourage you. After I had been telling people for years that LEAs didn't give discretionary grants for A-levels because after all, they could be taken by evening classes or by distance learning, one Leicestershire student wrote triumphantly to tell me that she had a mature student's discretionary grant to take three A-levels part time. And following the publication of last year's edition a reader wrote to tell me that Essex County Council were particuarly generous with regard to grants for Open University students attending summer school.

Access course students are often sympathetically received if they apply for discretionary grants. A special effort is made to take into account any factors that may have made it difficult for a student to acquire conventional qualifications at the conventional time. Students from ethnic minority groups for whom English is a second language, and who therefore might not have known enough English to do themselves justice at school are an example of a group who would be given careful consideration.

Many courses attract *mandatory* grants. This means that if you are accepted for a designated course, you will get a grant, provide you meet the residence requirements and educational requirements, and you have not already had a mandatory grant (or used up part of one). It is means-tested, which, for adult students (26 and over) means that instead of taking into account your parents' income, they will take into account that of your husband or wife, if you have one.

DESIGNATED COURSES
So what does the term 'designated course' describe?

A designated course is one that appears in an official list issued by the Department of Education and Science and available at local authority education offices. As this book goes to press it is being revised. But basically, a designated course is a full-time or sandwich first degree course; a full-time or sandwich Higher National Diploma course; or a high-level professional course, such as Graduateship in Music at one of the famous music colleges. If you look in college prospectuses, they usually tell you the good news if a course attracts mandatory grants. If they don't mention mandatory grants, start your own enquiries. (Sometimes a precedent has been set by a local authority giving a discretionary grant to a student on a particular course. That's always worth following up.)

HOW MUCH?
Rates of mandatory grant are revised each year, but as I write, the rates quoted are:
free tuition
maintenance (London) £2425
maintenance (outside London) £2050
maintenance (living at home) £1630

There are extra allowances if you are 26 or over before the beginning of the course and have worked for at least three years, earning at least £12,000 in total. The Older Students' Allowance is £215 a year, rising to £740 for students aged 29 or over. Extra payments may be made if you have dependents. *Changes in the amounts for maintenance come into force at the beginning of September each year.* A free booklet: *Grants to Students* is available from the Department of Education and Science, Room 2/ll, Elizabeth House, York Road, London, SE1 7PH. For Scotland, write to the Scottish Education Department, Awards Branch, Haymarket House, Clifton Terrace, Edinburgh EH12 5DT.

EMPLOYMENT TRAINING

(Forget about anything you once heard of 'TOPS' or the 'MSC' or the 'Job Training Scheme'. These schemes have all been discontinued and replaced by the scheme described below):

The main training programme for adults operated by the Training Agency (formerly MSC) is Employment Training. It is, generally, open to people who have been unemployed for at least six months, though there are certain categories of people exempt from this condition, including people with disabilities, returners to the labour market, ex-offenders and people intending to train in skills which are in short supply.

People in Employment Training receive an allowance based on the benefits they were receiving before they joined the programme, plus a training premium of £10 a week. In addition, trainees are reimbursed travel costs in excess of £4 a week and can be paid lodging costs of up to £50 a week if they have to move to another area in order to train. They are also provided free of charge with any tools or equipment they may require, and can qualify for a training bonus after a minimum of 3 months on the programme. Lone parents in Employment Training can receive help with necessary child care costs.

DEPARTMENT OF HEALTH BURSARIES

For certain paramedical professions for which courses are listed in this booklet – occupational therapy, physiotherapy and radiography – Department of Health bursaries are normally available. For students aged over 25 who have been financially independent for a minimum of three years, parental income is ignored and a mature student supplement may be payable. The rate of grant is variable, but as an example, the South East Thames Radiotherapy Education Centre sent details of grants payable to students studying radiotherapy at St. Thomas's Hospital. The rate for students living at home was from £1630 to £2291 a year. For students living in lodgings (in London) the rate was from £2425 to £3636 a year. (Rates of support for students living in lodgings outside London are likely to be lower.)

EUROPEAN SOCIAL FUND

Our membership of the EEC means that we are entitled to a share of the funds made available for retraining some categories of unemployed people or women 'returners'. The actual regulations are so complicated that colleges submitting courses for ESF sponsorship usually have at least one person who is an expert on them, and woe betide any college which loses its expert. However, if the description 'ESF-sponsored' appears in front of a course, it normally means that it is free, with travel costs paid where necessary, and *possibly* a training allowance.

ANY OTHER POSSIBILITIES?

Ex-Service personnel may be able to obtain financial help with retraining through service organisations. Charities sometimes have funds available to help people train for new careers, or they will support particular courses. For example, MENCAP funded the first students on the Further Education and Training of Mentally Handicapped People scheme.

Grants or bursaries may be available from groups concerned with special interests. The Arts Council offers various bursaries for students in the music, art, film-making and similar fields. Drama schools may have scholarships. You should find that the college you approach has knowledge of opportunities of this kind. They tend to keep records of organisations which have helped to fund students in the past.

Scholarships and bursaries may be 'closed', that is to say, open only to people who have attended certain schools or belonged to certain trades unions, or are the sons or daughters of people in particular occupations. When you are looking through prospectuses, always look up scholarships. The talent that wins you an extra £100 a year to spend on train fares could well have nothing to do with your course (e.g. you may get a music bursary though you're a law student), but it's none the less valuable for that.

Sometimes there are special awards to attract people to particular courses. For instance, the University of Salford has competitive scholarships for women who want to study Engineering, and there are 'enhanced' Department of Education and Science grants for people retraining in the shortage areas of maths, physics and craft, design and technology.

Many libraries keep the reference books, *Charities Digest*, published by the Family Welfare Association, and *Directory of Grant-Making Trusts*, published by the Charities Aid Foundation. You may find a philanthropic organisation offering an award for which you are eligible. It might only be a small sum, but if it covers the cost of a couple of reference books, it will be a help.

People threatened by redundancy may find their professional institute or trades union has funds for helping people who are retraining. Even when there is not a formal scheme for all members made redundant, there may be a loan scheme which individual members can use.

The government scheme of Career Development Loans has been very successful since it was piloted in Aberdeen, Bristol/Bath, Greater Manchester and the Reading/Slough areas. Career Development Loans are now available everywhere. They provide sums between £300 and £5000 to people who want to take up job-related training and finance it themselves. The government pays interest on the training loan during the period of training and for up to 3 months afterwards. The individual then takes over responsibility for repayment. Three banks are involved – Barclays, the Clydesdale and the Cooperative.

Any course is eligible provided it is job related, lasts for at least a week and not more than a year, and does not attract a mandatory student award. Full-time, part-time, weekend and open or distance learning courses (like The Open College or Open University courses) can be considered, and courses in private colleges and training schools as well as in the public sector.

At the end of 1988 in a review of the scheme, John Cope MP, the Minister of State for Employment said 'There is a surprisingly wide range of subjects. Courses ranging from archeology to accounting, hotels and catering to health visiting and wildlife management to word processing are all being paid for through Career Development Loans.' A free booklet with full details can be obtained from any Jobcentre, participating bank branch or by ringing (free of charge) 0800 585 505.

There are also bank loan schemes quite separate from Career Development Loans, such as the Midland Bank's loan scheme for certain business studies and accountancy courses, and the National Westminster Bank's scheme to help medical students with the cost of necessary books. If your bank doesn't offer any kind of loan scheme for study, they may be able to advise you on government finance sources, such as the Enterprise Allowance scheme for people setting up in business (see also 'Small Business and Self-Employment Courses').

In conclusion, the Citizens Advice Bureau (address of the nearest one in your local phone directory) can usually advise on grants, allowances, awards and concessions. When the person on the spot doesn't know, then, given time, authorities will be contacted who *will* know if there are any sources of funds you haven't tried for a grant, scholarship or bursary. When you think you have found out as much as you can, double-check with your CAB. Because their information services are so regularly updated, they are often the first to know of new awards, government schemes or concessions being made available nationally, or for special groups.

Information Sources

Throughout *The Mature Student's Handbook* whenever it's seemed useful, I have directed people to books, but listing *all* possible sources of extra information each time might have been confusing. Therefore I have compiled this list of information sources that you can tap into to extend your knowledge in the areas that tie in with your own plans.

SOURCES OF IDEAS

Always ask the library if they have the latest edition of a book; it's really important in the education and careers field, where changes can be rapid.

Careers A-Z (Collins) Quick-reference, easy-to-read paperback based on answers to Daily Telegraph Careers Information Service readers; hence concise explanations of job content, course choices and acronyms like AGCAS, BTEC, COIC.

Equal Opportunities (Penguin) Careers guide which grew out of *Careers for Girls* so very strong on opportunities for women, and on 'late start' opportunities and age limits. Good, clear job descriptions – valuable if you don't know what a quantity surveyor or legal executive might do all day.

Careers Encyclopedia (Cassell) Close-packed pages of detailed information on every conceivable job from archivist to zoo-keeper. Strongly recommended for useful forecasts of demand in occupations (you can avoid jobs likely to be overtaken by technology). Also helps you track down courses, naming colleges.

Careers In... series (Kogan Page). Separate careers booklets on every occupation you might have considered from Alternative Medicine to Careers in Crafts (two of my favourites as they include unusual occupations). Very useful preliminary reading when you're trying to decide between retraining courses,

Working In... series (COIC). Separate, illustrated, magazine-style booklets on occupational areas, rather than separate jobs. For instance *Work with*

Animals, Farms & Forests, The Boating Industry. Personal case-histories are augmented by very good information source lists.

SOURCES OF COURSES

Residential Short Courses (National Institute of Adult Continuing Education). Lists weekend and one-week study courses that could let you sample a new skill before you commit yourself to training for it – cookery, furniture restoration, bookbinding, photography, foreign languages, writing etc. Two issues a year (summer and winter courses) £1.50 inc. postage from NIACE, 19b De Montfort Street, Leicester LE1 7GE.

Educational Credit Transfer Handbook Gives details of concessions in entry requirements or course content allowed by certain universities, poly-technics, professional organisations to mature students of diferent kinds. Compiled from the ECCTIS database at the Open University. (Try your library; if they don't have a copy, ask them to redirect you to the Educational Guidance Service,or if there isn't one, to the Careers Service Office.)

Second Chances (COIC). Excellent source book of factual information on everything from YTS scheme to courses for retired people; includes personal development courses, leisure courses and learning through radio and TV as well as all the sorts of career change course listed here.

Directory of Further Education (CRAC/Hobsons). Extensive coverage of courses in local authority sector nationwide. Very useful for anyone who wants to track down a particular subject, be it fashion writing or sports studies, and who's willing to go to where the course is offered and compete with school-leaver students for places. Includes some independent colleges.

Directory of Independent Training & Tutorial Organisations (Careers Consultants). Extensive coverage of courses in the private sector, including unusual options like training to be a butler, male model or aromatherapist. Ideal for people looking for courses to match specific needs – 'crash' courses, distance learning, residential training etc.

Open Learning Directory (COIC) lists over 1500 courses and suppliers of open learning materials, together with advisory centres where students can go for advice, support and hands-on experience of open learning techniques and equipment. Try your Jobcentre for access to this if the public library doesn't have it, as it's an expensive purchase.

University Entrance – The Official Guide (Sheed & Ward). Will tell you where you can take a university degree in anything from Accountancy to Avionics or Victorian Studies to Virology. Mainly for young applicants but useful reference also for mature entrants. Cross-reference with *The Student Book* and *Degree Course Offers* (see below).

Polytechnic Courses Handbook (Committee of Directors of Polytechnics). Lists full-time, sandwich degree, HND and other advanced courses in polytechnics. Use with free *Directory of First Degree & Higher Diploma Courses* (includes *part-time* courses) available from the Council for National Academic Awards, 344 Gray's Inn Road, London, WC1X 8BP.

Colleges and Institutes of Higher Education (Standing Conference of Principals). Lists and describes all the higher education colleges whose degrees are validated by universities or the CNAA and gives usefully detailed information about courses and options. Use in association with *Degree Course Offers* and *The Student Book*.

The Student Book (Papermac). Lively university, polytechnic, college descriptions to give you the 'feel' of individual institutions. Highlights courses for which a college is noted, good on social life and on factors that you might find important, i.e. do most students go home at weekends?

Degree Course Offers (Careers Consultants). Another guide primarily aimed at young candidates, but this year with comments about attitudes to mature students and always has useful comments from authorities, e.g. *Psychology* – Bristol … 'Nursing qualifications are acceptable as well as A-levels or equivalent qualifications' … Manchester Polytechnic … 'All suitable applicants are sent a questionnaire and asked to write an essay on their choice of psychology. Selection is based on their answers' … Nottingham (and others) 'Preference is given to local applicants.' Also quotes percentages of mature students on named courses. Examples of interview questions very useful; can help you realise what sort of course you are applying for and if it's what you want before you fill in your application form.

British Qualifications (Kogan Page). The book to check if you want to establish which qualifications are recognised nationally. Covers all fields of work including conventional ones like accountancy and engineering as well as the more off-beat activities like musical instrument making and timber technology.

Working for Yourself (Kogan Page). Full of facts and ideas for self-employment or setting up in business. Not quite the same as *Going Freelance* (also Kogan Page) by the same author, Godfrey Golzen, where the emphasis is on sidelines and ways of earning at home. Together, both very good for people trying to decide *how* to switch from employment to self-employment. Use in conjunction with *Down to Business* (COIC) which is a simple, step-by-step guide to all the tasks you'll be taking on when you decide to go it alone.

Ask your Jobcentre for a free leaflet on the Enterprise Allowance Scheme (that's the one where you can get £40 a week for 52 weeks to help you establish your business). NB: You'll stand a better chance if you read the books first and an even better one if you take a short course.

Directory of British Associations (CBD Research Publications). Kept in public library reference rooms, this lists professional, trade, commercial and employers' associations with addresses and phone numbers, so if you need to check on whether a course is recognised or to find out where job vacancies are advertised in a particular occupation, this can be your starting point.

The Yearbook of Recruitment & Employment Services 1987 (Longman). Another big reference book listing all the independent employment agencies in the UK classified as to location and the types of job(s) each one handles. If you want to talk over the job prospects you might have after taking a course that appeals to you, you could do worse than call in on a placement agency (not at a rush time, like lunch-hour) and get their views.

EDUCATIONAL GUIDANCE SERVICES

For personal, face-to-face advice, local authorities are increasingly making the effort to fund Educational Guidance Services. The extent to which they operate, and the times they are able to open will really depend on how much money is available in your local authority's kitty, but ask at the public library if your area has an EGA – they'll know the address. Don't forget help available from Jobcentres and the increasing number of Jobclubs, and if in any doubt, get an authoritiative view of any course from the appropriate trade union or professional institute. Again, the librarian in the reference section of your local public library will be able to help you find the right organisation and the right address.

Addresses

LONDON

Birkbeck College, University of London, Malet Street, London WC1E 7HX

Bloomsbury College of Nurse Education, Division of Basic Nurse Education, Minerva House, 1-4 North Crescent, Chenies Street, London WC1E 7ER

Brent & Harrow School of Nursing, Harrow Nurse Education Centre, Northwick Park Hospital, Watford Road, Harrow, Middx HA1 3UJ

British Isles Study Programme, 150 Conway Crescent, Perivale, Greenford, Middx UB6 6JE

Camberwell Health Authority: King's College Hospital School of Radiography, King's College Hospital, Denmark Hill, London SE5 9RS

Camden Training Centre, 57 Pratt Street, London NW1 0DP

Central London Adult Education Institute, (formerly the City Lit) Stukeley Street, Drury Lane, London WC2B 5LJ

Central London : Polytechnic of Central London, 309 Regent Street, London WlR 8AL

Central Middlesex and Hammersmith Hospital Schools of Radiography and Radiotherapy, Acton Lane, London NW10 7NS

Charing Cross School of Nursing: Riverside Health Authority, Claybrook Road, London W6 8LN

Chelsea School of Art, Manresa Road, London, SW3 6LS

City & East London College, Pitfield Street, London N1 6BX

City University, Northampton Square, London EC1V OHB

College for the Distributive Trades, 30 Leicester Square, London WC2H 7LE

Cordwainers College, Mare Street, Hackney, London E8 3RE

Ealing Health Authority School of Nursing, Ealing Hospital – General Wing, Uxbridge Road, Southall, Middx UB1 3HW

Enfield & Haringey School of Nursing: North Middlesex Hospital, Edmonton, London N18 1QX

Goldsmiths' College, University of London, Lewisham Way, London SE14 6NW

Guy's Hospital School of Physiotherapy, Shepherd's House, St Thomas Street, London SE1 9RT

Guy's Hospital Radiography Education Centre, St Thomas Street, London SE1 9RT

Hammersmith Hospital School of Nursing, Hammersmith Hospital, Du Cane Road, London W12 OHS

Hospitals for Sick Children: Charles West School of Nursing, 24 Great Ormond Street, London W1N 3JH

Hounslow & Spelthorne Health Authority: West Thames School of Nursing, West Middlesex University Hospital, Isleworth, Middx TW7 6AF

Islington & Hampstead School of Radiography: The Royal Free Hospital, The Hoo, 17 Lyndhurst Gardens, London NW3 5NU

King's College London, Admissions Adviser – Physiotherapy, Normanby College Campus, King's College Hospital, Denmark Hill SE5 9RS

London College of Fashion, John Princes Street, London W1M 9HE

London College of Printing, Elephant & Castle, London, SE1 6SB

London Foot Hospital and School of Chiropody, Fitzroy Square, London, W1P 8AY

London Hospital School of Radiography and Radiotherapy, The Luckes Home, Whitechapel, London, E1 1BB

London School of Economics & Political Science, Houghton Street, London, WC2 2AE

London School of Occupational Therapy: West London Institute of Higher Education, Lancaster House, Borough Road, Isleworth, Middx TW7 5DU

London: University of London, Senate House, Malet Street, London WC1E 7HU

London: University of London, Secretary for External Students, Room 204, Senate House, Malet Street, London, WC1E 8HU

Middlesex Hospital School of Physiotherapy, Arthur Stanley House, Tottenham Street, London W1P 9PG

Middlesex Polytechnic, 114 Chase Side, London, N14 5PN

Middlesex & University College Hospitals Schools of Radiography, The Middlesex Hospital, Mortimer Street, London, W1N 8AA

Morley College, 61 Westminster Bridge Road, London, SE1 7HT

Newham Community College, (amalgamation of East Ham & West Ham Colleges) Welfare Road, Stratford, London, E15 4HT

North London College, 444 Camden Road, London N7 0SP

North London: Polytechnic of North London, Holloway, London N7 8DB

Paddington College, 25 Paddington Green, London W2 1NB

Paddington College: Chelsea School of Chiropody, 25 Paddington Green, London W2 1NB

Pitman Central College, 154 Southampton Row, London WC1B 5AX

Polytechnic of East London, Longbridge Road, Dagenham, Essex RM8 2AS

Queen Mary College: University of London, Mile End Road, London E1 4NS

Royal Free Hospital and Friern School of Nursing, The Royal Free Hospital, Pond Street, London NW3 2QG

Royal Holloway & Bedford New College: University of London, Egham Hill, Egham, Surrey TW20 0EX

Royal Marsden Hospital School of Radiotherapy, Downs Road, Sutton, Surrey SM2 5PT

St Bartholomew's School of Nursing: St Bartholomew's Hospital, West Smithfield, London EC1A 7BA

St Mary's College, Strawberry Hill, Twickenham, Middx TW1 4SX

St Mary's Hospital School of Physiotherapy, St Mary's Hospital, Praed Street, London W2 1NY

St Thomas' Hospital School of Physiotherapy, St Thomas' Hospital, London SE1 7EH

St Thomas' Hospital: South East Thames Regional Radiograpy Training Centre, St Thomas' Hospital, London SE1 7EH

South Bank Polytechnic, Borough Road, London SE1 0AA

South East London College, Breakspeare Road, Lewisham Way, London SE4 1UT

South London College, Knights Hill, London SE27 0TX

South West London College, Tooting Broadway, London SW17 0TQ

Thames Polytechnic, Wellington Street, London SE18 6PF

Thomas Guy & Lewisham School of Nursing, Guy's Hospital, London SE1 9RT

Tottenham College of Technology, High Road, Tottenham N15 4RU

Tour Management Training Centre (Europe), 85 St George's Square Mews, London SW1V 3RZ

University College, University of London, Gower Street, London WC1E 6BT

Uxbridge: Brunel – the University of West London, Middx UB8 3PH

Uxbridge College, Park Road, Uxbridge, Middx UB8 1NQ

Waltham Forest School of Nursing: Whipps Cross Hospital, London E11 1NR

West London Institute of Higher Education, Lancaster House, Borough Road, Middx TW7 5DU

West Middlesex Hospital School of Physiotherapy;, West London Institute of Higher Education, Lancaster House, Borough Road, Isleworth, Middx TW7 1PT

Westminster College, Battersea Park Road, London SW11 4JR

Westminster Hospital School of Radiography: Riverside Health Authority, Udall Street, London SW1P 2PP

Willesden College of Technology, Denzil Road, London NW10 2XD

SOUTHERN AND EASTERN ENGLAND

Ashford: South East Kent School of Nursing, Education Centre, The William Harvey Hospital, Kennington Road, Willesborough, Ashford, Kent TN24 0LZ

Aylesbury College, Oxford Road, Aylesbury, Bucks HP21 8PD

Barnet School of Nursing, Barnet General Hospital, Wellhouse Lane, Barnet, Herts EN5 3DJ

Basildon College of Further Education, Nethermayne, Basildon, Essex SS16 5NN

Basingstoke Technical College, Worting Road, Basingstoke,Hants RG21 1TN

Bedford College of Higher Education, Polhill Avenue, Bedford MK41 9EA.

Bognor Regis – see Chichester

Borehamwood: De Havilland College – see Welwyn Garden City

Bracknell College, Church Road, Bracknell, Berkshire RG12 1DJ

Brighton Polytechnic, Moulescoomb, Brighton, East Sussex BN2 4AT

Brighton Polytechnic Department of Chiropody, Leaf Hospital, St Anne's Road, Eastbourne BN21 2HW

Brighton: University of Sussex, Sussex House, Falmer, Brighton BN1 9QN

Bromley College of Technology, Rookery Lane, Bromley Common, Kent BR2 8HE

Bromley School of Nursing, Education Centre, Farnborough Hospital, Farnborough Common, Orpington, Kent BR6 8ND

Cambridge College of Further Education, Newmarket Road, Cambridge CB5 8EG

Cambridgeshire College of Arts & Technology, East Road, Cambridge CB1 1PT

Cambridge Health Authority School of Physiotherapy, Education Centre, Addenbrooke's Hospital, Hills Road, Cambridge CB2 2QQ

Cambridge & Huntingdon Department of Nurse Education, Education Centre, Addenbroke's Hospital, Hills Road, Cambridge CB2 2QQ

Cambridge: University of Cambridge, Intercollegiate Applications Office, Kellet Lodge, Tennis Court Road, Cambridge CB2 1QJ

Canterbury: Christ Church College, North Holmes Road, Canterbury CT1 1QU

Canterbury College of Art – see Kent College of Art

Canterbury College, New Dover Road, Canterbury, Kent CT1 3AJ

Canterbury: University of Kent at Canterbury, Canterbury, Kent CT2 7NX

Carshalton: Merton & Sutton Health Authority: Carshalton School of Nursing, Queen Mary's Hospital for Children, Carshalton, Surrey SM5 4NR

Chatham – Mid Kent College of Further & Higher Education, Horsted, Maidstone Road, Chatham, Kent ME5 9QU

Chelmsford: Mid Essex School of Nursing, Broomfield, Chelmsford, Essex CM1 5LG

Chichester: West Dean College, Chichester, West Sussex

Chichester: West Sussex Institute of Higher Education, College Lane, Chichester, West Sussex P019 4PE

Colchester Institute, Sheepen Road, Colchester, Essex C03 3JL

Colchester: University of Essex, Wivenhoe Park, Colchester C043 3SQ

Crawley College of Technology, College Road, Crawley, West Sussex RH10 1NR

Croydon College, Fairfield, Croydon CR9 1DX

Dunstable College, Kingsway, Dunstable, Beds LU5 4HG

Eastbourne: Sussex Downs School of Nursing, General Training Department, District General Hospital, Kings Drive, Eastbourne BN21 2UD

Eastleigh College of Further Education, Chestnut Avenue, Eastleigh S05 5HT

Egham: Royal Holloway & Bedford New College, Egham Hill, Egham. Surrey TW20 OEX

Epsom: North East Surrey College of Technology, Reigate Road, Epsom, Ewell, Surrey KT17 3DS

Guildford College of Technology, Stoke Park, Guildford GU1 1EZ

Guildford: Regional Radiotherapy Education Centre, St Luke's Hospital, Warren Road, Guildford, Surrey GU1 3NT

Guildford: South West Surrey College of Nursing, Guildford Nurse Education Centre, St Luke's Hospital, Warren Road, Guildford, Surrey GU1 3NT

Guildford: University of Surrey, Guildford, Surrey GU2 5XH

Hastings College of Arts and Technology, Archery Road, St Leonard's on Sea, East Sussex TN38 0HX

Hatfield Polytechnic, PO Box 109, Hatfield, Herts

Havering Technical College, Ardleigh Green Road, Hornchurch, Essex RM11 2LL

Hemel Hempstead: Dacorum College, Marlowes, Hemel Hempstead, Herts HP1 1HD

High Wycombe: Buckinghamshire College of Higher Education, Queen Alexandra Road, High Wycombe, Bucks HP11 2JZ

Ipswich: East Suffolk Health Authority School of Nursing, Education Centre, Ipswich Hospital, Heath Road, Ipswich, Suffolk IP4 5PD

Ipswich: Suffolk College of Higher & Further Education, Rope Walk, Ipswich, Suffolk IP4 1LT

Kent College of Art & Design (Amalgamation of Canterbury College of Art, Maidstone College of Art & Medway College of Design) – New Dover Road, Canterbury, Kent CT1 3AN

Kingston Polytechnic, Henry House, Kingston Hill, Kingston-upon-Thames, Surrey KT2 7LB

King's Lynn: Norfolk College of Arts & Technology, Tennyson Avenue, King's Lynn, Norfolk PE30 2QW

Luton College of Higher Education,Park Square, Luton, Beds LU1 3JU

Luton & Dunstable School of Radiography, St. Mary's Hospital, Dunstable Road, Luton, Beds LU1 1BE

Maidstone: Mid Kent College – see Chatham

Merton College,Morden Park, London Road, Morden, Surrey SM4 5QX

Merton Institute of Adult Education, Whatley Avenue, London SW20 9NS

Milton Keynes: The Open University, Walton Hall, Milton Keynes, Bucks MK7 6AA

Mendlesham: RTT Training Services Ltd., Mendlesham Training Centre, Norwich Road, Mendlesham, Stowmarket, Suffolk IP14 5ND

Newbury College, Oxford Road, Newbury, Berkshire RG13 1PQ

Norwich: Broadland Centre of Nursing & Midwifery Education, Broadland Nurse Education Centre, Administration Block, Norfolk and Norwich Hospital, Brunswick Road, Norwich NR1 3SR

Norwich City College of Further & Higher Education, Ipswich Road, Norwich NR2 2LJ

Norwich: University of East Anglia, Norwich NR4 7JT

Peterborough & Stamford Department of Nurse Education, Thorpe Road, Peterborough PE3 6DA

Portsmouth College of Art, Design & Further Education, Winston Churchill Avenue, Portsmouth, Hants P01 2DJ

Portsmouth Health Authority: Portsmouth District School of Nursing, Queen Alexandra Hospital, Cosham, Portsmouth, Hants P06 3LY

Portsmouth: Highbury College of Technology, Cosham, Portsmouth, Hants P06 2SA

Portsmouth Polytechnic, Museum Road, Portsmouth, Hants P01 2QQ

Portsmouth & South East Hampshire Health Authority School of Radiography, Saint Mary's Hospital, Milton Road, Portsmouth, Hants P03 6AD

Reading College of Technology, Crescent Road, Reading, Berkshire RG1 5RQ

Reading: University of Reading,Whiteknights, Reading, Berkshire, RG6 8AH

Richmond Adult and Community College, Clifton Road Centre, Clifton Road, Twickenham TW1 4LT

Rochester: Mid Kent College – see Chatham

Romford College of Nursing and Midwifery, Gubbins Lane, Harold Wood, Romford RM3 0BE

St Albans City College, 29 Hatfield Road, St Albans, Herts AL1 3RJ

St Albans: Hertfordshire College of Art and Design, Hatfield Road, St Albans, Herts

St Albans: Hertfordshire Centre for Building Studies, Hatfield Road, St Albans, Herts AL1 3RX

Slough: Langley College of Further Education, Station Road, Langley, Slough, Berkshire SL3 8BY

Southampton Institute of Higher Education, East Park Terrace, Southampton, Hants S09 4WW

Southampton School of Radiography, D.8 West Wing, Southampton General Hospital, Southampton, Hants

Southampton Technical College, St. Mary Street, Southampton, Hants S09 4WX

Southampton University Hospitals Combined School of Nursing, Academic Building, General Hospital, Tremona Road, Southampton, Hants S09 4XY

Southampton: University of Southampton, Southampton, Hants S09 5NH

Southend College of Technology, Caernarvon Road, Southend-on-Sea, Essex SS2 6LS

Stevenage College, Monkswood Way, Stevenage, Herts SG1 1LA Surbiton: Hillcroft Adult College, Surbiton, Surrey KT6 6DF

Sutton College of Liberal Arts, St. Nicholas Way, Sutton, Surrey SM1 1EA

Tonbridge/Tunbridge Wells: West Kent College, Brook Street, Tonbridge, Kent TN9 2PW

Tunbridge Wells Health Authority: Pembury Hospital School of Nursing, Pembury, Tunbridge Wells, Kent TN2 4QJ

Watford: Cassio College, Langley Road, Watford, Herts WD1 3RH

Watford College, Watford, Herts WD1 2NN

Watford: West Hertfordshire School of Nursing, Peace Prospect, Off Hempstead Road, Watford, Herts WD1 3HA

Welwyn Garden City: De Havilland College, The Campus, Welwyn Garden City, Herts AL8 6AH

Wimbledon: Pitman Wimbledon College, Alwyne Road, Wimbledon SW19 7QQ

Wimbledon School of Art, Merton Hall Road, Wimbledon SW19 4QA

Winchester: King Alfred's College, Sparkford Road, Winchester, Hants S022 4NR

Worthing District School of Nursing, Southlands Hospital, Shoreham-by-Sea, Sussex BN4 6TQ

CENTRAL ENGLAND

Abingdon College of Further Education, Northcourt Road, Abingdon, Oxfordshire OX14 1NA

Abingdon: The Open College, Freepost, P.O. Box 35, Abingdon, Oxfordshire OX14 3BR

Birmingham: Bournville College of Art, City of Birmingham Polytechnic, Bournville, Birmingham B30 1JX

Birmingham: Bournville College of Further Education, Bristol Road South, Birmingham B31 2AJ

Birmingham: Matthew Boulton College, Sherlock Street, Birmingham B5 7DB

Birmingham: Matthew Boulton College School of Chiropody, Hope Street, Birmingham B5 7DB

Birmingham: Newman and Westhill Colleges, Genners Lane, Bartley Green, Birmingham BT32 3NR

Birmingham Polytechnic, Perry Barr, Birmingham B42 2SU

Birmingham: Queen Elizabeth School of Nursing, Queen Elizabeth Medical Centre, Edgbaston, Birmingham B15 2TH

Birmingham School of Physiotherapy, Queen Elizabeth Medical Centre, Edgbaston, Birmingham B15 2TH

Birmingham School of Radiography, Masscroft, 13 Pritchetts Road, Edgbaston, Birmingham B15 2QU

Birmingham: South Birmingham Health Authority School of Nursing, Selly Oak Hospital, Raddlebarn Road, Birmingham B29 6JD

Birmingham: University of Aston, Gosta Green, Birmingham B4 7ET

Bridgenorth & South Shropshire College of Further Education, Stourbridge Road, Bridgenorth, Shropshire WV15 6AL

Chesterfield College of Technology & Arts, Infirmary Road, Chesterfield, Derbyshire S41 7NG

Corby: Tresham College – see Kettering

Coventry: Henley College, Henley Road, Bell Green, Coventry, West Midlands CV2 1ED

Coventry Polytechnic, Priory Street, Coventry, West Midlands CV1 5FB

Coventry Polytechnic School of Occupational Therapy, Priory Street, Coventry, West Midlands CV1 5FB

Coventry Polytechnic School of Physiotherapy, School of Health Sciences, Coventry Polytechnic, Priory Street, Coventry, West Midlands CV1 5FB

Coventry School of Nursing, Walsgrave Hospital, Clifford Bridge Road, Coventry, West Midlands CV2 2DX

Coventry School of Radiography, Coventry and Warwickshire Hospital, Stoney Stanton Road, Coventry, West Midlands CV1 4FH

Coventry Technical College, Butts, Coventry, West Midlands CV1 3GD

Derby: Derbyshire Royal Infirmary School of Radiography, London Road, Derby DE1 2QY

Derby: Derby School of Nursing, Southern Derbyshire Health Authority, Boden House (4th Floor), Main Centre, Derby DE1 2PH

Derbyshire College of Higher Education, Kedleston Road, Derby DE3 1GB

Dudley College of Technology, The Broadway, Dudley, W. Midlands DY1 4AS

Grantham College of Further Education, Stonebridge Road, Grantham, Lincolnshire NG31 9AP

Hinckley College of Further Education, London Road, Hinckley, Leicestershire LE10 1HQ

Keele: University of Keele, Staffs ST5 4BG

Kettering: Tresham College, St. Mary's Road, Kettering, Northamptonshire NN15 7BS

Kidderminster College, Hoo Road, Kidderminster, Worcestershire DY10 1LX

Leamington Spa: Mid-Warwickshire College of Further Education, Warwick New Road, Leamington Spa, Warwickshire CV32 5JE

Leicester: Charles Frears School of Nursing, 266 London Road, Leicester LE2 1RQ

Leicester: Leicester Royal Infirmary Schools of Radiography, Leicester LE1 5WW

Leicester: University of Leicester, The University, Leicester LE1 7RH

Lichfield College, Cherry Orchard, Lichfield, Staffs WS14 9AN

Lincoln: Lincolnshire School of Radiography, St George's Hospital, Long Leys Road, Lincoln

Loughborough Co-Operative College, Stanford Hall, Loughborough, Leicestershire LE12 5QR

Loughborough Technical College, Radmoor, Loughborough, Leicestershire LE1 3BT

Loughborough: University of Technology, Loughborough, Leicestershire LE11 3TU

Mansfield: Mansfield & Worksop School of Nursing, Avenue House, Ashfield Avenue, Mansfield, Notts NG18 2AE

Newcastle-under-Lyme College, Liverpool Road, Newcastle-under-Lyme, Staffs ST5 2DF

Newark Technical College, Chauntry Park, Newark, Nottinghamshire NG24 1PB

Northampton Adult Education Centre, Military Road AE Centre, Military Road, Northampton NN1 3ET

Northampton: Nene College, Moulton Park, Northampton NN2 7AL

Northampton: Nene College/Northampton School of Chiropody, Nene College, Park Campus, Northampton NN2 7AL

Northampton School of Radiography, Crockett Block, Northampton General Hospital, Clifton Ville, Northampton NN1 5BD

Northampton: St Andrew's School of Occupational Therapy, St Andrew's Hospital, Northampton NN15 DG

Nottingham School of Physiotherapy, Hucknall Road, Nottingham, NG5 1PC

Nottingham School of Radiography, Queen's Medical Centre, Nottingham NG7 2UH

Nottingham: The Hogarth School of Radiotherapy, Thornton House, Park Terrace, Nottingham NG1 5GP

Nottingham: South Nottinghamshire College of Further Education, Greythorne Drive, West Bridgford, Nottingham NG2 7GA

Nottingham: Trent Polyechnic, Burton Street, Nottingham NG1 4BU

Oswestry College, College Road, Oswestry, Shropshire SY11 2BA

Oswestry and North Staffordshire School of Physiotherapy, Robert Jones and Agnes Hunt Orthopaedic Hospital, Oswestry, Shropshire SY10 7AG

Oxford: Dorset House School of Occupational Therapy, 58 London Road, Headington, Oxford OX3 7PE

Oxford: Plater College, Pullens Lane, Headington, Oxford OX3 0DT

Oxford Polytechnic, Gypsy Lane, Headington, Oxford OX3 0BP

Oxford Regional School of Radiography, Academic Centre, John Radcliffe Hospital, Headington, Oxford LX3 9DU

Oxford: Ruskin College, Walton Street, Oxford OX1 2HE

Oxford: University of Oxford, Oxford Colleges Admissions Offices, University Offices, Wellington Square, Oxford OX1 2JD

Redditch College, Peakman Street, Redditch, Worcs B98 8DW

Retford: Eaton Hall International, Retford, Nottinghamshire DN22 0PR

Retford: Rampton Hospital School of Nursing, Retford, Nottinghamshire DN22 OPD

Shrewsbury College of Arts & Technology, London Road, Shrewsbury, Shropshire SY2 6PR

Shrewsbury: Royal Shrewsbury Hospital School of Nursing, Education Centre, Royal Shrewsbury Hospital North, Myton Oak Road, Shrewsbury, Shropshire

Solihull College of Technology, Blossomfield Road, Solihull, West Midlands B91 1SB

Stafford College of Further Education, Earl Street, Stafford ST16 2QR

Stafford: Mid-Staffordshire School of Nursing, David Hollin Building, Staffordshire General Infirmary, Foregate Street, Stafford, Staffordshire ST16 2PA

Stoke-on-Trent: Cauldon College of Further & Higher Education, Stoke Road, Shelton, Stoke-on-Trent, Staffs ST4 2DG

Stoke-on-Trent: North Staffordshire School of Nursing and Midwifery, City General Hospital, Newcastle Road, Stoke-on Trent, Staffs ST4 6QG

Stoke-on-Trent: Staffordshire Polytechnic, College Road, Stoke-on-Trent, Staffs ST4 2DE

Stourbridge College of Technology & Art, Hagley Road, Stourbridge, West Midlands DY9 1LY

Stratford-upon-Avon: South Warwickshire College of Further Education, The Willows, Alcester Road, Stratford upon Avon, Warwickshire CV37 9QR

Sutton Coldfield College of Further Education, Lichfield Road, Sutton Coldfield, West Midlands B74 2NW

Tamworth College of Further Education, Upper Guingate, Tamworth, Staffs B79 8AE

Thame: Rycotewood College, Priest End, Thame, Oxfordshire OX9 2AF

Walsall: Sister Dora School of Nursing, Manor Hospital, Moat Road, Walsall, West Midlands WS2 9PS

Walsall: West Midlands College of Higher Education, Gorway, Walsall, West Midlands WS10 OPE

Warley: Sandwell College (amalgamation of Warley College of Commerce and West Bromwich College of Technology) Woden Road South, Wednesbury, West Midlands WS10 OPE

Warwick: University of Warwick, Coventry, West Midlands CV4 7AL

Warwick: Warwickshire School of Nursing, Nurse Education Centre, Central Hospital, Birmingham Road, Hatton, Near Warwick, West Midlands CV35 7EE

Wellingborough College, Church Street, Wellingborough, Northants. NN8 4PD

Witney: West Oxfordshire Technical College, Holloway Road, Witney, Oxon OX8 7DE

Wolverhampton: Bilston Community College, Westfield Road, Wolverhampton, West Midlands WV14 6ER

Wolverhampton Polyechnic, Molineux Street, Wolverhampton, West Midlands WV1 1SB

Wolverhampton School of Nursing, Education Centre, New Cross Hospital, Wolverhampton, West Midlands WV10 0QP

Wolverhampton: Wulfrun College of Further Education, Paget Road, Wolverhampton, West Midlands WV6 0DU

Worcester District School of Nursing, Newton Road, Worcester SR5 1HT

NORTHERN ENGLAND

Accrington and Rossendale College, Sandy Lane, Accrington, Lancashire BB5 2AW

Altrincham: South Trafford College of Further Education, Manchester Road, West Timperley, Altrincham, Cheshire WA14 5PQ

Ashington: Northumberland College of Arts and Technology, College Road, Ashington, Northumberland NE26 9RG

Ashton-under-Lyme: Tameside College of Technology, Beaufort Road, Ashton-under-Lyme,Tameside, Greater Manchester OL6 6NX

Barrow-in-Furness College of Further Education, Howard Street, Barrow in Furness, Cumbria LA14 1NB

Barrow-in-Furness: South Cumbria School of Nursing, Education Centre, Furness General Hospital, Barrow-in-Furness, Cumbria LA14 4LF

Bishop Auckland: County Durham School of Nursing, Nurse Education Headquarters, Group Offices, General Hospital, Bishop Auckland, Co Durham DL14 6AD

Blackburn College, Fielden Street, Blackburn, Lancashire BB2 1LH

Blackpool & Fylde College of Further and Higher Education, Ashfield Road, Bispham, Blackpool, Lancashire FY2 0HB

Bolton Institute of Higher Education, Deane Road, Bolton, Greater Manchester BL3 5AB

Bradford Hospitals School of Physiotherapy, Bradford Royal Infirmary, Bradford, West Yorkshire BD9 6RJ

Bradford School of Nursing, Nursing Careers Advice Department, Nurses Home, Little Horton Lane, Bradford, West Yorkshire BD5 0JJ

Bradford & Ilkley Community College, Great Horton Road, Bradford, West Yorkshire BD6 1AY

Bradford: University of Bradford, Bradford, West Yorkshire BD7 1DP

Bridlington – East Yorkshire College of Further Education, West Street, Bridlington, North Humberside Y015 3EA

Burnley College, Shorey Bank, Ormerod Road, Burnley, Lancashire BB11 2RX

Chester College, Cheyney Road, Chester CH1 4BJ

Chester District School of Nursing, Nurse Teaching Department, Countess of Chester Hospital, Lierpool Road, Chester CH1 3QR

Consett: Derwentside College, Park Road, Consett, Co Durham DH8 5EE

Dewsbury College, Halifax Road, Dewsbury, West Yorkshire, WF13 Dewsbury, West Yorkshire WF13 2AS

Doncaster: Doncaster Health Authority Department of Nurse Education, Doncaster Royal Infirmary, Thorne Road, Doncaster, South Yorkshire DN2 5LT

Doncaster: Humberside College – see Hull

Douglas, IoM: Noble's Isle of Man Hospital School of Nursing, Westmoreland Road, Douglas, Isle of Man

Durham: New College Durham, Framwellgate Moor Centre, Durham DH1 5ES

Gateshead Technical College, Durham Road, Gateshead, Tyne & Wear NE9 5BN

Grimsby: Humberside College – see Hull

Halifax: Calderdale College, The Percival Whitley Centre, Francis Street, Halifax, West Yorkshire HX1 3UZ

Huddersfield Health Authority School of Nursing, General School, The Royal Infirmary, Lindley, Huddersfield, HD3 3EA or Psychiatric School, Storthes Hall Hospital, Kirkburton, Huddersfield HD8 0PT

Huddersfield Polytechnic, Queensgate, Huddersfield, West Yorkshire HD1 3DH

Huddersfield Polytechnic School of Chiropody, The Polytechnic, Queensgate, Huddersfield, West Yorkshire HD1 3DH

Hull District School of Nursing, Hull Health Authority, Victoria House, Park Street, Hull, North Humberside HU2 8TD

Hull: Humberside College of Higher Education, Cottingham Road, Hull, North Humberside HU6 7RT

Hull School of Radiography, John Symons House, Park Row, Park Street, Hull, North Humberside HU2 8TD

Kirby College of Further Education, Cherryfield Drive, Kirby, Merseyside L32 8SF

Lancaster College of Adult Education, St. Leonard's House, St. Leonardgate, Lancaster LA1 1NN

Lancaster & Morecambe College of Further Education, Morecambe Road, Lancaster, Lancashire LA1 2TY

Lancaster: North West Lancashire School of Radiography, Lancaster Moor Hospital, Lancaster LA1 3JR

Lancaster: St Martin's College, Lancaster LA1 3JD

Lancaster School of Nursing, Royal Albert Hospital Grounds, Ashton Road, Lancaster LA1 5AX

Lancaster: The University, Lancaster LA1 4YW

Leeds: East Leeds School of Radiography, Seacroft Hospital, York Road, Leeds LS14 6UH

Leeds: Jacob Kramer College, Vernon Street, Leeds LS2 8PH

Leeds: Park Lane College of Further Education, Park Lane, Leeds LS3 1AA

Leeds Polytechnic, Adult Training Unit, 22 Queen Square, Leeds LS2 8AF

Leeds: Trinity & All Saints College, Brownberrie Lane, Horsforth, Leeds LS18 5HD

Leeds: Western Health Authority School of Physiotherapy, The General Infirmary at Leeds, Great George Street, Leeds LS1 3EX

Leeds: Western Health Authority School of Radiography, Clarendon Wing, The General Infirmary at Leeds, Belmont Grove, Leeds LS2 9NS

Leeds: Western Health Authority School of Radiotherapy, Cookridge Hospital, Leeds LS16 6QB

Leigh College, Railway Road, Leigh, Lancashire WN7 4AH

Lincoln: North Lincolnshire College, Cathedral Street, Lincoln LN2 5HQ

Liverpool Institute of Higher Education, PO Box 6, Stand Park Road, Liverpool L16 9JD

Liverpool: Merseyside School of Radiography, Royal Liverpool Teaching College, Prescot Street, Liverpool L7 8XR

Liverpool School of Nursing, Royal Liverpool Hospital College, Prescot Street, Liverpool L7 8XN

Liverpool: Sefton School of Nursing, South Sefton (Merseyside) Health Authority, Walton Hospital, Rice Lane, Liverpool L9 1AE

Liverpool: South Mersey College, Childwall Abbey Road, Liverpool L16 0JP

Liverpool: The University, PO Box 147, Liverpool L69 3BX

Manchester Polytechnic, All Saints, Manchester M13 9PL

Manchester: Manchester Royal Infirmary School of Physiotherapy, Oxford Road, Manchester M13 9WL

Manchester: North Manchester School of Nursing, North Manchester General Hospital, Central Drive, Crumpsall, Manchester M8 6RB

Manchester: School of Therapy Radiography, Christie & Clatterbridge Hospitals, Christie Hospital & Holt Radium Institute, Wilmslow Road, Withington, Manchester M20 9BX

Manchester: South Manchester Community College, Barlow Moor Road, West Didsbury, Manchester M20 8PQ

Manchester: South Manchester School of Nursing, Mauldeth House, Mauldeth Road West, Manchester M21 2RL

Manchester: South Manchester School of Physiotherapy, Withington Hospital, West Didsbury, Manchester M20 8LR

Manchester: The University, Manchester, Extra-Mural Department, Oxford Road, Manchester M13 3PL

Manchester: University of Manchester Institute of Science & Technology, PO Box 88, Sackville Street, Manchester M60 1QD

Manchester: Moseley Road Centre for Community Education, Moseley Road, Fallowfield, Manchester M14 6WQ

Middlesbrough: Cleveland School of Radiography, South Cleveland Hospital, Marton Road, Middlesbrough, Cleveland TS3 4BW

Middlesbrough: Longlands College of Further Education, Douglas Street, Middlesbrough, Cleveland TS3 2JW

Middlesbrough: Teesside Polytechnic, Brough Road, Middlesbrough, Cleveland TS1 3BA

Morpeth: Northumbria College of Nursing Studies, Northgate Hospital, Morpeth, Northumberland NE61 3BP

Nelson and Colne College, Scotland Road, Nelson, Lancashire BB9 7YT

Newcastle-upon-Tyne Polytechnic, Ellison Building, Ellison Place, Newcastle-upon-Tyne NE1 8ST (This address is correct if you wish to apply for details of the Diploma in Occupational Therapy or the Graduate Diploma in Physiotherapy).

Newcastle-upon-Tyne School of Nursing, General Nurse Education, Freeman Hospital Teaching Centre, Newcastle-upon-Tyne NE7 7DH

Newcastle-upon-Tyne Schools of Radiography, The Royal Victoria Infirmary, Queen Victoria Road, Newcastle-upon-Tyne NE1 4LP

Northallerton: Friarage Hospital Nurse Education Department, Northallerton, North Yorkshire DL6 1JG

Oldham Centres for Community Education, Chaucer Street, Oldham, Greater Manchester OL1 1BA

Ormskirk: Edge Hill College of Higher Education, St Helen's Road, Ormskirk, Lancs L39 4QP

Ormskirk: West Lancashire Nurse Education Centre, Ormskirk & District General Hospital, Wigan Road, Ormskirk, Lancashire L39 2AZ

Peterlee College, Peterlee, Co. Durham SR8 1NU

Preston College, St Vincent's Road,Fulwood, Preston, Lancashire PR2 4UR

Preston: Lancashire Polytechnic, Preston PR1 2TQ

Rotherham College of Arts & Technology, Eastwood Lane, Rotherham, South Yorkshire S65 1EG

Rotherham: Rockingham College of Further Education, West Street, Wath-upon-Dearne, Rotherham, South Yorkshire S63 6PX

Runshaw Tertiary College, Longdale Road, Leyland, Preston, Lancashire PR5 2DQ

St Helen's College, School of Management Studies, Water Street, St. Helen's, Merseyside WA10 1PZ

Salford College of Technology, Frederick Road, Salford M6 6PU

Salford College of Technology: Manchester School of Radiography, Frederick Road, Salford M6 6PU

Salford College of Technology: Northern College of Chiropody, Frederick Road, Salford M6 6PU

Salford College of Technology: School of Occupational Therapy, Frederick Road, Salford M6 6PU

Salford College of Technology: School of Physiotherapy, Centre for Health, Social Work and Paramedical Studies, Frederick Road, Salford M6 6PU

Salford: The University of Salford, Salford M5 4WT

Scarborough: York and Scarborough School of Nursing, York District Hospital, Wigginton Road, York Y03 7HE, and Scarborough Hospital, Scalby Road, Scarborough Y012 6QL

Scunthorpe: Scunthorpe and Goole School of Nursing, Scunthorpe General Hospital, Cliff Gardens, Scunthorpe, Humberside DN15 7BH

Sheffield City Polytechnic, Pond Street, Sheffield S1 1WB

Sheffield: Loxley Tertiary College, Myers Grove Lane, Sheffield S6 5JL

Sheffield: North Trent Schools of Radiography, 21 Claremont Crescent, Sheffield S10 2TA

Sheffield: Parkwood College, Shirecliffe Road, Sheffield S5 8XZ

Sheffield: Rother Valley College of Further Education, Doe Quarry Lane, Dinnington, Sheffield S31 7NH

Sheffield: Stradbroke College, Richmond Centre, Spinkhill Drive, Sheffield S13 8FD

Shipley College, Exhibition Road, Shipley, West Yorkshire BD18 3JW

Skelmersdale College, Northway, Skelmersdale, Lancashire WN8 6LU

Southport College of Arts & Technology, Mornington Road, Southport, Merseyside PR9 OTT

Stockport: Stockport Department of Nurse Education, Stepping Hill Hospital, Stockport, Greater Manchester SK2 7JE

Sunderland Polytechnic, Langham Tower, Ryhope Road, Sunderland, Tyne & Wear SR2 7EE

Wakefield: Bretton Hall College, West Bretton, Wakefield, West Yorkshire WF4 4LG

Wakefield: Pinderfields College of Physiotherapy, Pinderfields General Hospital, Aberford Road, Wakefield, West Yorkshire WF1 4DG

Warrington: North Cheshire College, Padgate Campus, Fearnhead, Warrington, Cheshire WA2 ODB

Widnes: Halton College of Further Education, Kingsway, Widnes, Cheshire WA8 7QQ

Wigan College of Technology, (Trace Ltd.) Parsons Walk, Wigan, Lancs WN1 1RR

Wirral School of Nursing, Arrowe Park Hospital, Upton, Wirral, Merseyside L49 5PE

York: College of Ripon & York St John, Lord Mayor's Walk, York Y03 7EX. (Write to Department of Occupational Therapy if this particular course interests you).

WALES AND WESTERN ENGLAND

Aberystwyth: Ceredigion College of Further Education, Llanbardan Colleges, Llanbardan Fawr, Dyfed SY23 2BP

Aberystwyth: University College Aberystwyth, The University of Wales, PO Box 2, Aberystwyth, Dyfed SY23 2AX

Bangor: Gwynedd School of Nursing, St David's Drive, Bangor, Gwynedd LL57 4S1

Barnstaple: North Devon College, 01d Sticklepath Hill, Barnstaple, Devon EX31 2BQ

Bath College of Higher Education, Newton Park, Bath, Avon BA2 9BN

Bath: Norton Radstock College, South Hill Park, Radstock, Bath, Avon BR3 3AW

Bath School of Physiotherapy, Manor House, Combe Park, Bath BA1 3NW

Bath School of Radiography, Royal United Hospital, Combe Park, Bath BA1 3NG

Bath: The University of Bath, Claverton Down, Bath BA2 7AY

Bridgwater College, Bath Road, Bridgwater, Somerset TA6 4PZ

Bristol: Avon School of Nursing, Bristol and Weston Centre, Eugene Street, Bristol BS2 8HW

Bristol: Brunel Technical College, Ashley Down, Bristol BS7 9BU

Bristol: Filton Technical College, Filton Avenue, Filton, Bristol BS12 7AT

Bristol Polytechnic, Coldharbour Lane, Frenchay, Bristol BS16 1QY

Bristol Schools of Radiography, Bristol Royal Infirmary, Bristol BS2 8HW

Cardiff: South East Wales School of Radiography, Combined Training Institute, University Hospital of Wales, Heath Park, Cardiff CF4 4XW

Cardiff: South Glamorgan Health Authority School of Physiotherapy, Combined Training Institute, University Hospital of Wales, Heath Park, Cardiff CF4 4XW

Cardiff: South Glamorgan Institute of Higher Education, Western Avenue, Llandaff, Cardiff CF5 2YB

Cardiff: South Glamorgan Institute of Higher Education School of Chiropody, Department of Clinical Health Studies, Llandaff, Cardiff CF5 2YB

Cardiff: South Glamorgan School of Nursing, Combined Training Institute, University Hospital of Wales, Heath Park, Cardiff CF4 4XW

Cardiff: South Wales School for Therapeutic Radiography, Velindre Hospital, Whitchurch, Cardiff CF4 7XL

Cardiff: University of Wales College of Cardiff, PO Box 78 Cathay's Park, Cardiff CF1 1XL

Cheltenham: College of St Paul and St Mary, The Park, Cheltenham, Glos GL50 2RH

Chippenham Technical College, Cocklebury Road, Chippenham, Wilts SN15 3QD

Dolgellau: Meirionnydd College, Coleg Meirionnydd, Dolgellau, Gwynedd LL40 2YF

Exeter College, Hele Road, Exeter, Devon

Exeter: Devonshire College of Nursing and Midwifery, Mowbray House, Butts Road, Heavitree, Exeter EX2 5BA

Exeter: The University of Exeter, Northcote House, The Queen's Drive, Exeter EX4 4QJ

Gloucester: Gloucester Health Authority School of Radiography, Collingwood House, Horton Road, Gloucester

Gloucester: The Gloucestershire School of Nursing, Great Western Road, Gloucester GL1 3NN

Haverfordwest and Neyland: Pembrokeshire College, off Dew Street, Haverfordwest, Dyfed SA61 1SZ

Lampeter: St David's University College, Lampeter, Dyfed SA48 7ED

Llanelli: Carmarthenshire College of Technology & Art, Llanelli Campus, Alban Road, Llanelli SA15 1NG

Newtown: Montgomery College of Further Education, Newtown, Powys

Plymouth College of Further Education, Kings Road, Devonport, Plymouth PL1 5QG

Plymouth College of Further Education School of Chiropody, North Road West, Plymouth PL1 5BY

Plymouth: Cornwall and Plymouth Schools of Nursing and Midwifery, Education Centre, Derriford Hospital, Plymouth PL6 8DH

Plymouth: Polytechnic South West, Drake Circus, Plymouth PL4 8AA

Plymouth School of Radiography, 8 Woodside, Plymouth PL4 8QE

Pontyclun: Mid Glamorgan Health Authority School of Nursing, Hensol Hospital, Nr Pontyclun CF7 8YS

Pontypool College, Blaendare Road, Pontypool, Gwent NP4 5YE

Pontypridd: Polytechnic of Wales, Llantwit Road, Treforest, Pontypridd, Mid-Glamorgan CF37 1DL

Poole: Dorset Intitute of Higher Education, Wallisdowne Road, Poole, Dorset

Rhyl: Clwyd School of Nursing, Bodelwyddan, Rhyl, Clwyd LL18 5UJ

Salisbury College of Technology, Southampton Road, Salisbury, Wilts SP1 2LW

Salisbury School of Nursing, Harcourt Terrace, Salisbury, Wilts SP2 7SZ

Street: Strode College, Church Road, Street, Somerset BA16 OAB

Swansea: Gorseinon College, Belgrave Road, Gorseinon, Swansea, West Glamorgan SA4 2RF

Swansea: South West Wales School of Radiography, Morriston Hospital, Swansea, West Glamorgan SA6 6NL

Swansea: University College of Swansea, Singleton Park, Swansea, West Glamorgan SA2 8PP

Swansea: West Glamorgan School of Nursing, Department of Nurse Education, Parc Beck, Sketty Road, Swansea SA2 9DX

Swindon School of Nursing, Princess Margaret Hospital, Okus Road, Swindon, Wiltshire SN1 4JU

Taunton: Somerset College of Arts & Technology, Wellington Road, Taunton, Somerset TA1 5AX

Taunton: Somerset School of Nursing, Musgrove Park Hospital, Taunton, Somerset TA1 5DA

Tiverton: East Devon College of Further Education, Bolham Road, Tiverton, Devon EX16 6SH

Torquay: South Devon College of Arts and Technology, Newton Road, Torquay, Devon TQ2 5BY

Totnes: Dartington College of Arts, Totnes, Devon TQ9 6EJ

Truro: Cornwall School of Radiography, 24 Falmouth Road, Truro, Cornwall TR1 2HX

Weymouth College, Cranford Avenue, Weymouth, Dorset DT4 7LQ

Wrexham: North Wales School of Radiography, Wrexham and East Denbighshire War Memorial Hospital, Wrexham, Clwyd LL11 1EG

Yeovil College, Ilchester Road, Yeovil, Somerset BA21 3BA

SCOTLAND AND NORTHERN IRELAND

Aberdeen College of Commerce, Holburn Street, Aberdeen AB9 2YT

Aberdeen: Grampian School of Occupational Therapy, Woolmanhill, Aberdeen AB9 1GS

Aberdeen: Grampian School of Physiotherapy, Aberdeen Royal Infirmary, Woolmanhill, Aberdeen AB9 1GS

Aberdeen: Robert Gordon's Institute of Technology, Schoolhill, Aberdeen AB9 1FR

Alloa: Clackmannan College of Further Education, Branshill Road, Alloa, Clackmannanshire FK10 3BT

Antrim: Northern Area College of Nursing, Area Hospital Site, Bush Road, Antrim BT41 2QB

Belfast College of Mental Health Nursing, Purdysburn Hospital, Saintfield Road, Belfast BT8 8BH

Belfast College of Technology, College Square East, Belfast, NI BT1 6DJ

Belfast College of Technology: Northern Ireland School of Chiropody, College Square East, Belfast, NI BT1 6DJ

Belfast Southern College of Nursing, Belfast City Hospital, Lisburn Road, Belfast BT9 7AB

Belfast: Stranmillis College, Stranmillis Road, Belfast, NI BT9 5DY

Clydebank College, Kilbowie Road, Clydebank, Strathclyde G81 2AA

Coleraine: University of Ulster, Cromore Road, Coleraine, Co. Londonderry BT52 1SA

Dumfries & Galloway College of Technology, Heathall, Dumfries DG1 3QZ

Dundee: Duncan of Jordanstone College of Art, Perth Road, Dundee DD1 4HT

Dundee: The University, University Tower Building, Nethergate, Dundee DD1 4HN

Edinburgh: British Isles Study Programme, (Iain Hobbs, Principal in Scotland), 150 Conway Crescent, Perivale, Greenford, Middx UB6 8JE

Edinburgh College of Art, Lauriston Place, Edinburgh EH3 9DF

Edinburgh: Heriot-Watt University, Riccarton, Edinburgh EH14 4AS

Edinburgh: Napier Polytechnic of Edinburgh, Collinton Road, Edinburgh EH10 5DT

Edinburgh: Queen Margaret College, 36 Clerwood Terrace, Edinburgh EH12 8TS

Edinburgh: Queen Margaret College Department of Physiotherapy, 36 Clerwood Terrace, Edinburgh EH12 8TS

Edinburgh School of Diagnostic Radiography, 79 Lauriston Place, Edinburgh EH3 9HY

Edinburgh: Telford College of Further Education, Crewe Toll, Edinburgh EH4 2NZ

Edinburgh: The University, 01d College, South Bridge, Edinburgh EH8 9YL

Fermanagh College of Further Education, Enniskillen, Co Fermanagh BT74 6AE

Glasgow: Anniesland College, Hatfield Drive, Glasgow G12 0YE

Glasgow Business School of the University of Glasgow, The University, Glasgow G12 8QQ

Glasgow Northern College of Nursing and Midwifery, 30O Balgrayhill Road, Glasgow G21 3UR

Glasgow: The Queen's College, 1 Park Drive, Glasgow G3 6LP

Glasgow: The Queen's College School of Physiotherapy, 1 Park Drive, Glasgow G3 6LP

Glasgow: The Queen's College School of Radiography, Smith Building, Jordanhill College of Education, Southbrae Drive, Glasgow G13 1PP

Glasgow School of Chiropody, 757 Cookston Road, Glasgow G53 7UA

Glasgow: The University, Glasgow G12 8QQ

Glasgow: The University of Strathclyde, 16 Richmond Street, Strathclyde, Glasgow G1 1XW

Inverness College of Further & Higher Education, 3 Longman Road, Longman South, Inverness IV1 1SA

Kilmarnock: Ayrshire and Arran College of Nursing and Midwifery, Crosshouse Hospital, Crosshouse, Kilmarnock KA2 0BE

Kirkcaldy: Fife College of Nursing and Midwifery, Forth Avenue, Kirkcaldy, Fife KY2 5YS

Lisburn College of Further Education, Castle Street, Lisburn, Co. Antrim, NI BT27 4SU

Melrose: Scottish Borders College of Nursing, Education Centre, Borders General Hospital, Huntlyburn, Melrose TD6 9BD

Motherwell College, Dalzell Drive, Motherwell ML1 2DD

Newcastle College of Further Education, Donard Street, Newcastle, Co. Down, NI BT33 0AP

Newry: The Continuing Education Programme, Southern Education and Library Board, Downshire Road, Newry, Co. Down BT34 1EE

Newtownabbey College of Further Education, Shore Road, Newtownabbey, Co. Antrim, NI BT37 9RS

Paisley College of Technology, High Street, Paisley, Renfrewshire PA1 2BE

Perth College of Further Education, Brahan Estate, Creiff Road, Perth PH1 2NX

St Andrews: The University of St Andrews, College Gate, St Andrews, Fife KY16 9AJ